CHALLENGING THEOCRACY

Ancient Lessons for Global Politics

Commonly perceived as a direct threat to the practice of liberal democracy, the global re-emergence of theocratic claims to political rule is a misunderstood development of twenty-first-century politics. Analysing the relationship between religion and politics throughout the Middle East, Africa, and the United States, as well as classical and medieval political philosophical sources, *Challenging Theocracy* critiques the contemporary formation of theocracy.

The chapters in this volume provide an account of the origins of theocracy and explore ancient texts that articulate the theocratic political ideas which continue to influence political life today. In an effort to consider how regimes extend beyond their immediate institutional and legal forms and find their foundation in timeless ideas, the contributors examine ancient and modern political thought to better understand its persistent power and impact on global politics.

DAVID EDWARD TABACHNICK is a professor in the Department of Political Science, Philosophy, and Economics at Nipissing University.

TOIVO KOIVUKOSKI is an associate professor in the Department of Political Science, Philosophy, and Economics at Nipissing University.

HERMÍNIO MEIRELES TEIXEIRA is an assistant professor in the Department of Political Science, Philosophy, and Economics at Nipissing University.

EDITED BY DAVID EDWARD TABACHNICK,
TOIVO KOIVUKOSKI, AND HERMÍNIO
MEIRELES TEIXEIRA

Challenging Theocracy

Ancient Lessons for Global Politics

UNIVERSITY OF TORONTO PRESS
Toronto Buffalo London

ISBN 978-1-4426-4929-3 (cloth)   ISBN 978-1-4426-2667-6 (paper)

Library and Archives Canada Cataloguing in Publication

Challenging theocracy : ancient lessons for global politics / edited by
David Edward Tabachnick, Toivo Koivukoski, and Hermínio Meireles
Teixeira.

Includes bibliographical references and index.
ISBN 978-1-4426-4929-3 (cloth). – ISBN 978-1-4426-2667-6 (paper)

1. Theocracy – History.   2. Religion and politics – History.   3. Political
science – Philosophy.   4. Philosophy, Ancient.   5. World politics – 21st
century.   I. Tabachnick, David, editor   II. Koivukoski, Toivo, editor
III. Teixeira, Hermínio Meireles, 1961–, editor

JC372.C53 2018   201'.727   C2017-907034-7

University of Toronto Press acknowledges the financial assistance to its
publishing program of the Canada Council for the Arts and the Ontario
Arts Council, an agency of the Government of Ontario.

Canada Council   Conseil des Arts
for the Arts   du Canada

ONTARIO ARTS COUNCIL
CONSEIL DES ARTS DE L'ONTARIO
an Ontario government agency
un organisme du gouvernement de l'Ontario

Funded by the   Financé par le
Government   gouvernement
of Canada   du Canada

Canada

Contents

Preface

DAVID EDWARD TABACHNICK, TOIVO KOIVUKOSKI,
AND HERMÍNIO MEIRELES TEIXEIRA

Though distinguished by the separation of church and state and the legitimation of regimes by consent of the governed to their government, modern liberal democracies have been challenged by the ascendancy of theocratic mandates to rule, both domestically and in foreign relations. For although there has been progress at the normative level in the advancement of a human rights agenda premised on the idea that human beings are essentially free and equal, and in practice through the spread of democratic institutions, de-colonialization, and popular confrontations with tyrannical regimes, the notion that there is a political power more august than the will of the people is having its resurgence. This idea that the right to rule is not contingent on the active and informed consent of the people governed, but derives from some supposed higher power, has obvious instantiations in regimes that trace their legitimacy to a mandate given by God, as well as in ideologies of sovereignty which make the state into a mortal god on earth, thus challenging the rightness of liberal democracy both from within and without.

The global re-emergence of theocratic claims to political rule and authority is perhaps the most pressing and misunderstood development of twenty-first-century politics. A generation ago, the Iranian Revolution of 1979 was looked upon as an anomaly in a rapidly secularizing society. A growing separation of church and state was thought to correspond to globalizing economics and democratic politics. Now, however, while globalization and democracy have flourished, there are proliferating efforts to establish religiously based political and legal systems in countries around the world. This largely unanticipated development suggests the need to give an account of the new rise of theocratic regimes. *Challenging Theocracy: Ancient Lessons for Global Politics* is intended to provide this needed account of the origins and influence of theocracy through an exploration of ancient texts that articulate as well as critique theocratic political ideas.

With recognition given to the foreign policy dimensions of the rise of theocratic regimes whose interests are at odds with liberal democracies, this volume is not intended as a catalogue of ascendant theocratic regimes the world over. Rather, the focus remains on how theocratic aspirations challenge the core principles of liberal democracy. In light of these encounters with decidedly illiberal legitimations of regimes, derived not from the inherent freedom and equality of peoples but from their relations to the divine, it may be helpful to see what can be learned from this challenge so as to deepen the bonds of civil society and democratic culture. For there may be some truths in the critiques offered towards liberal democracy and free market economics: that a condition of political plurality may degenerate into an inchoate mass society, that multiculturalism may be levelled out into an indifferent field of cultural differences, and that a mindless freedom to buy and sell as one chooses may not satisfy the needs of the human spirit for meaning found in concert with others and directed towards the cultivation of public virtues. There may be good reason to consider how our civil society could be buttressed by a civil religion appropriate to these tasks, and suited to the perpetuation of liberal democracy through a set of shared beliefs, something deeper than commitment to freedom conceived as licence, and more humanistic than devotion to a power beyond the capacities of political discourse to articulate. Indeed, Western liberal democracies are not so devoid of the ethical and spiritual dimensions as radical theocratic critics would aver. Answering the challenges posed by those who question the separation of church and state requires this kind of critical self-reflection from within the traditions of liberal democracy.

In the same way that earlier "Ancient Lessons for Global Politics" volumes treated a range of regimes in *On Civic Republicanism*,[1] *On Oligarchy*,[2] *Enduring Empire*,[3] and *Confronting Tyranny*,[4] *Challenging Theocracy* considers the theocratic regime not simply as an historical event or a kind of politics characterized by a particular set of institutions and laws, but instead as a political possibility that can manifest itself in a variety of contexts. Like other regimes, theocracy exists under the surface of political life, in thoughts and practices that stay relatively autonomous, even when an official regime may be constituted specifically to deter them. All told, one must consider how regimes extend beyond their immediate institutional and legal forms and find their foundations in timeless ideas. By studying the earliest sources of these ideas, we can better understand their persistent power and the impact they have on global politics.

As suggested above, theocratic ideas, especially more recently outside of the West, have coalesced into official theocratic regimes: political rule directly inspired and decided by the omnipotence and omniscience of the divine. One sees *direct* theocratic rule not only in the unexpectedly durable Shi'a radicalism of the Ayatollahs in Iran, but also in the unfolding tensions of Islamism in Egypt, the Wahhabi rule of Saudi Arabia, the strict governance of the Taliban in Afghanistan and its resurgence, as well as in political parties, non-state and trans-national actors throughout much of the Middle East, Turkey, Pakistan, Bangladesh, and Northern and Central Africa. Contemporary theocracy is not limited to Islamic cases but is also found in the papal decrees of Vatican City, the monks of Tibet, the growing role of Hasidim in the government of Israel as well as the political influence of Mormon and radical evangelical communities in the United States.

There have been some excellent individual studies of these contemporary theocracies. For example, Carrie Rosefsky Wickman's recent *The Muslim Brotherhood: Evolution of an Islamist Movement*,[5] Said Amir Arjomand's definitive *The Turban and the Crown: The Islamic Revolution in Iran*,[6] and the collection of essays in *Religion and Politics in Saudi Arabia: Wahhabism and the State*[7] provide detailed discussions of the relationship between religion and politics in Egypt, Iran, and Saudi Arabia. There has also been growing concern about the rise of theocracy within traditionally secular states. The influence of Islamism on Turkish politics is explored in *Muslim Nationalism and the New Turks* by Jenny White[8] and religion in Israeli politics in *Israel's Higher Law: Religion and Liberal Democracy in the Jewish State* by Steven Mazie.[9] Similarly, some interesting and mostly critical popular and academic work has been done on the influence of theocratic ideas on American politics.[10] And of course, there is Huntington's now infamous account of a supposedly immanent conflict between the West as such and ascendant Islamist regimes, with their irreconcilability apparently ensured by divergent religious beliefs,[11] an account belied by the presence of diverse theocratic elements – both secular and sacred – in Western liberal democracies as in the majority of Islamic regimes. Although calling attention to these conflicting mandates to rule may point to potential conflicts with core principles of liberal democracy, it does not help us make sense of fratricidal violence within religions, where civil wars rather than civilizational clashes seeming to be the more pressing sources of conflict. Still, an open-eyed awareness of the violent potentials of zealotry, whether it be ideological or religious, offers a framework for reflection more adequate to the actual challenges faced by liberalism than blithe claims that we have arrived at the end of either history or ideology. We must, therefore, seriously consider the apparent diversity among regimes and the various legitimations of rule from which they are derived.

In general, while many of these books do review the theological foundations of these political movements as well as cultural and social reasons for their increased popularity, there remains the challenge of explaining the unanticipated overturning of the confident Enlightenment judgment that religion would be inevitably purged from the modern state. This is all the more problematic because many of these books either suggest or explicitly argue that the rise of theocracy represents a threat to the practice of liberal democracy. Some contemporary sources on religion and American politics do weigh the writings of the American founding fathers, early texts on republicanism, and the First Amendment of the US Constitution but, for the most part, do not consider the deeper history of considerations of and warnings against theocratic elements in politics. *Challenging Theocracy: Ancient Lessons for Global Politics* aims to provide this critical ballast through a consideration of classical and medieval sources of political philosophy for understanding the contemporary formation of theocracy as well as its critique.

For example, if modern ideas about the separation of church and state are not entirely sufficient as criticism of theocracy, the division of divine rule from the governance of things argued for in classical political theory will help identify why public life should be founded on rational and humanistic grounds. Aristotle and Plato both argued that, while respect for one's community as a basis for a good and virtuous life does approach something like a civil religion, there can be no political *theoi-kratoi* or rule by the gods as such. Aristotle clearly distinguished between political rule among equals and the sort of autocratic or kingly *techne* associated with divine power. A leader who rules with god-like authority is not engaged in political relationships with citizens, but instead in something akin to a parental relationship with children.[12] This is problematic not only because it provides no public role for subjects, but also because there is no requirement for transparency or accountability from those in charge. Still, Plato explained that the worship of the divine does play a role in public life to encode the goods of political community as articles of faith, bringing a sense of reverence to the life of the *polis*. So a kind of political theology is crafted as part of the "city in speech" in the *Republic*, though with formative myths pared down into rational archetypes for behaviour, with the gods and demi-gods turned into spectres of reason serving the public good.[13] Likewise, in the *Euthryphro*, if Homeric myths are invoked as sources of arbitration in human affairs they are very much rationalized myths,[14] open to critique on the basis of their usefulness and consistency, with any claim to authority based on faith reducible to platitudes, along the lines of "something of the kind must be true," at bare minimum taking it as a matter of faith that some form of public order is necessary, however diverse the forms that regimes may take.

At least here, at the origins of Western political thought, the suggestion is that theocratic claims were part of our accounts of the political and, in turn, could never be entirely expelled from the state. Even though in the Age of Reason and Enlightenment political philosophers called for the end of divine right as the basis for political authority, the relationship between "city and man" was still founded upon a mythic or religious notion. As Carlos Fraenkel explains in his recent *Philosophical Religions from Plato to Spinoza*,[15] the medieval and classical traditions wrestled with the relationship between reason and religion in the formation and practice of government and law. Averroes and Maimonides, in their explanations of the need for *sharia* and *torah*, argued, similarly to Plato, that divine law is necessary as a guide "for members of the community who are unable to attain *perfect* self-rule."[16] And, in the same way classical political philosophers presented the divine *nomoi* as accessible only through our rational capacity, these medieval thinkers argued that the true nature of the laws of Muhammad and Moses could only be reached through reason.

A similar kind of approach is also found in recent work by prominent scholars such as Agamben, Butler, Santner, Reinhard, and Žižek (among others), but with a marked critical difference.[17] In part following the seminal work of Walter Benjamin,[18] they examine how these rational traditions that are said to limit and govern the role of the theological in politics,[19] in fact found their power and authority in the event(s) of an exception within the order of sovereign law (i.e., real and/or perceived security crises, tumults, or emergencies); namely, in exceptional moments where reason and norms of law are suspended so as to found and/or restore sovereign law in the pure, brutal "force [violence] of the law."[20] They therefore explore what might be called *indirect* theocratic rule in what was above called "political theology." This work suggests the need to explore the ways theocratic ideas have developed into an understanding of modern state sovereignty as the omnipotence of political decisions on life itself.

All told, the main goal of *Challenging Theocracy* is to show how "ancient lessons" from classical and medieval political thought can help us better understand the influence of theocratic ideas in the development and function of the modern state as well as the recent rise of theocratic regimes in global politics.

Theocracy in Ancient Political Thought and Practice

Theocracy is a contested concept, as it takes on many different forms, but most importantly the concept itself engenders action. Fred Dallmayr argues that theocracy, when matched with the rationalizations of secularism, transforms structures into totalitarian regimes. Returning to the ancient, theocratic writings of St Paul, Dallmayr asks a pointed question: What are we to do in these imperial dystopias? Following Paul's testimonies, he directs us to the word of God as an illustration of the idea of "beyond theism."

A similar tension between rationalist philosophy and received religious authority is of political significance in part since it pertains to questions of what are pious and just modes of behaviour for human beings. This tension can be played out even in regimes that are not explicitly theocratic. Mark Lutz explores this relation at the origins of political philosophy, with a focus on Socrates' critical examination of the authorities of Athens and the virtues that ought to undergird claims to moral and political legitimacy. Lutz argues that although the trial of Socrates may have been influenced by the philosopher's political associations, the theological dimensions of the charges would have been very real, rooted in deeply felt notions of civic piety.

Religion and politics intersect for Socrates upon occasions of doubt, where it is not clear what to do, when the human powers to act and to understand meet their limits. At these junctures, we have the Socratic dictum that knowledge pertains to one's own defining limits – the I know that I do not know – serving as both moderating influence against overreaching claims to knowledge and as a caustic influence on received religion. Adding to the quarrel between philosophy and religion are Socrates' efforts to rationalize the Greek gods, and in Lutz's view to import an austere new god of philosophy into the city through the insistence that for the sake of ontological stability and their own perfection, the gods cannot be at odds with one another or change their views out of the fickleness of sentiment. And although political philosophy can be said to begin at this original encounter, the potential for conflict between these two rival claims to authority is perennial and shared between cultures, arising out of the philosophic demand that authorities give an account of themselves.

The differences between philosophy, religion, and politics serve not simply to delimit the respective spheres, but to enervate these distinctly human capacities. For the partitioning out of human experience is not premised on the assignation of exclusive territories to each – that is, schools, places of worship, and the public – but includes those liminal grounds where these practices overlap, with aspirations shared in common between orders. In an inquiry into the parities between Platonic political philosophy and the Eleusinian mysteries, Steven McGuire notes that while Plato's aim may have been to criticize authorities inherited from mythic traditions, myth remains very much at play in his philosophy and in philosophy's original perspective on the political. Drawing on Voegelin and Schelling's readings of the mysteries and of Plato, McQuire argues that "politics always takes place between the secular and the sacred, and, as such, we should be wary of regimes that would attempt either to reduce politics to a purely immanent activity or seek to use it as a means to achieve a transcendent end."

What this means is that the tension between politics and religion is formative for each domain, with spiritual aspirations underlying any political community, and with a kind of civic spiritedness informing communities of faith. Even inasmuch as Platonic philosophy presses hard on the demand to rationalize the life of man, it recognizes its own limits in doing so, acting more as go-between to the secular and sacred orders than as intellectual architect of archetypal forms for each to assume. In McQuire's reading, this philosophical form of self-knowledge registers the limits of reason, tracing *logos* – the internally consistent word, capable of giving an account of itself – back to a ground in the very *mythos* that it would critique. This grounding of reason in myth comes to prominence in the rites of the Eleusinian mysteries, which broke through the rigidly assigned territories of Olympian deities in a way that anticipated the kind of transcendence promised by philosophy, while assuring initiates of the shared ground of human experience in the fecundity of a natural order.

The affinities between Platonic political philosophy and the Eleusinian mysteries are also a focus of Toivo Koivukoski's chapter, wherein
the author argues that the specific value of that ancient Greek religious
practice was to at once intimate a source of civic solidarity while delimiting the powers of rational speech to describe the grounds of public
communion. While we may share in the spontaneous beneficence of
nature, in the mysteries that source of shared being was kept secret,
with the punishment for leaking the secret teachings being erasure of
a person from the community. It may be that the similarities between
those beliefs and the secret teachings that the interlocutors in the *Symposium* were initiated into may have figured into the charges against
Alicibiades, along with political suspicions about the plots of an oligarchical cabal.

If the political value of religion for Plato functions in this sense of
describing the limits of what can be said and done in public, for Aristotle religion serves an analogous function, with the gods acting as archetypes for humankind. Specifically, Koivukoski points to the patterns
of political succession, varied claims to legitimacy, counsel among the
gods, and power sharing in ancient Greek theology as being archetypal
for politics among human beings also, in the arts of "ruling and being
ruled in turn," with religion not performing a rigidly prescriptive role
so much as describing the boundaries of what any decent political order
might look like.

In terms of what kind of civic virtue may attend a decent society, and
what may be its sources, Jeremy Neill points to Christian and Muslim
adoptions of virtue ethics from Aristotle. The Philosopher was a key
source for medieval theologians looking to spell out what makes for
a good life and a just community, combining reason with virtue in an
endorsement of those kinds of human excellence that contribute to the
integrity of the community as a whole. And while Aristotle's virtue ethics may not be specifically religious in his formulation, derived rather
from reason, experience, and the rule of the middle way, they do at
times complement explicitly religious codes of conduct with prescriptions as to how to live well.

This reaching back behind modern Enlightenment ideas of the common good considered in terms of the realization of human freedom
answers certain persistent critiques of the modern project, both inasmuch as they pertain to what is worth doing with our freedom, and
what kind of common good could direct and give purpose to our individual energies and talents. Restoring the significance of these origins

of political science in Aristotle could answer the critiques of modernity arising out of resurgent religious traditions, with a re-adoption of a kind of civil religion from pagan philosophy back into liberal modernity. To this end, Neill points to the ethical value of property ownership in both Aristotle and early modern political and economic theory, underlining that custom as a necessary precondition for the cultivation of public virtues, with theology learning a lesson in civic virtue from secular philosophy.

And yet still, there is clearly a divide between the classical disposition towards a politics informed by some kind of common good requiring habituation in virtue ethics and the modern acceptance of peaceful coexistence among freedom-loving equals as the nearest, realistic approximation of shared purposes for society. The ancient, classical approach discriminates against private goals that are vulgar, denigrates the pursuit of wealth beyond what is necessary to the attainment of leisure and public virtue, and sorts aspirations into those of intrinsic value and those that ought to be subordinated as being instrumental to higher ends. Quite differently, these kinds of hierarchical orderings of individual purpose mandated by public institutions of government and education, wherein the political community directs citizens as to how to be good in their private lives, have no place in a liberal society premised on the freedom and equality of citizens.

It seems clear to us, therefore, that the theological power and authority of theocratic forms of political rule do not necessarily end with a supposed historical obsolescence of the latter types of regimes. Scholars of the political history of Western regimes have had to come to terms with, and "take seriously" as Tracy B. Strong argued, the scholarship and political theology of the former Nazi jurist Carl Schmitt.[21] It was he who demonstrated that secular, Western concepts such as sovereign authority and the rule of law remain profoundly theological in practice.[22] With this insight in mind, Westerners should not be surprised that non-Western parts of the world, especially Islamic ones, most often astutely oppose the spread of Western, modern state secularism with the principled practices of theology. If certain contemporary state regimes (Iran) and religiously inspired non-state political movements (Boko Haram) make theocratic claims to power, one must take their ancient theological claims seriously and avoid the dangerous reduction of these to mere geo-political analyses. This is exactly what the authors of our next four chapters do with respect to contemporary Islamic and secular claims to theocratic rule.

Theocracy and Modern State Politics

Houchang Hassan-Yari's chapter engages the question of Islamic theocracy in Iran, but in a different direction that is reminiscent of the chapters by Allan Mittleman and Hermínio Meireles Teixeira. Although he focuses on Islamic theocracy in the Shia traditions of Iran, and not on Jewish and Christian theocratic traditions (as did the aforementioned authors), Hassan-Yari contends that Shi'ite theocracy – especially its belief in the event of the 12th Imam and its "period of occultation" – in fact opposes and deposes the claims of Islamic legitimacy in contemporary Iranian regimes. He demonstrates that, at least since the Khomeini regime of the 1979 Islamic revolution, Iranian regimes have been clerical but certainly not theocratic. These clerical leaders and the Islamic people of Iran are said to "walk in opposite directions." They rule in favour of a political "maslaha" (expediency) most often translated into an authoritarian politics that compromises the theocratic essence of Shi'ite Islam. Most concerning, writes Hassan-Yari, is that these clerics are making politically expedient decisions on theological matters when they are supposed to be, at the most, preparing the physical conditions for the return of the 12th Imam from his period of "Major Occultation." In Hassan-Yari's depiction of this rupture in leadership, Shi'ite theocracy therefore appears as the enduring potential of an Islamic deposing of existing regimes.

In his chapter on Islamism in North Africa, Jeffry Halverson traces the relationship between religion and state and the process of secularization while illustrating how the revival of theocracy came to be. Islam was a fundamental part of society and integral to the state as law and governance were established through religion. The return to theocracy was born out of crisis. It was an identity crisis engendered through secularization that reinvigorated nationalism, pan-Arab ideology, and a return to traditional Islamism. This new theocracy is radically different than when church and state were simply embedded in one another. Halverson examines how militant Islamist ideology characterized this return to Islam in the attempt to destroy secularism and the perceived break between religion and state. Therefore, the idea that secularism is the condition for the revival of theocracy emerges and presents itself as an important factor in understanding Islam today.

Alan Mittleman examines the origins of the term theocracy and traces this through Judaism, where theocracy was once used as a method of critique, understood to be inherently anti-monarchical, and as a method of politics. Theocracy in the Jewish context contains a different meaning and is not associated with a religious authority for the state. Mittleman argues that theocracy does not exist in the modern Jewish world, but rather that there are tenets of a theocratic impulse. Theocracy in the Jewish context pertains to a critical approach to politics. Theocracy does not concern the relation between religion and the state; rather, it is simply a feature of interest politics in modern democracy. This understanding of theocracy is important in understanding the contemporary conflicts regarding the Jewish Home.

In almost a specific instance of Mittleman's insights into the critical "theocratic impulse" of Jewish theology, Hermínio Meireles Teixeira examines the political potency of such an impulse in the crucial encounter between Walter Benjamin and the Nazi jurist and political philosopher, Carl Schmitt. Returning to the testimonies of St Paul, he specifies Benjamin's reading of Paul's theocracy as an affirmation of "anomic" events in the experiences of profound spiritual and political transfiguration. There is nothing less here, so Teixeira argues, than the transmission of a transformative politics where the irruptions and repetitions of the anomic prove to be the very core of any legal-political regime's claim to decisive powers over life.

Responding to the Challenges of Theocracy

Theocracy is clearly a challenge to modern politics. Peter Simpson begins with Aristotle and the separation of the modern and pre-modern world, where religion is a necessary component of both worlds or else there can be no claim to the good. His chapter presents the separation of church and state as unusual and unnatural, if you will, and problematizes our self-championing of this distinction in the modern landscape. Simpson points out an inherent paradox of liberalism, which is the relentless pursuit of passion combatted with coercion, where coercion itself becomes the object of politics. There is an additional paradox, which complicates the first, and it is the way liberalism posits a perceived denial of theocracy, while at the same time engendering a division between society and religion. This division between society and religion merely re-appropriates theocracy into the domain of the liberal under the guise of a new secular form. Simpson argues that the spiritual is needed once again and his analysis shifts to examine power and the idea that power must be divided into the temporal and the spiritual in order to release the reins of control that coercive power has yielded through liberalism.

In her chapter, Yvonne Sherwood argues that there is a new form of theocracy, which is located in law, economy, and the indisputable virtues of democracy as these forces mobilize as the same omniscient totalizing power of theocracy. Sherwood examines a brief history of the concept of theocracy and argues that there has been a shift in the term; where it was once exclusively applied to theological-political structures, through secularization theocracy has become more than religion. While at first this seems contradictory, this is precisely the problem that Sherwood is drawing out, as it is the convergence between illegitimate divine power and the terrain of the secular state, where theocracy is reinvigorated and garners a new form – god has re-emerged. The living theocracy is now and, while the old gods are dead, the modern divine represents itself in the ideological claim to neo-theistic rule.

Similarly, James Franke and Laurie M. Johnson mark the ideological differences between contemporary Islamic theocracies and liberal democracies, arguing that the goals of shaping law by religious dictate and of cultivating individual character through virtue education draw political Islam away from modernity and closer to the ancients. The authors use this ideological distinction to explain the ideological impasse between Western and Islamic regimes, where the core purposes of the state are understood in essentially different ways. Drawing on the early modern critiques of classical political philosophy and the incorporation of that form of liberalism into the "American Way" by the Founding Fathers, Franke and Johnson depict a stark divide between states devoted to the preservation of individual liberties, and those directed towards the inculcation of virtue in citizens through divinely sanctified laws. Between those two poles, compromise may be difficult to achieve.

Church and state may be separate in the American constitution, but they have overlapped historically in American political culture, with recurrent debates as to the kind of influence that religion should have in the public sphere. By exploring the origins of the separation of church and state in communities of dissent in the mid-Atlantic colonies, in the liberal political philosophy of John Locke, and in the constitutional convention of 1789, Scott Hibbard adds the ballast of history to an often rancorous and roiling disagreement. Steadied by the perspective offered by this history of ideas, Hibbard offers that the dispute at the centre of America's "culture wars" need not be polarized between the religious right advocating for a renewed public role for Christianity as a foundation of national identity and the secular left seeking to do away with religion altogether in public discourse, but that a centrist position of ecumenical secularism is possible. Any honest account of American politics would have to admit the role that religion plays in it, even given the constitutional separation of church and state. Hibbard notes that there is an avowedly religious dimension to the doctrine of American "exceptionalism" that has historically informed American foreign policy with a sense of purpose, at times even transcending national interests. And while the state may not have a role in shaping the religious beliefs of its citizens, it can and does cultivate a sense of civil religion that provides unity to the body politic. The author quotes Eisenhower's comment that "America makes no sense without a deeply held faith in God – and I don't care what it is." This public value of religion requires a concomitant tolerance for diversity of faiths, as well as respect for the freedom of conscience of others as the proper grounds of civil religion.

Ronald Beiner begins his chapter with the observation that theocracy evidently remains a very real possibility in contemporary politics, scanning the horizon for such ascendant regimes in Iran, the so-called "Islamic State," Afghanistan, and Palestine, as well as noting the influence of religion in outwardly secular regimes. Beiner argues that if theocracy remains an enduring possibility, then the canon of political philosophy offers a valuable guide for identifying these kinds of perennial tensions, specifically through reflection on attempts to domesticate the public influence of faith into some form of civil religion, enlisting energies of communion without having religious fervor tear apart the body politic. This aim has been central in early modern republican efforts at shaping shared belief into some form of civically useful religion, an effort which can be traced back even further to the civil cults that bound together ancient polities with shared practices and perceptions. For the moderns, "Civil religion in its essence means that religion is too dangerous to be left in the hands of churches and priests, and since it cannot be conjured away, it ought to be deposited in the hands of the state (which would put religion to good civic purposes and guarantee religious toleration among all citizens)." While such an effort to tame religion in the public sphere may or may not be a vigorous enough response to regimes marked by rabid religiosity, the tension between religion and politics is clearly enduring. What can and should be done in any particular political circumstance is contingent on the means available and the culture within which one may act, but the questions that action seeks to answer have a certain consistency throughout the history of political thought, hence the significance of the canon in framing those debates.

Beiner draws attention to Shaftesbury's reflections on the proper relation between religion and politics, with the question arising in the eighteenth century "from the troubling thought that Christianity no longer
supplied the unshakeable cultural and moral foundations that, in his
view and the view of virtually all his contemporaries, were required as
the condition of having a coherent society." If religious authorities could
no longer bully belief into a set of orthodox aspirations and taboos, then
reason would have to step in, shoring up civil religion in such a way
as to make room for critique and scepticism. The author suggests that
Shaftesbury's own critique of the political influence and amassment of
property by Egyptian priests could be applied also to Hebrew, Roman,
and Christian priests, inasmuch as their power and privilege were
based in populations duped by ignorance, superstition, and zealotry. If
political philosophy cannot turn around the souls of people en masse,
it can show up the pathologies of priestcraft for what they are, while
holding out the possibility of a harmonious society informed by both
faith and reason as a standard by which to judge theocratic regimes.

This "showing up" of contemporary forms of "priestcraft" allows us
a concluding affirmation of what is perhaps the most unique contribution of this volume: that the theocratic claims of regimes are both *direct*
and *indirect*, and that the non-juridical forms of the latter, especially as
they are housed in secular forms of juridical rule, help us in the struggle
to uncover the theology of political regimes that claim *post-theocratic*
power and legitimacy. Was this not what Michel Foucault bequeathed
to us in his later work? It was he who warned the coming scholarship
with the injunction: "I'm afraid that we still have not cut off the head
of the king."[23]

NOTES

1 Geoffrey C. Kellow and Neven Leddy, eds, *On Civic Republicanism: Ancient
Lessons for Global Politics* (Toronto: University of Toronto Press, 2016).
2 David Edward Tabachnick and Toivo Koivukoski, eds, *On Oligarchy: Ancient
Lessons for Global Politics* (Toronto: University of Toronto Press, 2011).
3 David Edward Tabachnick and Toivo Koivukoski, eds, *Enduring Empire:
Ancient Lessons for Global Politics* (Toronto: University of Toronto Press, 2009).
4 Toivo Koivukoski and David Edward Tabachnick, eds, *Confronting
Tyranny: Ancient Lessons for Global Politics* (Lanham, MD: Rowman and
Littlefield Publishers, 2005).

5 Carrie Rosefsky Wickman, *The Muslim Brotherhood: Evolution of an Islamist Movement* (Princeton: Princeton University Press, 2013).

6 Said Amir Arjomand, *The Turban and the Crown: The Islamic Revolution in Iran* (Oxford: Oxford University Press, 1988).

7 Mohammed Ayoob and Hasan Kosebalaban, eds, *Religion and Politics in Saudi Arabia: Wahhabism and the State* (Boulder, CO: Lynne Reinner, 2009).

8 Jenny White, *Muslim Nationalism and the New Turks* (Princeton: Princeton University Press, 2012).

9 Steven Mazie, *Israel's Higher Law: Religion and Liberal Democracy in the Jewish State* (Lanham, MD: Lexington, 2006).

10 These studies tend to overemphasize the religious right's power over American government, especially during the Bush Administrations. They also tend to restrict the concept of theocracy to traditional, juridical types of political regimes. See, for example: Kevin Phillips, *American Theocracy: The Perils and Politics of Radical Religion, Oil, and Borrowed Money* (New York: Viking Press, 2006); Michelle Goldberg, *Kingdom Coming: The Rise of Christian Nationalism* (New York: W.W. Norton, 2006); James Rudin, *The Baptizing of America: The Religious Right's Plans for the Rest of Us* (New York: Thunder's Mouth Publishing, 2006); Randall Balmer, *The Kingdom Come: How the Religious Right Distorts the Faith and Threatens America: An Evangelical's Lament* (New York: Basic Books, 2006); JoAnn M. Macdonald, *Democracy versus Theocracy* (Charleston: Booksurge Publishing, 2008).

For a notable exception to the above texts, and one highly suitable to the themes of this text, see Ran Hirshl, *Constitutional Theocracy* (Cambridge: Harvard University Press, 2010). Hirshl examines how "pre-modern" sources of theocratic rule are contained within the historical evolution of modern constitutionalism and integral to its latter-day functioning.

11 Samuel Huntington, *The Clash of Civilizations and the Remaking of World Order* (New York: Simon and Schuster, 1996/2011).

12 *Politics*, 1259b.

13 *Republic*, III.

14 *Euthyphro*, 5c–d.

15 Carlos Fraenkel, *Philosophical Religions from Plato to Spinoza: Reason, Religion, and Autonomy* (Cambridge: Cambridge University Press, 2013).

16 Ibid., 3.

17 See Giorgio Agamben, *Homo Sacer: On Sovereign Authority and Bare Life* (Palo Alto: Stanford University Press, 1998); Giorgio Agamben, *The State of Exception* (Chicago: Chicago University Press, 2005); Eric Santner, *On Creaturely Life* (Chicago: University of Chicago Press, 2006); Eric Santner, K. Reinhard, and Slavoj Žižek, *The Neighbor: Three Inquiries in Political*

Theology (Chicago: University of Chicago Press, 2007); Judith Butler, *Frames of War* (New York: Verso, 2009); Judith Butler, H. de Vries, and L. Sullivan, eds, *Political Theologies: Public Religions in a Post-Secular World* (New York: Fordham University Press, 2006); Judith Butler, *Precarious Life* (New York: Verso, 2004).

18 For the key works of Walter Benjamin that animate much of the work cited in footnote #17, see Walter Benjamin, *Origins of German Tragic Drama* (New York: Verso, 2009), and Benjamin, "Theses on History," in *Illuminations* (New York: Shocken Books, 1968).

19 Namely, and within the continuities and discontinuities of their histories, traditions from the classical (Greco-Roman) to the medieval, Renaissance, and Enlightenment epochs.

20 Carl Schmitt, *Political Theology: Four Chapters on Sovereignty* (Chicago: University of Chicago Press, 2005), 14. For a critical explanation of the significance of Schmitt's emphasis on the "force" of law, see Georgio Agamben's second chapter of *State of Exception* (Chicago: University of Chicago Press, 2005), 32–40.

21 Tracy B. Strong, "Forword: Dimensions of the New Debate around Carl Schmitt," in Carl Schmitt, *The Concept of the Political*, expanded edition, trans. George Schwab (Chicago: University of Chicago Press, 1996). See pp. ix–xxxi for Strong's argument that we must take Schmitt's political theology "seriously" as a prevailing form of secular rule.

22 For Schmitt's classic formulation that the most essential concepts of the modern, sovereign state are in fact secularized theological concepts, see Carl Schmitt, *Political Theology: Four Chapters on the Concept of Sovereignty*, trans. George Schwab (Cambridge: MIT Press, 1985), 36. For his more decisive claim that concepts of the modern state are "superficial secularizations of the omnipotence of God," see Schmitt, *The Concept of the Political*, 42.

23 Michel Foucault, *La volonté de savoir: Histoire de sexualité*, vol. 1 (Paris: Gallimard, 1976), 117. See also Foucault, "Entretien avec Michel Foucault," in *Dits et écrits*, vol. 3 (Paris: Gallimard, 1994), 150.

CHALLENGING THEOCRACY

Ancient Lessons for Global Politics

PART ONE

Theocracy in Ancient Political Thought and Practice

1 Theocracy as Temptation: Empire and Mindfulness[1]

FRED DALLMAYR

> Too long have I dwelled
> among those who hate peace.
> I am for peace; but when I speak,
> they are for war.
>
> Psalm 120:6–7

"Theocracy" – meaning God's rule or rulership – is a deeply ambivalent and contested concept. Depending on the meaning assigned to it, the term is liable to generate fierce emotions and antagonisms. To an extent, this outcome may seem surprising. Approached in a calm and dispassionate spirit, the idea of "theocracy" is nothing other than what religious believers – in diverse formulations – routinely affirm. Thus, practising Christians are wont to recite daily, and perhaps even several times daily, words contained in the "Lord's Prayer" which state: "Your kingdom come, your will be done in heaven as it is on earth." Words or sentiments to a similar effect can be found in several other world religions – without occasioning alarm or disturbance. Here as elsewhere the rub, of course, comes when one tries to define or interpret properly the precise meaning of words. Questions instantly proliferate: What or where is God's kingdom and who is in charge? And even if one grants that God's will should be done in heaven, how can it be done on earth, or who will be the legitimate stand-in for God on earth?

Thus, as one can see, a seemingly routine formula quickly opens a Pandora's box and even a minefield of queries. Surely, it is proper to tread very cautiously in this field, while searching for reliable guideposts. One such guidepost can be found in the gospel of Matthew in the passage dealing with the temptation of Jesus. Actually, the text mentions several kinds of temptations, but culminates in the offer to Jesus of a spectacular type of theocracy. As we read (Matthew 4:8–10), the tempter took him to "a very high mountain" and showed him "all the kingdoms of the world and the glory of them," offering them all to Jesus in return for subservience (a seemingly unequal bargain). We know that the offer was rejected by Jesus firmly with the words: "You shall worship the Lord your God and him alone shall you serve." The passage in Matthew mentions several other tempting offers, such as the promise of food and sustenance – surely an enticing gift after a fasting period of forty days – and probably of an abundance of "consumer items" desirable for commodious living in the world. This offer too, we recall, was rejected with the words that humans "live not by bread alone, but by every word that proceeds from the mouth of God."

All temptations listed by Matthew are memorable; but most memorable and thought provoking is surely that offer of world dominion or domination. This offer is particularly thought provoking because it was not made to just anyone but to Jesus. Now, for Christian believers, Jesus was not only an exemplary and even perfect human being – as such he is recognized also by non-Christians – but rather Christ, the "son" of God, or God seen as a human person. It is the same Christ who exhorted his followers to pray that God's "kingdom" may come and God's will be done on heaven and earth. Something curious thus happens in the story of Matthew: for there Christ rejects precisely the opportunity of world domination which might have seemed the most expedient and promising way to establish God's "kingdom" on earth. Surely, something must dawn on us at this point: namely, that God's kingdom (as invoked in the Lord's Prayer) is something entirely different from world rule or world domination. Differently put: God rules entirely otherwise than worldly potentates, kings, or emperors. This difference was in fact explicitly stated by Jesus in another passage (Matthew 20:25–6): "The rulers of the Gentiles lord it over them, and their great men exercise authority over them. It shall not be so among you."

Biblical stories are sometimes treated as far-off legends, as fables from a bygone era. The same happens to the passages in Matthew's gospel. The story of the temptations is sometimes viewed as a distant saga, as an exotic event that happened – and could only have happened – to Jesus. Tucked away as a museum piece it remains without consequences. But how is this possible – as long as Christians are expected not only to pay lip service to, but to follow in the footsteps of their Lord? (And even those who regard him as an exemplary person will surely want to learn from this example). Thus, seeing that Christ rejected world domination

as a temptation and sinful abomination, why would Christians everywhere not also join in this rejection – no matter by what potentates
(kings or emperors) this domination is exercised or attempted to be
exercised? How can Christians – or mindful people anywhere – become
accomplices in the establishment and expansion of this kind of abomination? Should they not pay heed to the exhortation of Jesus that only
the divine (the just and pure) deserves to be worshipped and served?
And does this not require of all mindful people a kind of turning or
"mind-fasting" as an antidote to the powerful temptation?

To be sure, in our modern world, theocracy comes in many different shapes and forms; not all of them are infested with the same kind
of danger or temptation. One way in which theocracy has traditionally manifested itself is in absolutist clerical regimes, that is, in regimes
where religious authorities wield absolute or near-absolute political power. Fortunately, under the impact of modern democracy, such
regimes are waning (although they have by no means disappeared).
In my view, the term should not be applied in situations where religious institutions simply exercise ritual and educational functions in
civil society without wielding public control. Unfortunately and dis-
tressingly, modern times have generated the near-reversal of traditional
(clerical) theocracies: namely, the erection of basically "secular" regimes
into quasi-religious, totalitarian structures fuelled by comprehensive,
sometimes millenarian ideologies. This was the case in the well-known
totalitarian systems of the twentieth century. Unhappily, the demise
of these systems has not put an end to totalizing global aspirations.
The technological "advances" of our time have put at the disposal of
political elites unprecedented weapons of mass destruction as well
as unheard of instruments of mass surveillance and mind control. In
the case of some elites, these advances have unleashed the dystopia of
world-empire, of a total control of the world based on the monopoly of
all available knowledge or information as a premise of absolute power.
Using the terminology commonly applied to the traditional image of
God, one can characterize the dystopia as the linkage of "omniscience"
and "omnipotence" – which in turn yields the formula of a "pseudo-
theocracy" or sham-theocracy.

What are people placed within the ambit of this imperial dystopia
supposed to do? What else, but what Jesus did: dismiss it and move
on. A halfway sane or mature person would not wish to waste time in
pursuit or in support of worthless affairs. To be sure, there is no point –
for mindful individuals – to butting their heads against the ramparts

of empire. Given its formidable arsenal of armaments – from nuclear weapons to drones to hidden torture chambers – direct confrontation can only result in self-destruction. At this point, another part of Matthew's story of the temptations of Jesus becomes relevant: where the tempter dared Jesus to throw himself down from the pinnacle of the temple, trusting to be rescued by God's angels (Matthew 4:6–7). This part of the story, in my view, is a warning against willful self-sacrifice or martyrdom, an action which flies in the face of the commandment against killing and self-killing and of the principle of the sacredness of human life. Jesus's clear response to the tempter is that one should not recklessly put God's mercy to the test. If there is not the possibility of direct confrontation – because of its lethal effects – there remains only the possibility of circumspect action, of subterfuge and non-violent resistance, or something which Buddhists traditionally have called "skillful means" (*upaya*).[2]

Given the close connection between world-empire and advanced modern technology, skillfulness here resembles the attitude which Martin Heidegger recommended for the encounter between human beings and the "enframing" power of *Gestell*. Instead of either assaulting that power or pliantly submitting to it, Heidegger counselled a stance of mindful "releasement" or *Gelassenheit*, a stance granting a limited niche to technology in one's life, while otherwise just letting it be or leaving it to its own devices. Left to its own devices and bereft of sustaining enthusiasm, technology's and empire's power might possibly relent and perhaps ultimately subside. Leaving be, one should note, does not in any way signal abandonment of the hope for a different alternative: the hope for something which is the very reverse of pseudo-theocracy or sham-theocracy. This is the hope which animates the search for God's genuine "kingdom," a search which – in the words of St Augustine – unites people "from all nations and all tongues" into a "harmonious pilgrim band" journeying towards the promised place. Elaborating on Augustine's words, religious philosopher Richard Kearney stresses that the promised abode can neither be engineered or controlled nor be abandoned by human beings: it "can never be fully possessed in the here and now, but always directs us toward an advent still to come."[3] In the here and now, all we can do is keep searching and move on. In this respect, we need to emulate the "wise men from the East" after their visit to Bethlehem: for, knowing about King Herod's cruel designs, "they went to their homes by another way" (Matthew 2:12).

NOTES

1 This chapter is reprinted from Fred Dallmayr, *Mindfulness and Letting Be: On Engaged Acting and Thinking* (Lanham: Rowman and Littlefield, 2014) with kind permission of the publisher.

2 Compare Michael Pye, *Skillful Means: A Concept of Mahayana Buddhism*, 2nd ed. (New York: Routledge, 2003) and John W. Schroeder, *Skillful Means: The Heart of Buddhist Compassion* (Honolulu: University of Hawaii Press, 2001). In many ways, skillful means is similar to the Aristotelian notion of prudent judgment (*phronesis*). One important kind of "*upaya*" was the Gandhi-inspired "non-cooperation movement" with British imperialism in 1920–2. Another form is the effort to resist and liberate oneself from the pervasive mind control imposed by empire. International politics expert Hans Köchler speaks in this context of the need to deflate dominant clichés leading to the "deconstruction of imperial myths." See Köchler, "Self-Determination in the Age of Global Empire," http://i-p-o.org/Koechler-Self_Determination -Global_Empire-IPO-OP-2013.htm.

3 See Richard Kearney, *The God Who May Be: A Hermeneutics of Religion* (Bloomington: Indiana University Press, 2001), 108, 110; St Augustine, *City of God*, trans. Gerald G. Walsh et al. (Garden City, NY: Image Books, 1958), 465 (book 21, chapter 17). Compare also my "Religious Freedom: Preserving the Salt of the Earth," in *In Search of the Good Life: A Pedagogy for Troubled Times* (Lexington: University of Kentucky Press, 2007), 205–19.

2 The Confrontation between Classical Political Philosophy and the Gods of the City

MARK J. LUTZ

In North America, Europe, and East Asia, defenders of divine law or *shari'a* have joined those in the Middle East who forcefully challenge the legitimacy of Western institutions and political principles. These defenders claim that divine law is the highest authority not only in how we should worship God but also in political and moral affairs. They say that what we know from reason does not conflict with what we know from divine law. But divine revelation, along with its attendant tradition of religious faith and learning, is based on a wisdom about what is truly just and good that is unavailable to those who rely solely on human reason and experience.

Among the influential thinkers associated with the revival of Islam, especially in its more radical forms, is Sayyid Qutb. According to Qutb, the West has mastered material nature and recklessly gratified a full range of bodily appetites, but it has achieved this by neglecting loftier needs and responsibilities. The West's spiritual emptiness makes clear the need for a turn to Islam or that it is now time for Islam to take its "turn."[1] But to turn to Islam, he says, it is not sufficient to worship God and to follow the Qur'an on one's own; one must live under a state that is guided only by *shari'a*. While Qutb is a critic of Western rationalism, he is not blind to its achievements. He argues that God has revealed Himself through nature, and it is necessary to study those sciences that reflect what God has made.[2] Consequently, it is useful and even necessary to take up those Western sciences that focus on non-human subjects, like mathematics or chemistry. But philosophy and the social sciences are more problematic. He argues that our understanding of what transcends material nature is necessarily dim and that we cannot fully understand many important truths if we try to grasp them through merely "human" thought.[3] It is therefore deeply misleading and impious to study any human or social science that has been developed and advanced by those who are not steeped in divine law.[4]

In light of these practical and theoretical challenges to the West's tradition of political philosophy, we might expect the inheritors of that tradition to offer a stout defence of political rationalism. We might hope that leading contemporary political theorists would initiate a dialogue with defenders of divine law so that each side might listen to, learn from, and come to respect the other. Such a dialogue might contribute greatly to Western society's stability, intellectual openness, and spiritual health. But contemporary rationalists tell us that all thinking, including the thinking that emerges from the Western tradition of political philosophy, rests on assumptions about what counts as knowledge that are neither demonstrable nor self-evident.[5] According to this understanding, it would be impossible for defenders of political rationalism to justify their way of thinking or their way of life to advocates of divine law. At most, we can point to areas of political agreement or common ground and tolerate any disagreements that arise. Even when thinkers such as Habermas and Rawls grant that we need to include members of religious traditions in our deliberations about politics and ethics in order to give greater substance to those deliberations, they caution that we can include in these deliberations only religious thinkers who acknowledge Western political principles such as universal human rights and who accept the authority of modern science.[6] Thus, leading political rationalists see little room for serious dialogue with the most strident critics of Western rationalism and of the politics and morality that are grounded in that rationalism.

This is not the first time that vigorous advocates of divine law have challenged the authority and legitimacy of political rationalism. In the medieval era, Islamic, Jewish, and Christian philosophers offered a powerful defence for relying on philosophy to illuminate and supplement religious texts and doctrines and to guide politics and law. Great Islamic philosophers such as al-Farabi, Avicenna, and Averroes took as their model Plato, for they saw in him a philosopher who not only established a searching dialogue with believers in divine law, but also used that dialogue to justify philosophy to those who defend the authority of divine law and religious faith. Thus, thinkers such as Leo Strauss, who turned to the medieval philosophers to find a tenable defence of philosophic reason, ultimately looked back to Plato, for in Plato we find the medieval philosophers' original model for inquiring into divine law.[7]

Socrates and the Perilous Condition of Classical Philosophy

Political philosophy is one of the few disciplines that has an identifiable beginning: it was founded by Socrates, who is said to have been the first to compel philosophy to turn from studying the heavens and to inquire instead into cities and households.[8] In its classical form, political philosophy seems to offer a great benefit to political life. It promises to replace opinions about justice, law, and other matters of practical importance with knowledge about these subjects. But instead of welcoming whatever rational guidance Socrates could offer, the city of Athens tried, convicted, and executed him for doing injustice, impiety and for corruption of the young.[9] According to Plato, the prosecution of Socrates for these crimes is no accident; it takes place within the context of a deep and essential conflict between philosophy and civic piety. The philosopher, who takes his bearings from his own reasoning and experience, is confronted by the city and its gods, who object both to his apparent disdain for the authority of law and to his efforts to pry into secrets that the gods wish to leave hidden. Even a city as enlightened as Athens cannot put up with Socrates' unorthodox beliefs about the gods or with his relentless public examinations of his fellow citizens about political, moral, and religious matters.

Even though Plato presents Socrates being persecuted and prosecuted for his alleged injustice and impiety,[10] some scholars claim that he was put to death for narrowly political reasons. Commentators such as John Burnet, A.E. Taylor, and I.F. Stone, Jr contend that he was prosecuted on religious charges by political partisans who sought to discredit and punish anyone who was associated with the tyrant Critias and with the would-be tyrant Alcibiades.[11] These scholars underestimate, however, how deeply and inextricably politics was linked to religion and faith in the classical city. Fustel de Coulanges famously describes the city as a religious cult in which the citizen is defined by his participation in the religion of his city.[12] According to the classical citizen, the gods care deeply about the city and its laws. Some cities, such as Crete and Sparta, lived under extensive codes of law that they traced back to the gods themselves. In Crete, it was accepted that king Minos conversed with his father, Zeus, and learned from him how to make laws for the city. The Spartan king Lycurgus travelled to Crete to study the laws of Minos and, after consulting with the god Apollo, elaborated a new, complete, and divine code of law for his city. Not every polis, of course, lived under a complete code of divine law. In other cities, the citizens themselves crafted many of their own laws. As Toivo Koivu-koski points out in this volume, religion did not guide the Athenians in the manner of a prescriptive law. More generally, he says, religion gave the Athenians models to emulate and limits to avoid rather than strict directions and rules. But even self-legislating democracies such as Athens continued to respect a set of ancient laws that were said to be laid down and enforced by the gods. After Pericles compelled rural citizens from around Attica to abandon their traditional, rustic ways and to move within the walls of the city, those citizens longed for the ancient modes of worship, and they continued to believe that the gods hate those who transgress ancient laws against crimes such as murder, incest, and father beating.[13] In commercial Athens, debtors took oaths before the gods to repay their creditors.[14] The connection between the gods and the city extends beyond making and enforcing ancient laws. When deciding momentous policy questions, the ancient Greeks often sought guidance from oracles, dreams, and other divine signs. When deliberating whether to go to war, statesmen consulted oracles and debated how those oracles should be interpreted.[15] After declaring war against the Athenians, the Spartans failed to prosecute the war to the fullest because they suspected that their cause was not entirely just and therefore the gods could not favour them.[16] In the midst of campaigns, they allowed their belief in the significance of signs, such as earthquakes and eclipses, to alter their strategies.[17] Before and after battle, the ancient Greeks made prayers and sacrifices to their gods. On occasion, they found that victories were marred by impieties that were committed while securing them. In the *Apology*, Socrates alludes to the trial of the ten generals from the victory over the Spartans at Arginusae, when Athens sentenced ten victorious generals to death because they failed to recover Athenian corpses after a decisive naval victory.[18] While elite elements of a city such as Athens may have doubted conventional beliefs about the gods, most Athenian citizens never ceased to believe that the gods are at the heart of civic life.[19]

Centuries before Socrates' birth, philosophy emerged from cities such as these. But even though the first philosophers sometimes expressed their thoughts in poems that speak about the gods, they depart from non-philosophers by taking their bearings from their own study of nature rather than from law. Wishing to know themselves and the world that they live in through their own intellect, they sought to know the lasting, intelligible necessities that compel everything that is to come into being and to pass away. This led them to look behind the surface of things, to set aside what law or custom tells us, and to seek with their own intellects to discern deeper, hidden, and yet thoroughly intelligible causes of all that is. They developed sciences such as geometry, astronomy, and geology in the course of their greater endeavour to discover the natural order that underlies the whole. As they made progress in discovering this natural order, they called into question the existence of mysterious, purposive, providential gods. They were able to attribute climatic phenomena such as rain, thunder, and earthquakes to the workings of a mechanistic "ethereal vortex," or to even more fundamental elements such as the atoms, rather than to willful gods.[20] As Plato's Athenian Stranger explains in the *Laws*, the natural philosophers believe that everything that exists emerges out of the random motion of matter. They believe that each thing that comes into being does so through some combination of nature, chance, and art.[21] By nature, they say, certain elements collide randomly with one another to form various composite beings, some of which are living and some of which are not. According to his argument, there is no divine intelligence giving order or movement to the heavenly bodies or to anything else in the cosmos. The sun and moon are merely stones that arbitrarily have come to be in a circular motion.[22] Some things come into being through human art, but these things have far less dignity than what comes into being through nature and chance alone. Some of the arts, such as medicine, farming, and gymnastics, serve natural ends, and they can be worthy of some seriousness.[23] But other arts, including most of the political art, merely conceal what is natural.[24]

While classical political philosophers such as Xenophon, Aristotle, and Cicero suggest that the pre-Socratic natural philosophers fail to give "the human things" any serious attention, a brief survey of the pre-Socratics' surviving works reveals that they developed a cohesive critique of the city's laws, morality, and gods. Examining the fragments of their writings, we find that they sharply criticize traditional, authoritative poets such as Homer and Hesiod,[25] and call into question the city's account of justice and nobility.[26] In the *Clouds*, the comic poet Aristophanes lays out the philosophers' and sophists' critique of traditional moral life. Aristophanes portrays Socrates openly denying the existence of Zeus, and his companion, the Unjust Speech, denying the existence of justice.[27] The sophistic Unjust Speech easily wins his debate with the old-fashioned Just Speech by showing that traditional morality promises us that virtues such as courage or moderation will bring rewards, but the rewards that it brings are easily eclipsed by those that come from successful vice.[28] In dialogues such as the *Gorgias* and the *Republic*, characters such as Callicles and Gorgias recount subtle, psychological explanations of how human beings were initially moved by selfish, sub-moral concerns to conceive of justice and to take it seriously.

Shocked and outraged by such teachings, the classical cities often persecuted the philosophers for impiety and for corrupting the young. In Sicily, the philosopher Pythagoras and his followers were persecuted and killed by their fellow citizens. In Colophon, the philosopher Xeno-phanes was exiled. Anaxagoras moved from Asia Minor to Athens and lived there for thirty years. But after he became a friend and teacher of the great statesman Pericles, he was arrested for impiety and eventually fled the city in fear for his life. The sophist Damon and the philosopher Protagoras also lived in Athens and befriended Pericles, but they, too, were forced into exile. In addition, the philosopher Diagora was forced to flee Athens after being sentenced to death. And while the Athenians may have come to regret executing Socrates soon after his death, a few years later both Plato and Aristotle were compelled to flee Athens. These examples show that even where philosophy was tolerated in ancient Greece, it remained controversial and was frequently perse-cuted by defenders of the city's laws and gods.[29] As Socrates' compan-ion Cebes observed on the day of Socrates' execution, the many believe that philosophers deserve to die.[30]

The Socratic Turn

Despite the manifest gravity of the charges against philosophy, a num-ber of contemporary scholars maintain that Socrates was a rationalist who never stopped to ask himself how he knows that he should be guided by his own philosophic reason rather than by inspired poems and laws or by oracles, dreams, and other forms of prophecy. Focusing on how Socrates is portrayed by Xenophon and by the so-called 'early' dialogues of Plato, Gregory Vlastos argues that Socrates has a general "commitment" to reasoned argument as well as a secondary commit-ment to obeying commands that reach him through "supernatural" or "extra-rational" channels.[31] Socrates reconciles the two commitments by assuming that the gods who communicate through oracles, dreams, and disembodied voices are moral beings whose morality is fully intel-ligible to rational human beings. When Socrates applies his reasoning to the obscure and puzzling prophecies that are sent by the gods, he discovers that they are intelligible and coherent.[32] He "assumes" that the commitment to reason and to supernatural command are in "perfect harmony" and that piety has an "essence of its own which is as normative for the gods as it is for us."[33] Vlastos's portrait of Socrates implies that Socrates fails to seek, let alone to find, evidence that it is pious and just to "rationalize" the gods. Vlastos's Socrates makes so many assumptions about piety and the gods that he comes to light as more of a dogmatic rationalist than as someone who leaves no aspect of his life unexamined.[34] According to Vlastos, Socrates' devotion to philosophy is a kind of faith, and he never recognizes the need to respond to the challenges posed by theocracy and divine law.

Mark McPherran follows Vlastos in claiming that Socrates takes for granted that piety can be defined in universal terms and that the gods follow intelligible moral principles.[35] McPherran claims that Socrates never asked himself why his examinations succeed or fail.[36] McPherran also follows Vlastos in believing that the dogmatically rationalist Socrates subjects communications from extra-rational sources to rational scrutiny, but McPherran qualifies this by saying that Socrates does this "whenever possible."[37] This qualification is important because, he says, extra-rational communications have a "genuine epistemic role in Socratic thought."[38] According to McPherran, the philosopher Socrates is also a "religiously oriented reformer of Greek religion" who believes in providential gods and who gives credence to their communications even when he cannot fully support what he learns from those communications with what he knows through his own reasoning.[39] Thus, in McPherran's view, Socratic philosophy is based not only on a faith in philosophy but also on religious faith.[40] McPherran's position is, however, exposed to two significant problems. The first is that philosophy distinguishes itself from other ways of life by taking its bearings only by what is evident to the philosopher himself and only by those things for which he can give an account.[41] On the basis of this evident knowledge, the philosopher tries to give an account of philosophy's necessity.[42] According to this understanding, McPherran's Socrates is a man of faith rather than a philosopher. Moreover, McPherran's Socrates would have no grounds for challenging anyone who claims to have extra-rational knowledge that philosophy is impious and unjust. Like Vlastos, McPherran presents Socrates as leading a philosophic life without ever recognizing and responding to the charges levelled against it by theocracy and religious orthodoxy.[43]

Plato's dialogues, however, present us with a Socrates who is always alert to the challenge posed by theocracy. As perilous as philosophy's position may have appeared to the Pre-Socratics, Socrates believes that it is even more precarious than they realized. Socrates recognizes that the natural philosophers brush aside their fellow citizens' charges that they disdain the gods and their laws because they are confident that they have a compelling, rational account of the natural necessities that govern the whole in which providential gods have no place and in which conventional morality and law have no intrinsic dignity. But Socrates is keenly aware of essential limits to what anyone can know through natural philosophy. He recognizes that the natural philosophers do not have at their disposal the complete account of the whole that would decisively refute claims by those who defend divine law or religious faith. Lacking evidence for such a refutation, he further sees that the Pre-Socratic, natural philosophers' attempts to explain – and to explain away – how non-philosophers understand political, moral, and spiritual phenomena fall short of their goal. The philosophers are too quick to attribute such phenomena to hidden but underlying causes, and so they fail to address fully what the city says or claims about justice and the gods. Perhaps they do not understand everything that is or that comes into being and passes away. Perhaps the gods are angry at them, and perhaps the gods will vent their anger in an afterlife. Furthermore, the philosophers need to consider the possibility that they have not yet fully understood matters such justice and piety, and so they may have neglected moral and spiritual obligations that any serious human being would feel. Having discovered these limitations to what a rational mind can know with certainty about nature as a whole, Socrates devised a new approach to the study of all things, and this new approach led him to found classical political philosophy.

Socrates describes what led him to undertake the "turn" that led him to found political philosophy in Plato's *Phaedo*. On the day of his execution, Socrates discusses his early life with a small group of admirers. He says that when he was young, he studied nature and thought it was a magnificent thing to know the causes of all the beings.[44] He sought to know what causes each of the beings to come into being, endure, and perish. He wants to show that every effect has a discernible cause or that no being comes into being out of nothing. Regarding growth, he attempts to show that everything can be traced back to unchanging, fundamental elements, but his argument raises questions both about the changes that take place during growth and also about the origin or cause of the elements themselves. As Socrates presents it, the natural philosopher needs to trace each of the elements back to some primary, underlying, material necessity, or, as he calls it, to "an Atlas" that must "embrace and hold together all things."[45] If the philosopher can show the existence of such a fundamental necessity, he will have found what the early philosophers call "nature." If he can also show that everything comes into being from and through this primary necessity, he will have shown that nothing comes into being spontaneously or mysteriously. He will have shown that everything that comes into being, endures, or passes away has a cause that is necessary and intelligible to the human intellect without the assistance of any god or prophet sent by a god.

As Socrates recounts his thinking, he finds several important problems with this project. The first is a difficulty associated with causation itself. Socrates says that he could not find a single cause that completely accounts for how one and one become two. While one and one become two through the combining of one unit with another unit, we can also make two things out of one by separating some one unit into two halves. The difficulty that this raises is that two seems to come into being through two opposite kinds of causes, and so we cannot say that we know of one, single cause that is always and that is simply the cause of what is two.[46] This points to the impossibility of ascribing a single cause for any effect and thus of nailing down a single, decisive account of anything that comes into being, endures, and passes away. He alludes to a second difficulty in other dialogues, such as the *Republic*. There, he indicates that the attempt to discover a fundamental, first cause, which he calls not an "Atlas" but the idea of the good, is that the philosopher would have to know this immediately, fully, and without condition.[47] But if we come to know each being by identifying the causes of it being what it is and that prevent it from becoming something else, then we could know this Atlas only because we knew of some prior cause or causes that compel it to be what it is. And so, the natural philosopher falls into an infinite regress of causes that prevents him from acquiring a comprehensive account of the whole.[48]

Lacking a decisive account of what causes all things to come into being, endure, and pass away, Socrates recognizes that the philosophers cannot rely solely on their inquiries into material nature to refute decisively claims made by defenders of divine law and religious faith. The natural philosopher can give persuasive accounts of meteorological phenomena, and he can point out that the gods do not seem to punish those who do injustices. But he cannot dismiss out of hand claims that the whole is ordered for the good and that the gods reward the just but punish the wicked in the afterlife. Furthermore, he recognizes that he must defend himself and philosophy before the bar of the city and its gods on the terms set by the city and its gods.[49]

In Socrates' account of how he turned towards political philosophy, he emphasizes that this turn does not require him to abandon altogether the study of nature. Rather, he says that he came to approach the study of all things in a new way that we now call "the theory of the ideas." Undertaking a "second sailing," Socrates stopped looking for a decisive account of the whole among causes that are hidden from us in ordinary life. Instead, he turned his attention towards "speeches."[50] Using speech to investigate each of the beings, he seeks out the "look" or "shape" or "form" (*idea*) of each being in order to learn the class characteristics that enable us to recognize that a particular thing belongs to a given class. He would not inquire into the origins of each being, but would focus on *what* it is or on how it manifests itself in ordinary life. Insofar as each form limits what comes into being as a member of a class, that form is a cause of what comes into being, endures, and passes away. Thus, knowledge of this sort of cause would give the philosopher some knowledge of a part of the whole.[51] Now, knowledge of this sort of cause does not provide an exhaustive account of the whole. It cannot determine whether any particular thing will come into being or pass away. Nor can it inform us about the purpose of the whole. But it is evidence that the beings come into being, endure, and pass away in conformity to some intelligible, lasting, and thus natural limitation.

When Socrates turns to the substance of the speech that he examined, he says that he focuses on the study of the idea of the noble or beautiful (*to kalon*), the idea of the good, and the ideas of similar matters.[52] Thus, Socrates begins to ask "What is noble?" to discern the idea of the noble and "What is good?" to know the idea of the good. He does not explain why he focuses on these "human" concerns nor does he say whether he took up from the start questions about piety and the gods. Yet the context of the *Phaedo* reminds us that Socrates was always confronted with questions about the piety and justice of his way of life and that he was keenly aware of the need to address them in a sufficient way. Even in the passage under examination, his remark that he seeks to know the ideas of the beautiful and the good implies that he examined what we know about the gods, insofar as the gods are said to be surpassingly beautiful and good.[53] In other dialogues, Socrates says explicitly that he regards it as important to know divine matters.[54] Moreover, when Socrates does examine what a god is and what a god would require of us, he would inevitably ask questions about what is noble and what is good because these are among the things that pious critics say the philosophers neglect and misunderstand.

In seeking out the ideas of what is noble, what is good, and other such things, Socrates indicates that it is possible to make progress in knowing these things. Even our most confused or obscure opinions about these things somehow glean or "divine" something about the phenomena that can be clarified and thought through. Upon discovering that certain of our opinions contradict one another, we can ask ourselves which seem to be more important and truer. And by thinking these matters through, Socrates can ascend from having a mere opinion of what is noble or what is good to a true opinion or perhaps even to knowledge of these things. Armed with such knowledge, he might effectively show philosophy's critics that philosophy helps rather than hinders us from knowing what is truly noble and good. And insofar as the study of these ideas is truly a second sailing, then it continues his efforts to know nature or some aspect of nature. As he says in the *Phaedo*, those who study the beings in speeches are not looking at (mere) images any more than are those who study the beings in (visible) deeds.[55] The turn to speeches about those things that morally serious people take seriously suggests that studying the human soul is our best access to the study of nature, simply.

The drama of the *Phaedo* suggests that Socrates made some progress in this study. He is confident that the philosophic life leads to true virtue,[56] and he dies in relative peace, evidently persuaded that he will not be punished by vengeful gods in the afterlife.[57] Moreover, in the *Apology* he makes numerous, positive claims to know things of great importance, such as that the soul exists and that the virtue of the soul is more important than the goods of the body.[58] And he asserts famously that the philosophic life is the greatest good for a human being and that the unexamined life is not worth living.[59] His second sailing seems to have taught him enough to conclude that his way of life is good for him and that it is neither unjust nor impious in the eyes of the gods.

In light of such comments, Socrates seems to have learned enough to defend the philosophic life before the bar of the city and its gods. But, as we have noted, his second sailing cannot provide him with a comprehensive knowledge of the whole, but at most with knowledge of the ideas or with "partial knowledge of parts" of the whole. Or does he have even partial knowledge of these matters? After all, Socrates is especially famous for his professions of ignorance, especially in the *Apology*, where he appears to affirm that he knows nothing at all. The

Apology is especially important to any inquiry into Socrates' turn to political philosophy because it contains a second account of how he came to lead his distinctive way of life. Thus, it is useful for those who are inquiring into Socrates' answer to charges of impiety and corruption to consider what he says there about how and why he became the Socrates known to us through Plato's dialogues.

In the *Apology*, Socrates says that he undertook that way of life in response to classical Greece's most revered spiritual authority, the Oracle at Delphi. He claims that his companion Chaerephon, whom Aristophanes linked to Socrates in the *Clouds* twenty years earlier, travelled to Delphi and asked the Oracle if anyone is wiser than Socrates. When Socrates heard that the Oracle answered "No," Socrates was perplexed because he knew that he was not wise, and so he set out to refute the Oracle. He says that he wanted to find someone wiser than him so that he could confront the Oracle with this evidence and demand an explanation. But, he says, he found that none of the Athenians who are respected for their wisdom know anything about what is "noble and good" nor about "the greatest things." He concluded that he really is the wisest insofar as he alone does not suppose that he knows what he does not know about these matters. This insight, he says, is the basis of his human wisdom. He further claims that he spends his life in service to the god, showing others that they are not wise even though he incurs their anger and envy for exposing their ignorance. He explains that those who are angry and envious accuse him of being an atheistic natural philosopher and a teacher of rhetoric, largely because these accusations have been circulating against all philosophers and especially against him since the performance and publication of the *Clouds*.[60]

This famous account of how Socrates came to examine and refute his fellow citizens is manifestly incomplete. It does not explain what Socrates did that led Chaerephon to travel to Delphi to ask the Oracle his question nor how Socrates knew from the start that he was not wise in any way. But Socrates' account in the *Phaedo* of his early life supplies an explanation: his youthful inquiries into natural philosophy would have impressed Chaerephon and his insights into the limits of natural philosophy would have persuaded him that he, as a philosopher, is necessarily far from being altogether wise. Therefore, Socrates' account of his early life in the *Apology* seems to recount his thinking after he began his "second sailing" or after he began his own inquiry into speeches about what is noble and about other matters of practical importance to human things. The account in the *Apology* says little about what

Socrates learned about such matters from thinking these things through on his own. Manifestly, he did not believe that anything that he learned about the idea of the noble or the just constituted complete wisdom about these or other matters. But he does indicate in the *Apology* that he saw that he needed to test whether those who are not philosophers, especially those who are most respected by the city, might have some wisdom that has escaped his notice. He would be especially curious to learn whether they have learned from the gods or from the laws established by gods some divine wisdom that he lacks.

Still, does not Socrates openly declare in the *Apology* that he knows nothing? But if he is thoroughly ignorant, as he seems to say, how does he answer the charges against him? How does he know that he is not committing impieties by carrying out his investigations? How does he know that Pythian Apollo meant him to undertake the subsequent mission to examine others that he devised on his own? A careful examination of what Socrates says reveals that he does not claim to be altogether ignorant. In saying that he knows that he is ignorant, he indicates that he knows what it would mean for him to have knowledge. Moreover, he specifies what he does not know in a variety of ways. In his first admission, he says that he does not know the virtue of "a human being and a citizen."[61] In order to unpack what he means in saying this, it is useful to note that he later says that he knows that his preoccupation with philosophy has not allowed him the leisure to be a good citizen.[62] And, as we have noted, he also affirms that he knows that his way of life is the greatest good for a human being and that the unexamined life is not worth living.[63] These statements suggest that he knows what the virtue of a human being would be and what the virtue of a citizen would be, but he does not know how to live the life of a virtuous citizen while at the same time living the life of the good human being, which is the life of the philosopher.[64]

Similarly, Socrates also says that he does not know what is "noble and good."[65] This term is used ordinarily to describe a gentleman or moral man. In the *Apology*, Socrates does not say precisely why neither he nor his interlocutors know what is noble and good, but, like the "virtue of a human being and citizen," being "noble and good" seems to mean bringing two things together. But what is the distinction between what is noble and what is good? In yet a third account of his youth, Socrates says in the *Symposium* that he once investigated what is noble by consulting a foreign priestess named Diotima. In their conversation, he agreed that we love good things because we seek to be happy. But he says that he cannot explain what we seek in loving what is noble or what is beautiful (*to kalon*). According to Diotima, we love the noble for the sake of our own immortality, in the hope that by devoting ourselves to what is noble we somehow gain a share in what never perishes.[66] As she continues to describe what she calls the noble itself or the one idea of the noble, she indicates that we consider most noble those things that have nothing to do with the body or with anything particular, including with our particular bodies and with our particular selves.[67] By this account, to live a life of complete nobility would be to dedicate ourselves to what is noble, to the exclusion of everything else, and thus to live without regard for our happiness. One manifest problem is that it becomes difficult to understand how anyone could live a life that is both noble and good, since this would require such a person to know that he devotes his life to what is noble, to what is not concerned with his own happiness, while at the same time knowing that this dedication will be the source of his own, individual happiness.[68] In saying in the *Apology* that no one knows what is noble and good, Socrates is suggesting that none of the Athenians has seriously considered how to combine a life of genuine nobility that is at the same time a life that meets our needs and is good and knowable for us. Just as Socrates says regarding the virtue of the human being and citizen, he indicates in the *Apology* that he knows what is noble: he says that the poets say many noble things and that the artisans make many noble things.[69] And, as we said before, he says that he knows of a way of life that is truly good for a human being. But he does not know what is noble and good in the strictest sense.

Socrates' other professions of ignorance include him saying that he does not know anything "so to speak."[70] But there is a great difference between not knowing anything simply and not knowing anything in a manner of speaking. His ignorance is qualified because, in some respects, he knows something about the matters under investigation. In his final remarks about his ignorance, Socrates says that he found that even though the artisans proved to know many things, they did not know the "greatest things," even though they supposed that they knew them. He concluded that he was better in not supposing that he knows these things than they were in supposing mistakenly that they did know them.[71] In light of what he indicates about his knowledge of the virtue of human beings and citizens and about his knowledge of the noble and good, Socrates' claim that he knows nothing about the greatest things appears to mean that he knows why the way of life that morally serious citizens aspire to lead is more difficult and questionable than any of them recognize.

By confirming that his fellow citizens do not know what is noble and good and that they do not know the greatest things, Socrates brings to light a stunning implication: even though the Athenians have been educated by their city's laws, culture, and religious customs, none of them knows anything about those things that matter most to morally serious human beings. Even though most of them were raised in an atmosphere of proud, democratic self-rule mixed with deep civic piety, not a single Athenian has been taught any knowledge about virtue nor about any other important thing, evidently including the gods – insofar as the gods would be included among the beings that are noble and good or among the things that are greatest. More generally, Socrates indicates that none of them has received any wisdom from any divine source, such as from prophecy, poetry, or divine law, and thus he also implies that their accusations against Socrates and the other philosophers are deeply problematic.

It is true that Socrates says that he examined and refuted the politicians, poets, and artisans, but he does not mention questioning any of Athens's religious or spiritual authorities. But this may be a case where Socrates wishes to downplay – but not completely conceal – this most controversial aspect of his investigation. Socrates is more forthcoming about his examinations of the religious authorities a few pages later, when he describes his examination of the poets. He reports that the poets say many noble things without knowing them, through some sort of inspiration, just like the "diviners" and those who interpret oracles.[72] Through his almost offhand comparison, Socrates indicates that he also examined the diviners, oracle interpreters, and perhaps other priestly authorities and found that they do not know what they claim to know about the greatest things.[73]

In the *Phaedo*, Socrates says that when he turned to speeches or to the ideas, he focused on those matters that human beings take seriously, such as what is noble and what is good. In the *Apology*, he indicates that he examined not only himself but also those non-philosophers who are reputed to be wise about what is noble, about what is good, and about those things of practical importance to most human beings. He concludes from this that he alone has human wisdom, and whatever else this might mean, it indicates that none of those who accuse him or any other philosopher do so on the basis of any wisdom concerning virtue or the gods.

The Examination of a Diviner in Plato's *Euthyphro*

Plato does not present us with examples of Socrates examining the politicians, poets, or artisans. He does, however, provide us with an account of Socrates' examination of a "diviner" or prophet (*mantis*). The *Euthyphro* contains Socrates' examination of a man who claims to have prophetic wisdom and to be able to teach it to others. But when Socrates asks Euthyphro to teach him the idea of piety, Euthyphro proves unable to do so. As the only representative of the diviners to appear in Plato's dialogues, Euthyphro's failure to define piety seems to signal that none of those who call themselves diviners or prophets actually are. But there are two difficulties with such an analysis of the dialogue. The first is that Euthyphro is extremely eccentric: he pursues an unseemly and dubious prosecution of his father for the murder of a near stranger on the grounds that the gods hate murderers and those who fail to prosecute them.[74] By casting doubts on Euthyphro's knowledge of piety and the gods, Socrates appears as a defender of common decency and ordinary religious sensibilities. By challenging the wisdom of so odd a figure, Socrates seems to defend common decency. But he also would not seem to shed much light on the wisdom of diviners as such. Yet the drama points to the possibility that Socrates conducted similar examinations of much more respectable diviners and interpreters of oracles and suggests how he called their much more respectable beliefs into question.

The second, graver, difficulty is that Euthyphro does not seem to become as unsettled as Socrates says his interlocutors usually become after he examines them. In the *Apology*, Socrates emphasizes that his interlocutors tend to grow angry when he shows them that they are ignorant because he believes that their anger is very telling. Their angry reactions show that they acknowledge, if only implicitly, that they need but lack a coherent account of the things that are most important to them.[75] For if their ignorance were not genuine or if they did not regard it as a serious deficiency, then they would simply shrug off their failure to answer Socrates. In the *Apology*, Socrates indicates that they do not shrug it off, and he associates their anger with their ignorance or with their refusal to acknowledge that ignorance.[76] In the *Euthyphro*, however, Euthyphro seems to shrug off Socrates' arguments when Socrates points out that he has not been able to define piety adequately. The inquiry into piety begins when Socrates asks Euthyphro to teach him the idea of piety. When Euthyphro says that piety is what the gods love, Socrates asks him whether the pious is what the gods love or whether the gods love what is pious.[77] This question raises what is called the "Euthyphro problem," which is the question whether the gods establish standards for what is pious without looking to anything beyond their own love or will or, by contrast, whether the gods recognize some independent and intelligible standard of piety and whether their love conforms to that standard. As Peter Simpson reminds us in this volume, the question whether a divine being establishes the highest principles or whether those principles exist independently to limit and direct divine beings has been taken up by a long series of important thinkers in the Western tradition.[78]

In response to Socrates' question about which of these two alternatives is true, Euthyphro endorses the former. But he cannot provide an account of what that standard might be and keeps returning to the claim that piety is what the gods love. When Socrates shows him that he has failed to identify the idea of piety, Euthyphro seems to be untroubled. He blames Socrates for the circularity of their arguments.[79] Insofar as Euthyphro is never troubled by his failure to define piety, he seems to believe that his knowledge of piety is profound even if he cannot put it into words for Socrates. He speaks, in other words, as if he has a kind of wisdom that comes to him from the gods that need not be fully articulated through the philosopher's reasoned speech. If he is, and remains, untouched by Socratic dialectics, then this suggests that political philosophy cannot inquire fully into claims made by diviners or prophets. This leaves open the possibility that they possess a divine wisdom that is inaccessible to the rationalist philosopher.[80]

While we cannot undertake a detailed examination of the Euthyphro here, we can note that by the end of the dialogue, Socrates' questions manage to disturb Euthyphro to the point that he must suddenly leave in what he calls a "serious hurry."[81] This latter part of the dialogue differs from the first, in part, because here Socrates asks about the relation between piety and justice. From the start of the dialogue, Euthyphro has consistently associated impiety with injustice.[82] Bearing this in mind, Socrates asks if justice is a part of piety or if piety is a part of justice. Socrates is asking if piety is rooted in justice, so that what we owe the gods is based on and conforms to pre-existing standards of justice. The alternative would be that justice is part of piety, so that what we regard as just is rooted in and shaped by our reverence and duties to the gods. To explain what he is asking, Socrates compares the relation between piety and justice to the relationship between fear and awe. He claims that we can fear without experiencing awe, but we never feel awe unless we also feel fear. This leads us to wonder if fear is a cause of awe and, if so, if justice is also a cause of piety.[83] By suggesting that justice is a cause of piety, he raises the possibility that our beliefs about justice shape our beliefs about what the gods are and about what we owe them. In keeping with this suggestion, Socrates could test to see if he can shake Euthyphro's confidence in his knowledge of justice and if this leads Euthyphro to doubt what he claims to know about the gods.

In response to this question, Euthyphro answers that piety is part of justice. Rather than directly explore and try to shake Euthyphro's understanding of justice, Socrates asks Euthyphro why we owe the gods prayers and sacrifices. Euthyphro answers that we owe the gods thanks for saving our households and cities. When Socrates asks whether the gods love our prayers and sacrifices because these things satisfy some need of the gods, Euthyphro answers that the gods have no needs, so they evidently love them and regard them as pious simply because they love them and regard them as pious. When Socrates points out once again that Euthyphro fails to trace what is pious to any independent and intelligible standard of piety, Euthyphro rushes away. Euthyphro is more troubled this time because Socrates has led him to wonder whether he truly knows what is just and thus whether he can be certain that his prosecution of his father is loved by the gods.[84] Indeed, the fact that he changes his earlier claim that piety is what is loved by the gods to the claim that piety is what the gods happen to love suggests that he does not have a firm grasp on what piety is. The action of the *Euthyphro* thus suggests that Socrates could, if he chose to, lead Euthyphro or any of Athens's other diviners, oracle interpreters, and spiritual leaders to wonder what they truly know about piety and the gods.

While Socrates' examinations may show that those non-philosophers who claim to know divine matters do not know what they claim to know about the gods, we wonder what Socrates can claim to have learned about the gods through his second sailing that gives him confidence that philosophy is not impious or unjust and that a god would not oppose those who lead a philosophic life. How does Socrates know that philosophy helps us to understand what a god is and what a god would require of us? How does he rule out the possibility that mysterious, purposive gods intervene in nature and in our lives? If our beliefs about the gods tend to be grounded in and sometimes garbled by our confused beliefs about justice, what can we come to learn about the gods if we are clear-sighted about justice?

The Theology of the *Republic*

At the end of his life, Plato's Socrates says openly in the *Euthyphro* and the *Apology* that he lacks wisdom about piety and the gods. Yet, in the *Republic*, which is set years before the *Euthyphro* and *Apology*, Socrates is willing to outline, in his own name, an account of what a god is and of how a god should be worshipped. While elaborating the laws that would shape the education of the guardians, Socrates openly challenges the teachings about the gods found in authoritative poets such as Homer and Hesiod, teachings that shape Athens's official rituals and laws. But Socrates declares that much of what they say about the gods and heroes are lies. They lie, he says, about the gods when they say that the gods feel enmity towards one another and fight one another. They also lie when they say that the gods sometimes send us evils along with goods.[85] In place of what traditional authorities teach about divine matters, Socrates lays out the fundamental principles of what will be taught about the gods. This leads him to offer what his companion Adeimantus calls "theology," an account of the gods based on what we can know about them through our own reasoning and experience about them. While it is true that he says that what they teach young people about the gods will have to be a mixture of truth and falsehood since young people cannot understand the truth on its own, he also wins Adeimantus' agreement that what they teach about the gods must be true.[86]

Socrates begins his account of the gods by securing Adeimantus' agreement that the gods are good and that they are the source of only good things and never of the evil things that befall us. If the gods do send us any evils, it is in order to teach us not to do wrong.[87] Adeimantus accepts this first principle and agrees with Socrates' observation that if the gods cannot send us evils, then the gods are not omnipotent.[88] Socrates' second theological principle is that contrary to what Homer teaches, the gods do not alter their forms to deceive human beings. Socrates supports this by saying that the gods' condition is beautiful and in every way the best. Being without any needs, they would never change in any way since any change in their condition would make them worse.[89] This argument leads us to wonder if the gods vary their movements in order to exercise any sort of particular providence. The example that Socrates chooses to illustrate his second principle is that the gods would not lie because they have no need that would compel them to lie. He adds that the gods would not lie to help those who are in need, such as the foolish or insane, because the gods are not friends to those who are foolish or insane.[90] Thus, the gods come to sight as benign beings who nonetheless remain at a distance from our everyday lives: it is a question when or if they intervene to help those who are in need.

This theology is to form the basis of the earliest childhood education of the guardian class. In order to help the young to accept this teaching about the gods, Socrates elaborates an education in the arts that will make help them become courageous or stout-hearted and capable of steely self-control. Later, we will find that the young who have learned to revere these remote, unchanging gods will help them to accept the teaching in books 5 and 6 that the remote, unchanging ideas are the highest objects of study and the highest beings in the cosmos.[91] Yet these theological gods who conform to intelligible principles are not merely akin to but are even limited by the ideas.

As crucial as Socrates' theology is to the *Republic* as a whole, we wonder how Socrates knows that it is true. How does he know that the gods must conform to principles of morality that we recognize and follow? How does he know that they cannot be whatever they might want to be? What Socrates shows in early books of the *Republic* is that morally serious men take justice seriously, and they believe that justice is intelligible to us on its own and not through prophecy or divine law. Adeimantus is among those who believe that justice is good for the just and of those who are friends of the just.[92] Dismissing conventional stories about gods who are indifferent to justice, he is prepared to accept what Socrates says about the gods' beneficence because he believes that a true god would be just and that justice is good and beneficent.[93] Consequently, Socrates is able to show that Adeimantus' beliefs about the gods and about what they require of us are shaped by his beliefs about justice.[94] In this respect, at least, the argument and the action of the *Republic* bear out the hypothesis in the *Euthyphro* that piety is a part of justice.

Adeimantus is, however, less open to Socrates' subsequent claim that the god never change their forms and never lie to help those who are foolish or insane. In order to explain why Socrates ascribes this second principle to the gods, it is useful to consider Socrates' subsequent claim that justice "in truth" is having a harmony or good order in the soul.[95] According to Socrates' definition of justice at the end of book 4, the just man harmonizes the parts of his soul, and the resulting harmony is justice. This internal activity takes place prior to any external action, including any political action.[96] By inviting us to think through how Socrates arrives at this paradoxical account of the "idea" of justice,

Plato offers us the further opportunity to confirm for ourselves whether our beliefs about justice shape our beliefs about the gods and whether becoming more clear-sighted about the former can help us to become more clear-sighted about the latter.

Plato's Inquiry into the Claims of Divine Law

One of the central themes of Plato's dialogues is that Socrates founded political philosophy in order to vindicate the life of philosophy against powerful critics who claim that it is impious and unjust. In dialogue after dialogue, Socrates shows that people who claim to know the greatest things do not know what they claim to know. He shows that none of his interlocutors has a divine wisdom that is not accessible to the rationalist philosopher. In the *Republic*, he uses his own reason to elaborate an account of the gods that, on reflection, seems at odds with what Athens and other cities believe about the gods. His gods resemble what came to be called the philosopher's gods: remote, austere objects of contemplation that do not appear to intervene in the daily lives of human beings. As far as these gods may be from the gods of Athens, Socrates is able to show that the morally serious people with whom he speaks in the dialogue will accept, if only implicitly, such gods insofar as he can show that such gods conform to the principles of justice that they themselves put forward. In other dialogues, Socrates shows that a rationalist philosopher like himself can know the very roots of civic piety. In the *Alcibiades Major*, the *Minos*, and other dialogues, he is able to awaken in others a deep concern for the gods by making them aware of their needs and their ignorance about the greatest things.

As thorough as Socrates' examination of his fellow citizens may be concerning their knowledge of divine matters, it does not fully meet the challenge posed by the very existence of divine law. The classical political philosopher cannot vindicate political philosophy against its most serious critics until he addresses claims that law-giving prophets have established codes of divine law whose wisdom and justice surpasses anything that can be known through rationalist philosophy. Plato undertakes precisely this challenge in the *Laws*. In the *Laws*, the Athenian Stranger travels to Crete to learn about the laws that Zeus gave to Crete through his son, King Minos. Engaged in a probing dialogue with Kleinias, an elderly Cretan statesman, he finds that the laws of Minos aim at producing battlefield courage, but not at the whole of virtue.[97] When the Athenian Stranger asks Kleinias if a genuine code of divine law must aim at the whole of virtue, Kleinias answers that it must, and he acknowledges that the laws of Minos, as currently understood, cannot be divine.[98] By a somewhat less direct route, the elderly Spartan statesman Megillus makes the same concession about the laws that Lycurgus gave to Sparta.[99] Both grant that neither the laws of Crete nor those of Sparta can have come from a god.

When it emerges that Kleinias has been charged with helping to lay out the laws for a new colony of Crete's, he asks the Athenian Stranger to help by continuing to lay out his own account of a truly divine law. With Kleinias and Megillus serving as his touchstone, the Athenian outlines an extensive legal code for the new colony. It is significant that he does not speak to his interlocutors as a philosopher but as a diviner or prophet.[100] The dialogue culminates in book 12, where the Athenian Stranger says that the law requires a saviour because even the divine code that he has elaborated fails to aim at a single goal.[101] He indicates that the saviour must be a philosopher,[102] and his elderly interlocutors enthusiastically ask him to guide the city in securing such a saviour. The drama of the dialogue shows that the philosopher knows what inspires the believer in divine law: he knows what they hope for and expect from divine law. Moreover, he knows that they recognize, explicitly or only implicitly, that divine law must aim at intelligible goals and that such a law needs philosophy, the intellect, to help it achieve those goals. In the end, the opposition to philosophy is not only unwarranted but also an obstacle to the success of divine law.[103] Taken together with Plato's other dialogues that portray Socrates examining non-philosophers who are reputed to be wise, the Laws offers powerful evidence that political philosophy is so far from being impious and unjust that it is necessary for us to know what is truly pious and just.

However much political philosophy may need to answer its contemporary secular and non-secular critics, questions can be raised about whether Plato is a suitable model or guide for mounting a credible defence of political rationalism today. Some might object that Plato may have displayed brilliance in thinking through the conflict between philosophy and revelation in his own day, but a deeper and more complicated conflict comes into sight when philosophy encounters the Biblical God or the Qur'anic God. Limited by his historical situation to knowing only pagan gods, Plato could neither anticipate nor reflect on the possibility of a holy, omnipotent, and ultimately unfathomable God.[104] In this volume, Peter Simpson's essay "Theocracy's Challenge" nicely exemplifies this approach to Plato. Simpson acknowledges that Socrates exposes "the incoherence and hypocrisy in prevailing religious belief and practice" by pointing to something "plainly" better and more intelligent. But, he adds, Socrates' wisdom is "only knowledge of ignorance." He says that when Plato "dares" to teach, he can teach only "theology." Simpson defends this by saying that the Platonic Ideas "are, after all, children of the gods" and that "the Platonic myths repeat, if in sophisticated fashion, what the pagan myths taught: a life after death where the just are rewarded and the unjust punished." Plato's reliance on such myths means that philosophy needs a theology that it can "point to" but cannot substantiate. But Socrates' "knowledge of ignorance" is neither as simple nor as absolute as Simpson assumes. As we have observed, Socrates says in the *Apology* that he knows nothing "so to speak."[105] Later, he says that examining himself and others about virtue and other important matters is the greatest good for a human being, and he asserts in his own name that this is true.[106] In the *Symposium*, he claims that he has expert knowledge in "erotic matters," and this knowledge consists of insight into the most powerful human longing and into what links the human to the divine.[107] In the *Republic*, he claims to have discovered what justice is and never retracts the definition.[108] Rather than reflect on what is behind such claims, Simpson identifies the Platonic Socrates' positive knowledge with the theory of the ideas, a theory that he says is derivative from pagan gods. But unlike the willful, providential pagan gods who came into being out of nothing, the ideas are intelligibly permanent and permanently intelligible beings that are never said to will or even to think.[109] If the ideas are the only intelligible causes of what comes into being and passes away, then they do not merely stand in for the pagan gods: they supplant them by being the standards for all action and by strictly limiting what can come into being and pass away.[110] It is true that Socrates sometimes supplements what he says about justice and the ideas with myths about providential gods.[111] But he presents these stories as myths intended to lead non-philosophers to live justly rather than as supports for his own philosophic activity.[112] As Socrates indicates in the *Apology*, he has evidence for believing that his way of life is good for him whether or not there is an afterlife.[113] This is not to say that Plato's thinking about the ideas makes it impossible for him to anticipate the biblical God. Early fathers of the Church such as Origen and Ambrose enthusiastically draw on Plato's thinking to elaborate their teachings about God. Learning from Platonists such as Cicero and Plotinus, Augustine concludes that Plato is able to know much about God through philosophy alone.[114] According to the great Islamic philosophers of the medieval era, Plato's account of the philosopher-king is, in fact, an account of the Prophet, and the *Republic* as a whole is a model for understanding divine law and establishing.[115] Avicenna says that Plato's books on the laws, that is, the *Laws* and the *Republic*, are "the treatment" of prophecy and divine law.[116] These philosophers found in Plato a model not only for inquiring into divine law, but also for establishing a serious and productive dialogue with defenders of divine law. Contemporary thinkers who yearn for a similar dialogue with contemporary defenders of divine law, or of religious orthodoxy generally, might look to Plato, and to classical political philosophy as a whole, for similar guidance.

NOTES

1 Sayyid Qutb, *Milestones* (USA: SIME Publishing, 2005).
2 Sayyid Qutb, *In the Shade of the Qur'an* (Leicestershire: Islamic Foundation, 2000), 6.
3 Sayyid Qutb, *The Islamic Concept and Its Characteristics* (Plainfield, IN: American Trust Publications, 1991), 11.
4 Helpful studies include John Calvert, *Sayyid Qutb and the Origins of Radical Islamism* (Oxford: Oxford University Press, 2009); and Roxanne Euben, *Enemy in the Mirror* (Princeton: Princeton University Press, 1999).
5 Michael Lynch, *In Praise of Reason* (Cambridge: MIT Press, 2012).
6 Jürgen Habermas, "An Awareness of What Is Missing," in *An Awareness of What Is Missing* (Malden, MA: Polity Press, 2010); John Rawls, *The Law of Peoples* (Cambridge: Harvard University Press, 1999).
7 Leo Strauss, "Preface" to *The Argument and Action of Plato's Laws* (Chicago: University of Chicago Press, 1975); Leo Strauss, *Philosophy and Law* (Ithaca: State University of New York Press, 1995), 74, passim.
8 See Cicero, *Tusculan Disputations*, 5.10–11, and Xenophon, *Memorabilia*, 1.11.
9 See Plato, *Apology of Socrates*, 24b–c, and Xenophon, *Apology of Socrates*, 10. According to Diogenes Laertius in his "Life of Socrates," the indictment read that Socrates does injustice by not believing in the gods of the city and by corrupting the young and leading in new daimonic things.
10 Plato, *Apology*, passim; *Euthyphro*, 2c–3b, 6a; *Seventh Letter*, 325b5–c1.
11 For a helpful discussion of the scholars who advance this claim, see Peter J. Ahrensdorf, "The Question of Historical Context and the Study of Plato," *Polity* 27.1 (1994): 124. See also G.R. Morrow, *Plato's Cretan City* (Princeton: Princeton University Press, 1993), 471–2.

12 Fustel de Coulanges, *The Ancient City* (Baltimore: Johns Hopkins University Press, 1980), 185, 192–3.

13 Aristophanes, *Clouds*, 1445–78; Plato, *Euthyphro*, 5d–e.

14 Aristophanes, *Clouds*, 1226–7.

15 Herodotus, 1.67, 5.63, 7.178, 8.35–9; Thucydides, 1.25.1–2, 1.103.2, 1.118.3, 3.92.5.

16 Thucydides, 7.18.2.

17 Thucydides, 3.89.1, 7.50.4.

18 Plato, *Apology*, 32b–c.

19 Thucydides, 5.105.2–3.

20 *Clouds*, 188–200, 366–425.

21 *Laws*, 888e.

22 Plato, *Apology*, 26d; Plutarch, "Life of Nicias," 23.

23 *Laws*, 889d.

24 *Laws*, 889d–e.

25 Heraclitus, 40, 42, 56, 57, 106.

26 Antiphon, 44–61; Empedocles, 4, 9, 1, 128, 134, 137; Heraclitus, 5, 14, 24, 32, 33, 34, 44, 52, 94, 102, 124, 128.

27 *Clouds*, 367, 900–9.

28 *Clouds*, 1050–82.

29 Ahrensdorf, "The Question of Historical Context and the Study of Plato," 119–20.

30 *Phaedo*, 64a–b.

31 Gregory Vlastos, *Socrates Ironist and Moral Philosophy* (Princeton: Princeton University Press, 1991), 157, 167.

32 Ibid., 170.

33 Ibid., 157, 165.

34 Ibid., 157, 162, 170.

35 Mark McPherran, *The Religion of Socrates* (University Park: State University of Pennsylvania Press, 1996), 38.

36 Ibid., 297.

37 Ibid.,12, 183, 187.

38 Ibid., 190–1, 194–208.

39 Ibid., 6, 8.

40 Ibid., 81, 82, 252, 268.

41 *Crito*, 46b; *Phaedo*, 76b.

42 Leo Strauss, "Progress or Return?" in *The Rebirth of Classical Political Rationalism* (Chicago: University of Chicago Press, 1989), 255, 269.

43 For a lively debate about McPherran's account of Socrates among scholars such as C.D.C. Reeve, Paul Woodruff, and McPherran himself, see

Nicholas D. Smith and Paul Woodruff, eds, *Reason and Religion in Socratic Philosophy* (Oxford: Oxford University Press, 2000).

44 Plato, *Phaedo*, 96a6–10. Unlike scholars such as Vlastos and McPherran who seek the "true" Socrates in Plato's "early" dialogues such as the *Apology, Crito, Euthyphro, Laches, Charmides,* and *Lysis,* Plato expressly presents an "early" or "young" Socrates only in the *Parmenides* and in parts of the *Phaedo, Symposium,* and *Apology.*

45 *Phaedo*, 99b–c3.

46 *Phaedo*, 96e–97b.

47 Cf. *Republic*, 511b–c.

48 *Phaedo*, 96b–c; *Republic*, 506c–7a, 509c; Aristotle, *Metaphysics*, 984a16–b1.

49 Heinrich Meier, "Why Philosophy?" *Review of Metaphysics* 56.2 (2002): 395–6.

50 *Phaedo*, 90d–e.

51 Leo Strauss, *What Is Political Philosophy?* (Chicago: University of Chicago Press, 1959), 39.

52 *Phaedo*, 100b.

53 *Phaedo*, 80d; *Republic*, 379b, 381b.

54 *Euthyphro*, 5a.

55 *Phaedo*, 99d.

56 *Phaedo*, 69d.

57 See also *Apology*, 40c–41c.

58 *Apology*, 29d–30b.

59 *Apology*, 38a.

60 *Apology*, 20e–23e.

61 *Apology*, 20b.

62 *Apology*, 31d, 32e, 36c1.

63 *Apology*, 38a.

64 Excellent, new discussions of the *Apology* include David Leibowitz, *The Ironic Defense of Socrates* (Cambridge: Cambridge University Press, 2010) and Thomas Pangle and Timothy W. Burns, "Plato's *Apology of Socrates,*" in *Key Texts of Political Philosophy* (Cambridge: Cambridge University Press, 2015).

65 *Apology*, 21d.

66 *Symposium*, 203.

67 *Symposium*, 211.

68 Mark J. Lutz, *Socrates' Education to Virtue* (Ithaca: State University of New York Press, 1997), 102, 164–5. For an alternative approach, see Elizabeth S. Belfiore, *Socrates' Daimonic Art* (Cambridge: Cambridge University Press, 2012).

69 *Apology*, 22c–d.

70 *Apology*, 22d1.

71 *Apology*, 22d–e.

72 *Apology*, 22b–c.

73 Leibowitz, *The Ironic Defense of Socrates*, 74, 89.

74 *Euthyphro*, 5d–e.

75 Leibowitz, *The Ironic Defense of Socrates*, 79–80.

76 *Apology*, 21c–e, 22e–23a, 23c–d.

77 *Euthyphro*, 10.

78 For a recent interpretation of the *Euthyphro* see Ronna Burger, *On Plato's Euthyphro* (Munich: Carl Friedrich von Siemens Stiftung, 2015).

79 *Euthyphro*, 10e–11c.

80 For an effective statement of a different approach to how Plato understands the relationship between the philosopher and the divine, see Steven F. McGuire's essay in this volume, "Between Rationalism and Theocracy."

81 *Euthyphro*, 15e.

82 *Euthyphro*, 4b–e, 5d–e, 8b.

83 Christopher Bruell, *On the Socratic Education* (Lanham, MD: Rowman and Littlefield, 1999), 131–2.

84 Consider *Euthyphro*, 14b.

85 *Republic*, 377d–78d.

86 *Republic*, 379a.

87 *Republic*, 380a–b.

88 *Republic*, 380c.

89 *Republic*, 381a–c.

90 *Republic*, 382e.

91 *Republic*, 500b–d, 504d–e, 508a, 509a, 509c1–2.

92 *Republic*, 366e.

93 *Republic*, 365d–66c.

94 See also *Republic*, 330d–31d1.

95 *Republic*, 443c–44a.

96 *Republic*, 443e1–2.

97 *Laws*, 626b–27c, 631b–d.

98 *Laws*, 630d, 631b, 634c.

99 Mark Lutz, *Socrates' Education to Virtue* (Ithaca: SUNY Press, 2012), 54–89.

100 See Leo Strauss, *The Argument and the Action of Plato's Laws* (Chicago: University of Chicago Press, 1975), 11, 16, 49, 58, 149.

101 *Laws*, 961c, 962b–c, 963a–65a.

102 *Laws*, 965c, 967c–d, 969c.

103 *Laws*, 967c–d.

104 See, e.g., Silvio Montiglio, *Silence in the Land of Logos* (Princeton: Princeton University Press, 2010).

105 *Apology*, 22d1.
106 *Apology*, 38a.
107 *Symposium*, 177d; also *Phaedrus*, 257a.
108 *Republic*, 443c1–44a1.
109 Hesiod, *Theogony*, 116–25.
110 *Phaedo*, 96a, 99d–100b.
111 See, e.g., *Republic*, 614b–21d; *Gorgias*, 523a–24a.
112 *Republic*, 614b, 621c–d; *Gorgias*, 527a.
113 *Apology*, 38a, 40d, 42a.
114 Augustine, *City of God*, 5, 8, 11.
115 Al-Farabi, *The Virtuous City*, 1–2.
116 Avicenna, *Divisions of the Rational Sciences*, 108.

3 Between Rationalism and Theocracy: Plato, the Mysteries, and F.W.J. Schelling's Analysis of the Modern State

STEVEN F. McGUIRE

The logic of the secular rational state, which attempts to exclude religion from the theory and practice of politics, would suggest that we should reject theocracy as a primitive and dangerous regime type.[1] In fact, proponents of secular rationalism consider it to be the only reasonable alternative to a politics of religiously motivated coercion and violence.[2] If, however, we follow F.W.J. Schelling's analysis of the modern state, we will find that to draw such a strict dichotomy between secular rationalism and theocracy demonstrates a failure to understand the enduring relationship between religion and politics. This is because Schelling argues that all political regimes, even those that separate church and state, interpret themselves as representing a spiritual stance towards reality. Secular rationalists might not care to speak of the "supremacy of God," but they nevertheless believe their regime represents the truth of existence.[3] Thus, the tension between secular rationalism and theocracy as regime types is not about whether theology and metaphysics should influence politics but, rather, which (as well as how) theologies and metaphysics should have influence. If this is true, then instead of simply rejecting theocracy (or secular rationalism) as inherently objectionable, we should seek to distinguish between those regimes that adequately balance the relationship between religion and politics and those that do not. It is the latter that should truly concern us.

As Eric Voegelin argues, Schelling operates within a tradition of political thought going back to Plato and Augustine that identifies the "spiritual substance" of a community as the primary question of political theory.[4] Like those great thinkers, he recognizes that political communities are defined much more fundamentally by their spiritual commitments than they are by their formal organizations of power and authority. Voegelin points to Schelling's analysis of the Eleusinian mysteries, Platonic philosophy, and the crisis of the ancient Greek polis as an illustration of this point. Although the mysteries were incorporated into Athens's sacred calendar, they contributed to the development of an eschatological consciousness that transcended the mythology of the traditional polis religion and thereby led to the breakdown of the polis as a political form. Plato, who himself acknowledges a connection between the mysteries and philosophy, advances this eschatological consciousness and takes the further step of openly breaking with the mythology of the polis. This can be seen clearly in the *Republic*, in which the soul of the philosopher displaces the Homeric gods as the rightful source of order in the polis. For Plato, the spiritual discovery had an inherently political dimension, as the discovery of a new source of moral-spiritual order demanded expression in the polis. At the same time, without having yet developed the institutional separation of church and state, Plato recognized the limits of this possibility. Schelling himself cites the *Republic* as a warning against attempting to implement a perfect state.

At the foundation of Plato's and Schelling's political thought is their shared recognition that human reason is not immanent and self-grounding, but, rather, open to a reality that transcends it. In Plato's case, this interpretation is supported by references to the mysteries in the *Phaedrus* and *Symposium*. In drawing an analogy between the mysteries and philosophy, Plato highlights the spiritual character of philosophy as pursuit of a transcendent source of order. Of course, the medium of philosophy, unlike the mysteries, is reason, but Plato shows that reason is itself open to the same spiritual reality that is more inchoately sensed in the mysteries. Schelling, likewise, recognizes that the efforts of the German Idealists (including his younger self) to offer a completely rational and systematic account of reality can never succeed so long as we are in history. Reason is always a step behind the historical unfolding of reality and thus always remains responsive to a reality it cannot fully contain.

For both Plato and Schelling, the implications of their analyses of reason and its limits extend to politics. Each argues in his own way that political regimes are ordered towards but cannot fully contain transcendent truth, which means that politics always takes place between the secular and the sacred. It follows that we should be wary of regimes that claim to reduce politics to a purely immanent activity, as well as those that seek to use the state to achieve a transcendent end. It is evident enough that the world could never successfully accommodate regimes and movements of the latter type such as the Taliban, Al-Qaeda, and the Islamic State, given their destructive, apocalyptic ideologies. But secular rationalism pursued to the extreme can also inspire spiritual revolt and be politically destabilizing. Many people (including many Westerners themselves) find the idea of a strict separation of politics and theology to be deeply dissatisfying, and they also recognize that claims to religious neutrality mask the fact that secular rational states advance their own particular conceptions of reality that challenge other views and ways of life. For these reasons, it seems unlikely that France, for instance, will be able to maintain its policy of laïcité and integrate its growing Muslim population. Likewise, in the United States, the recent ruling of the Supreme Court concerning same-sex marriage represents to many religious believers the latest step in a movement towards a secular liberalism that is hostile towards their faith. Examples such as these illustrate that Schelling correctly saw that the modern separation of church and state did not completely sever the ancient connection between religion and politics.

The Eleusinian Mysteries and the Polis

Religion and politics were much more compactly related in the ancient Greek polis than they are in the modern age. The polis was the institutional context in which the Greeks participated in religion, and, in turn, it was ordered by the religious beliefs and practices of the community.[5] The polis was imbued with spiritual meaning: more than a merely secular or mundane political unit, it was understood to be an analogue for the cosmos, creating a "shelter" of order and meaning against a backdrop of chaos. It thus provided at once the political, legal, moral, and spiritual framework for ancient Greek life. It is the model for Voegelin's claim that every political society is "a little world, a cosmion, illuminated with meaning from within by the human beings who continuously create and bear it as the mode and condition of their self-realization."[6]

According to Schelling, the Eleusinian mysteries presented a challenge to the traditional order of the polis, and Voegelin uses Schelling's account of this challenge to illustrate the inherent link between politics and spirituality. Both Schelling and Voegelin believe that the mysteries threatened the order of the polis because they represented a new eschatological consciousness among the ancient Greeks that challenged the cosmological order associated with the Olympian gods. As Voegelin remarks in his discussion of the mysteries, "the Hellenic late civilization had developed a strong eschatological consciousness, a consciousness of the impending twilight of the gods, and with them of the polis."[7] Contemporary scholars are less inclined to recognize such a tension between the mysteries and traditional polis religion, noting that ancient Athens incorporated the mysteries into its sacred calendar. But the distinctiveness remains evident for a variety of reasons: non-Athenians, women, and slaves could be initiated; initiation was optional; the mysteries were shrouded in secrecy; and the spiritual purpose, blessings in the afterlife, were deeply personal. Each of these facts points to a distinct spiritual experience that broke the mould of the traditional polis religion.

Yet, the mysteries and the traditional polis religion were able to coexist. As Voegelin argues, it is Plato who clearly and openly questions the traditional order of the polis: "The open break with the traditional spiritual substances comes with the death of Socrates and the Platonic myth of the soul, and in the end the idea of the polis dies in the apoliticism of the Cynic, Stoic, and Epicurean schools."[8] Thus, Platonic philosophy does not represent a break with religion *tout court*, but, rather, a continuation of the spiritual movement more inchoately present in the mysteries. With the mysteries and then with Platonic philosophy the source of divine order is no longer found in the traditional mythology and rituals of the polis, but instead in the experience of initiation (in the case of the mysteries) or in the practice of philosophy (in Plato's case). As mentioned in the introduction, the break is clear in the *Republic*, where the soul of the philosopher, rather than the Olympian gods, is the source of moral and political order in human existence. But, according to Schelling and Voegelin – and Plato, who employs the mysteries to explain philosophy in both the *Symposium* and the *Phaedrus*, as will be discussed below – the mysteries represent an important step towards that break.

The Eleusinian mysteries are notorious for their secrecy (it was a crime to profane them), so, while scholars have collected many details about them from various ancient sources, it is not possible to explain the rituals with complete confidence, and certainly their meaning is a matter of interpretation and even speculation. Nevertheless, it is possible to offer a reasonably thorough account of how the mysteries likely transpired, of which a brief overview will suffice for present purposes.[9]

The mysteries were divided into two stages, the lesser and the greater. The lesser mysteries were preparatory to the greater, and they involved purifications and perhaps some instruction or other rites that took place near Athens, likely at Agrai by the Ilissos River in the Attic month of Anthesterion (February/March). The greater mysteries, which took place in Boedromion (September/October), began with a procession from Eleusis to Athens, and included rituals of purification, a time of fasting, a procession of the initiates from Athens to Eleusis, and then finally the events at Eleusis itself. The final revelations took place in the *Telestrion*, a large building dedicated to Hades which could hold a few thousand people. The only ones permitted to enter were the *mystai*, those initiates entering for the first time, and the *epoptai*, for whom it would be at least their second experience (initiates could re-experience the mysteries as many times as they wished; they had to go through the process at least twice to become an *epoptēs*). Each *mystai* had a *mysta-gogos*, someone who had been previously initiated and would lead the new initiate through the rites and into the site of the mysteries at Eleusis. In the centre of the *Telestrion* was the *Anaktoron*, a rectangular structure with a door at one end where the Hierophant's throne was placed. A fire burned on top of the *Anaktoron*; otherwise, it was dark until a flash of light emerged as the Hierophant emerged from the *Anaktoron*. It is unclear exactly what took place at this point, but it is suggested that the initiates witnessed things done, shown, and said. There is, for instance, mention of the re-enactment of a sacred marriage. One source reports that "the Athenians, celebrating the Eleusinian mysteries, show to the *epoptai* the great, admirable, most perfect epoptic secret, in silence, a reaped ear of grain."[10] But scholars are uncertain about both the veracity and the possible significance of accounts such as this one. The final revelations have been kept remarkably secret.

Further light is shed on the rituals and their meaning by the *Hymn to Demeter*, an ancient poem which ties the mysteries to an ancient myth about the goddess Demeter's search for her daughter, Persephone, who had been kidnapped by (and married to) Hades. The *Hymn* suggests that the mysteries were established to comfort the anxieties of human beings. As the *Hymn* reads:

> Mortals are ignorant and foolish, unable to foresee
> Destiny, the good and the bad coming on them.
> You are incurably misled by your folly.
> Let the god's oath, the implacable water Styx, be witness,

I would have made your child immortal and ageless
Forever; I would have given him unfailing honor.
But now he cannot escape death and the death spirits.
Yet unfailing honor will forever be his, because
He lay on my knees and slept in my arms.
In due time as the years come round for him,
The sons of Eleusis will continue year after year
To wage war and dread combat against each other.
For I am honored Demeter, the greatest
Source of help and joy to mortals and immortals.
But now let all the people build me a great temple
With an alter beneath, under the sheer wall
Of the city on the rising hill above Kallichoron.
I myself will lay down the rites so that hereafter
Performing due rites you may propitiate my spirit.[11]

Human beings exist in a mortal condition characterized by ignorance and folly. Implicit in the passage is the recognition that we experience this condition as inadequate, that we seek immortality, and that we fear falling out of favour with the divine source of order in the cosmos, which is represented here by the goddess Demeter. The mysteries are instituted to save us from such a misfortune. The importance of initiation is emphasized by the power that Hades grants to Persephone, his abducted bride and Demeter's daughter, when he releases her from the underworld:

You will have power over all that lives and moves,
And you will possess the greatest honors among the gods.
There will be punishment forevermore for those wrongdoers
Who fail to appease your power with sacrifices,
Performing proper rites and making due offerings.[12]

The end of the *Hymn* confirms that initiation was believed to secure a blessed state in this life and in the next. It also explains that the mysteries are to be kept secret. The *Hymn* relates that Demeter

... revealed
the conduct of her rites and taught her Mysteries to all of them,
holy rites that are not to be transgressed, nor pried into,
nor divulged. For a great awe of the gods stops the voice.

Blessed is the mortal on earth who has seen these rites,
But the uninitiated who has no share in them never
Has the same lot once dead in the dreary darkness.[13]

Thus, the mysteries offer initiates an opportunity to gain personal assurance that they are on good terms with the gods and will experience the benefits of that relationship in the afterlife. But why were the mysteries to be kept secret?

Schelling's argument in this regard is idiosyncratic and speculative and, as others have noted, the details likely do not stand up to contemporary philological scrutiny, but his general idea might have some truth to it.[14] He argues that the mysteries both recognized the legitimacy of the traditional gods of the polis, but also sought to move beyond them into a new age of spiritual understanding; thus, the mysteries could be incorporated into the religious activities of the polis, but only so long as the challenge to the traditional gods remained silent. As Edward Beach explains, by Schelling's account, the mysteries represented "the self-overcoming of the mythological consciousness" and the "inmost secret of the Mysteries represented the longing for a new religion that would surpass and replace the old religion."[15] Thus, the polis could only tolerate the mysteries so long as they were not openly discussed. Schelling almost certainly overstates the conflict between the mysteries and the polis, but it is still likely correct to see in the mysteries the beginning of an eschatological consciousness that would eventually challenge the traditional religion of the polis.

Even if this account is true, however, it still does not answer an even more puzzling question, that is, why were the rites never fully divulged in the writings of some impious soul who had at one time participated in the mysteries? Walter Burkert, a leading authority on ancient Greek religion, has suggested that the secret was ordered and kept because the significance of the rites simply could not be revealed to the uninitiated. As he explains,

Two adjectives, *aporrheta* ("forbidden") and *arrheta* ("unspeakable'"), seem to be nearly interchangeable in this usage, hinting at a basic problem inherent in the "secret" of mysteries: a mystery must not be betrayed, but it cannot really be betrayed because told in public it would appear insignificant; thus violations of the secrecy that did occur did no harm to the institutions, but protection of the secrecy greatly added to the prestige of the most sacred cults.[16]

This suggests that in order to fully understand the mysteries, one would have to participate in them. Because the meaning of the mysteries was found in the experience, the incomplete record of what actually happened during the rituals may not necessarily be the greatest obstacle to our understanding their meaning. In the words again of Burkert:

> If we had a fuller account [of the Mysteries at Eleusis], or even a filmed record such as modern anthropologists provide to document exotic customs, we would still be baffled. The gap between pure observation and the experience of those involved in the real proceedings remains unbridgeable. Who can tell what the experience is like without having undergone days and days of fasting, purifications, exhaustion, apprehension, and excitement?[17]

In short, the only way to truly understand the mysteries would be to enter into them. They offered initiates an experience that could not simply be revealed in language; rather than communicating a secret doctrine, they conducted a movement of the soul.

There is other ancient evidence to suggest that the point of the mysteries was the experience rather than a secret doctrine. In a fragment, Aristotle wrote that the initiates did not learn (*mathein*), but experienced (*pathein*) the mysteries and were brought to an appropriate state of mind,[18] and Sopatros says, "I came out of the mystery hall feeling like a stranger to myself."[19] Contemporary classicist Helene Foley agrees that the mysteries did not transmit to the initiates any knowledge as we normally understand it: "The secret rites did not pass on any secret doctrine or worldview or inculcate beliefs … Its blessings came from experiencing and viewing signs, symbols, stories, or drama and bonding with fellow initiates."[20] Thus, it seems that the mysteries were secretive because they could not be revealed to the uninitiated; one had to go through the process of initiation in order to understand the meaning of the revelation. Plato appears to have thought this a key point of connection between the mysteries and his philosophy.

The Mysteries and Plato's Political Philosophy

The mysteries were incorporated into the Athenian sacred calendar. Platonic philosophy, by contrast, explicitly seeks to replace the traditional religion of the polis and openly recognizes the transcendent *Agathon* as a new and superior source of personal and political order. Yet, in so doing it operates in continuity with the mysteries, as it further differentiates and builds on the eschatological consciousness they represent. Plato himself recognizes the connection between philosophy and the Eleusinian mysteries in several of his dialogues; the *Phaedrus* and the *Symposium*, in particular, both reference and even structurally mimic the themes and rituals of the mysteries.[21] Of particular interest is the fact that in both cases the language of the mysteries is used in passages that refer to the highest philosophical vision, as will be detailed below. This suggests that the practice of philosophy culminates in an experience that is analogous to the experience of mystery initiates. Indeed, Plato indicates that the experience of the philosopher, like the experience of the initiate, is one that can be understood only by becoming a philosopher. Moreover, he suggests that philosophy, like the mysteries, is eschatological and therefore spiritual in character: philosophy is not simply an intellectual discipline, but a spiritual experience that has a "saving" function. Finally, he also makes clear (perhaps most evidently in the *Republic*) that this experience peaks in the recognition of a source of order (moral, political, and spiritual) that transcends Homeric mythology. Taken together, these similarities to the mysteries suggest that philosophizing leads to a life-altering spiritual experience of a transcendent source of order that has profound consequences for both personal and political life.

It can be firmly established that the *Symposium* and the *Phaedrus* reference the mysteries at Eleusis through Plato's use of certain terms that are associated only with those specific rites. In the *Symposium*, the language of the mysteries appears in Diotima's speech when she says, "Even you, Socrates, could probably come to be initiated [*myētheiēs*] into these rites of love. But as for the purpose of these rites when they are done correctly – that is the final and highest mystery [*ta de telea kai epoptika*]."[22] The Greek verb *myētheiēs* is related to the noun *myesis*, which was the first level of initiation into the Eleusinian mysteries. And *epoptika*, here translated as "the highest mystery," is related to the noun *epoptēs*, which means in general "watcher" or "witness," but is also the name for those who have achieved the highest level of initiation in the Eleusinian mysteries. *Epoptēs* appears not to have been used in reference to any other mystery rite.[23] Thus, Plato is referencing specifically the highest revelation in the Eleusinian mysteries.

Similarly, in the *Phaedrus* Socrates employs Eleusinian terminology to describe the culmination of philosophical experience in his mythical account of the ascent of souls to a vision of that which is beyond being. Socrates says:

> As is just, only the [understanding] of a philosopher, the one who is in love with wisdom, grows wings. For thought is always, according to her capability through memory, near to those things, and by this nearness a god is divine. And only a man who correctly handles such reminders and is perpetually initiated into the perfect mysteries is truly perfect [*teleous aei teletas teloumenos, teleos ontōs monos gignetai*]. But standing apart from zealous human pursuits and being near to the divine, he is admonished by the many for being deranged, because they fail to see that he is divinely possessed, having the god within.[24]

That the reference is to Eleusis is confirmed in the next passage when Plato again refers to the idea of the *epoptēs*:

> Formerly ... it was possible to look upon beauty in its radiance when in a blessed chorus-dance we in Zeus' entourage, and others in the company of other gods, witnessed a blest sight and spectacle and we were initiated into what it is lawful to call the most blest of the mysteries. Celebrating these inspired rites, we were whole and untouched by those evils which lay in wait for us later. Being fully initiated and looking [*epopteuontes*] upon the whole, simple, unchanging, and blessed visions in pure light, we were ourselves pure and unmarked by what we now carry around and call a body, a thing which imprisons us like an oyster shell.[25]

Thus, in the *Phaedrus*, as in the *Symposium*, Plato uses the language of the Eleusinian mysteries as an analogy for the height of philosophical experience. The overall structures of the dialogues appear to be tied to the mysteries as well, as it could be argued that each dialogue involves a process of purification followed by an attempt by Socrates to lead one or more interlocutors into the deepest mystery of philosophy. Moreover, the would-be philosopher is guided by one who is already initiated; just as a *mystes* had a *mystagogos*, so the student of philosophy has a *psychagogos*.[26]

A further similarity is found in the secrecy that surrounds the wisdom of the philosopher. In both the *Symposium* and the *Phaedrus* the process of initiation into philosophy is described as a difficult process that ends in a vision that only a few can achieve. Likewise, in the *Republic*, Socrates does not describe the good directly, but only through simile and allegory. In the *Seventh Letter*, Plato attributes his silence to reasons similar to those used by Burkert in relation to the mysteries:

> There is no writing of mine about these matters [philosophical knowledge], nor will there ever be one. For this knowledge is not something that can be put into words like other sciences; but after long-continued intercourse between teacher and pupil, in joint pursuit of the subject, suddenly, like light flashing forth when a fire is kindled, it is born in the soul and straightway nourishes itself. And this too I know: if these matters are to be expounded at all in books or lectures, they would best come from me. Certainly I am harmed not least of all if they are misrepresented. If I thought they could be put into written words adequate for the multitude, what nobler work could I do in my life than to compose something of such great benefit to mankind and bring to light the nature of things for all to see?[27]

In parallel to Diotima's experience in the *Symposium* and the experience of the souls in the *Phaedrus*, here Plato writes that the highest philosophical knowledge cannot be transmitted to the uninitiated simply and directly.

These parallels between Platonic philosophy and the Eleusinian mysteries suggest that the common tie between them is their spiritual and, specifically, eschatological, character. To be sure, philosophizing and initiation into the mysteries are very different experiences, but Plato believed they both pointed to human participation in a reality that transcends the polis and its gods. Of course, in philosophy, unlike in the mysteries, this movement takes place through reason. The philosopher seeks to become self-reflectively aware of the nature and mode of his participation in reality in a way that the mystery initiate does not. At the same time, philosophy leads to participation in a reality that reason cannot render transparent. For Plato, human beings exist in *metaxy* – "between" mortality and immortality, ignorance and knowledge, injustice and justice – and reason is a movement of the soul by which we participate in a reality that is lasting, true, and good.[28] However, even as the soul of the philosopher ascends to these heights and becomes the new standard for moral and political order, Plato also recognizes our limited ability to implement it in personal and political life. The "between" nature of the human condition is not broken by Plato's discovery of a source of order beyond it.

The new spiritual standpoint of philosophy and the attendant analysis of the human condition become the basis for Plato's political theory. Plato's own experience of philosophy in relation to the Homeric myth suggests the political implications: the new standard of order both illuminates the nature of politics and becomes the basis for evaluating political regimes. Plato observes, first, that regimes are distinguished most fundamentally by the spiritual stance of the souls who lead them. Aristocracies are ruled by aristocrats, oligarchies by oligarchs, and so forth. Thus, Plato recognizes that the spiritual condition of a community is ultimately the source of its political order. Moreover, the new spiritual standpoint of the philosopher becomes the standard by which he evaluates and ranks the various regimes. Plato's political theory is at once descriptive and normative. From this perspective he sees that the crisis of ancient Athens is first and foremost due to the moral and spiritual poverty or corruption of its leaders. At the same time, he recognizes that political life takes place in *metaxy*, which means that every regime is likely to fall short of the philosophical idea of the polis that he articulates in the *Republic*. In what follows we will see that Schelling analyses the modern state in similar terms.

Schelling on the Modern State

In his *Stuttgart Seminars* of 1810 Schelling develops a critique of the political thought of his contemporaries that, according to Voegelin, shows he "has reestablished the theory of politics on the level of Plato and Saint Augustine." The key point, Voegelin argues, is Schelling's recognition that

> political theory is not exhausted by reflections on absolute and constitutional monarchy, on republic and democracy, on administration and rule of law, on executive, legislative, and judiciary powers, etc., but that the secular state must be understood in its very secularity, that is, in its relation to the spiritual substance of the community. Not the internal organization of the state, but the relation of the differentiated, secularized, political unit to the spiritual substance (to the idea, in Schelling's terminology) is the primary political problem. In this relation are rooted the problems of stability and instability, political rise and decay, change and evolution, revolution and crisis. If the secularized state is not placed in the context of the spiritual history of the modern world, the political phenomena of an age of crisis must remain utterly incomprehensible.[29]

For Schelling, as for Plato, the character of a regime is defined more fundamentally by the spiritual stance of the community than by its institutional arrangements.

More immediately, Schelling's political thought is grounded in the historical-metaphysical account of human existence that he developed as he moved beyond the philosophical paradigm of German idealism. Schelling himself is best known as one of the great German idealists (he knew and collaborated with both Fichte and Hegel), and many of his early works are important contributions to that school of thought, but the majority of his work belongs to the post-idealist period of his life. By his early thirties he had begun to question the possibility of offering a completely rational and systematic account of reality. His eventual break with idealism was precipitated by his conclusion that it could account for neither the reality of evil nor, by extension, true moral freedom. In his 1809 *Philosophical Investigations into the Essence of Human Freedom*, a watershed in his intellectual development, Schelling suggests that moral freedom is possible only because human existence takes place between the light of reason and a dark ground that is impenetrable to reason. Hence, there is a fundamental contingency in the nature of things that resists rational systematization and leaves open a living space for human freedom. With this insight Schelling also challenges the idea of freedom as autonomy by subjecting human beings to a reality they do not author and cannot rationally master. He would continue to explore the relationships between reason and contingency in his remaining decades; his efforts ultimately took the form of a philosophy of mythology and revelation in which he attempted to test his philosophical account of reality (reason) through an empirical investigation of history (contingency). He remained convinced that reason was not self-grounding because it is embedded in and responsive to a reality that it cannot fully explain or make transparent to itself.

Schelling's reflections in the *Philosophical Investigations into the Essence of Human Freedom* form the basis for his analysis of the modern state in the *Stuttgart Seminars* of 1810. He begins with a similar account of the human condition, arguing that human beings are free because they exist in a "middle-ground between the nonbeing of nature and the absolute Being = God."[30] As he further explains, the human being is "free from God by virtue of possessing an independent root in nature and free from nature by virtue of the fact that the divine has been kindled within him; that is, he is in the midst of, and simultaneously above, nature."[31] This, then, leaves open a space for moral freedom because we are compelled to follow neither the will of God nor the mechanism of nature. Schelling then goes on to argue that human beings currently exist in a fallen condition. Originally and finally destined to freely subordinate themselves to God, they have misused their freedom to assert themselves against God, leading to a breakdown in the order of being. Schelling's account is clearly reminiscent of the Christian account of the Fall, but he does not simply rely on the authority of revelation for his account. Rather, he believes it is empirically evident that the world is corrupted, citing as evidence the "opaqueness," "contingency," and "unrest" in nature, as well as, and perhaps most importantly, the existence of evil.[32] For Schelling, we experience these things as disordered because we judge them from the perspective of our participation in reason.

In this context Schelling interprets the modern state as a necessary but inadequate replacement for the spiritual unity that human beings enjoyed before they fell away from God. The state is an inadequate replacement because it does not achieve the inner or spiritual unity that has been lost (one based on free will), but it at least provides an external or natural unity as a substitute. As Schelling explains, "God can no longer be their [human beings'] unity, and hence they must search for a natural unity that, because it cannot be the true unity of free Beings, remains but a temporal and finite bond."[33] He continues: "The natural unity, this second nature superimposed on the first, to which man must necessarily take recourse, is the [modern] state; and, to put it bluntly, the [modern] state is thus a consequence of the curse that has been placed on humanity. Because man no longer has God for his unity, he must submit to a material unity."[34] The state orders the outward interactions of human beings (through coercion and force, if necessary) in order to maintain a semblance of the unity that once existed (or should exist) through freedom.

In Schelling's analysis, then, the state is a response to a spiritual problem, and it is ordered towards a spiritual end, even if it cannot fully achieve that end itself. It therefore must be understood in relation to the church, which represents the spiritual unity human beings seek. As Schelling observes, "The [modern] state, when viewed as an attempt to produce the merely external unity is opposed by another institution, one based on revelation and aimed at producing an inner unity or unity of the mind; namely, the *Church*."[35] Schelling thus recognizes the separation of church and state, but he also claims that there is a fundamental connection between them, since they are both ordered towards the same end. He further argues that the state cannot rely on force and coercion alone to maintain unity; it must also rely on and cultivate a moral and spiritual unity that supplements and supports the legal unity sought through the institutions of government:

> The idea of the state is marked by an internal contradiction. It is a natural unity, i.e., a unity whose efficacy depends solely on material means. That is, the state, even if it is being governed in a rational manner, knows well that its material power alone cannot effect anything and that it must invoke higher and spiritual motives. These, however, lie beyond its domain and cannot be controlled by the state, even though the latter boasts with being able to create a moral setting, thereby arrogating to itself a *power* equal to nature. A free spirit, however, will never consider [such] a natural unity sufficient, and a higher talisman is required; consequently, any unity that originates in the state remains inevitably precarious and provisional.[36]

Thus, he concludes, "the state ought to cultivate the religious principles within itself."[37] This is not a call for theocracy, but a recognition of something akin to Aristotle's idea of *homonoia*, or like-mindedness. The state governs and is governed by human beings, who are both rational and material beings. Therefore, even though the state aims at material unity, it also depends on some spiritual support in order to pursue that unity. Force and coercion will not be enough to hold the community together if its inhabitants do not willingly believe that it aligns with the truth of existence as they understand it.

Having established his understanding of the state and its proper relation to the church, Schelling proceeds to critique his contemporaries' attempts to harmonize individual freedom and political community as a failure to balance their spiritual longings and political reality. It is reasonable to say that this is Schelling's critique of secular rationalism, although he does not use the term. He argues that such a harmonization is impossible because all attempts to achieve it must either deny the right of the state to use force or maintain that right and thereby compromise freedom. As he writes, "We all know of the efforts that have been made, especially since the advent of the French Revolution and the Kantian concepts, to demonstrate how unity could possibly be reconciled with the existence of free beings ... Quite simply, such a state is an impossibility. Either the state is deprived of proper force or, where it is granted such [force], we have despotism."[38] Citing Fichte in particular, he concludes that "it is quite natural that at the end of this period during which people have been talking of nothing but freedom, the most consequent minds, in their pursuit of the idea of a perfect state, would have arrived at the worst kind of despotism."[39] Rather than recognizing the state's trajectory towards the transcendent truth represented by the church, these modern political thinkers have abstracted from the church and attempted to find spiritual fulfilment within the state. Here Schelling appeals to the *Republic*, noting that "Plato has shown what we are to think of the idea of a rational state, of the ideal state, although he did not pronounce it expressly. The true state presupposes a heaven on earth, and the true *politeia* exists only in heaven."[40]

Schelling's reference to the *Republic* suggests that Voegelin is correct to identify Schelling with the ancient tradition of political thought. Like Plato, Schelling recognizes that political regimes should be defined primarily according to their spiritual commitments. Moreover, Schelling recognizes in his own way the "between" character of human existence and, by extension, politics. In terms of reason, he expresses this insight in his recognition that it is always subject to a reality that is greater than itself and which continues to be revealed in history. In terms of politics, he recognizes that the state is simultaneously ordered towards transcendent reality and constitutionally incapable of fully implementing that reality. Finally, from this standpoint, Schelling critiques the modern rationalist conception of reason and the political thought that follows from it. His essay on freedom suggests that the very idea of reason as systematic is inimical to freedom because a closed rational system does not leave room for moral freedom. And in the *Stuttgart Seminars*, as has just been discussed, he observes that a state that is closed to the church will either undermine itself or the freedom of its population. In sum, while Schelling's analysis is not strictly speaking Platonic, it clearly operates in that tradition of political thought. Both Plato and Schelling understand that human beings seek a higher reality that remains elusive but nevertheless serves as the source of order for individual and communal existence.

Between Rationalism and Theocracy

We who live in secular rational states have trouble recognizing the connection between politics and spirituality because we live in an age in which the various dimensions of human existence have been so successfully differentiated from one another. So, for instance, we see much more readily the grounds for the institutional separation of church and state than we do the ongoing overlap of their jurisdictions in concrete reality. But the differentiation of these aspects of human existence does not undermine their interaction in the unity of concrete existence. Every human being and every human community still participates in both the political and spiritual dimensions of human experience and these overlap in lived experience as they always have. The connection is clearly illustrated by the crisis of the ancient polis: the eschatological consciousness represented by the mysteries and Platonic philosophy eventually unsettled the order of the polis by challenging the Homeric mythology that governed it. But, as Schelling shows, even the secular rational state represents a particular spiritual stance towards reality.

In his critique of secular rationalism Schelling follows Plato's recognition of the limits to ordering the city according to transcendent truth. With the analogy to the mysteries Plato portrays the philosopher as someone who seeks a truth that proves to be elusive. The beautiful in the *Symposium*, the beyond in the *Phaedrus* (and the good in the *Republic*) symbolize the truth in which the philosopher participates but cannot simply communicate. The truth of philosophy is transcendent, and reason, for Plato, is not simply a capacity of the human mind, but a movement of the soul towards ultimate reality. In the Platonic scheme, to confine reason to the immanent world (or to expect it to escape the limits of that world) would be to deform it. The human being and human reason live and move between immanence and transcendence. Likewise, the state cannot perfectly represent transcendent order, but it is ordered towards and dependent on it. The beautiful city of the *Republic* is the form of the city, but, as a form, it is not observable in the world.

Schelling demonstrates the significance of these ancient insights for understanding contemporary politics, especially potential conflicts between secular rationalism and theocracy. For the Schelling, the modern state is a kind of spiritual halfway house. It exists to order human beings externally towards God because we have failed to maintain our unity (with one another and with God) internally. The state by its nature cannot replace the church because it cannot bring about that internal unity which must be a matter of free will. Yet it is ordered towards the transcendent good represented by the church and depends for its existence on the community's continued recognition of that higher good. Therefore, while Schelling recognizes the institutional separation of church and state, he argues that they must cooperate with one another for the good of the community. Even in the modern age the state retains a spiritual character. Thus, whether a state interprets itself as representing the truth of existence or not cannot serve as a basis for distinguishing between good and bad regimes. It also seems unlikely that disagreements about the formal organization of power (secular rationalists separate the institutions of church and state, whereas theocrats do not) should be decisive. The real danger comes from those regimes that fail to maintain a balance between their spiritual longings and political reality, whether those longings are expressed in religious terms (as in the various Islamist movements) or secular ones (as is somewhat evident in the foreign policy prescriptions of American progressives and neoconservatives, although these cannot in any way be morally equated to the former). This might be a problem to which theocracies are particularly prone, but Schelling critiques the political thought of his contemporaries for this very reason, and surely it is possible for a theocratic regime to be politically responsible. Thus, the distinction between secular rationalism and theocracy does not necessarily determine whether a regime is inherently dangerous or not.

As is suggested by Schelling's critique of Enlightenment rationalism and political thought, the particular danger we face in modernity is the tendency to juxtapose rather than simply differentiate faith and reason. Rather than recognizing the legitimacy of both, secular rationalists are inclined to assert reason against faith and to argue that politics should operate in abstraction from religion and the church. And then theocrats who do precisely the opposite arise in response. On an international level we see this in the conflict between Western liberal democracies and various Islamist movements such as the Taliban, Al-Qaeda, and the Islamic State. It is also evident in domestic tensions, such as those between secularists and Christian fundamentalists (especially in the United States) or Muslims (in France and other parts of Europe). These conflicts result in part because the modern attempt to separate religion and politics encourages us to fall into the categories of fideism and rationalism.[41] Both are problematic because they obscure the other as a fundamental part of human experience, and, in so doing, they aim to establish a more certain connection between spiritual truth and political order than is possible in reality. Moreover, the dichotomy itself is dangerous because it divides the political world into two camps that are fundamentally opposed to one another and have no shared basis for community. For these reasons, it seems imperative that we attempt to recover a proper sense of the enduring and necessary relationship between religion and politics.

Conclusion

There is a growing recognition among Western elites, especially since the attacks of 11 September 2001, of a need to re-evaluate the possibility of secular rationalism and to reconsider the role of religion in public life. Jürgen Habermas, for instance, has modified his earlier commitment to strict secular rationalism and suggested that the great religious traditions have something to contribute to contemporary public discourse.[42] Schelling's analysis of the modern state shows why this re-evaluation is necessary. The crisis of the ancient Athenian polis wrought by the eschatological consciousness represented by the mysteries and Platonic philosophy clearly demonstrates that the spiritual condition of a community is inherently linked to its political order. Schelling sees that this is still a truth of the human condition in modernity: the institutional separation of church and state does not dissolve the relationship between religion and politics in concrete reality. The particular danger of the secular rational state is that it will fail to understand itself as participating in a transcendent source of order. Theocracy, by contrast, might struggle to accept the limits of political existence. In either case, however, the source of the problem – a failure to maintain balance between the sacred and the secular – is the same, as is the potential consequence: dangerous and likely destructive politics.

NOTES

1 Mark Lilla, *The Stillborn God: Religion, Politics, and the Modern West* (New York: Vintage Books, 2008).
2 William T. Cavanaugh, *The Myth of Religious Violence: Secular Ideology and the Roots of Modern Conflict* (New York: Oxford University Press, 2009).
3 Ronald Weed and John von Heyking, eds, *Civil Religion in Political Thought: Its Perennial Questions and Enduring Relevance in North America* (Washington: Catholic University of America Press, 2010).
4 Eric Voegelin, *The Collected Works of Eric Voegelin*, vol. 25: *History of Political Ideas*, vol. 7: *The New Order and the Last Orientation*, ed. Jürgen Gebhardt and Thomas Hollweck (Columbia: University of Missouri Press, 1999), 227.
5 Christiane Sourvinou-Inwood, "What Is *Polis* Religion?" in *Oxford Readings in Greek Religion*, ed. Richard Buxton (New York: Oxford University Press, 2000).
6 Eric Voegelin, *The New Science of Politics: An Introduction* (Chicago: University of Chicago Press, 1987), 27.
7 Voegelin, *The New Order and the Last Orientation*, 229.

8 Ibid., 227–8.
9 For accounts of the mysteries and the ancient sources relating to them, see
   Walter Burkert, *Ancient Mystery Cults* (Cambridge: Harvard University
   Press, 1987); Burkert, *Greek Religion* (Cambridge, MA: Harvard University
   Press, 1985); Helene P. Foley, ed., *The Homeric Hymn to Demeter: Translation,
   Commentary, and Interpretive Essays* (Princeton: Princeton University Press,
   1994); George Mylonas, *Eleusis and the Eleusinian Mysteries* (Princeton:
   Princeton University Press, 1974); Karl Kerényi, *Eleusis: Archetypal Image of
   Mother and Daughter*, trans. R. Mannheim (New York: Bollingen Foundation,
   1967); Robert Parker, *Polytheism and Society at Athens* (New York: Oxford
   University Press, 2005); Jan N. Bremmer, *Initiation into the Mysteries of
   the Ancient World* (Boston: Walter de Gruyter, 2014); Kevin Clinton, "The
   Sanctuary of Demeter and Kore at Eleusis," in *Greek Sanctuaries*, ed. Nanno
   Marinatos and Robin Hägg (New York: Routledge, 1993).
10 Hippolytus, *Refutation of All Heresies*, 5.8.39f., quoted in Burkert, *Ancient
   Mystery Cults*, 91.
11 *Homeric Hymn to Demeter*, 256–74. Translation from Foley, *The Homeric
   Hymn to Demeter*.
12 Ibid., 365–9.
13 Ibid., 475–82.
14 Barry Cooper, *Eric Voegelin and the Foundations of Modern Political Science*
   (Columbia: University of Missouri Press, 1999), 408.
15 Edward Allen Beach, *The Potencies of God(s): Schelling's Philosophy of
   Mythology* (Albany: State University of New York Press, 1994).
16 Burkert, *Ancient Mystery Cults*, 9.
17 Ibid., 91.
18 Burkert, *Greek Religion*, 286.
19 Quoted in Foley, *The Homeric Hymn to Demeter*, 69.
20 Ibid., 70.
21 On the Eleusinian mysteries in the *Phaedrus* and *Symposium*, see Michael
   L. Morgan, *Platonic Piety: Philosophy and Ritual in Fourth-Century Athens*
   (New Haven: Yale University Press, 1990); Anne Mary Farrell, "Plato's
   Use of Eleusinian Mystery Motifs," PhD diss., University of Texas at
   Austin, 1999; Nancy Evans, "Diotima and Demeter as Mystagogues in
   Plato's Symposium," *Hypatia* 21.2 (2006): 1–27; Max Nelson, "The Lesser
   Mysteries in Plato's Phaedrus," *Echos du Monde Classique* 44 (2000): 25–43;
   Doug Al-Maini, "Opening the Kiste: Religion, Politics, and Philosophy
   in Plato's Phaedrus," PhD diss., University of Guelph, 2004; Michael A.
   Rinella, "Supplementing the Ecstatic: Plato, the Eleusinian Mysteries and
   the Phaedrus," *Polis* 17 (2000): 61–78; Barbara Sattler, "The Eleusinian
   Mysteries in Pre-Platonic Thought: Metaphor, Practice and Imagery for

Plato's Symposium," in *Philosophy and Salvation in Greek Religion*, ed. Vishwa Adluri (Boston: Walter de Gruyter, 2013); Kevin Clinton, "Stages of Initiation in the Eleusinian and Samothracian Mysteries," in *Greek Mysteries: The Archaeology of Ancient Greek Secret Cults*, ed. Michael B. Cosmopoulos (New York: Routledge, 2003).

22 Plato, *Symposium*, trans. Alexander Nehamas and Paul Woodruff (Indianapolis: Hackett Publishing, 1989), 209e–10a.

23 Burkert, *Ancient Mystery Cults*, 92, 172. Burkert only ever uses *epoptēs* and its variants in reference to Eleusis; in his "Index of Greek Terms" in *Ancient Mystery Cults*, *epopteia* is defined as "watching; experience of *epoptes* at Eleusis," *epoptes* is defined as "watcher; highest degree at the Eleusinian mysteries," and, finally, *epopteuein* is defined as "to watch; to become *epoptes* at Eleusis" (172).

24 Plato, *Phaedrus*, trans. Stephen Scully (Newburyport: Focus Publishing, 2003), 249c–d.

25 Ibid., 250b–c.

26 Ibid., 271c.

27 Plato, "Seventh Letter," in *Plato's Epistles*, trans. Glenn R. Morrow (New York: Bobbs-Merrill Co., 1962), 237–8.

28 Eric Voegelin, "Reason: The Classic Experience," in *The Collected Works of Eric Voegelin*, vol. 12: *Published Essays, 1966–1985*, ed. Ellis Sandoz (Baton Rouge: Louisiana State University Press, 1990), 279.

29 Voegelin, *The New Order and the Last Orientation*, 227.

30 F.W.J. Schelling, "Stuttgart Seminars," in *Idealism and the Endgame of Theory: Three Essays by F.W.J. Schelling*, trans. T. Pfau (Albany: State University of New York Press, 1994), 223.

31 Ibid., 225.

32 Ibid.

33 Ibid., 226–7.

34 Ibid., 227.

35 Ibid., 228.

36 Ibid., 227.

37 Ibid., 229.

38 Ibid., 227.

39 Ibid.

40 Ibid.

41 As Joseph Ratzinger argues in his contribution to Jürgen Habermas and Joseph Ratzinger, *The Dialectics of Secularization: On Reason and Religion* (San Francisco: Ignatius Press, 2006).

42 See his contribution in the same work.

4 The Place of Religion in Politics: On Analogous Gods and the Piety of the Unspoken

TOIVO KOIVUKOSKI

The most sensible of the philosophers who have reflected on the nature of God have said that he is a being of supreme perfection, but have seriously misused this concept. They have enumerated all the perfections that man is capable of possessing or of imagining, and have applied them to the idea of divinity without realizing that these attributes are often incompatible, and cannot subsist in the same subject without invalidating the other.

Montesquieu, *Persian Letters*[1]

Sappho says that to die is evil: so the gods judge. For they do not die.

Aristotle, *Rhetoric*[2]

The category of theocracy does not appear in either Plato's or Aristotle's classifications of regimes, and when we think of the politics of fourth- and fifth-century Athens we tend to consider it in terms of either democracy or oligarchy. The same could be said of our time also, with the politically contested question being whether it is democracy or oligarchy that presently prevails as governing regime. And yet, in that ancient example, when it came to Athens's two most notorious political prosecutions, the trials of Socrates and Alcibiades, religion figured prominently, as it appears also in contemporary global politics with a resurgence of claims to theocracy.

In the case of Alcibiades, though one could point to abundant secular reasons why the general could have been accused, including treason and desertion, it was his supposed profaning of the Eleusinian Mysteries that roused the *demos* to anger. Those charges are in this sense like the ones against Socrates, with religion brought to bear not so much as a set of prescriptive standards directing the political, but rather as a set of unspoken codes and authorities that ought not to be questioned in public.[3] In this chapter I will explore the relation between religion and politics through a consideration of the importance that the esoteric Eleusinian mysteries had for Athenian political life, serving as common rites and rituals that induced a profound sense of fellow feeling, but which could not be discussed openly on threat of execution and erasure of the person from the community.

Considering what of these ancient rites and myths can be practically incorporated as lessons for contemporary consideration, the lessons must be by analogy; Zeus of course wields little religious influence today, proving that there is something mortal about even the gods, though the stories about them may endure. In terms of the exoteric Greek myths about the gods, of which we do have lasting, iterative retellings – echoing as myths do through history – theology served an analogous rather than a prescriptive public role, tracing out the frames of political possibilities where succession, power sharing, and counsel among the gods were archetypal for politics among human beings. I will argue that religion can possess these kinds of enduring political values, encoding underlying expectations for civility and power sharing, specific values of civil religion that are perverted when translated into overly prescriptive codes for public conduct.

If one considers the current scourge of fundamentalist religious movements with global political aspirations, then in terms of a response from within the Western tradition of political thought there is value in a reconsideration of the origins of the dynamic between religion and politics, with us going back even further than the early modern separation of church and state in order to explore forms of civil religion and community in classical Greek political thought, asking why a politically constituted people would worship in common, or how one could read an ethic of rule from out of the lives of gods. While it is necessarily difficult to ascertain what happened in the ancient rites of the Eleusinian mysteries themselves, we can come to know the legacy that those mysteries took on in the history of ideas, and the meanings and virtuous beliefs, which, as Aristotle indicates, were attributed to gods by people. It is indeed probable that Plato's use of myth as a "likely story" and limit of rational discourse, as well as Aristotle's assessment of religion as analogue to human nature, would have been at odds with the self-understandings of religious devotees to Demeter or Zeus in their time. The point of this chapter rather is to explore how religious sensibilities could be adopted into a political regime without compromising the rational underpinning of civic association. To these ends, I will consider Plato's use of myth and the place of the Eleusinian mysteries in the charges against Socrates and Alcibiades, along with Aristotle's account of the gods as analogues of human powers and virtues, as ways of relating the political and the religious so as to respect the differences between our mortal arts – such as the art of politics – and a divine order of things.

If the gods cared for politics,[4] and were of a civil spirit, exerting some kind of order upon the affairs of humankind, then one might expect more peace and unanimity within this sphere of the human condition. But the reality is that the sacredness of the political has more to do with honours and recognition shared among human beings than with a sharing of divine and secular mandates to rule. For it is a perennially messy obligation to speak and act on the behalf of others, requiring the ongoing and constitutive discourses of public deliberation. Quite differently, deriving some supposed right to rule from a god would short-circuit the talk among citizens that makes a political community what it is.

In lieu of the inherent imperfection of political compromise, rule by divine fiat would effectively depoliticize the political community, unfolding in a pattern of subservience more suited to saints or to slaves than to free and equal human beings. Even if a claim to supreme religious authority did not degenerate into a mask of tyranny (which would be quite a natural consequence of the conflation of particular interests with a supposedly supreme Good), still a benevolent theocrat or caste of worthy priests ruling with a view to the perfection of the divine would deprive human beings of what is at once a hallmark of our imperfection and our secular saving grace, that is our capacity for convincing, rational speech in the absence of absolute authority, this being a necessary instrument for that pattern of *politeia*, "ruling and being ruled" in turn, which the philosopher Aristotle identifies as being basic to our human nature.[5]

It is noteworthy that the category of "theocracy," or rule by the gods, does not appear in either Aristotle's or Plato's classifications of regimes. Given the intended systematic application of Aristotle's categories of regimes or *politeia*, one can assume that the reality of a regime claiming divine right to rule could be accommodated in more precise and discernible language, namely, in terms of the number and class of those who share in political power, and whether those who have a hand in public affairs do so for their own private benefit or for the common good. Thus, a claim to theocracy could be distilled into more scientific underpinnings, described in actuality as being a monarchy, a tyranny, an aristocracy, oligarchy, polity, or mob rule.

That said, a religious sensibility is certainly inflected into classical political philosophy, which is not without its orientations towards the divine. By way of analogy: the natural orientation that would align one's body towards the warmth of the sun does not mean that the sun rules over the person warmed by its power. Humankind obviously owes its being to the sun, as we do to the whole of nature, but that pattern of indebtedness is quite different from the relations between creditors and debtors, or public authorities and citizens within a society. In the case of the natural order of things, life is a gift beyond compensation, and so is outside of the negotiation of interests and benefits that characterize the political and economic realms. If we owe our being to nature – whether its being is a divine creation or otherwise – nature as such need not know this, and is as such not a subject itself. Nature certainly enframes the political, though existing on another order of reality, as different as are the doings of gods and men.

It would be more accurate to describe the orientation of classical political philosophy towards the divine as a matter of theological speculation than of direct theocratic rule. For what remains of the divine in politics, properly so called, has more the character of a limit condition than of prescriptive rule: with the terms of the sacred outlining what may not be discussed or done more so than what is to be done.[6] This appears to be Plato's perspective on the relation of religion and politics, as in the *Republic, Gorgias, Phaedo*, and *Symposium*, in a "something of the kind must be true" mythical moment in the dialogues that is, in effect, the trailing off of the capacities of rational speech, reverting from *logos* to *mythos*.[7] After all, Socrates' *daimon* only acts as a restraining voice, and only as an indication of what should not be done, rather than what is to be done. Or, as in Aristotle, the relation between politics and religion is analogous: human affairs can be compared to a sacred order of things, where we make the gods after our own images, with archetypes suited to virtues being useful in legitimizing political authority.

Here, at the limits of the political there are two distinct emphases in Plato and Aristotle, with Plato drawing out the mythic dimension of religiosity through "likely tales" that carry on where rational speech cannot, and with Aristotle keeping more firmly within the secular realm by making the Greek gods into analogues of our political nature. The first approach is evinced in the Greek belief in the Eleusinian mysteries, of which Plato was a devotee (though Socrates was not), public rites that were thought to sustain political communities with a feeling of fellowship, but which forbade any public articulation of the grounds of the union beyond the initiates, with the mysteries being too deep a matter of discussion for the hurly burly of politics, though sustaining that possibility of public discourse all the same. Here I will examine Plato's presentation of theology as a "likely story" and limit of political discourse through a consideration of the charges against the Athenian general Alcibiades, in the company of the philosopher Socrates, the former for the supposed profaning of the Eleusinian mysteries, the latter for bringing new gods into the city.

The second, comparative approach enlisted by Aristotle points to analogous qualities between the theological and human orders, whereby we make the gods after our own image, and thus, in terms of classical theology, see a similar contestation and sharing of power played out among the gods as between human beings. In terms of Aristotle's analogous approach to the comparison of divine and human orders, I will examine the succession of power within the Greek pantheon, and consider what those stories say about questions of legitimate authority and the willing succession of power.

Profaning the Mysteries

In reference to the political context of Plato's *Symposium*, Allan Bloom makes the intriguing suggestion that the charges against Alcibiades may be traceable to rumour and innuendo over what went on prior to and at that particular party, the *Symposium*.[8] The party is recollected and narrated sometime after the fact, about fourteen years later and at a moment of spiritual decline for the Athenians, having lived under occupation, embittered by the reign of the Thirty Tyrants and suffering class divisions between oligarchs and the *demos*. The night of the party itself coincided with the height of the Athenian empire, the year of the ill-fated Sicilian expedition and the charges against Alcibiades, who was accused of having profaned the Eleusinian mysteries, defaced statues of Hermes, and plotted against the Athenian democracy.[9]

What Bloom intimates is that those charges had something to do with suspicions surrounding what was said and done at the party to celebrate Agathon's winning tragedy at the festival of Dionysus. Those suspicions could have been raised by the people who were then gathered, as well as by the subject of the dialogue itself. We know that Socrates was suspect by association, along with some of his students, of having supporting the Spartan regime over Athenian democracy, a suspicion that may have informed the charges later brought against him: of impiety and fomenting insurrection among the youth.[10] However frustrated a student he may have been, Alcibiades certainly gave some grounds for these suspicions when he fled from prosecution and aided the Spartans in their war on Athens, as did Critias and Charmides through their participation in the oligarchical regime installed by Sparta after its victory over Athens.

But at a deeper level, in consideration of the supposed profaning of the Eleusinian mysteries, it may have been the subject matter of the *Symposium* itself that raised suspicions that an oligarchical cabal had, on that particular night, parodied the mysteries behind closed doors. Perhaps, on the way to the party uninvited, Alcibiades and his band of drunken revellers had knocked the phalluses off statues to Hermes at the doorsteps of Athenian households as they caroused through the city. If they had indeed done so, they would have been making a mockery out of what was considered highest and most noble, in a kind of reversal of values that would make the vulgar out of the divine, and comic affront out of tragic nobility.

The speeches about the god Eros in the *Symposium* would have been both inscrutable and infamous, having taken place in the privacy of Agathon's home yet involving some of the most well known of Athenian public figures, the speeches were evidently so intriguing that people would be gossiping about what was said more than a decade after the party.[11] The titillating speeches would have borne outward similarities to the Dionysian and Eleusinian mysteries, considering the connection between the festival to Dionysius, a festival to the dramatic arts, and the topic of Eros. In Diotima's speech, Eros is connected to reproduction, specifically birth and a bringing forth out of life: "His nature is neither immortal nor mortal; but sometimes on the same day he flourishes and lives, whenever he has resources; and sometimes he dies, but gets to live again,"[12] quite like the god who dies and is reborn; or too, like the goddess Demeter who makes her annual descent into the underworld, rescuing her daughter Persephone to be reborn into the fecundity of spring. The kind of praise offered to the largely unrecognized god Eros in the *Symposium* would sound quite familiar to a devotee to Dionysus or to an initiate of the Eleusinian mysteries.[13]

Then there is the philosophical appropriation of religious sensibilities: at the core of the Platonic dialogue there is the mystery teaching revealed by a priestess to initiates (a secret poorly kept within the precinct of the schools of philosophy). The mystery teaching bears witness to a beauty that all beautiful beings partake in, but which subsists in and of itself irrespective of the modes of partaking in the beautiful. Here we have an idea of beauty very much like the many manifestations of Dionysus – one god in many forms – with his universality somehow undiminished and pure in each instantiation, with many local deities taking on his name and many roving congregations singing his praise.[14]

Because this particular god was also a man, it was possible for the congregation to experience his enthusiasm directly, such that they would each and all become *en-theoi*, having the god within them. There is in this sense an opening for the principles of universality, equality, and solidarity in that most embodied, and at once outlier, god in the Greek pantheon; for having no well-defined territory among the Olympian gods, Dionysus is free to connect multitudes in a way that the settled gods with their sovereign territories could not. It is as if this most irrational seeming of the Greek gods broke through the logic of pantheism, which portioned out divine powers within their precincts, in such a way as to appropriate pagan cults for a monotheistic end. Along this line of thought, Cornford suggests that "Teaching the unity of all life, it disposes of polytheism by the doctrine that all the Gods are only diverse shapes of one divine principle, 'one nature with many names.'"[15] It may be too much to suggest the anticipation of monotheism from out of polytheism, but what remains from both the secret teachings of Dionysus and Diotima is this mysterious participation of a multitude in unity, wherein the universal is not diminished however much the multitude partake in it.

It was rumoured outside of its sacred precinct that the Eleusinian mysteries generated a feeling of sympathetic union among fellow citizens, promising a bond of sociability more basic than the terms any social contract could offer. Much as in the nocturnal rites of the Dionysian mysteries, the secret, mass rites at Eleusis promised a sense of the spontaneous beneficence of nature and redemption through life's patterns of birth, death, and rebirth, joining the initiates in a sympathetic union more singular than a social order premised on the calculation of interests. Thus, in consideration of which kinds of worship to allow by legislation, Cicero has Marcus recommend to Atticus that "Your beloved Athens seems to me to have brought forth many superb and divine things and given them to human life, but nothing is better than the Mysteries through which we have been developed and civilized

from a rustic and crude existence into humanity."[16] Echoing that historical resonance of these myths into modernity, in his dramatized encyclopedia of classical thought the Abbé de Barthélemy likewise extols
initiation into the mysteries of Eleusis and the dissemination of that
civil religion, observing that "wherever it has been introduced by the
Athenians, it has diffused a spirit of union and humanity; that it purifies
the soul from its ignorance and pollution; that it procures to the initiated the peculiar aid of the gods, the means of arriving at the perfection
of virtue, the serene happiness of a holy life, and the hope of a peaceful
death and endless felicity."[17]

There are these perennial promises of religion – to be of good hope
towards death and to enjoy communion in the gifts of life. And it is
perennial also that these hopes and aspirations would be at times
oppressed politically in the lives of men and women. For the source
of the longing for justice – what is the political core to any theocratic
order – is precisely that absence, that deeply felt knowledge that something unjust has occurred, even if our words and reasons, our laws and
our social codes are not up to the order of a divine justice. This is why
religious codes cannot be politically prescriptive; rather, their sole justifiable political influence should be to set the unspoken limits of a political order, that is, that which cannot be discussed or done in public.[18]
That this would confirm a juridical order, as in the prohibition of homi-
cide, for example, speaks, if not to the natural-law tradition directly,
then at least to the mythic undercurrent of our unconscious common
sense. Our reasons have deeper roots than rational thought can express.
Behind every "I know that I do not know" spoken by Philosophy there
is a "Something of the kind must be true" spoken by Myth. Thus, religion is helpful to bridge that gap between self-conscious knowledge
and the ecstatic revelation of truth, drawing as it does on the quite natural human longings for justice, truth, and beauty. There is this erotic
quality to religion, teasing the spirit's hopes along through earthly life.
Dionysus was just such an erotic, earthly god: "a mediator between
God and Nature, some daemonic power, half-natural, half-divine, an
Eros who will fill up the chasm, and bind all things again into one."[19]

This is much like the god that Alcibiades, that most erotic of the
Greek youth, supposedly profaned, akin to the god Eros eulogized in
the *Symposium*, likewise a god in – between the human and the divine.
That mediation of heaven and earth suggests the possibility of bringing religion to bear on the political in a most circumspect of ways,
with the divine indicating the limits of what human beings may do,

in an intimation of perfection reserved to the margins of the human-made world.

There is a kind of moderation and openness built into the ancient Greek consideration of the sacred limits of the political that may be helpful in our contemporary circumstances, with the civilized world beset by millenarian death cults and gnostic fanatics. For it is apparent that a host of diverse religious sensibilities and practices were accommodated within and between ancient Greek cities: witness Socrates' observation of something like a condition of multiculturalism on the Mediterranean, where he bears witness to a foreign Thracian moon goddess being worshipped at the port of Athens alongside of a native procession, and judges both to be equally fine.[20] This possibility cues into the political function of religion not as a replacement for human-made laws and customs, but as their outermost limit. If, in a free society religion cannot function prescriptively as a set of marching orders for collective life, it could still ground the possibility of consensus building and the negotiation of diverse interests with an underlying common sense, delimiting that which could not be questioned in public so as to set the terms of plurality and what can be contested.

This truce between the religious and political orders could provide a realistic response to the kinds of fundamentalist political movements that are running roughshod over communities where political processes for the settling of differing interests are absent or failing, whether this is the so-called Islamic State in Iraq and Syria, Boko Haram in Nigeria, or al-Shabaab in Somalia. It is likely not sufficient to simply decry these nascent theocracies as anathema to the modern separation of church and state, at the risk of contributing to an apparently powerful narrative that would depict the modern state as nothing more than an arbitrary instrument for the production of security. The kind of ideology that would see perpetual war against unbelievers and the genocidal cleansing of apostates as somehow appropriate world historical goals for a religion needs strong rebuttals at the ideological level. For religion can promise powerful bonds of community and purpose, and it does provide grounds for resistance to human-made tyrannies – two perspectives shaped by an uplifting of collective purposes, with our human aims directed towards higher ends through shared belief. Answering that apparent lapse in failed security states and beleaguered tyrannies would be helped through a reconsideration of the place of religion in politics, of the value of civil religion and belief in gods analogous to our human natures.[21]

Analogous Gods

The gods who populated the ethical imaginations of the ancient Greeks were paradigmatically political, images of a human order retroactively divined onto the origins of gods and the cosmos. In the ancient Greek theogonies the familial succession of right to rule is explicitly analogous to political order, wherein the head of the divine household governs as "ruler of the universe."[22] Thus, the *kosmos* is described by Apollodorus not as the creation of Ouranos, but as his dynasty. If the god creates, it is inasmuch as he begets. For what is remarkable is this fecundity of the Greek gods, including the amazing plurality of divinities that their begettings brought forth. So, we have the lists of unions and births that spell out the literal theogony, a process of birthing begetting the conditions for birth, where what is born are the gods who will rule over humans, enjoying their sacrifices and looking over their own children. In this literal sense, these gods are very much like humans, though unconditioned by a mortality that would limit their powers in any terminal or essential way.

For when it comes to the limits of gods' powers, in ancient Greek theology the specific portioning out of the relative domains of gods had a clearly provisional and political aspect to it. All the Greek theogonies bear on how power is shared among the gods and how power is transferred from one regime to the next – two perennially quite dangerous kinds of events politically, testing the limits of shared trusts. There is for this reason good cause to reflect on how power was shared and transferred in the mythic past, in order to understand those mythic prehistories that encode the very basis of the possibility of power sharing, wherein an almost genetic pattern of social relations grounds humanmade covenants. For if the gods can make promises, and hold council, and share power among themselves, then analogously so too can human beings.

Though the *Library* that is attributed by custom (and error) to Apollodorus is arguably already somewhat distant from a living myth, related in a spirit not so much of wonder as of encyclopedic interest, what remains clear in the retelling are these genealogical relations of succession and power sharing, political arrangements that are confirmed in acts of the gods that very much resemble the customs of men. Here the truth of myth consists not in any specific instructions relayed from gods to men, but in the analogous sense of the stories that constitute myth. This is also why, however lacking in drama or poetry the *Library* may be, and however uncertain its authorship, the myth still remains a cosmos unto itself, a divine frame for mortal doings. In this sense, "Zeus caused oaths to be sworn,"[23] and so too can human beings, whatever oaths may be made and specific promises fulfilled or broken. In explicitly political terms, the pseudo-Apollodorus relates a myth of origins wherein the Titans "entrusted sovereignty to Cronos,"[24] unwisely as events turned out, whereas in more politically articulate form the Olympian gods "shared power between themselves by casting lots."[25] In this succession of regimes there seems to be a kind of improvement in divine political affairs from Ouranos to Cronos to Zeus, moving from tyranny and paranoia to shared custom and established trusts. For however capricious the Olympian gods may have been, for example switching allegiances from side to side during the Trojan War, they are clear about their respective provinces and powers. If they are susceptible to the entreaties of priests and supplicants, it is because they are somehow like us. As Homer has Zeus say to his brother Poseidon, "I care for them, even though they die."[26] And laterally, among the gods themselves, as in human affairs, the succession of divine authority can be very much a contested matter. There is the violence that can accompany the transfer of authority, as generation wars on generation with each claiming the right to rule itself, whether by old customs or new ones. In its worst instantiations, father will kill son and son will kill father for that power, such that justice becomes an afterthought to a politics of uncivil war. If these old gods are not exemplary, it is because they so resemble realities of politics, hard truths as persistent now as millennia ago.

If this kind of violent underpinning of ethical codes reveals the original perversity of patriarchal rule, then it is a patriarchy that is clearly threatened by the generation to follow. The original regime in the Greek pantheon serves as the model of a paranoid tyranny, compelled by fear of a prophecy that would have the child unseat the parent from power, aiming thus to kill that very child pre-emptively, with all living progeny of the original gods doomed by this ruthless strategy for holding onto power.

The three generations of Greek gods that begin the line of succession pass power off to the next generation in a variety of ways, some perhaps more civil and just than others, with each of the three regimes effectively becoming criminal in the eyes of the next, imprisoned by the succeeding regime. If one were to read a political ethic from out of the three transfers of authority, it would likely be the valorization of the willing power sharing and voting by lot practised by the Olympian gods. Zeus's rebellion against his father Cronos seems justified by the crimes of the father, while Zeus's pre-eminence among his brother and sister gods looks like a vindication of his deeds of liberation. In these senses, there seems to be a course of improvement in that classical theogony, where the original gods, all-powerful as they may have been, cannot embody properly archetypal models for humanity. It is as if the union of Sky and Earth, Ouranos and Ge, is too elemental and austere a vision of the divine to stabilize a civilizational order. What is missing is the kind of condition of true plurality necessary to ground a civilizational order attuned to human nature. What matters in terms of the actual practices and perceptions that undergird an ethos of a civil religion is that the gods deserve remembering and respect in part because of how they came to deserve power. The portioning out of reciprocal dues is more developed than the sheer awe experienced in being beset by the heaven and earth, two elements that make the range of human choices and powers seem rather insignificant. For though one can tremble before the thundering heavens, one cannot ask questions and expect answers from those elemental gods. What develops then in the Greek pantheon is precisely this political aspect of reciprocity, as in the portioning out of divine powers – to Zeus the heavens, to Poseidon the waters of the world, and to Pluto the underworld[27] – and a pattern of accountability so that human beings can ask of the gods and hope to receive. Thus, as in Giambattista Vico's reading of original myth, prayer becomes more than a mimetic trembling before Jove's thunder, endeavouring entreaties to the divine that would reflect the actual social and historical conditions of humanity.[28] Vico argues, contra mystic appropriations of myth as serving some transcendent end, that myth is very much of humanity. "For the wisdom of the ancients was the vulgar wisdom of the lawgivers who founded the human race, not the esoteric wisdom of great and rare philosophers."[29] Because of this vulgar source of religious sentiment, the frames provided by myth have correspondingly simple relevance for human affairs, such that all civilizations pay respect to the dead through rites, observe the sacredness of marriage, and share in some religion. Outside of civilized society, barbarity is defined by the lapse of those grounding customs, with those rites being so helpful for there to be civil trusts. Religion does indeed bear upon the political, not in the sense of dictating a legal code, but in making the political articulation of laws and the autonomy they allow possible. Vico criticizes interpretations of myths that would confer some hyperbolic or gnostic cause to the religious, writing that

> the philosophers have not yet contemplated His providence in respect of that part of it which is most proper to men, whose nature has this principal human property: that of being social. In providing for this property God has so ordained and disposed human affairs that men, having fallen from complete justice by original sin, and while intending almost always do something quite different and quite the contrary – so that for private utility they would live alone like wild beasts – have been led by this same utility and along the aforesaid different and contrary paths to live like men in justice and to keep themselves in society and thus observe their social nature.[30]

Hannah Arendt makes much of Vico's reading of human history as source of a *verum factum* from and for humanity, observing that "history is made by man as nature is made by God."[31] On this human scale of religion, Vico's reading of religion as analagous myth provides for a ground of civility more accessible to common sense than alien gods and death cults could ever be. And although his attempted resuscitation of the political value of myth contra zealotry and millenarian fantasy took place within the context of a simultaneous critique of the overreaching qualities of modernity, which could produce barbarisms of its own through an excess of rationality, one finds quite similar assessments of the *sensus communis* in classical Greek interpretations of the tradition, where gods are seen as perhaps the personifications of natural powers, or as the deification of past heroes through their remembrance in myth.[32] Yet even at that margin of *mythos* and *logos* in the classical tradition where myth became a mere story and fantastic embellishment of a half-forgotten past, a core presence of myth remains in the portrayal of gods who are very much of this world, a divine genealogy of begetting that begets begetting and a cosmos held together by animate powers attuned to human nature.

The patterns of succession and power sharing described in the classical theogony lay out architectonic structures for the political orders that they ground. The way in which divine order is portioned out and preserved over time becomes paradigmatic for human orders, tracing out a political frame for common sense within which differences would be mediated. But that is not to say that the archons are in every instance exemplary models for conduct themselves. The ancient Greek gods do shameful things,[33] they deceive,[34] they go to war with one another,[35] they mock the crippled among them and attempt to exterminate their own monstrous births.[36] They are more capable of avarice than mortals are by virtue of their immortal lives, more prone to violence out of an absence of a fear of death. There is a cautious truth in Socrates' indictment against the Homeric gods, for whom fighting, conniving, and jealous love affairs were fixtures of the divine drama.[37] The cause for caution in these violent exchanges, civil wars, and lovers' feuds has less to do with Socrates' epistemological uncertainty as to precisely what piety is, and more to do with the apparently political relations within the pantheon, with the gods no more bound to a principle of logical non-contradiction and ontological stability than the political is.

The significance of this analysis of theocracy as a regime is that the various theocracies represented in the classical tradition – the three ages of the gods, Heaven, Time, and Zeus – manifest various modes of political ordering or regimes, different kinds of political succession and means of legitimation. So Ouranos, Heaven, the original patriarch, claimed indiscriminate right to do his will unto his own. For example, he sends his first monstrous births with Ge down into Tartarus. The original god in the theogony claims total right to rule, a claim disputed by his partner and their children, who are disposed by his claim to absolute sovereignty to revolt against the father. This incomplete legitimation of authority – a rule supposedly as self-evident as the sky is over the earth – leads to violent reactions and non-consensual transfers of authority. The father is castrated by the son, and a generational succession broken by the act of patricide. This particular mode of succession, with all the uncertainty and capriciousness that violence involves, would be echoed in the next generation of dynastic succession, as the *archon* reflects on his own tyranny and how that may be in turn usurped. He imagines his children after the model of his own actions, and takes an initiative against fate to pre-emptively detain his progeny en masse. But as with all pre-emptive actions, the future vision of Cronos is imperfect, and his wife Rhea manages to steal the child away from fate and the designs of the god of time, with the mother hiding the son until he can make war on his father.

What distinguishes Zeus from the two patriarchs before him is his apparent willingness to share power, deciding among sibling gods by casting lots.[38] Zeus is a moderate god compared to the original deities, governing within the kind of customary limits to power that would make human society possible.[39] The common-sense notion that democracy is preferable to tyranny, even if that democracy is still explicitly hierarchical, resonates from out of these stories of origins. Zeus offers the first oath in the theogony, binding his actions by promises made, and bestowing honour through the recognition of other gods. In this self-moderated conduct where rule fixes its own limits, the capriciousness of absolute sovereignty is stabilized by power sharing and promises. If these are not political directives drawn directly from classical theology, they do trace out what would be common-sense frames of understanding pertaining to power and its limits. Though the ancient Greek gods were worldly divinities, their constitutive power was not so much to dictate law as to affirm that there ought to be law governing the wills of men, and that power ought to be shared between men as between the gods.

The architectonic function of the pantheons from all three theocratic regimes grounds the limits and possibilities of political action. It is not so much a divine law to be read into the political world as it is a frame within which lawful relations may be understood. By this token the theocratic element in classical political theology works by omission as much as by specification in describing the boundaries of common sense. Thus, the punishment meted out for the profaning of the Eleusinian mysteries – execution – with the religious element of the law pertaining to that which may not be discussed in public.

The three generations of ancient Greek gods, each with their respective claims to rule and patterns of succession in between, can thus be taken to stand in as archetypes of the human experience, much as Aristotle theorizes: "The fact that men were generally governed by kings in ancient times, and that some still continue to be governed that way, is the reason that leads us all to assert that the gods are governed also by a king. We make the lives of the gods in the likeness of our own – as we also make their shapes."[40]

What makes this junction of the divine and the human orders ontologically well founded is the fact that these gods had lives, *tous bios taōn theaōn*, that are in ways exemplary representations of the human condition. The particular consonance between the human and the divine reflects the recurrences of certain traits and types, as in Aristotle's political categories of regimes, with the real question pertaining not to how the gods rule over men, but whether the divine archetypes are tyrannical, monarchical, aristocratic, or democratic in their formation.

There is genuine truth in Socrates' critique of the Homeric gods, namely, that they are unaccountable for their behaviours and act at odds with any rational principle of creed or purpose. And yet, though human beings may need some collective relation to the divine, the gods don't need religion themselves; nor do the Homeric gods appear to need to be good if by the Good we mean, after Plato, logical, principled behaviour. Those old gods obviously manifest a whole host of contradictory behaviours. One of the most hallowed deities for the Athenians, the goddess Demeter, whose effects on the collective belief of her day were remarkable for inducing a sense of solidarity in the Eleusinian mysteries, teaching agriculture to her people and encouraging celebration of the cycles of the seasons, was famed as a mothering goddess. Yet in her effort to liberate her daughter Persephone from the underworld and bring the springtime back from death and darkness, the divine mother proved herself to be capable of killing as well as mothering care. Demeter was beneficent to her hosts the Eleusinians, giving them the arts of cultivation as a kind of blood money repayment for her indiscriminate killing of an Eleusinian child.[41] For the hosts to the wandering goddess to then celebrate the fecundity of the seasons in Demeter's name thus becomes a kind of collective acceptance of apology for the crimes committed *en route* to the liberation of her daughter. These analogous gods cannot be taken simply and un-problematically as instructive models to emulate, as in "What would Demeter do?" These are gods rather that express the sorts of contradictions that beset the human condition. The god Apollo apparently learned the arts of divination from Pan, sun-like reason tutored by a half-human, half-animal thing.[42] If the gods have their contradictions, bridging the rational and the irrational, it is because they are much like us in that respect. The divine archetypes ought to be imagined not as literal standards to be strictly represented in human affairs, but as projections of our contradictory natures, analogues of the divine in humanity, reflections on the defining limits and inspiring potentials that are embedded in our human nature.

In defence of philosophy, the words that Montesquieu has the Persian prince Usbek say on the relation between humans and the divine – "that these attributes are often incompatible" – are in a sense correct, though for reasons untrue to these two domains and their proper relation. From Usbek's perspective God is so inscrutable that the only virtue ethic to be gathered from his gnostic metaphysics is humility, the sole political consequence of religion, servility. Rather, the separation should be understood as architectonic, and in such a way as to allow for analogy between politics and religion without permitting their conflation. For it is precisely the difference between the two orders – between the eternal and the mortal – that would define the limits of the political while uplifting human spirits, promoting civility while curbing the imposition of civil custom as law, in what are foundational separations for a free and just civilization.

NOTES

1 Montesquieu, *Persian Letters*, trans. C.J. Betts (London: Penguin, 1993), l. 69.
2 Aristotle, *Rhetoric*, 1398b = Sappho fr. 201 Voigt in Anne Carson, *If Not, Winter: Fragments of Sappho* (New York: Random House, 2002), xiii.
3 In terms of Athenian laws pertaining to public religion Barthélemy observes that "the reigning religion is totally external. It holds out no body of doctrine, no public instruction, no rigorous injunction to participate, on stated days, in the established worship." Jean-Jacques Barthélemy, *Travels of Anacharsis the Younger in Greece, During the Middle of the Fourth Century before the Christian Aera*, vol. 2, trans. Jean Denis Barbié Du Bocage (London, 1825), 341.

   In this spirit of a civil religion that respects the basic political condition of plurality, Socrates' defence in Xenophon's *Apology* emphasizes the bare minimum requirements for pious citizenship, namely, belief in the divinities of one's city and some observance of public religious rites. Xenophon, *Apology*, trans. O.J. Todd (Cambridge: Harvard University Press, 1997), 11.
4 Plato, *Republic*, trans. Allan Bloom (New York: HarperCollins, 1991), 365e.
5 Aristotle, *Politics*, trans. Carnes Lord (Chicago: University of Chicago Press, 1984), 1284a1.
6 This is the perhaps suspect and appended subtitle of Plato's dialogue, the *Crito*: *or On What Is to Be Done*, with the subtitle describing Socrates' ultimate test of the bonds of civility and duty, taken to their logical limits in a refusal to act against the laws precisely so as to demonstrate the injustice of their application.
7 Consider the epistemological allowance for myth in the *Gorgias*, where Socrates says: "Give ear then, as they say, to a right fine story, which you will regard as a fable [*muthon*], I fancy, but I as an actual account; for what I am about to tell you I mean to offer as the truth [*legein*]." Plato, *Gorgias*, trans. W.R.M. Lamb (Cambridge: Harvard University Press, 1925), 523a.

   On his deathbed, Socrates finishes his tale of another world suited to an immortal soul with the modest proviso: "Now to insist that those things are just as I've related them would not be fitting for a man of intelligence; but that either that or something like it is true about our souls and their dwellings, given that the soul evidently is immortal, that, I think, is fitting and worth risking, for one who believes that it is so – for a noble risk it is – so one should repeat such things to oneself like a spell; which is just why I've so prolonged the tale [*muthon*]." Plato, *Phaedo*, in Catalin Partenie, *Plato: Selected Myths* (Oxford: Oxford University Press, 2009), 114d.

In this sense of myth as truth that Socrates describes on his death bed, the truth as myth fills in where *logos* cannot go, suited as a form of expression to mediating between temporal and eternal orders, being not bound by the principle of non-contradiction as *logos* is, not referring to its truth according to some adequacy of correspondence, but rather calling truth into being like a spell, where by its repeated invocation the myth, and the people who are its retellers, become real and endure in their retelling.

8 Allan Bloom, "The Ladder of Love," in Plato, *Symposium*, trans. Seth Benardete (Chicago: University of Chicago Press, 2001), 72.

9 Thucydides, *History of the Peloponnesian War*, trans. Richard Crawley (Vermont: Everyman, 1993), 6.27–9.

10 Plato, *Apology*, trans. Thomas and Grace West (Ithaca: Cornell University Press, 1998), 33a.

11 Bloom puts the date of the party itself at 416 BCE, on the authority of Athenaeus and the recorded date of the festival of Dionysius Linaea, at which Agathon won his prize for best tragedy (Athenaeus, *Deipnosophists*, 5.217A.). While certainly no stenographic account of that specific historical event, given the *Symposium*'s four-times-removed narration, this political context to the dialogue, taking place on the eve of the Sicilian expedition, would have heightened the public intrigue about what was said and done in Agathon's home that evening, with Socrates' mystery teaching, relayed from a priestess to the party gathered, sounding very much like a secular retelling of the Eleusinian mysteries outside of their sacred precinct.

12 *Symposium*, 203e.

13 Diotima indicates by inference that Eros is an older god than Dionysus, begat from Need and Resource in a drunkenness brought on by divine nectar, but not by wine, in an era of older gods predating the culture and worship of the vine and the grape (*Symposium*, 203b). There is debate on the indigeneity of Dionysus to Greece, whether he arrived as a barbarian outlier or was a chthonic god (M. Rostovtzeff, *Rome*, trans. J.D. Duff [London: Oxford University Press, 1960], 93–4). In a sense, with its roaming god and congregation the cult of Dionysus doesn't lend itself to that kind of spatial ordering; he has an inherently outlier status – whether he is considered as an indigenous or a foreign god – that is typified in his exclusion from the Olympian pantheon. His "one nature, many names"

ephemerality would have been caustic to the politicized territories of the Olympian gods, appealing rather to the marginalized and democratic, women and slaves. The Dionysian experience of the divine is the spirit of mob enthusiasm and ecstatic revelry, and so he is in this sense very much like a god born out of human life, hence also the god's paradoxical autochthony and outlier status.

14 Or much as Steven McGuire suggests in this volume, "The practice of philosophy culminates in an experience that is analogous to the experience of mystery initiates."

15 F.M. Cornford, *From Religion to Philosophy: A Study in the Origins of Western Speculation* (Princeton: Princeton University Press, 1991), 113.

16 Cicero, *On the Laws*, trans. James G. Zetzel (Cambridge: Cambridge University Press, 2002), 2.36.

17 Barthélemy, *Travels of Anacharsis the Younger*, 5.213. The Abbé's account of classical Greek philosophy, politics, and society as seen through the eyes of an outsider was a popular source of philhellenism in modernity, demonstrating the continuing resonance of ancient Greek myths not only as matters of antiquarian interest, but as living stories with contemporary relevance.

18 Or as Mittleman observes in this volume, "Politics in this sense may be licensed by a sacred script, but it doesn't follow one."

19 Cornford, *From Religion to Philosophy*, 214.

20 Plato, *Republic*, trans. Bloom, 327a.

21 As Ronald Beiner comments in this volume, the ancient Greek polities were in this sense crafted in part by an endeavour "to domesticate religion for political purposes."

22 Apollodorus, *The Library of Greek Mythology*, trans. Robin Hard (Oxford: Oxford University Press, 2008), 1.1.1.

23 *Library*, 1.2.5.

24 *Library*, 1.1.4.

25 *Library*, 1.2.1.

26 Homer, *Iliad*, trans. Stanley Lombardo (Indianapolis: Hackett, 1997), 20.23.

27 *Gorgias*, 523b.

28 Giambatista Vico, *The New Science*, trans. Thomas Goddard Bergin and Max Harold Fisch (Ithaca: Cornell University Press, 1948), §448.

29 *The New Science*, §384.

30 *The New Science*, §2.

31 Hannah Arendt, *The Human Condition* (Chicago: University of Chicago Press, 1958), 298n.

32 Paul Veyne and Paula Wissing, *Did the Greeks Believe in Their Myths?* (Chicago: University of Chicago Press, 1988), 134n35.

33 Homer, *Odyssey*, trans. Stanley Lombardo (Hackett: Indianapolis, 2000), 8.287–395.
34 *Iliad*, 14.334.
35 *Iliad*, 20.34–5.
36 *Iliad*, 18.425–6; Apollodorus, *Library*, 1.1.2.
37 *Euthyphro*, 6b–c.
38 *Library*, 1.21.
39 *Iliad*, 16.416–19.
40 Aristotle, *Politics*, trans. Ernest Barker (Oxford: Oxford University Press, 1958), 1.2.
41 "Hymn to Demeter," in *Homeric Hymns, Homeric Apocrypha, Lives of Homer*, trans. M.L. West (Cambridge: Harvard University Press, 2003), 1.1.5.
42 *Library*, 1.4.1.

5 The Aristotelian Roots of Religious Governance Approaches

JEREMY NEILL

In this chapter I will argue for two theses, with the intention of improving our understanding of the recent revival of religious approaches to governance. As for the first, I will assert that one reason why religious approaches have undergone a revival in recent decades has been that they have been perceived by their proponents to be capable of improving the opinions and morals of persons, in a way that liberal models cannot. My second thesis will be that the roots of this transformative social view are discernible in the classical era – most notably in Aristotle's *Politics* and *Ethics* – in a way that, likewise, has not so far been adequately acknowledged by liberal political theorists. To strengthen this second thesis, I will explicate the property distribution scheme which Aristotle outlines in the *Politics* in support of his plan for the moral improvement of citizens, and I will reference Thomas Aquinas as a medieval transitional figure who was influenced by Aristotle and whose transformative governance ideas have been updated in recent years by Christian philosophers.

Moral Development: An Attraction of Religious Governance Approaches

One reason for the attractiveness these days of religious governance approaches is that such approaches, typically, purport to be able to improve the dispositions of persons. Many contemporary religious philosophers hold a perfectionist view of morals: they think that there is a particular lifestyle that is superior to other lifestyles, and that humans do best when they are operating in accordance with this superior lifestyle. They see their perfectionist assumptions as entailing that governments ought through moral, financial, or legal incentives to encourage the superior lifestyle that they favour. In their view, governments ought to seek to improve the dispositions of citizens and in particular to align the dispositions of citizens with the superior lifestyle. In this first section I will describe some of the conceptual commitments of these religious philosophers, including especially the foundations of their lifestyle perfectionism, and also the reasons why they think that the social infrastructure ought to be set up to promote dispositional changes. My goal in part is to develop a better understanding of their governance views. But at the same time, I am laying a foundation for my second thesis: my claim that the roots of this religious governance approach are traceable to Aristotle. I will be focusing primarily on the ideas of Christian theorists, and I will be thinking primarily of some of the more academic representatives of this religious-political mindset– theorists like Robert George, John Finnis, Richard John Neuhaus, Gerard Bradley, J. Budziszewski, and Frank Beckwith – all of whom are conscientious scholars, and all of whom have in their writings endeavoured to acknowledge the limitations and difficulties of their views.[1]

For starters, imagine a stock contemporary character – the perfectionist Christian – as a stand-in for the Christian theorists whom I am referencing. She believes that the Bible contains the essential truths of life and salvation, and that governments are responsible to God for putting biblical precepts into practice. Governments whose laws promote biblical values will inherit the blessing of God. But governments that facilitate pornography, abortion, promiscuity, homosexuality, or similar such extra-biblical practices will inherit the judgment of God. The Christian believes on the basis of her biblical commitments that humans are sinful creatures whose behaviours require regulation so that they do not destroy themselves through bad choices. She believes also that it is meritorious for Christians – like herself – to employ the policies of governments to minimize the pernicious effects of human nature. The Christian wants the government to intervene far more frequently in the lives of her fellow citizens than is typical today in liberal democracies. The cooperative traits that she thinks ought to be promoted are very different than the traits of Rawls's overlapping consensus and Habermas's deliberative public sphere.

At the heart of the Christian's view of governance is her belief that persons flourish most when they are operating in accordance with the classical moral vision that has been offered to them, by God, through divine revelation. Also central to her thinking is her belief that persons are frail and that it is easy for them to stray from this ideal lifestyle. Thus, persons require some cocktail of education, guidance, and coercion in order to live well. Whenever they stray too far from the ideal lifestyle, the responsibility of governments is to educate, lead, and (at times) even force them once again to appreciate it. The reason why the Christian thinks that it follows from her belief in the existence of a superior lifestyle that governments ought to promote such a lifestyle is that she thinks that when humans are living in accordance with the superior lifestyle it simply is a better state of affairs, on balance, than when they are not. The Christian believes that governments should – at least at some level – seek to promote the superior lifestyle, through educational and legal measures that seek to habituate people into better dispositional shape, and ultimately that facilitate the better state of affairs. For the Christian, the point of the education and legal measures is to settle people down and, especially, to facilitate their mastery of their desires. In sum, the Christian believes that there is a certain lifestyle that is superior to other lifestyles, that the social infrastructure ought to support this superior lifestyle, and that it is possible for education and the legal code to promote the disciplines of personal mastery and, ultimately, a better life.

To be sure, there are limits to the coercive efforts that are considered to be acceptable among conscientious Christian scholars. Each of the scholars I have referenced, being a person of good will, has acknowledged in his professional writings the limitations and difficulties of his opinions. Each, being cognizant that the tools of governments – financial incentives, prison sentences, and legal restrictions – are blunt and general-purpose kinds of things, has been at least to some extent wary of the efforts of governments to promote a particular understanding of morality through the legal code. In fact, speaking more generally, the attempts that have been made in recent liberal democratic history to promote a particular vision of human morality have only rarely accomplished the goals for which they were intended. Consider, as an example, the American prohibition era – an initiative which was promoted, with good intentions, largely by religious persons. It was instituted by the Eighteenth Amendment in 1919 and repealed later in 1933 by the Twenty-First Amendment. The American prohibition experience is thought today by most historians to have been a precarious and unsettling time in the country's history. It suggests that our efforts to promote morality through the legal code have at times been too clumsy to be able to bring about the behavioural changes that they were supposed to produce. Often also it is possible for laws that are aimed at facilitating better forms of personal morality to have unforeseen and undesired effects. During the 1960s in America the assumption of the Johnson administration was that the war on poverty would develop a mindset among impoverished Americans that they could, through governmental assistance, extricate themselves from their disadvantaged circumstances. There were many who did just this. But at the same time, there were many others who did not develop this mindset. Instead, they became even more dependent than they previously had been on government handouts.

The point is just that there are these days a healthy number of religious theorists, who, being conscientious, would not consider it reasonable for our public morality promotions to be ambitious. Thus, Princeton philosopher Robert George worries in a passage in which he speaks favourably of Aquinas that "laws which the multitude of a people generally find too difficult to comply with will produce a negative attitude toward the law in general, and lead to resentment and hardening of hearts, and possibly even rebellion."[2] Frank Beckwith, an ally of George and a prominent pro-life theorist, has similarly argued vis-à-vis cases in which having a child might bring hardship to the mother, that "those in the religious and charitable communities should help lend financial and emotional support to the family."[3] For thinkers like George and Beckwith, our efforts at promoting a particular understanding of morality – by means of the legal code – ought not to probe too deeply into the minds and hearts of the citizens. To be sure, theorists like George and Beckwith do advocate a legal code on which the morality that they favour is promoted. But at the same time, they also seem to think that laws have limitations and that in practice the laws that they favour might turn out to be less transformative than they hope. Sometimes in their writings they even say that the laws ought only to proscribe those behaviours that are already considered to be unacceptable by citizens. Thus, George asserts at one point that "the prudent legislator will be careful to make the law fit the condition of the people, and not to make legal prohibitions too onerous."[4] That is, for George the laws ought only at most to prohibit a society's most egregious wrongs: the behaviours that are duplicitous – embezzling corporate funds; murderous – killing a spouse or child; conniving – plotting to overthrow the government; or destructive – setting large grass fires. The core idea for George (and the others) still seems to be that regimes that have morality commitments are better than other regimes at preventing irreversible personal harms: drugs, alcohol, sexual addictions, and interpersonal conflicts. At the same time, however, for both George and Beckwith, historical experiences – like the American prohibition era – suggest that citizens need to be inclined at least to some extent to obey their country's morals laws, and that the most that governments ought to do to facilitate a particular lifestyle is to prohibit its most onerous vices.

Thus, there are today in the academy some prominent and conscientious religious philosophers who think, in a rather traditional fashion, that humans are frail and that they need education, guidance, and coercion in order to flourish. At the same time, as illustrated by George and Beckwith, at least some of these thinkers are social realists and are willing to acknowledge the limitations of such legal intrusions. They know, from historical experience, the prudence of not being too ambitious and of not infringing upon citizens' personal freedoms. So, in advocating a moralistic governance approach they probably are not intending for the tools of governments to be intrusive or minute, but instead are asserting only that governments ought to provide the citizens with outer-level behavioural boundaries. They typically believe themselves to be honourable in their advocacy of laws that promote morality: their desire is to improve the lives of their peers, since, in their minds, for their peers to think and act in accordance with the moral ideals that they favour is for their peers to flourish.

Finally, note that George, Beckwith, Neuhaus, and most of the other religious philosophers I have referenced here are opposed to post-Rawlsian forms of liberalism because of their belief that there is a certain lifestyle that is superior to other lifestyles, and that humans flourish best when they are operating in accordance with this superior lifestyle. They would certainly agree with many of the criticisms that are raised by Peter Simpson in "Theocracy's Challenge," a first-rate essay for this volume which chronicles a variety of the ills that political liberalism produces in its efforts to restrict comprehensive religious and moral topics to a private sphere. While Rawls of course does endorse a minimal understanding of the good, he does not seek to promote that understanding through thick or robust governance structures, and does not want the state to be non-neutral with respect to that good.[5] Little wonder that religious philosophers like George and Neuhaus do not think it possible for liberal governance theories, like Rawls's, to facilitate the perfectionist lifestyle that they advocate: "Once religion is reduced to nothing more than privatized conscience, the public square has only two actors in it – the state and the individual. Religion as a mediating structure – a community that generates and transmits moral values – is no longer available as a countervailing force to the ambitions of the state."[6] The fear of a thinker like Neuhaus, the author of this quote, is that when governments are too neutral with respect to the good, the state will grow too powerful and citizens will slip into moral degeneracy. In general, the form of governance that is valued by Neuhaus, George, and the others is governance that promotes the ideal lifestyle that they favour. They believe that the moral improvement that they favour ought in some way – even if only minimally – to be promoted by the legal system. They also think that the government ought to seek to develop in citizens a better understanding of the good life, and, ultimately, to facilitate in citizens a dispositional transformation.

Property Ownership in the *Politics*

As for this chapter's second thesis, my contention will be that it is possible to find in Aristotle's *Politics* some neglected roots of the distinctively modern and religious kinds of thought patterns that I have here referenced. In defending this thesis I do not of course mean to say that Aristotle's *Politics* is religious in the explicit sense of our representative Christian, but rather, as emphasized in Toivo Koivukoski's essay for this volume, that Aristotle opens politics to religion, to public speculations about theology and the good life, and especially to the possibility of human character improvement. That said, Aristotle divides happiness, the highest good for humans, into several different parts: rational activity, virtue, family, friends, wealth, health, and property.[7] He assumes that political communities ought to be organized around this highest good, or at least a variant thereof: "We see that every polis is a community of some sort, and that every community is established for the sake of some good."[8] Early in the *Politics* Aristotle asserts that governments ought to promote a particular understanding of that good: "Any polis which is truly so called, and is not merely one in name, must devote itself to the end of encouraging goodness. Otherwise, political association sinks into a mere alliance. Law becomes a mere covenant, a guarantor of man's rights against one another, instead of being – as it should be – a way of life such as will make the members of a polis good and just."[9] Thus, Aristotle in the *Politics* not only assumes that our political communities ought to be oriented towards the good life, but also that they ought to promote such a life among their members. The problem of politics is to determine the cooperative principles that would unite persons in a polis and facilitate their achievement of the good life.

In part, the reason why Aristotle endorses a transformative under-standing of governance – an understanding that promotes the good life, via education and coercion – is that he thinks that moral argumentation is limited in its capacity to bring about dispositional changes: "While [moral arguments] seem to have power to encourage and stimulate the generous-minded among our youth, and to make a character which is gently born, and a true lover of what is noble, ready to be possessed by virtue, they are not able to encourage the *many* to nobility and goodness."[10]

For Aristotle, a transformative infrastructure is a necessity because most persons, in its absence, would pursue lives of baseness and igno-rance: the many "do not by nature obey the sense of shame, but only fear, and do not abstain from bad acts because of their baseness but through fear of punishment."[11] Persons who do not by nature want to be virtuous ought, through education and legal strictures, to be taught to acknowledge the value of dispositional goodness:

> It is surely not enough that when they are young they should get the right nurture and attention; since they must, even when they are grown up, practice and be habituated to them, we shall need laws for this as well, and generally speaking to cover the whole of life; for most people obey necessity rather than argument, and punishments rather than the sense of what is noble.[12]

In fact, what has happened in history is that Aristotle's transforma-tive understanding of governance has become, over time, enormously influential in the Western and monotheistic worlds. Among Christian theorists it was the dominant view of governance up until the time of the Enlightenment, and it remains to this day an influential position among the adherents of many different religious world views. In this and the next section I will identify its roots in the *Politics* and the *Nicom-achean Ethics*.

Aristotle asserts in book 2 of the *Politics* that the polis is a natural, and not an artificial, arrangement, and that it ought to be led by the aristocracy and stabilized by the rule of law. His goal is to determine how it is possible for persons to unite in a political community and to aim together at the good life.[13] In part, he thinks that such a life is attain-able through a judicious plan of property distribution, where property is understood to include land, animals, slaves, and material goods. The reasons why he takes a judicious property distribution to be central to his analysis are that it is important for (1) infrastructure stability, and for (2) character formation.

In book 2 of the *Politics* Aristotle critiques his predecessors' descriptions of the ideal state and argues that a modified property system is more reasonable than a communal-style system as a way of distributing a polis's material resources. The system that he envisions is distinguishable from a communal-style system in that, in contrast to the latter, it does differentiate among the holdings of persons. That is, Aristotle's opinions about the property ownership topic are largely a reaction to the public ownership theories of Plato, who at one time depicted property as being a malicious distributive arrangement and as dividing the citizens from each other.[14] Aristotle does not think that the interests of his property holders would be inordinately divided. In fact, his view is that their pursuit of personal ownership would render the polis a more organized place. But Aristotle does, in book 2, think that there needs to be an elemental experience of unity in his polis, and as such he does investigate the Platonic proposal that children, women, and property ought to be held in common.[15] Aristotle also in book 2 finds a middle path between views of the polis that are overly unified and that would cause it to lose its diversity and creativity, and views of the polis which would make it so diverse and creative that its inhabitants would have little in common with each other.

For my purposes, the point is just that Aristotle does, at key junctures in the *Politics*, oppose the Platonic belief that greater unity is almost always and everywhere a good thing. In fact, there are numerous passages in the *Politics* in which Aristotle expresses doubts about the transformative capacities of Plato's communal-style property system: such communal legislation "may have a specious appearance of benevolence; men readily listen to it, and are easily induced to believe that in some wonderful manner everybody will become everybody's friend."[16] In part, the reason why Aristotle opposes communal-style property arrangements is because he thinks that such arrangements would undermine the cooperative capacities of citizens: while Plato's property abolition scheme ostensibly is aimed at unifying the state, in reality it would exacerbate citizen disputes. Aristotle also opposes communal-style arrangements because he thinks that their initial, utopian appearance would mask the incorrigibility of human character: "These evils, however, are due to a very different cause – the wickedness of human nature. Indeed, we see that there is much more quarrelling among those who have all things in common."[17] Yet at the same time, in spite of his criticisms of communal-style distribution systems, Aristotle does still, in the end, endorse the Platonic idea that a polis's system of property distribution is – and ought to be – transformative of the dispositions of persons.

Today, in the wake of Adam Smith's *Wealth of Nations*, our models of capital exchange have become predicated on the assumption that property possession means both private ownership and private forms of distribution and use – where private distribution and use includes a discretionary right on the part of the property owners to choose, if they so desire, not to distribute the benefits of their property among their neighbours. But the distributive program that Aristotle favours in the *Politics* is different from our contemporary and capitalistic distribution models by virtue of an interesting public twist.[18] In book five of the *Politics* Aristotle famously considers three different kinds of property arrangements: one in which the property is private and its use is common, one in which the property is common and its use is private, and one in which the property is common and its use is common.

Aristotle's own preference is for a hybrid scheme of private and public interests – one that integrates both a private form of ownership and a public form of distribution and use.[19] Martha Nussbaum has asserted for this reason that Aristotle is a proto-Marxist and that the common use that Aristotle envisions is intended to be enforced by the rule of law.[20] But Nussbaum's proto-Marxist gloss on Aristotle is not a widespread interpretation, and in fact what most of the other theorists in the field have thought that Aristotle is doing here is simply acknowledging that there are different degrees of common use: Aristotle's preference, among these different degrees, is that we ought to start by making things our own and then afterwards deploy them at will within our community. Thus, while he does think that political authorities ought for the sake of cultural unity to regulate his property dispersal scheme, nevertheless at the same time Aristotle's interest in public use is predicated primarily on private exercises, by citizens, of their personal volition.[21] He thinks that it is citizens' personal choices which ought to be the main catalysts for their public use of property.

Aristotle's classical distribution model also differs from our modern distribution theories in another sense: he does not seem to believe in an inherent right to property ownership.[22] So Aristotle's defences of property proceed on grounds that are otherwise than the modern discussion that has descended from Locke, and that assumes that humans have inherent resource rights. Aristotle's model also differs from our contemporary and capitalistic models in that it is predicated on the assumption that the dispositions of property owners are improved via their property ownership. Most of our contemporary property models are agnostic about this possibility. Particularly prominent for Aristotle is the idea that the social traits of the good life – including especially the traits of generosity and benevolence – are promoted by the opportunities that ownership offers for persons to disperse their holdings among their neighbours.[23] Aristotle thinks that it is possible through such dispersals for property-based systems to promote the virtues of temperance and liberality.

Thus, in the end, what Aristotle in book 2 is arguing is that the question of political unity is answerable, in large part, through a scheme of property distribution. The core of his argument is found in chapter 5, where, as Fred Miller has argued, Aristotle uses approximately five different arguments to defend the ownership and use of property: a private system of ownership and use is justifiable for Aristotle because it (1) promotes peace among the citizens,[24] (2) improves the property's upkeep,[25] (3) contributes to the development of friendships,[26] (4) maximizes natural pleasures (such as the love of self),[27] and (5) fosters the public expression of virtues of liberality and munificence.[28] Since several of these Aristotelian property defences are predicated on the assumption that altruism is incentivized via property ownership, the possibility of bringing about a social infrastructure that is transformative – an idea that Miller does not adequately emphasize – in fact appears to have been one of Aristotle's main conceptual motivations.

The first of Aristotle's private property arguments is that property ownership is justifiable because it promotes peace among the citizens. The argument is pitched, rhetorically, as a solution to the conflict problems that arise in circumstances of resource scarcity. It also is a response to Plato, who, as mentioned, believed that private ownership would do damage to the moral psychologies of citizens. Central to Aristotle's first defence of private property is his assumption that amid circumstances of resource scarcity the tendency of most persons will be to compete with each other. Most persons will seek to fight with each other and to take from each other more than they could otherwise obtain from their surroundings.[29]

More particularly, for Aristotle, most persons, when they are not being given the resources of their community in a manner that they feel is commensurate with their contributions, will become non-cooperative. The conflict will start when a small percentage of the citizenry chooses to forgo its work responsibilities, assuming that the others will carry the workload. But these malingerers will irritate their neighbours, and their neighbours, quarrelling with them, will see them as taking inordinate resources from the public trough.[30] The situation will only be resolved when everyone works together through a system of private ownership, role specialization, and public dispersal. Their effort to work together, and the harmonious outcome that Aristotle anticipates as resulting, suggest for him that their property ownership will transform their dispositions: it will alter their non-cooperative tendencies and instead will promote among them a mindset of orderliness and harmony. Thus, for Aristotle it is possible for a judicious system of property ownership to resolve the problem of interpersonal conflict, at least amid circumstances of resource scarcity. The key idea – one that Miller does not adequately emphasize – is that property ownership changes the characters of persons, facilitating their interpersonal harmony and making them no longer rivals to each other. Private ownership is valuable for Aristotle largely because he perceives it to be an instrumental good, of a kind that facilitates the formation of the soul.[31] Private holdings are distinct from communal-style systems in that they differentiate the property owners from barbarians and slaves, who are incapable of conscientious forms of cooperation. Ownership makes humans more cooperative than they would otherwise be if, say, in circumstances of communal-style distribution, they were compelled by their governments to get along and to share public resources.

Note that there is further evidence for this first argument's transformative view of property ownership in the limitations that Aristotle imposes upon his citizens' acquisition efforts. In *Politics* 1.8 and 1.9 Aristotle does say that it is reasonable for the resources that are available for acquisition to be limited. This limitation plan ought to be undertaken not only to maximize the general welfare, but also to benefit the individual property owners.[32] In support of this plan, in 1.9, Aristotle distinguishes between necessary and unnecessary forms of acquisition.[33] Necessary acquisition is the idea that some forms of property acquisition are natural – given by nature for humans and for the efforts of humans to flourish in accordance with their kind. Its practical manifestation is as the accumulation of goods for the sake of their intended purpose – in Aristotle's view, personal flourishing. By contrast, unnecessary acquisition is accumulation that goes too far and that is pursued for non-necessary ends that are beyond the goal of personal flourishing.[34] The zeal with which some persons pursue property acquisition is, in Aristotle's view, an indication of their confusion between necessary and unnecessary acquisition. Their concentration on unnecessary acquisition undermines their flourishing and their capacity for personal fulfilment. Thus, what motivates Aristotle to place limits on excessive property acquisition in *Politics* 1.8 and 1.9 is his goal of promoting the flourishing of his citizens. In particular, he wants to prevent persons from rendering themselves, through indulgences and personal excesses, unable to live the good life. Aristotle's property protection system is intended, in short, to transform their dispositions and to equip them to flourish in accordance with their kind.

Aristotle's second defence of private property is that property owners have stronger incentives to improve their property than they would otherwise have in communal-style distributive arrangements.[35] For Aristotle, Plato misjudged the value of property because he misunderstood human psychology. The psychological reality, for Aristotle, is that persons are self-interested and are not naturally desirous of being productive, communal-style participants: that is, it is not typical for them to want selflessly to devote themselves to the preservation of communal-style property arrangements. Their instinct instead is to neglect the public properties and to turn away, towards their own affairs.[36] As such, in Aristotle's view a private distribution system is better than a public one at fostering citizen productivity because it assumes a more realistic human psychology and because it offers more direct forms of control over one's holdings. Aristotle seems to see persons as being more motivated to improve the resources they are using – and to maximize their economic efficiency – when they are the owners of their property.[37] Presumably, it is their capacity to benefit themselves more directly through their property cultivation efforts that he sees as increasing their motivation to work. Thus, the second of Aristotle's defences is that his modified private property system is likely to do better, on balance, than a communal-style system at promoting economic health because it more effectively acknowledges the motivation of persons to improve their property when they are the owners of the resources that they are using.

Aristotle's third defence is that private property is justifiable because it facilitates friendships of virtue. The pleasure that virtuous agents take in their own dispositions, and in the dispositions of their friends, is more naturally manifested in a private ownership system than it is in other kinds of resource distributions. Aristotle's understanding of friendship in both the *Politics* and the *Nicomachean Ethics* is centred on a shared conception of the good.[38] In the *Ethics* he divides friendships into three kinds – pleasure, utility, and virtue, with the first two being inferior to the third.[39] Pleasure and utility, the inferior Aristotelian friendships, are based on self-interested goods: persons are friends of pleasure because they derive pleasure from each other's company; and they are friends of utility because they find each other to be useful.[40]

But since friendships of virtue are based on a perfectionist under-standing of the good, they are for Aristotle more stable and lasting than are other such friendships, and their participants are more capable of pursuing the good and of intending what is best for each other with respect to that good: "Perfect friendship is the friendship of men who are good, and alike in virtue; for these wish well alike to each other *qua* good, and they are good in themselves."[41] Friends of virtue are marked by their love for each other, for each other's sake, and by their devo-tion to a perfectionist understanding of life.[42] Their attention is oriented towards virtue, and as such the commonality on which they concen-trate is an objective good, superior to other such goods. Thus, for Aris-totle, the perfect friendship that he celebrates is related to the natural affection of virtuous agents for their own excellences. Their love of their own virtue – a love which is derived from their knowledge of the value of the good life that they are pursuing – for Aristotle enables them to appreciate the traits of their virtuous friends.[43]

The role that is played in the friendships of goodness of the *phronemoi*, by their love of their own virtue, is augmented by their property own-ership: that ownership puts them in a better position, at least in a dis-positional sense, to appreciate their friends of virtue. In part, this is because it enables them to display their virtue more publicly than they could otherwise do, thus facilitating their efforts to focus on virtue as a commonality of friendship. Aristotle seems also to envision a lending process, in which friends of virtue share their possessions for the sake of mutual use and enjoyment. For even though property ownership offers persons control of a set of resources, nevertheless in order to facilitate their friendships of virtue by means of property acquisition they must still be willing to give their friends opportunities to use such resources. It thus is possible in Aristotle's view for property ownership to improve the dispositions of persons, at least with respect to their ability to be friends of virtue.

The fourth of Aristotle's private property defences is predicated on the assumption that it is valuable, as such, for persons to take pleasure in themselves and in their own capacities. In fact, the reason why Aristotle is opposed to communal-style property arrangements, in part, is because he believes that the natural pleasures of persons increase in circumstances in which they can call things their own.[44] The chief of these natural pleasures is self-love: the healthy esteem that accompanies the success of one's thoughts and actions.[45] One manifestation of self-love is the satisfaction of property ownership.[46] For Aristotle, property ownership is valuable in part because it highlights the natural pleasure of virtuous citizens for themselves and their own capacities. The advantage of such a system is that it taps into a tendency of the human condition, which, for Aristotle, is for humans to take pleasure in their possessions. Through property, humans can take pleasure in knowing that nature is providing them all that is necessary for them to live and to attain their natural end, in keeping with their pursuit of happiness and their practice of moral virtues.

How does Aristotle see natural pleasure as supervening on property possession? His argument in book 2 seems to be – and some of the argument here proceeds via assumptions – that persons have a natural affection for themselves and that the things which facilitate that affection, such as property ownership, are pleasing. That is, persons naturally take pleasure in the property ownership that makes their self-actualization and self-enjoyment possible. Aristotle does likewise emphasize in the *Nicomachean Ethics* the importance of financial success – and of taking pleasure in such success – in one's quest for the good life. Perhaps the way in which Aristotle sees property ownership as supporting the self-love of agents is that it enhances one's capacity for contemplation. Or perhaps he is assuming that the joy of ownership and of calling things one's own is, in itself, pleasurable. Whatever the mechanism, the point is that for Aristotle property ownership offers greater pleasures than do other, different distribution systems.[47]

Aristotle argues in a fifth defence of private property that when a community's property arrangements are preserving both private ownership and public use they provide the citizens with more promising venues than would otherwise be available for the exercise of liberality.[48] High-minded citizens who are endeavouring to actualize themselves and to appreciate their own virtue are in need of a public outlet for their generosity.[49] In the absence of such an outlet they could not otherwise be meaningfully altruistic, in a way that would impact their quest for the good life. Their noble aspirations and upright dispositions could not otherwise find appropriate and public forms of philanthropic expression. Thus, Aristotle depicts an institutional experience of property ownership as being a precondition for the exercise of philanthropy: in order to express our generosity we need to be capable of deploying our resources in a manner that is under our own power. We can, when we are endeavouring to offer the benefits of property to others, attain a more appropriate level of generosity when we own our property than we could otherwise do if we were merely the purveyors of properties that are not our own. In part, the point is that the public deployment (and, ultimately, public recognition) that is essential to liberality must, in order to be genuine, proceed from a platform that is under our control. The individual agents must be able deploy the resources at their disposal from a standpoint which makes those resources actually, in practice, under their control.

Thus, for Aristotle, property ownership gives persons more promising opportunities than they would otherwise have to acknowledge their own magnanimity. The high-minded recognition of one's personal virtue, realized through property ownership and altruistic resource dispersals, would not be similarly possible if persons did not own the property whose benefits they were seeking to disperse.

The point is that Aristotle envisions the psychologies of his property owners as being sophisticated and malleable, and as promoting by means of appropriate (and public) benefit dispersals the ideals of munificence and self-development. His fifth defence thus is that property ownership is a soul-crafting enterprise, and that it educates persons in the virtues. For Aristotle, liberality facilitates political unity because it ties together the interests of citizens. Wealth and property are external goods which enable one to be virtuous, in ways that fulfil one's function and facilitate happiness. They are necessary conditions for happiness, although not the central components of that happiness.

The emphasis of the fifth Aristotelian defence on dispositional alteration is evidence that Aristotle envisions the psychologies of his property owners as being malleable. The first defence – the promotion of social harmony, the second defence – the improvement of natural resources, and the third defence – the cultivation of friendship, are likewise predicated on the possibility of dispositional malleability. Thus, in at least four of his five defences Aristotle is assuming that human dispositions can be altered and improved via the social infrastructure. In particular, property ownership is a system that habituates agents out of their primitive moral egotism. While their moral egotism might at first be what motivates them to pursue property ownership, nevertheless the fact of that ownership, once achieved, transforms their dispositions and facilitates their social virtues.

Moral Psychology in the *Nicomachean Ethics*

Further evidence that Aristotle intends for private ownership to facilitate the citizens' dispositional transformation is discernible in his treatment of virtue in the *Nicomachean Ethics*. The transformative vision of human dispositions that appears in the *Ethics* was intended by Aristotle to be continuous with the dispositional improvement program that is outlined in his private property defences in the *Politics*.[50] The point is that the defences of property ownership in the *Politics* are supposed to be similar to Aristotle's arguments in the *Ethics* about the importance of public magnanimity, and that in the *Ethics*, as in the *Politics*, Aristotle intends for the social infrastructure to facilitate dispositional improvement.[51]

The agents of the *Ethics* can undergo a program of dispositional improvement, and ultimately of achieving the good life: a life of rational activity, in accordance with the intellectual and moral virtues.[52] They might initially be non-cooperative and, as such, not at first interested in practising such virtues. In fact, in his depictions in the *Ethics* of the moral psychologies of children Aristotle does stress their primitive egotism which, being undesirable, must be remedied via a program of virtuous habituation.[53] For Aristotle what can bring about their dispositional improvement is their repetition of virtuous deeds.[54]

While personal excellence is featured in the *Ethics* as the goal of the *phronimos*, the *phronimos* is not portrayed by Aristotle as being a narrow-minded egotist. Through dispositional education the self-focus of the *phronimos* comes to be on his personal excellence, rather than on self-indulgence. The *phronimos* comes to see happiness as being primarily a function of his personal excellence. And in focusing on his personal moral improvement, the *phronimos* is equipping himself for a life of flourishing – and not a life in which he privileges his own interests at the expense of others. He is by means of this moral improvement – and this is the part of the *Ethics* that is important for our understanding of how Aristotle's moral improvement program illuminates our understanding of the transformative governance view of the *Politics* – seeking to equip himself to facilitate in others a capacity for flourishing. The virtue of generosity seems in particular to be intended by Aristotle to be a part of the pursuit by the *phronimos* of his personal excellence:

after all, "it is the nature of a liberal man not to look to himself."[55] Thus, Aristotle's understanding of eudaimonism is intended to include altruistic ventures, and does mean paying attention to the needs of others: it is in particular pitched by Aristotle as being an attempt to focus on oneself and one's character improvement in a way that facilitates such improvement and, ultimately, imparts the benefits of liberality and magnanimity to one's community.[56]

Moreover, in the *Ethics*, as in the *Politics*, since there is a role in the *phronimos*'s quest for a life of activity and general interests, his neighbours are supposed to be his partners in his quest for the good life.[57] Thus in the *Ethics*, as in the *Politics*, Aristotle is envisioning a social infrastructure that crafts the soul. The most prominent venue in which Aristotle envisions the virtuous development and actions of the *phronimos* as taking place is the public realm.[58] What Aristotle emphasizes in his description of liberality are the ways in which it is possible for the *phronimos* to direct his resources towards larger, more community-style purposes, and the fact that the *phronimos* feels pain and pleasure in the right ways: "But if he happens to spend in a manner contrary to what is right and noble, he will be pained, but moderately and as he ought; for it is the mark of virtue both to be pleased and to be pained at the right objects and in the right way."[59] The flourishing of the *phronimos*, which is just as much a matter of looking after the needs of others as it is a matter of pursuing the traits of self-control and proper pride, is made possible in large part by a judicious social infrastructure.

Aristotle's Influence on Contemporary Religious Philosophers

To be sure, not all of Aristotle's opinions have been influential in the recent theocratic revival. Aristotle differs in some major ways from the contemporary religious philosophers I have referenced: for instance, in a way that would be abhorrent to such thinkers, Aristotle considers slavery to be foundational to his system of property ownership.[60] Aristotle's elitist and xenophobic assumptions are likewise unacceptable in the modern conversation – among both religious and non-religious thinkers alike. Again, Aristotle was not a religious personalist and his theological convictions – he appears only to have believed in a deistic first mover – were in numerous ways unlike the religious opinions of the contemporary thinkers whom I have cited.

Nevertheless, in spite of these differences I think that the main point of my narrative remains intact: that Aristotle sought to embed a particular understanding of the good in his social infrastructure, that he sought to promote this good in a transformative way through institutions like property ownership, and that today there are numerous religious theorists who are his intellectual descendants and who are advocates of a similar embedding process. Their endorsement of transformative governance and of a social infrastructure that promotes a particular understanding of the good is, ultimately, traceable to Aristotle's property views. This can in part be seen from the way that the time in Western history that they characteristically reference – when Aristotle's influence was at its zenith – was, through and through, a religious age: the medieval era, when thinkers like Albert the Great and Thomas Aquinas sought explicitly to link Aristotle's dispositional teachings to Christian theology. Today, the governance opinions of many of our religious thinkers are drawn directly from the medievals, and as such the medievals are worth a brief mention as transitional figures in the development of more modern ideas of law and social cooperation. For the Christian thinkers whom I have referenced above, Thomas Aquinas is the especially central figure.

Like Aristotle, Aquinas believed that the social infrastructure ought to be aimed at improving the dispositions of the citizens: "The perfection of virtue must be acquired by man by means of some kind of training."[61] Aquinas's political writings focused on the formation of laws – including especially laws that would facilitate the citizens' moral improvement. Being a medieval, he favoured monarchy as a governance system and argued that the king ought to promote virtues among the people. The way in which the king ought to do this is by offering social conditions that facilitate the virtuous life: the king should "by his laws and orders, punishments and rewards … restrain the men subject to him from wickedness and induce them to virtuous deeds."[62] In holding this conviction Aquinas was making the goals of his social infrastructure similar to the goals of Aristotle's system of private ownership: to transform the dispositions of the citizens and to facilitate their personal flourishing. Aquinas's rigorous defences of these convictions ultimately became central in the medieval effort to appropriate classical forms of political thinking.

Consider also a contemporary religious thinker who has drawn from Aquinas and whose governance opinions are ultimately traceable to Aristotle: Robert George, a Catholic Christian. George advocates a "pluralistic perfectionist" view of governance that is aimed at the improvement of the citizens' character.[63] George takes his inspiration from

Aquinas's belief that there are basic goods which are – or ought to be – acknowledged by humans and which thus should also be recognized in the state's legal code. George rejects liberal views that depict the state as being a peace agreement between contending parties. Instead, siding with Aristotle and Aquinas, he argues that the state ought to promote these basic goods among the citizens. Being a classical liberal, he does of course accept the existence of civil liberties. But at the same time, he grounds these liberties in an understanding of the good – and of the importance of promoting the good – which is reminiscent of Aristotle's justification of his modified private property system.

What the examples of Aquinas and George illustrate is that even though Aristotle was not himself a religious thinker, nevertheless his influence on religious thinkers down through the centuries has been profound. The Christian thinkers of the medieval era, the ancestors of many of today's religious philosophers, were especially strongly impacted by his governance views. Aristotle's beliefs that there is an ideal lifestyle and that the social infrastructure ought to be transformative were widespread in medieval days and have again become widespread today as well. Aristotle is thus the intellectual grandfather of those religious thinkers like George, Finnis, and Neuhaus who today trace their lineage to the medievals and who are endeavouring to promote a particular lifestyle over other lifestyles. The burden of this essay has been to show that the connection between Aristotle's transformative governance views and the governance opinions of such thinkers is particularly discernible in his understanding of the polis and of private property.

NOTES

1 Representative works include Robert George, *Making Men Moral* (Oxford: Oxford University Press, 1993); John Finnis, *Natural Law and Natural Rights*, 2nd ed. (Oxford: Oxford University Press, 2011); Gerard Bradley and Robert George, "Marriage and the Liberal Imagination," *Georgetown Law Journal* 84 (1997): 301–20; J. Budziszewski, *Written on the Heart: The Case for Natural Law* (Westmont, IL: Intervarsity Press, 1997); Frank Beckwith, *Defending Life: A Moral and Legal Case against Abortion Choice* (Cambridge: Cambridge University Press, 2007).

2 George, *Making Men Moral*, 32.

3 Beckwith, *Defending Life*, 98.

4 George, *Making Men Moral*, 33.

5 John Rawls, *Political Liberalism*, 2nd ed. (New York: Columbia University Press, 2005), 190–200; also Alan Patten, "Liberal Neutrality: A Reinterpretation and Defense," *Journal of Political Philosophy* 20 (2012): 249–72; and Jeremy Neill, "Rawls and Acceptable Dispositional Standards: A Feasible Public Space?" *Philosophia Christi* 17.1 (2015): 31–52.

6 Richard John Neuhaus, *The Naked Public Square* (Grand Rapids, MI: Eerdmans, 1984), 82.

7 The idea that Aristotle did not think that happiness consisted in the rational activity of the soul alone is part of an inclusivist reading of what Aristotle means by happiness and is identified approximately as the "Hegelian" approach in Nicholas White, "Conflicting Parts of Happiness in Aristotle's Ethics," *Ethics* 105 (1995): 258–83. The fact that Aristotle believed happiness to include wealth and property is evident from the *Rhetoric* (*Rhetoric*, 1360). See also Jeremy Neill, "Aristotle and American Oligarchy: A Study in Political Influence," in *On Oligarchy: Ancient Lessons for Global Politics*, ed. David Tabachnick and Toivo Koivukoski (Toronto: University of Toronto Press, 2011), 24–46.

8 Aristotle, *Politics*, 1252a1–2. Quotations are from Richard McKeon, *The Basic Works of Aristotle* (1941) (New York: Random House Publishers, 2001).

9 *Politics*, 1280b6–9.

10 Aristotle, *Nicomachean Ethics*, 1179b7–11.

11 *Nicomachean Ethics*, 1179b11–12.

12 *Nicomachean Ethics*, 1179b37–80a4.

13 Eugene Garver, *Aristotle's Politics: Living Well and Living Together* (Chicago: University of Chicago Press, 2011).

14 Quality treatments of this topic can be found in Lenn Goodman and Robert Talisse, eds, *Aristotle's Politics Today* (New York: State University of New York Press, 2007); and Mary Nichols, *Citizens and Statesmen: A Study of Aristotle's* Politics (Savage, MD: Rowman & Littlefield, 1992).

15 *Politics*, 1261a4–6.

16 *Politics*, 1263b15–17.

17 *Politics*, 1263b22–5. For Aristotle, no one, "when men have all things in common, will any longer set an example of liberality or do any liberal action; for liberality consists in the use which is made of property" (*Politics*, 1263b12–14). Likewise, every "man should be responsible to others, nor should any one be allowed to do just as he pleases; for where absolute freedom is allowed there is nothing to restrain the evil which is inherent in every man" (*Politics*, 1318b37–19a1). Also, "Most men tend to be bad … [As] a rule men do wrong to others whenever they have the power to do it" (*Rhetoric*, 1382b4–10).

18 I of course do recognize the difficulty of attempting to juxtapose Aristotle's "property ownership" and our modern "private property." There are differences between the two. For instance, central to our own "private property" is the notion of private ownership and private use; by contrast, Aristotle's classical theory assumed that private ownership meant that the noble Athenian man had private possession but was involved in public use and enjoyment of his property. Prominent contemporary Aristotle scholars – including, most notably, Fred Miller – have articulated for us in detail what it is that is the same and different between Aristotle's property ownership ideas and contemporary views: Fred Miller, "Aristotle on Property Rights," in *Essays in Ancient Greek Philosophy IV: Aristotle's Ethics*, ed. John P. Anton and Anthony Preus (Albany: State University of New York Press, 1991), 227–47. Aristotle does not favour a system in which property is held privately and used privately: Robert Mayhew, *Aristotle's Criticism of Plato's Republic* (Lanham, MD: Rowman and Littlefield, 1997); also, Robert Mayhew, "Aristotle on Property," *Review of Metaphysics* 46 (1993): 803–31; and Terence Irwin, "Generosity and Property in Aristotle's *Politics*," in *Beneficence, Philanthropy and the Public Good*, ed. Ellen Frankel Paul et al. (New York: Basil Blackwell Inc., 1987).

19 In Aristotle's own words, "The criterion of 'security' is the ownership of property in such places and under such conditions that the use of it is in our power; and it is 'our own' if it is in our power to dispose of it or keep it" (*Rhetoric*, 1361a18–22).

20 Martha Nussbaum, "Aristotelian Social Democracy," in *Liberalism and the Good*, ed. Henry Richardson et al. (New York: Routledge, 1990); also, Martha Nussbaum, "Nature, Function, and Capability: Aristotle on Political Distribution," *Oxford Studies in Ancient Greek Philosophy* (1988): 145–84.

21 *Politics*, 1329b40–30a3.

22 Fred Miller, *Nature, Justice, and Rights in Aristotle's* Politics (Oxford: Clarendon Press, 1995), 312. Miller, in contrast to my views, believes that it is intelligible to speak of rights, including property rights, as being present in Aristotle's thought.

23 *Politics*, 1263a25–9, a38–40.

24 *Politics*, 1263a8–21, 27–8, b23–7.

25 *Politics*, 1261b33–40, 1263a28–9.

26 *Politics*, 1263a29–40.

27 *Politics*, 1263a40–b5.

28 *Politics*, 1263b5–14.

29 *Politics*, 1263b22–5.

30 Elsewhere Aristotle underscores these sentiments: "And those who have been wronged, or believe themselves to be wronged, are terrible; for they are always looking out for their opportunity" (*Rhetoric*, 1382b12–13).

31 Jill Frank, "Integrating Public Good and Private Right: The Virtue of Property," in *Aristotle and Modern Politics*, ed. Aristide Tessitore (Notre Dame, IN: University of Notre Dame Press, 2002).

32 *Politics*, 1256b31–2.

33 In matters of wealth, "there is a boundary fixed, just as there is in the other arts; for the instruments of any art are never unlimited, either in number or size, and riches may be defined as a number of instruments to be used in a household or in a state." *Politics*, 1256b34–6.

34 *Politics*, 1256b34–6; also, as Aristotle says when he is attempting to explain how people confuse necessary wealth with unnecessary wealth, "In either [case], the instrument is the same, although the use is different, and so they pass into one another; for each is a use of the same property, but with a difference: accumulation is the end in the one case, but there is a further end in the other" (*Politics*, 1257b35–7; brackets mine).

35 *Politics*, 1263a8–21, 27–8, b23–7.

36 After all, "Every one thinks chiefly of his own, hardly at all of the common interest" (*Politics*, 1261b33–4).

37 *Politics*, 1263a27–9.

38 For Aristotle, friendship seems to emerge from the *phronimos*'s self-focus: "Therefore, since each of these characteristics belongs to the good man in relation to himself, and he is related to his friend as to himself (for his friend is another self), friendship too is thought to be one of these attributes, and those who have these attributes to be friends" (*Nicomachean Ethics*, 1165a29–33). Aristotle's discussion of friendship and self-love in *Nicomachean Ethics* 9.8 is a very significant passage that does seem to suggest egotism (of some kind). Moreover, in *Nicomachean Ethics* 10.6–8 he also seems to suggest that the flourishing life is one that has strong egoistic components.

39 *Nicomachean Ethics*, 1156a7; also, A.W. Price, *Love and Friendship in Plato and Aristotle* (Oxford: Oxford University Press, 1989), 131.

40 *Nicomachean Ethics*, 1156a14–19.

41 *Nicomachean Ethics*, 1156b7–11. The descriptive word that Aristotle attaches to this third kind of friendship is the Greek word *teleios*, which Jonathan Barnes, W.D. Ross, and A.W. Price translate as "perfect." Terence Irwin translates the word as "complete."

42 At times, Aristotle seems to take the "other's sake" to mean for the sake of the other's virtuous attributes. By this he seems to mean that each friend

loves the other for the other's upright and excellent character. Cf. Price, *Love and Friendship in Plato and Aristotle*, 104ff.

43 "Therefore, since each of these characteristics belongs to the good man in relation to himself, and he is related to his friend as to himself (for his friend is another self), friendship too is thought to be one of these attributes, and those who have these attributes to be friends" (*Nicomachean Ethics*, 1166a29–34).

44 *Politics*, 1263a40–b1.

45 "For surely the love of self is a feeling implanted by nature and not given in vain" (*Politics*, 1263b1–3); also, *Rhetoric*, 1371b12–23: "Everyone necessarily is a lover of self, more or less." Immediately thereafter, Aristotle does qualify his endorsement of self-interest: "Although selfishness is rightly censured; this, however, is not the mere love of self, but the love of self in excess" (*Politics*, 1263b1–3).

46 "Again, how immeasurably greater is the pleasure, when a man feels a thing to be his own; for surely the love of self is a feeling implanted by nature and not given in vain" (Aristotle, *Politics*, 1263a40–1).

47 *Politics*, 1263a43–b1.

48 Irwin, "Generosity and Property in Aristotle's *Politics*," 37–54.

49 *Politics*, 1263a33–5.

50 The argument that Aristotle's ethical and political thinking is seamless is pervasive in the contemporary literature: Paul VanderWaerdt, "The Plan and Intention of Aristotle's Ethical and Political Writings," *Illinois Classical Studies* 16 (1985): 231–53; A.W.H. Adkins, "The Connection between Aristotle's Ethics and Politics," in *A Companion to Aristotle's* Politics, ed. David Keyt and Fred D. Miller, Jr (Oxford: Blackwell Press, 1991), 75–93; Christopher Rowe, "Aims and Methods in Aristotle's *Politics*," in *A Companion to Aristotle's* Politics, ed. Keyt and Miller, 57–74; and Peter Simpson, *A Philosophical Commentary on the* Politics *of Aristotle* (Chapel Hill: University of North Carolina Press, 1998).

51 *Politics*, 1119b22–1123a33.

52 Sarah Broadie, *Ethics with Aristotle* (Oxford: Oxford University Press, 1991).

53 Also, *Politics* 1337a2–3.

54 *Nicomachean Ethics*, 1103a23–5; also, *Nicomachean Ethics*, 1103b7–9.

55 *Nicomachean Ethics*, 1120b23–6.

56 *Nicomachean Ethics*, 1120a6–7; "Magnificence is an attribute of expenditures of the kind which we call honorable, e.g. those connected with the gods – votive offerings, buildings, and sacrifices – and similarly with any form of religious worship, and all those that are proper objects of public-spirited ambition, as when people think they ought to equip a chorus or a trireme, or entertain the city, in a brilliant way" (ibid., 1122b18–24).

57 John Cooper, *Reason and Human Good in Aristotle* (Cambridge, MA: Harvard University Press, 1975), primarily chap. 1; Terence Irwin, *Plato's Moral Theory* (Oxford: Oxford University Press, 1977), 241 and 254–9; Irwin, *Aristotle's First Principles* (Oxford: Oxford University Press, 1988), 439–44.

58 *Nicomachean Ethics*, 1094a30-b12; also, *Politics*, 1252al–8, 1260a17–19.

59 *Nicomachean Ethics*, 1121a1–4; "And the liberal are almost the most loved of all virtuous characters, since they are useful; and this depends on their giving" (ibid., 1120a21–3).

60 *Politics*, 1256a1–2.

61 Thomas Aquinas, *The "Summa Theologica" of St Thomas Aquinas*, translated by the Fathers of the English Dominican Province (London: Burns, Oates & Washburn, 1915), I-II, q. 95, a. 1.

62 Thomas Aquinas, *St Thomas Aquinas on Kingship*, trans. Gerald B. Phelan (Toronto: Pontifical Institute of Mediaeval Studies, 1949), *De Regno*, iv (i. 15) [120].

63 Robert George, *Making Men Moral* (Oxford: Oxford University Press, 1993).

PART TWO

Theocracy and Modern State Politics

6 The Non-Theocratic Islamic Republic of Iran (IRI)

HOUCHANG HASSAN-YARI

Nothing appears more surprising to those who consider human affairs with a philosophical eye, than the easiness with which the many are governed by the few.

David Hume, *Of the First Principles of Government*

Islamic Republic is neither Islamic nor republic; it is a military government.

The Grand Ayatollah Hossein Ali Montazeri[1]

Several Islamic Republics exist among today's political systems. Afghanistan, Mauritania, and Pakistan are headed by civilian presidents. Iran is unique and the only Islamic republic whose leader is the Shias' Twelfth Imam. During Mohammad bin Hasan Al-Askari's occultation, otherwise known as Imam Mahdi,[2] the leadership of the Iranian people devolved upon a cleric appointed by the Assembly of Experts of the Leadership, an elected body of eighty-six clerics.[3] As a political project, the Islamic republic is still unfinished almost four decades after its creation. There is no serious indication which suggests an end to the confusion surrounding the nature of the Islamic regime. The name of the new regime, *Islamic Republic (of Iran)* is an oxymoron. The word *republic,* that is to say, the dominance of the public as source of legitimacy, is diluted in the adjective *Islamic,* which takes front stage and precedence.

Everything leads us to believe that, unlike caricatured representations that accept the clerical system's claim to have Islamized the Iranian people, there are many indicators showing that the Islamic regime and the Iranian people walk in opposite directions. This is especially true when it comes to implementing what the rulers want, and to gauging the Iranian people's understanding of such a regime. Clerics are in power, but Iran is not a theocracy.

The second Islamic republic under the rule of Seyyed Ali Khamenei – 1989 to present – is rather a hybrid authoritarian, totalitarian, and quasi-democratic system. Instead of defending and implementing an Islamic system of law, it is rather the latter that is called to serve politics. Religion is reduced to a single function of justifying a political system that wants to be seen as religious. The process of the sanctification of power that began under Ruhollah Khomeini has had its foundations consolidated under Khamenei.

God versus the Skirmishes of the People: The Roots of the Question

The question of the source of legitimate power in Iran remains unsettled. The confusion is embedded in the essence of the new regime and was created by Khomeini[4] himself when he invented the Islamic government based on the governance and guardianship of the jurist (*Velayat-e faqih*). Between the uprising and the fall of the monarchy in 1979, the idea of "government" evolved into the term "republic." As in Shi'a Islam, the question of authoritative guardianship is central to a community of believers that cannot be leaderless. Khomeini therefore opted for the rule of *foqaha* (Islamic jurists) during the absence of the Twelfth Imam.

Khomeini introduced the clergy to active politics. This development is remarkable because the majority of the Shi'a clergy showed very little interest in a political activism they considered impure. For centuries, the clerics were content to be functioning intermediaries between believers and their Allah. Clerics' disinterest in the practice of politics awarded them the vast space of religious activities. The institution of religion was largely respected by the kings, who enjoyed this division of labour. With Khomeini, politics was rehabilitated and no longer considered impure. He believed in the revival of Islam from its exile by introducing it to Muslims.

The Islamic Republic of Iran's (IRI) selective approach to Islam is not in line with what is expected from an Islamic state whose laws should be based on Sharia. Based on its practice of expediency, IRI is neither a theocracy nor a democracy because it imposes improvised laws and regulations passed through a questionable process.[5] It seems that the

IRI was successful in deepening the gap between many Iranians and Islam. Even several clerics confirm the relationship between people and religion was better before the revolution. As Mehdi Khalaji writes:

> In line with some of Khomeini's disciples, like Ahmad Azari Qomi, who claimed that the interests of the regime precede all Islamic principles and that, if necessary, Islamic principles – including the unity of God – can be suspended, Khomeini himself wrote that sharia is not binding for the jurist ruler, who has the right to ignore prayer and other rituals (known as the Pillars of Islam) in favor of the regime's needs. Despite the ground-shaking effects of Khomeini's stance, no other Iranian cleric dared oppose him openly.[6]

Is Iran Really a Theocracy?

First, we need to describe the characteristics of theocracy in the context of the Iranian post-revolutionary, political culture. Theocracy is non-existent in Aristotle's six forms of government.[7] They are: monarchy, tyranny, aristocracy, oligarchy/plutocracy (a group of a few wealthy people), polity, and democracy (all citizens). The authoritative sources of power are rule by the one, the few, or the many. As a concept, theocracy is a compound notion of the Greek words *theos* (god) and *kratia* (rule). It entails the rule of God by clerical intermediaries.[8]

There are several concepts pertinent to the case of Iran, whose political system has a great deal in common with theonomy,[9] a system of government in which primary scriptural sources (in Islam, the Quran, hadith and Sunnah, the Prophet's sayings and acts) are said to be adopted into law. In its chapter 1 (General Principles), article 4 (Islamic Principle) of the Constitution of the Islamic Republic of Iran stipulates: "All civil, penal, financial, economic, administrative, cultural, military, political, and other laws and regulations must be based on Islamic criteria. This principle applies absolutely and generally to all articles of the Constitution as well as to all other laws and regulations, and the wise persons of the Guardian Council are judges in this matter." Chapter 5 (The Right of National Sovereignty), article 56 (Divine Right of Sovereignty) states: "Absolute sovereignty over the world and man belongs to God, and it is He Who has made man master of his own social destiny. No one can deprive man of this divine right, nor subordinate it to the vested interests of a particular individual or group." The Islamic republic's theocrats claim that the Vali-e faqih has an absolute and exclusive right to rule in the name of God. This right is conferred on them by the grace of the Almighty. This devolution of the divine right to clerics is therefore consolidated in the IRI's constitution. Stripping man of his vested right, article 57 (Separation of Powers) of chapter 5 (The Right of National Sovereignty) avowed: "The powers of government in the Islamic Republic are vested in the legislature, the judiciary, and the executive powers, functioning under the supervision of the *absolute* religious Leader and the Leadership of the Umma, in accordance with the forthcoming articles of this Constitution."[10] In the realm of politics absolute power is always more formidable than rights.

"Mahdism," from Mahdi the hidden Imam, is a core component of the Iranian Twelver Shi'a ideology under the rule of the dominant clerics. It is an adapted version of the *apocalyptic theocracy*. It calls upon the *divine lieutenants* of the twelfth Imam to prepare the physical conditions for the Mahdi's return from his Major Occultation. Accompanied by his Iranian lieutenants, Mahdi will launch a campaign to purify the world of its sins. This was the theological basis for the Islamic republic's theocratic claims, and is mostly institutionalized in the framework of its constitution. The reality, however, depicts a very different picture.

From its inception in 1979, the Islamic Republic of Iran was Islamic in façade, but very pragmatic and sometimes *un*islamic in its approach to politics. Over time, it has become an ordinary authoritarian system like so many other regimes in the region. Instead of implementing a system of Islamic law, one based on a progressive reading of the Shi'a doctrine as promised by the founder of the new regime (Ayatollah Ruhollah Khomeini during the revolution), the new political elite put Islam in the service of the state. It did and does so under the guise of expediency and necessity. Religion is reduced to the single function of justifying a political system. The gradual resurgence of Islam will lead to the creation of new judicial, financial, economic, cultural, and political institutions. After the ground is prepared, Islamic government will one day be established.[11] In other words, the ultimate goal of the revival of Islam is to take political power and conduct its government by *foqaha*.[12]

Khomeini mastered this political and religious flip-flop throughout his public life. Before the 1979 revolution, he was in favour of monarchy by defending it as a model of government. He then reversed course on his initial opinion, arguing that it is against Islam. He did not act on his post-revolution promise to Iranians about free utilities (water, electricity).[13] In 1963 he issued a fatwa in direct contradiction of Mohammad Reza Shah Pahlavi's granting of women's suffrage.[14] After the revolution, he announced that women had the duty to vote and participate in all elections. The consumption of sturgeon that was forbidden by Khomeini and all Shiite jurists before the revolution became permissible in Khomeini's fatwa. Other practices permitted after the revolution included the following: autopsies, chess, women appearing on television and in movies, hearing a woman's voice on the radio, and listening to non-religious music.[15] In 1988 and after several setbacks on the warfront with Iraq, Khomeini "called off the eight-year holy war that he had vowed to wage until total victory was achieved."[16] He had promised to fight to the last drop of his blood and to his last breath. "Taking this decision was more deadly than taking poison. I submitted myself to God's will and drank this drink for his satisfaction,"[17] Khomeini said. Two years after the war started, Khomeini confirmed his refusal to make peace, "even if the whole world gathers." He argued that peace with the criminal Saddam Hussein was a crime against Islam. Drinking from a poisoned chalice by accepting the UNSC resolution 598 did not conserve Iran's territorial integrity or save the combatants from slaughter, because it was "based only on the interest of the Islamic republic."[18]

As the regime's survival is the ultimate objective of the Vali-e faqih, Khomeini's successor, Ayatollah Ali Khamenei, would in turn drink the poison by introducing the term "heroic flexibility"[19] to justify the painful compromises reached in the nuclear deal with the P5 + 1 (China, France, Russia, the United Kingdom, plus Germany). The term is a reference to the armistice agreed to by Hasan ibn Ali (625–70), the second Shi'a Imam. Khamenei described Imam Hasan's "peace accord" deal with Muawiya, his worst enemy, as "History's Most Glorious Exercise of Flexibility," necessary and very beneficial on certain occasions.[20] But how glorious was that flexibility when he was compelled to accept the armistice?

Similarities between the general theme of the Iranian nuclear deal and Hasan's truce treaty with Muawiya ibn Abi Sufyan (602–80, founder of the Umayyad Dynasty caliphate, caliph in Damascus) are striking. They amount to a giving away of rights in favour of survival. Like his father Imam Ali, Imam Hasan's succession to the caliphate was rejected by other contenders. When Hasan was deserted by his followers, including his cousin, and failed to secure the leadership of the Muslim community, abdication in favour of his (and his father's) arch enemy Muawiya became an absolute necessity to save his own life. He relinquished the power through a treaty, but obtained a few minor concessions from the new caliph: abandonment of the curse on his father, allowance of the practice of personal prayer, security for his loyal followers, and respect for the treaty with Muawiya. After his victory over Hasan and in an address to the faithful, Muawiya said:

> By God, I have not fought against you to make you pray, nor to fast, nor to make the pilgrimage, nor to pay zakat.[21] Indeed, you do that (already). I fought so that I might have power over you and God has given that to me when you were reluctant to (obey) Him. Indeed, I have been requested by al-Hasan ... (to give him) things and I have given things to him. All of them are now under my foot. And from now on I will not fulfil anything.[22]

Hasan was poisoned by his wife,[23] who was bribed by Muawiya with money and a promise to marry her to his son Yazid (647–83). In the end, Hasan lost power and his life, as well as the life of his younger brother Husain (626–80), the third Imam of the Shiites.

This remarkable adaptation that repudiated what was *wrong* in a particular context, claiming to make it *right* in a different environment, is a clear and powerful sign that political realities force leaders to change course, even at the expense of their religious credibility. The volte-face which is rendered necessary by the expediency of the Iranian government, by its reason of state, was not always practised by some Shiites. Khomeini believed the entire society, including all clerics, should obey the orders of the Leader since he gets his legitimacy directly from the Prophet Mohammad and represents the Twelfth Imam. At least in theory, the Leader has the ultimate authority over the spiritual and temporal life of the society.

In the original, theoretical system of Khomeini's understanding, Islam seeks to establish a theocratic political system. However, some powerful Great Ayatollahs opposed Khomeini's vision on political Islam. One of the most respected opponents of the clerical political leadership is the Grand Ayatollah Ali Sistani of Najaf, who has refused to endorse *velayat-e faqih* despite pressure from Tehran. He questions the managerial ability of clerics and believes that "the jurist needed something more than jurisprudence to manage the state. In other words, the state's legitimacy was not derived from jurisprudence."[24] As a Shi'a scholar, Sistani has to overcome a deeply rooted contradiction. On the one hand he recognizes pluralism as essential for the administration of the country, while on the other he regards Shi'a as rightful and, therefore, inherently in conflict with pluralism.[25]

Sistani is only one of many sceptics of the viability of a political system based on Islam. Muhammad Amien Rais, a prominent Indonesian politician and a denier of the Islamic state proposed by Khomeini, goes further than Sistani. He stated: "The Quran does not say anything about the formation as an Islamic state, or about the necessity and obligations, both moral and political obligations on the part of Muslims to establish a Sharia or Islamic state. Secondly, the Quran is not a book of law, but a source of law. If the Quran is considered a book of law, Muslims will become the most wretched people in the world."[26]

In order to overcome this philosophical contradiction of an Islamic state in Shiism, and to counter Khomeini's dogmatic imposition of militant political views on Iranian society, Sistani instead furthered reflection on the role of jurists in societal and political spheres. His pragmatic political doctrine, called *hekmat-e faqih* (wisdom of the cleric jurist), is neither the rule of the jurist nor an indifference to politics. It means prudence and paying attention to the interests and capacity of society.[27] This is a clear recognition of society's legitimate *right* to freely choose its political path. The consistency and moderation of his doctrinal approach earned him respect from Iraqi Shi'a and Sunni communities in the post-US invasion of Iraq in 2003. For Sistani, society should be ready to adhere to the rule of the jurist and not the other way around, as the Iranian model shows. The paralysis that still haunts Iran since the advent of the Islamic Republic occurred when Khomeini erected a political system without historical precedent, and then forced Iranians to adapt to this system.[28]

As a form of political regime, in theocracy the spiritual dominates the temporal and "the supreme religious leader is also the apex political leader."[29] The Islamic Republic of Iran is divine and belongs to the Hidden Imam, but is governed, on his behalf, by clerics whose supreme leader is regarded as divinely guided and immune from making any mistakes. In this system the leader is connected to the Almighty through the Prophet Mohammad and his descendent Imams. The judiciary system is based on religious law and the legislative apparatus's role is limited to extracting a body of laws from the Sharia. In a system based on this premise, clerics rule for life. From this perspective, theocracy as a political regime is hereditary like a monarchy. However, the difference between the two lies in the fact that in monarchies power remains in the same family tied by blood, while in the Iranian theocratic-like system it is the religious caste that shares power among its members and their ideological associates. Being ruled by clerics and having a written constitution does not make the IRI a "constitutional theocracy," where a

> formal separation exists ... between political leadership and religious authority. Power in constitutional theocracies resides in political figures operating within the bounds of a constitution, rather than from within the religious leadership itself. Basic principles such as the separation of powers are constitutionally enshrined. The constitution also typically establishes a constitutional court that is mandated to carry out some form of active judicial review.[30]

In Iranian clericalism, the political system implemented a systematic policy of supporting the *right* of the clergy to exercise power and influence in all matters. This creates a system of government where it is the responsibility of the rulers to make people pious by enforcing religious values that are believed to deliver believers into paradise. In reaction to the promotion of force by influential clerics in Iran against those people who do not comply with the state's unwritten religious rules, President Rouhani, himself a cleric, said: "Do not interfere in people's lives so much, even if it is out of compassion. Let people pick their own path to heaven. One cannot take people to heaven through force and a whip. The Prophet [Mohammad] did not have a whip in his hand."[31]

It is ironic that while the first, and only, Islamic republic in the Middle East moves away from its Islamic essence in the name of *maslahah*[32] (expediency) and is ready to suspend Islamic principles to save the regime, other nations in the region seek to replace dictatorships with Islamic regimes.

President Mohammad Khatami was another example of the lack of unanimity among clerics regarding the nature and essence of the Islamic republic. A middle-ranking reformist cleric and former president of Iran, Khatami introduced the notion of "civil society" that was supposed to be an integral component of the greater Muslim Ummah (community). Since the 1979 revolution, Iran has vacillated between two increasingly incompatible concepts. The debate is between those who define the Iranians as a distinct *nation* and others who see them as part of the *Ummah*.[33] To add to the confusion, Khatami tried to describe the political system in Iran as a "Religious democracy"; *religious* in its belief, while *democratic* in its exercise of polity. The confusion is enshrined in the IRI constitution. An unfinished battle between a dogmatic and rigid structure and a desire for an open, modern and progressive regime has consumed and constrained the potential of Iran since 1979. Elections are organized, but all candidates are vetted by a clerically dominated, non-elected body. Presidents and members of parliament remain relevant only if they act in the frame established by numerous non-elected centres of power, chief among them the leader and his followers. If the fundamental contradiction in the nature of this Islamic regime is not resolved, the deadlock could lead to a major confrontation between the forces in favour of the status quo and those who advocate reform. The violence that followed the presidential elections of 2009 is one of several serious occurrences that indicate the rupture between the state and its people.

Khomeini's solution for resolving the constitutional impasse was to introduce the concept of *maslahah* by creating the Expediency Discernment Council of the System, adding another layer to an already very fat administration. The attempt failed because the problem is fundamentally structural and cannot be resolved by cosmetic alterations. The regime's inability to overcome its contradictions became even more evident after Khomeini's death. Persistent quarrels among the different state agencies necessitate the ever-increasing interference of non-elected leaders in daily political and factional activities. This, as a result, further erodes the claim that the system is democratic and self-regulating. As Evangelina Axiarlis puts it, "The term 'Islamic state' refers to the official regime characteristics of the country. It is a theocratic regime that is organised by religious principles whereas its social, political and legal institutions have been Islamicised. Democratic process in the administration of the Islamic state is normally rejected, and totalitarianism and authoritarianism are governing features of the political landscape."[34]

A Hybrid System: Authoritarianism Predominance

The history of Persia has always been hectic, from the time of its expansive empires dominating the territories from present-day India to the Mediterranean Sea right through until today. For more than a century Iranians struggled against the despotism and absolute power of their rulers. The 1906 Constitutional Revolution[35] was the first attempt in their struggle. In nineteenth-century Iran, the clergy was very powerful. Several soft authoritarian Qajar Shahs were very incompetent and corrupt. The great powers, Russia to the north and Great Britain to the south, dominated not only the territory of Iran, but to a large extent its domestic and foreign policy. During this period of rampant colonialism, the concessions of a north-south corridor railway and tobacco cultivation were given to British companies, and customs to Belgians.[36] This was also the era of nationalism in Europe and its introduction to Iran. The first major concession of the government to clerics and their followers was the creation of a judicial system that had to avoid any discrimination and bias when treating the Shah's "subjects." This concession was made so as to abort a popular revolt.[37] Later on, the Shah issued a decree ordering a series of reforms, including the creation of a parliament and a body of laws in conformity with the Sharia.[38] The Constitutional Revolution resulted in the creation of several modern institutions which imitated the European model, but without importing the spirit and functionality of those institutions.

The Roots of Authoritarianism in Modern Iran

It was in the backdrop of a century-long struggle for good governance, freedom, and accountable government that Iranians revolted against the Pahlavi dynasty (1925–79). Since the 1979 revolution, Iran has invented a unique political structure. It is an Islamic republic theorized, legitimized and implemented by Ayatollah Ruhollah Khomeini, the Guide of the Revolution. The Guide's absolute *Velayat-e faqih* system is a rehash of seventh-century ancient Islam with a very pronounced Safavid Shi'a (1501–1736) makeup, combined with the nineteenth-century Qajar rule. These traditions were imposed on a twentieth-century partially secularized Iran and continue into the twenty-first century.

The new creature is called by the first president of the Islamic republic, Abolhassan Banisadr, a *Mollataria*, not a theocracy but a regime[39] governed by Mullahs, or clerics. Inspired by Max Weber's *Economy and Society*, Akbar Ganji, a prominent Iranian journalist and dissident, prefers the term Sultanism over authoritarianism, totalitarianism, or *Mollataria*. In his essay, Weber wrote: "Where it [a political system] indeed operates primarily on the basis of discretion, it will be called sultanism." Sultanism is both traditional and arbitrary, according to Weber, and expresses itself largely through recourse to military force and an administrative system that is an extension of the ruler's household and court.[40] Sultans sometimes hold elections in order to prove their legitimacy, but they never lose any power in them. According to Weber, sultans promote or demote officials at will, rob state bodies of their independence of action and infiltrate them with their proxies, and marshal state economic resources to fund an extensive apparatus of repression. Weber might have been describing Khamenei, Ganji confirms.[41] Although Weberian sultanism also encapsulates some characteristics of Khomeinism in Iran, there are quite significant nuances that distinguish them from each other. In other words, the Weberian framework cannot describe Khomeinism in all its dimensions.[42]

For Ganji, the Islamic government is neither totalitarian nor fascist, as many voices can be heard saying in Iran today. It is not a theocracy, as no single ideology dominates the country. The ruling religious fundamentalists lack a unified vision, and fundamentalist, traditionalist, and modernist versions of Islam compete for power. Diversity of opinion over interpretations of Islam brings no positive or substantial change in the spiritual or material life of the vast majority of the population not affected by sterile ideological debate.

Another point of dissimilarity with the confirmation of Ganji relates to his claim that there is competition within the camp of the so-called *principaliste*. The ultimate reference here remains Khamenei. If there is competition for power, it's certainly at a very low level that never worries the leader. Competition in this sense is more an effort to prove which subjects are more loyal and fulfilling of the leader's expectations. It is about the degree of subordination to the authoritarian ruler, not a challenging of him.

The survival of the regime is the red line for its leaders and followers. Religion has increasingly become an instrument of political power. Khomeini and his successor Ali Khamenei have confirmed that preserving "the state takes precedence over all the precepts of Sharia. The ruler can destroy a mosque or a house if it impedes the construction of a road ... The state can temporarily prevent the hajj [the pilgrimage to Mecca and Medina, an important religious duty] when it considers it to be contrary to the interests of the Islamic state."[43] Article 57 of the Iranian constitution grants the supreme leader absolute power.[44]

An analysis of the power structure in Iran clearly shows all powers lay, directly or indirectly, in the hands of the leader. A real functional republic cannot be run by an absolute leader who is neither elected nor accountable for his actions. The Islamic Republic of Iran's novelty and contribution to the field of political science and human political experience is the creation of a religious authoritarianism on the skeleton of democratic institutions. A parliament exists but takes its orders from the leader in important issues. A constitution exists to serve the purpose of the absolute Vali-e faqih, who controls all the levers of power. A police force and a very large security, intelligence, and military

(Islamic Revolutionary Guard Corps – IRGC), as well as close to five million Bassijis,[45] exist, not to protect the people, but to prevent them from disturbing the absolute rule of the leader.

The controversial and complex nature of the Islamic republic makes it very difficult to define or fit it in a single concept.[46] It is necessary to make a clear distinction between the formal rights of the people enshrined in the constitution and informal, unwritten, mechanisms that curtail these same rights. For example, a definition of authoritarianism states:

> The public does not play a significant role in selecting or removing leaders from office, and thus political leaders in authoritarian systems have much greater leeway to develop policies that they "dictate" to the people ... Authoritarian systems by their nature are built around the restriction of individual freedom. At a minimum, they eliminate people's right to choose their own leaders, and they also restrict to varying degrees other liberties such as the freedom of speech or of assembly. Authoritarianism's relationship to equality is less clear. Some authoritarian systems, such as communism, limit individual freedom in order to produce greater social equality. Others seek to deny equality, existing only to enhance the power of those in control.[47]

This definition does not adequately reflect the situation in Iran. For instance, despite the fact that restrictions exist for candidates to run for any office, from municipal elections to the Assembly of Experts, once candidates pass through a rigorous and highly politically biased vetting process, the election is relatively free. On the equality question, the Islamic republic has alienated the middle class – which was flourishing under the Shah's rule – in favour of the less fortunate people living in small towns and villages. Khomeini engineered a reverse equality scheme. One of the revolution's slogans was "We will destroy the city-south – with its poor neighbourhoods – to build a new neighbourhood similar to the north of the city – more affluent."

Many aspects of policies under Khomeini and Khamenei are totalitarian, inspired by a very strong ideology that seeks to transform fundamental aspects of the state, society, and economy through a wide array of organizations and applications of force, seconded by a strong populist discourse. In other words, the Islamic totalitarian system strives for the control and transformation of all aspects of the private and public life of Iranians according to a very austere and ideological understanding of Islam. Because of the ambitious goals of totalitarianism, violence becomes a necessary tool to destroy any obstacle to the changes imposed by its rule.[48] An illustration of this strong will to transform Iranian society from top to bottom over the past four decades is the attempt by the regime to Islamize all university curricula from mathematics courses to humanity and social sciences. All these attempts, like the imposition of a rigid dress code for women, have failed so far.

The most prominent features of authoritarianism in Iran are: 1. The existence of endemic violence and control. The Islamic regime has created a vast national network of intelligence surveillance, police forces, IRGC, and Bassij. Mosques and informers are omnipresent in every district of any town. An example of this kind of police control and securitization of society is the presence of the Ministry of Information posters in cities. The posters invite people to denounce anyone who can be seen as a threat to public safety. Arbitrary arrests, torture, murder, public hanging of "criminals," and kidnapping of suspects for interrogation are frequent. 2. *Velayat-e faqih* is a clientelistic mode of governance that sustains itself by providing incentives to its benefactors in exchange for their loyal service. It is a predominantly patriarchal system arranged for the advocacy of a guardianship-based political system. 3. Iranian authoritarianism endeavours to emulate the Chinese model of authoritarianism without being able to stimulate economic growth the way the reforms led by Deng Xiaoping did. Khamenei tries to establish a firm hold over the state and society. He controls political dissent, suppresses independent media, and deals with the pressures exerted by Western countries by preserving his ideological values and immunizing them against "westoxication."[49] The question is whether the Chinese model can provide helpful lessons for the Islamic republic's efforts to reinforce its monopoly of power in the archaic absolute *Velayat-e faqih* of twenty-first-century Iran. 4. Consistent with Shi'a traditions, the Islamic Republic is obsessed with the cult of personality. After the revolution, some people saw "Khomeini's picture in the moon."[50] Later on, he was titled "imam," a designation that was exclusively used by Shias for the descendants of Imam Ali, Prophet Mohammad's son-in-law and the first Shi'a Imam. A representative of Ali Khamenei in the holy city of Qom claims that when the future leader of the IRI left his mother's womb he said: "O Ali!"[51] A close supporter to Khamenei presents him as the successor of Prophet Mohammad and Imam Ali, implying his position of leader has been invested by God, who, in opposition to the people and republicanism, is the source of his legitimacy.[52] The leader is the centre of the circle and everything revolves around him. The logical consequence of this situation is that nobody will be capable of judging the pertinence of his decisions even if they go against the national interest of Iran. In the Shi'a theology, saints do not make mistakes, therefore Khamenei is always right. His office organizes routine meetings between him and groups of students, physicians, scientists, bazaaris, airline pilots, mollas, workers, women, poets, movie directors, even sometimes foreign ambassadors in post in Tehran. It is in these meetings that the leader provides direction to his audience on the ways to conduct their business. This is an attempt to present the leader's abilities as a broad knowledge capable of addressing all segments and concerns of the population. 5. There is an effort to prevent, by all means available, the creation of viable political parties that attract members and challenge the political status quo. There is no space for public demonstration if it's not in support of the regime's ideology. 6. The leader establishes the direction of the country's foreign, defence, economic, social, scientific, and cultural policies. 7. The principal mission of the government apparatus is to serve the leader and implement his views and decisions. All state institutions, including the presidency, parliament, Expediency Council, Council of the Guardian of the Constitution, and Assembly of Experts,[53] are empty shells and submissive to the leader's will. Khamenei exercises total control over all of Iran's elected institutions by virtue of a constitutional provision (article 110) that empowers him to set the state's general policies.

It is important to remember that despite the inefficiency of all state institutions, they are indeed needed to project the image of a system where different components of society participate in the decision-making process through their representatives. This illusion of effective participation in the decision-making process is exposed regularly when voters realize how limited the role of "their" elected representatives is in parliament and elsewhere. The threat of boycotting elections normally forces the leader to tactically retreat by making a few cosmetic concessions on the eve of elections to get a higher participation. More participation brings prestige and legitimacy for the Islamic regime in the eyes of the international community as well as the doubters of the authoritarian state. Once the goal of political participation is reached, the system returns to its true nature: arrests, repression, public invitations to attend executions of condemned prisoners, and exile.[54] The episodes of the presidency of Mohammad Khatami (1997–2005) and election of Hassan Rouhani (June 2013) have injected breaths of fresh air into the lungs of a tired authoritarian regime that survives from one crisis to the other.

In spite of the authoritarian state's resistance to global Information and Communication Technologies and their free and open media, normal interaction between Iranian and international non-governmental organizations (and the flux of people and ideas they bring) persist in the Iranian republic. The absolute *Velayat-e faqih*'s grip over society is continuously challenged by daughters and sons of the revolution who are eager to catch up with the global trend for a better life. The state's responses to all aspects of globalization show distinct signs of exhaustion and inefficiency: greater isolation, higher repression, and further control of information and communication. Religion has reached the limits of its usefulness as a factor that justifies the ineffectiveness of the Islamic Republic. The Islamic Revolution went through three stages of change in its evolution. 1. Before the victory of 1979, religion was presented by Khomeini and his loyal followers as a unifying, inclusive, and tolerant factor. 2. After the establishment of the Islamic regime, religion has become the engine of exporting the revolution as advocated by Khomeini. During the first republic (1979–89), the revolution took a radical turn that led to two major developments. First, there was the American hostage crisis that triggered Western sanctions against the new regime. The second event was the Iran-Iraq war that lasted eight years, with disastrous consequences for the Iranian and Iraqi peoples. These critical events allowed Khomeini to repress leftist, nationalist, secular, and moderate Islamist opponents, redirect popular mobilization at the "Great Satan," and monopolize state power.[55] Khomeini called the occupation of the "American spy den" "the second revolution," and the Iran-Iraq war "God's hidden gift." 3. The second republic (since 1989) resulted in an escalation of confrontation with the West, use of more force to legitimize the leader, and an equating of the state with Khamenei.

Khamenei is a new version of French king Louis XIV, who believed he was the state. The leader of the revolution who oversteps his authority is bound by no rules and has no limits in exercising his unchecked power. Mohsen Safaei-Farahani, former deputy minister of economy, has confirmed that 50 per cent of Iran's gross domestic product is controlled by 120 parastatal foundations and economic agencies.[56] All these agencies are under the leader's control and immune from any government scrutiny, even if they are budgeted by the government. The absolute power of the leader emboldens all units of the state under his control, including the Guardians of the Islamic Revolution, often called

Revolutionary Guards or Islamic Revolutionary Guard Corps. After ignoring Khomeini's warning not to meddle in the politics of the state, the IRGC, with the tacit approval of Khamenei, has played a significant role in the demise of reformist movements, as well as in limiting any attempts by Rouhani to discourage their political and economic role.

Encouraged by the nuclear deal, Rouhani began talking about the following possibilities: a détente with the United States, an effective separation of powers in Iran, and a return of the armed forces (IRGC) to their barracks. The presidential projects directly call into question the authority of Khamenei and are seen as a flagrant interference in the spheres of the leader's power. In the design of Khamenei's office, the president is merely executing the decisions taken by the state. As the leader has the monopoly of power and veto over all state agencies, there is no hope of reforming the Islamic system. It is Khamenei who determines where the interests of Islam and that of the nation lies.

NOTES

1 Mehdi Khalaji, "Islam vs. Iran's Islamic Republic," The Washington Institute, 2009. http://www.washingtoninstitute.org/policy-analysis/view/islam-vs.-irans-islamic-republic.
2 "The Guided One," the Hidden Imam, was born on 868 in Samarra (Iraq) and has been living in the Occultation since 872. He will re-establish the rightful governance of Islam and replete the earth with justice and peace. https://heavenawaits.wordpress.com/2014-2019-islams-shiite-countdown-to-the-12th-imam-mahdi/ and http://www.shia.org/mehdi.html.
3 For an analysis of the state institutions in Iran see Mehran Kamrava and Houchang Hassan-Yari, "Suspended Equilibrium in the Islamic Republic of Iran," Muslim World 94.4 (2004): 495–524.
4 Ruhollah Khomeini, Governance of the Jurist. Islamic Government. Tehran: Chamber Society, 1979.
5 The parliament is elected by the electorate, but is not sovereign in its decisions. It does not legislate, but interprets the Sharia. Its decisions can be overturned by an unelected higher authority. The Leader can stop its proceedings when considered unacceptable at any time.
6 Mehdi Khalaji, "Shiite Jurisprudence, Political Expediency, and Nuclear Weapons, Part 2," Washington Institute, 2011. http://www.thecuttingedgenews.com/index.php?article=52768.
7 http://www.nssa.us/journals/2007-28-1/2007-28-1-16.htm.

8 The Iranian brand of theocracy is distinguished from some other Asian theocracies because of the nature of its leaders, who come from the clergy. In Japan the emperors and in China the warrior kings were believed to be divine representatives of the Almighty. See Andrew J. Waskey, "The Political Theory of Theocracy," National Social Science Association. http://www.nssa.us/journals/2007-28-1/2007-28-1-16.htm.

9 For a definition of theonomy, see Greg Bahnsen, "What Is 'Theonomy'?" http://www.cmfnow.com/articles/pe180.htm.

10 Constitution of the Islamic Republic of Iran, http://www.iranonline.com/iran/iran-info/Government/constitution.html.

11 Waskey, "The Political Theory of Theocracy," 92.

12 Faqih (plural foqaha), a religious scholar, is a Muslim theologian and expert in fiqh, or Islamic jurisprudence. In Shi'a Islam Faqih has the exclusive right of interpretation in Islamic law. Paradoxically, that exclusiveness has sporadically been challenged by non-clerical scholars of Islam after the Islamic revolution in 1979.

13 M. Bakh, K. McIntyre, and J. Le Beau, *Escaping Islam: The Evil Might Not Be Realized Until It Is Too Late* (Bloomington, IN: AuthorHouse, 2009), 160.

14 In June 1963 Khomeini issued a fatwa equating women's franchise to prostitution, and was subsequently detained and exiled to Turkey and later Iraq. Reyhaneh Noshiravani, "Iranian Women in the Era of Modernization: A Chronology," Foundation for Iranian Studies, 2009. http://fis-iran.org/en/women/milestones/pre-revolution.

15 Khalaji, "Shiite Jurisprudence, Political Expediency, and Nuclear Weapons, Part 2."

16 Robert Pear, "Khomeini Accepts 'Poison' of Ending the War with Iraq; U.N. Sending Mission," *New York Times*, 21 July 1988.

17 Ibid.

18 Ibid.

19 Najmeh Bozorgmehr, "Ayatollah Invokes 'Heroic Flexibility' to Justify Iran Deal," *Financial Times*, 15 July 2015.

20 "Iran: 'Hello Diplomacy, So Long Martyrdom,'" *The Guardian*, 21 September 2013.

21 Zakat is the third pillar of Islam. It is a tax, comprising percentages of personal income of every kind for the relief of the poor. "Zakat means grow (in goodness) or 'increase,' 'purifying' or 'making pure.' So the act of giving zakat means purifying one's wealth to gain Allah's blessing to make it grow in goodness." http://www.zpub.com/aaa/zakat-def.html.

22 *Imam Hasan (as), a Brief Look into His Life.* https://www.al-islam.org/printpdf/book/export/html/14955.

23 "Mu'awiya's Plot to Poison Imam Hasan (as)." http://www.sibtayn.com/
en/index.php?option=com_content&view=article&id=5941:mu-awiya-s
-plot-to-poison-imam-hasan-as&catid=576&Itemid=671.

24 Mohammad Javad Akbarein, "Sistani: The Silent Ayatollah," *IranGeo.*
http://irangeo.net/sistani-the-silent-ayatollah/.

25 Ibid.

26 Alfred Stepan and Juan J. Linz, "Democratization Theory and the 'Arab
Spring,'" *Journal of Democracy* 24.2 (April 2013): 18.

27 Khomeini, *Governance of the Jurist.*

28 On 30 and 31 March 1979 a referendum was held to determine the nature
of the new political system. Voters were asked to say Yes or No to the
question of whether the "Islamic Republic" should replace the monarchy.
The people did not know much about the concept of an Islamic Republic,
which Khomeini – in whom the vast majority of Iranians invested their
confidence – did not see necessary to define. "Less than six months
later, in December of 1979, 75 percent of eligible voters [voted for] a new
constitution." For more details, see Yasmin Alem, *Duality by Design: The
Iranian Electoral System* (Washington, DC: International Foundation for
Electoral Systems, 2011), 65. In the euphoric revolutionary context of 1979
nobody dared to question Khomeini's choice of a new political system.
He famously proclaimed: "Islamic republic, not one word more, not one
word less." *RadioFreeEurope/RadioLiberty*, "Reformists Cling to Islamic
Republic Ideal as Khamenei Sounds the Death Knell." http://www.rferl.
org/content/Reformists_Cling_To_Islamic_Republic_Ideal_As_Khamenei
_Sounds_The_Death_Knell_/2067735.html; http://www.thecuttingedgenews
.com/index.php?article=52768.

29 See Ran Hirschl, "The Rise of Constitutional Theocracy," *Harvard
International Law Journal Online* 49 (2008): 73. http://www.harvardilj.org/
wp-content/uploads/2011/02/HILJ-Online_49_Hirschl.pdf.

30 Ibid.

31 *ISNA* (Islamic Society of North America), 25 May 2015. "We cannot impose
the heaven by force." Arash Karami, "Rouhani Under Fire for Saying
Heaven Can't Be Forced," *Al-Monitor*, 27 May 2014. http://www.al-monitor.
com/pulse/originals/2014/05/khatami-criticizes-rouhani-heaven-force
-whip.html#posted.

32 *Maslahah* is a complex concept defined by predominant Islamic scholars.
Abu Ḥamid Muḥammad ibn Muḥammad al-Ghazali (1058–111), a
theologian, jurist, philosopher, and a Persian Sufi dervish, has offered the
most comprehensive definition. According to Al-Ghazali, *maslahah* means to
"secure a benefit or prevent harm but is, in the meantime, harmonious with

the aim and objective of the sharia. These objectives consist of protecting the five essential values, namely religion, life, intellect, lineage and property. In Al-Ghazali's view, any measure, which secures these values, falls within the scope of Maslahah and anything, which contravenes them in *masfadah* (evil) while preventing the latter is also Maslahah." Elvan Syaputra, Faridl Noor Hilal, Muhammad Febriansyah, Issa Qaed, Muhammad Majdy Amiruddin, Muhammad Ridhwan Ab. Aziz, "Maslahah as an Islamic Source and Its Application in Financial Transactions," *Quest Journals Journal of Research in Humanities and Social Science* 2.5 (2014): 67.

33 This Umma versus nation dichotomy is not a mere intellectual exercise. It has serious consequences for Iran. A nation usually lives in demarcated borders, while the Umma lives as a large community that englobes the totality of Muslim lands from Morocco to Malaysia. Since the Umma does not recognize national borders, Iran would become a province in the ocean of 1.5 billion Muslims. The issue is the loss of Iranian identity that has survived centuries of Arab and Mongol invasions.

34 Evangelina Axiarlis, *Political Islam and the Secular State in Turkey: Democracy, Reform and the Justice and Development Party* (London: I.B. Tauris, 2014), 81.

35 For a description of root causes of the revolution, see Samih K. Farsoun and Mchrdad Mashayekhi, eds., *Iran: Political Culture in the Islamic Republic* (London: Routledge, 1992).

36 For the impact of colonial rivalries on Iran and an analysis of concessions, see Abdolreza Houshang Mahdavi, *History of Iran's Foreign Affairs from the Safavids to the End of World War II (1500–1945)* (Tehran: Amir Kabir Publications House, 1986).

37 For an account of this dynamic, see Vladimir Minorsky, "Iran: Opposition, Martyrdom, and Revolt," in *Unity and Variety in Muslim Civilization*, ed. G.E. von Grunebaum (Chicago, 1955). Also Nikki R. Keddie, *Religion and Rebellion in Iran: The Tobacco Protest of 1891–1892* (London: Frank Cass & Co. Ltd., 1966).

38 For a complete account of the Constitutional Revolution and the role played by clerics, see the two tomes of Ahmad Kasravi, *Constitutional History of Iran* (Tehran: Amir Kabir Publications House, 1958).

39 Trying to make a distinction between "regime" ("the patterns of allocation, use, and abuse of power in a polity") and "state" in Iran would be a futile effort as there is a fusion between regime and state; see Houchang Chahabi and Juan Linz, eds, *Sultanistic Regimes* (Baltimore: Johns Hopkins University Press, 1998).

40 Weber refers to the Ottoman state as an extreme case of the patrimonial state that makes administrative and military organization the purely

personal instruments of the master's arbitrary power. Sultanism is characterized by complete reliance on military force and arbitrary power, or despotism. The Ottoman sultan embodies both political and spiritual power. Hilal Inalcik, "Comments on 'Sultanism': Max Weber's Typification of the Ottoman Polity." http://www.inalcik.com/images/pdfs/72506692C OMMENTSONSULTANiSM.pdf.

41 Akbar Ganji, "The Latter-Day Sultan Power and Politics in Iran," *Foreign Affairs*, November/December 2008.

42 As an example, if we look at the ideal type of a contemporary sultanistic regime, described by Chahabi and Linz in *Sultanistic Regimes*, "it [the sultanistic regime] is based on personal rulership, but loyalty to the ruler is motivated not by his embodying or articulating an ideology, nor by a unique personal mission, nor by any charismatic qualities, but by a mixture of fear and rewards to his collaborators" (p. 7). This description of a sultanistic regime does not present an accurate image of the absolute Guardianship of Jurisprudence. The ideology of this regime (religion = Shiism) and Khomeini's charisma had been instrumental in rallying different segments of the Iranian population behind the Revolution Guide.

43 Akbar Ganji, "The Latter-Day Sultan: Power and Politics in Iran," *Foreign Affairs* 87.6 (November/December 2008).

44 Ibid.

45 The Bassij (volunteer), a multidimensional, multitask force, was created by Khomeini to protect the new regime and enforce the Islamization of schools, universities, state apparatuses, like the army, police, and society in general. A few years ago, the Bassij was armed and integrated into the IRGC land force. The IRGC and Bassij were instrumental in protecting the Islamic regime against popular protests following the 2009 elections.

46 Different authors have tried to classify the differences among types of authoritarianism. Barbara Geddes recognizes four: military, single-party, personalist, and amalgams of the pure types. See Geddes, "Authoritarian Breakdown: Empirical Test of a Game Theoretic Argument," http:// eppam.weebly.com/uploads/5/5/6/2/5562069/authoritarianbreakdown_ geddes.pdf.

47 "Authoritarianism." http://210.46.97.180/zonghe/book/207- Essentials%20of%20Comparative%20Politics-W.W.Norton%20&%20 Company-PATRICK%20O'NEIL/part05.htm#types_of_authoritarian_rule.

48 Ibid.

49 The terms "Westoxication" and "Weststruckness" are derived from the Persian term "Gharbzadegi" as conceptualized by Jalal Al-e Ahmad, an Iranian author. He "compares ghabzadegi to a disease which kills

wheat from within, to a disease with two faces: the West and the *gharbzadeh* ("Westoxicated" or "Weststruck" native). Brad Hanson, "The 'Westoxication' of Iran: Depictions and Reactions of Behrangi, al-e Ahmad, and Shariati," *International Journal of Middle East Studies* 15.1 (February 1983): 9. http://www.jstor.org/stable/162924. Al-e Ahmad believed the Westoxication process leads to the erosion of all walks of Iranian life including arts, culture, and education in favour of Western culture, goods and services. Jalal Al-I Ahmad, *OCCIDENTOSIS: A Plague from the West*, trans. R. Campbell, annotations and introduction by Hamid Algar (Berkeley, CA: Mizan Press, 1984).

50 Simin Redjali, *A Symphony of Life* (USA: Xlibris LLC, 2013).

51 Hojatoleslam Mohammad Saidi is the city's Friday prayer leader. "Khamenei said 'Ya Ali' at birth," *Al Arabiya News*, 16 April 2001. english.alrabiya.net/articles/2001/04/16/45602.html. See also http://compgovpol.blogspot.ca/2011/04/.

52 On the conservatives' belief that the "leader's legitimacy derives from God," see *BBC News*, 21 November 1997. http://news.bbc.co.uk/2/hi/world/analysis/33397.stm.

53 According to the constitution, the Assembly of Experts must supervise the leader's work and dismiss him if he fails to be just and up to the task of fulfilling his responsibilities. In reality, the only visible act of the assembly, which meets once or twice a year, is its meeting with the leader where the latter gives his opinion on the functioning of the assembly. This is a reverse role. Members of the assembly are all clerics and have only praise for the leader. The meeting is broadcast by state television.

54 For an analysis of electoral authoritarian regimes see Tulia G. Faletti, "Varieties of Authoritarianism: The Organization of the Military State and the Evolution of Federalism in Argentina and Brazil," *Studies in Comparative International Development* 46.2 (2011).

55 Arang Keshavarzian, "How Islamic Was the Revolution?" *Middle East Research and Information Project* (MERIP), 2009, published in MER 250.

56 *Khabaronline*, cited by *Gooya News*, http://news.gooya.com/politics/archives/2014/06/181270.php. Also see Steve Stecklow, Babak Dehghanpisheh, and Yeganeh Torbati, "Khamenei Controls Massive Financial Empire Built on Property Seizures," *Reuters Investigates*, 11 November 2013, http://www.reuters.com/investigates/iran/#article/, part 1; Parvin Alizadeh, Hassan Hakimian, and Massoud Karshenaeds, *The Economy of Iran: The Dilemma of an Islamic State* (London and New York: I.B. Tauris, 2000); Ervand Abrahamian, "Why the Islamic Republic Has Survived," *Middle East Research and Information Project*, 2009, MER 250.

7 Islamism in North Africa: From Cairo to Tunis

JEFFRY R. HALVERSON

In 1928, a school teacher in Ismailia, Egypt, named Hassan al-Banna (d. 1949) established a Sunni Muslim revivalist association known as the Muslim Brotherhood. The Muslim Brothers, or *Ikhwan al-Muslimun*, sought to restore and defend the Arab-Islamic identity of Egypt from Western encroachment, especially its secularism. At the time, Egypt was a colonial holding of the British Empire. The Muslim Brothers advocated Egyptian independence and the implementation of indigenous *shari'a* (Islamic law) in the post-colonial state. Today, the Muslim Brotherhood is recognized as the grandfather of all Islamist movements, even those factions hostile to it (e.g., al-Qaeda). It is the primary architect of the ideology known today as "Islamism." Much has been written about the history of the Muslim Brotherhood and its impact in the Arab East (*Mashreq*).[1] Far less work has explored its westward influence across the *Maghreb* (Arab West/North Africa). This chapter specifically addresses the Muslim Brotherhood's impact on the Maghreb, focusing on Ennahda ("The Renaissance") in Tunisia, once the Arab world's most secular state. Special attention is given to its primary ideologue, Rachid Ghannouchi, and the history of his intellectual development. By examining Ennahda, this analysis sheds light on the diverse forms that Islamism or Muslim "theocratic" systems have taken in the modern Arab Muslim world, including democratic and pluralistic ones that are often overlooked.

The political ideology articulated by the Muslim Brothers in Egypt, known as Islamism, posits that the nation state (a Western import) should be "Islamic." This meant principally that the modern state should implement laws derived from (or aligned with) the Qur'an and *Sunnah* (as derived from the Hadith). Islamism thus differs from classical Islamic systems of governance rooted in the premodern age of empires. And it certainly differs from the tribal city-state of Medina during the last decade of Muhammad's life (622–32 CE) in the seventh century. The Muslim Brothers said nothing of sultans and very little about caliphs. Instead, they spoke of parliaments, elections, centralized state governments with fixed state borders, and the rule of law. In fact, Hassan al-Banna and other members of the Muslim Brotherhood were already running as candidates in parliamentary elections in the 1940s, long before the Arab Spring. The broader imprint of the European colonial experience, despite the animosity it engendered, was clear. However, the Muslim Brothers saw European secularism as absolutely unacceptable and fundamentally foreign to Muslim societies. Perhaps, they argued, it was even a malicious plot by the Western colonial powers to weaken and divide the Muslim world. Thus, the "Islamic state" accorded sovereignty above all to the One God (*Allah*), and rejected the legislative desires and whims of human beings (i.e., republican governance) as a form of *shirk*, or idolatry, if placed on a par with God. Monotheism, or *tawhid*, in their purview, necessarily requires that God alone is sovereign and at the centre of all spheres of life, public and private. Although a fair degree of flexibility is accorded to juristic interpretation, especially as unprecedented matters arise, the core principle remains that the judgments of the created (i.e., humanity) may not abrogate or supersede those of the Creator (at least without making a sound legal case). And furthermore, the Qur'an is the final divine revelation to humanity, and Muhammad is the last prophet ("The Seal of the Prophets"). Therefore, no new revelations are forthcoming to guide modern societies and address their challenges.

This type of political system could be termed a "theocracy," but only with the important qualifier that Sunni Islam has no priesthood. It has no rituals or ceremonies requiring a specialist to act as an intermediary between God and the community of believers. There are credentialed scholars (*ulama*), comparable to rabbis in Judaism, trained in the various religious sciences (e.g., jurisprudence, Arabic grammar), and individuals who possess sufficient knowledge of the Qur'an (in Arabic) to lead congregational prayers (requiring recitation), but these are not priests in any conventional sense of the word. Thus, Sunni Muslims (in contrast to Shia Muslims and Christians) have not faced the same historic struggle with "priestcraft" that Beiner describes in his contribution to this volume. Indeed, the founder of the Muslim Brotherhood, Hassan al-Banna, was not an *alim*, or an official prayer leader (*imam*), but a primary school teacher. The same was true of his successors. The second leader or *Murshid* ("Guide") of the Muslim Brotherhood, Hassan al-Hudaybi (d. 1973), was a judge, and the third leader, Umar al-Tilmisani (d. 1986), was a lawyer. For lack of a better word, one could aptly describe the leaders and ideologues of the Muslim Brotherhood as "laypeople." The same is true of other notable Islamists movements, such as the Jamaat-e Islami in British India (now India and Pakistan).

Following the historic Arab Spring, a Muslim Brotherhood–affiliated movement, Ennahda, rose to power in Tunisia, led by the influential Islamist ideologue Rachid Ghannouchi. A small state of 11 million, Tunisia was the birthplace of the Arab Spring. Its "Jasmine Revolution" began in an impoverished town called Sidi Bouzid, where a young disgruntled merchant named Mohamed Bouazizi committed self-immolation on 17 December 2010. In weeks, massive protests across Tunisia toppled the Constitutional Democratic Rally (French acronym RCD) regime and sent President Zine Al-Abidine Ben Ali into exile. The regime toppled, and political exiles quickly came home, including Ghannouchi. On 30 January 2011, after twenty-two years of exile (mostly in London), Ghannouchi was welcomed at Tunis-Carthage International Airport by thousands of supporters. The re-entry of Islamists into Tunisian politics caused great angst, inside and outside the country. And indeed, Ennahda entered Tunisia's first free democratic elections in October 2011 and won convincingly.

Before the ascent of Ennahda, Tunisia was a secular-nationalist state. But it was a colonial possession of France before that period, and still previously a domain of the Ottoman Empire. Under the Ottoman Turks, imperial territories fell under the aegis of a highly bureaucratic empire in which *shari'a*, as administered by official Ottoman *ulama*, was central.[2] After the conquest of the Mamluk sultanate of Cairo in 1517, the Ottoman sultans, non-Arabs who reigned principally via the military prestige of their dynasty, adopted the mantle of the Caliphate – nominal political successors of the Prophet. The Ottoman conquest of Tunisia followed in 1574 after a brief period under Spanish Catholic rule. Under Turkish rule, Tunisia became a semi-autonomous *beylik* or province under a regional governor or *bey*, acknowledging the suzerainty of the Ottoman caliphs. This era of Islamic governance came to an end with the French conquest in 1881.

The architect of the new "Islamic" Tunisia, Rachid Ghannouchi, was born near the town of Hamma in the coastal governorate of Gabès. His earliest schooling came via his father, a devout Sunni Muslim recognized as the village *imam* (prayer leader), albeit one without formal religious training.[3] Ghannouchi's family also included Nasserists in their ranks, and Gamal Abdel-Nasser's (d. 1970) struggle against the Western imperialist powers reportedly fascinated him.[4]

Led by Nasser, the Egyptian "Free Officers" overthrew the British-backed monarchy in Cairo in 1952 and declared independence. The subsequent authoritarian regime led by Nasser espoused secular Pan-Arab Socialism ("Nasserism"). Charismatic and influential, he militantly condemned Western imperialism, especially Zionism, while courting the support of the Soviet Union. In much of the Arab world, Nasser was a hero and a source of pride until the catastrophe of the 1967 Six-Day War.

Tunisia's own independence (from French colonial rule) came on 20 March 1956. By July of that year, the monarchy was abolished and a republic was established. The leader of Tunisia's independence struggle, Habib Bourguiba (d. 2000), became president of the new republic. However, he quickly assumed the role of a secular autocrat. In his view, progress and development required emulating secular Europe as a model, even in its styles and dress.[5] Like the Republic of Turkey, however, Tunisia was not truly secular. The state and religion were not separate and autonomous. Rather, the state exercised firm control over religion in a complex, but generally antagonistic, relationship. Indeed, as Sherwood discusses in her contribution to this volume: "If secular politics comes into being by being defined against religion, then religion is always hovering in the wings." Pursuing a modernization project, Bourguiba gradually abolished Islamic laws and *shari'a* courts, eliminated religious instruction at the ancient al-Zaytouna seminary in Tunis, nationalized the *awqaf* (religious endowments), and discouraged individual religious practice, such as wearing the *hijab* (headscarf) or fasting during in the Muslim holy month of Ramadan.[6] Bourguiba saw these old traditions as unfit for a modern twentieth-century society. In fact, he reportedly referred to the *hijab* crudely as an "odious rag."[7] In addition, he publicly ridiculed the Qur'an and belief in the afterlife, denied miracles, and even boasted of his extra-marital affairs, clashing with traditional social taboos.[8] But arguably the most notable of Bourguiba's social reforms came in the form of the *Majallat al-Ahwal al-Shakhsiya* (Code of Personal Status), issued by decree in August 1956. The code greatly improved women's rights in virtually every area (the most progressive in the Arab world), abolished polygamy, prohibited forced marriages, legalized adoption, and granted women equal entitlement to divorce, among other reforms.[9] The code would remain a major point of tension in Tunisia's political arena for decades to come.

Despite independence, Ghannouchi's hometown of Gabès retained its colonial French character, and it was rare for young men to pray in the mosques.[10] Even Ghannouchi abandoned prayer (*salat*) and the Qur'an as a young man, preferring to read Western literature and play soccer. Looking back, Ghannouchi later explained that he did not yet understand that Islam is a comprehensive vision of life capable of comprehending and responding to the changing world.[11] Nevertheless, Ghannouchi yielded to his father and studied at al-Zaytouna in Tunis. His time there (1959–62) made him acutely aware of the "identity crisis [that] secularization had created in his country."[12] The traditional Islamic studies of the Maliki *madhhab* (legal school) at al-Zaytouna had no relevance to the rapidly changing modern world around him. Nasserism, by contrast, spoke to those challenges.

By 1964, Ghannouchi was living in Egypt and studying at Cairo University, eager to immerse himself in the Nasserist movement. But what Ghannouchi found in Cairo, Nasser's capital, was not what he had envisioned.[13] Worst of all, Nasser and Bourguiba, who were once bitter foes, secretly arranged to have all Tunisian dissidents sent back home.[14] "Bourguiba practiced repression in the name of national unity," Ghannouchi later wrote, "while Nasser did it in the name of liberating Palestine and uniting the Arabs."[15] Ghannouchi quickly left Nasser's Egypt for Syria in search of his Arabist ideals.

Syria was only years removed from its union with Nasser's Egypt (1958–61) as the "United Arab Republic." It was the birthplace of Baathism – a secular Arabist ideology (similar to Nasserism) that attempted to merge Marxist social theory with revolutionary Pan-Arab nationalism. At the time of Ghannouchi's stay, Syria was home to a range of activist trends. The state had yet to assume the authoritarian anti-Islamist form that characterized the later Assad regime. At Damascus University, where Ghannouchi studied philosophy, he witnessed the struggle between secularists and Islamists on campus.[16] The leaders of the Islamist camp were the Syrian *Ikhwan* or Muslim Brotherhood, an alliance of Islamist groups associated with Hassan al-Banna's better-known Egyptian group. The Syrian *Ikhwan* was established by the anti-colonial activist Mustafa as-Sibai in the 1940s. Now secularist and Islamist students debated subjects such as Palestine, Western science, and the traditional family unit in Arab society. While in Damascus,

Ghannouchi met a Nasserist named Hmida Ennaifer, who later co-founded the Tunisian Islamist movement with him in 1970.[17]

In the summer of 1965, Ghannouchi departed Syria and travelled throughout Europe.[18] Looking back, Ghannouchi claimed his impressions of the West, especially Western youth, matched Islamist portrayals of it.[19] The well-known Egyptian Islamist Sayyid Qutb (executed by Nasser in 1966) had a similar experience in the United States in the early 1950s. Like Qutb, Ghannouchi found the secular-nationalistic West to be a materialistic society driven by hedonism, consumerism, and the acquisition of wealth. The West was largely devoid of anything more than a superficial religiosity. Westerners had little interest in the values enshrined in God's revealed books, whether it was the Bible or the Qur'an. This impression informed Ghannouchi's study of nationalism in the Arab world thereafter. He came to reject the European (e.g., French) roots of the leading Arabist ideologies. Indeed, Syrian Arabist trends, like other ideologies of the Arab *Mashreq* (as distinct from the Maghreb), often opposed Islam, or simply religion in general. Ghannouchi saw this opposition as "another commodity imported from nineteenth-century European thought, impregnated with the problems and customs of foreign societies that underwent their own course of development."[20]

According to Ghannouchi's own account, 15 June 1966 was the night that he embraced Islamism. The Islam of his upbringing was one of custom, ritual, tradition, and certain ethical sensibilities. In his estimation, this was not "true Islam," because Islam was actually a complete way of life that informed an entire approach to the world. "That very night I shed two things off of me: secular nationalism and traditional Islam," he later recalled.[21] In an interview with scholar Azzam Tamimi during his exile, Ghannouchi described his conversion in almost mystical terms. He explained: "On that night I was reborn, my heart was filled with the light of God, and my mind with the determination to review and reflect on all that which I had previously conceived."[22] The experience narrated by Ghannouchi is reminiscent of one described by Umar al-Tilmisani, known as *Imam al-Zahid* ("the ascetic leader") among Egypt's Muslim Brothers, who described his own conversion to Islamism in 1933 (after previously being a nationalist Wafdist) by stating: "The latent religious passion in my heart broke out within me."[23]

The 1967 Six-Day War (known as *al-naksa* or "the setback") was a disaster for the Arab states, particularly Egypt. It delivered a heavy blow to the claims of the Nasserists and other Leftists, including the

Baathists. Indeed, it was a blow to secular nationalism in general. As the Egyptian al-Qaeda ideologue Ayman al-Zawahiri would later relate: "The direct influence of the 1967 defeat was that a large number of people, especially youths, returned to their original identity: that of members of an Islamic civilization."[24] However, Ghannouchi notably claims that he converted to Islamism in 1966, prior to the Six-Day War.

After Damascus, Ghannouchi associated with certain Salafi circles. The Salafi movement – rooted in the reformist teachings of Muhammad Abduh (d. 1905) and Rashid Rida (d. 1935) in the late nineteenth century – calls for a revival of Sunni Islam. This entailed returning to the way of the pious ancestors (al-salaf al-salih), meaning the first generations of Muslims in the seventh century. In the twentieth century, the Salafi movement became increasingly indistinguishable from Wahhabism, the eighteenth-century puritanical sect that now dominates Saudi Arabia. Ghannouchi carried these interests with him to Paris in 1968, where he reconnected with Hmida Enneifer, who was studying at the Sorbonne. In Paris, Ghannouchi's Salafi views left him predisposed to the teachings of a local branch of the Tablighi Jamaat.

The Tabligh is one of the largest Islamic movements in the world. Its annual gathering, the Bishwa Ijtema, in Tongi, Bangladesh, typically attracts some three million people. It was established by the Neo-Sufi Sunni revivalist Muhammad Ilyas in Mewat, British India, in 1926. Since its founding, the Tabligh has stressed personal spiritual outreach, proselytizing to existing Muslim communities and encouraging them to emulate the Prophet Muhammad. Notably, it strongly eschews political activity. The movement is global, but its adherents and missionary units are predominately South Asian. Thus, the Tabligh community in Paris was established in 1968 by Pakistanis who recruited North African laborers.[25] "Living with the Tabligh community," Ghannouchi recalled in 1995, "provided me with immunity and protection from fierce winds and added a new dimension to my molding."[26] Although not an Islamist group, the Tabligh provided Ghannouchi with an environment to observe strict Islamic practice, while other North Africans were immersed in liberal Parisian culture. In fact, his involvement with the Tabligh greatly concerned his family in Tunisia, and his elder brother was sent to retrieve him.

During the return journey, Ghannouchi passed through Algeria. The Muslim Brotherhood had reached Algeria by 1953 and helped rally opposition to French colonial rule, although the Leftist National Liberation Front (French acronym FLN) was dominant. It was preceded by the formation of a Muslim Brotherhood branch in Libya a few years prior, and succeeded by various Moroccan Islamist groups in the 1970s (e.g., *Chabiba al-Islamiyya*) and a Moroccan branch of the Muslim Brotherhood in the 1990s called *al-Islah w'al-Tajdid* (later *al-Tawhid w'al-Islah*). In Algeria, Ghannouchi met Muslim reformist Malik Bennabi (d. 1973), whose writings on the decline of Muslim societies appealed to him. Bennabi introduced Ghannouchi to the belief in the harmony of reason (*'aql*) and revelation (*wahy*), asserting that "neither may exist without the other."[27] This was an important development. Indeed, there is a strong correlation between Islamic rationalism (such as that found in *'ilm al-kalam*, or Sunni theology) and political moderation among certain Islamists like Ghannouchi or al-Tilmisani, in contrast to the textual absolutism (*Athariyya*) of extremists, such as al-Zawahiri.[28] Bennabi was a fierce critic of Sayyid Qutb's militant Islamist ideology, the dominant ideological trend among Islamist extremists today.[29] It was Bennabi's influence that led Ghannouchi to reject Qutb's ideology as a variant of Kharijism – a heretical seventh-century sect that declared Ali (the fourth Rightly-Guided Caliph of Sunni Islam and first Holy Imam of Shia Islam) to be an infidel (*kafir*) for perceived impropriety – and realize the inadequacy of his own earlier Salafi and *Tabligh* orientation for the existing circumstances in Tunisia.[30] The ultimate result was Ghannouchi's pragmatic localized concept of *al-khususiyya al-Tunisiyya*, or "Tunisian specificity" – the idea that Islam is dynamic and adaptive to different societies and cultures, including Tunisia.

In 1969, Ghannouchi met a law student named Abdelfattah Mourou, who was born in Tunis to a merchant family of Andalusian (i.e., Spanish) descent. Morou studied at Sadiki College – a modern bilingual school – and at the University of Tunis, where he trained as a lawyer.[31] Morou was active in Sufism early on, and his mystical approach to Islam influenced Ghannouchi as well. In 1970, Ghannouchi, Ennaifer (recently returned to Tunis), and Mourou established an Islamist organization called the *Jamaat Islamiyya*, or Islamic Group (IG).[32] The IG was initially confrontational with Tunisia's religious establishment (*ulama*) and the irreligious behaviour of the people. They preached wherever they could. They criticized the apathy and deviations of religious leaders from a *Tablighi* or Salafi perspective.[33] Then in 1973 the IG changed course and shifted to the political arena. Ghannouchi, Ennaifer, and Mourou decried the dominance of Leftists in the political opposition and the threat of communism. Aside from its atheism, communism was also a Western ideological import. In this endeavour, Bourguiba's secular regime, like other Arab regimes (e.g., Anwar Sadat's in Egypt), strategically tolerated Islamists for a time, especially on university campuses. "The university became the locomotive of the [Islamist] movement," Enneifer would later recall.[34]

The conflict between Leftists and Islamists in Tunisia soon erupted into violence. Leftist militants armed with weapons attacked Islamist student gatherings in 1977 and again repeatedly thereafter.[35] However, a Tunisian labour uprising led by the Tunisian General Labour Union (French acronym UGTT) in January of 1978 altered Ghannouchi's relationship with the Left. The Islamists now assumed a collision course with Bourguiba's secular authoritarian state.

During Bourguiba's reign, the Neo-Destour party consolidated power over the republic into a de facto single-party system. The state assumed authoritarian form as early as 1959 and extraordinary power was accorded to the presidency. Policy debate was a private matter among Neo-Destour cadres, and Bouguiba's decisions were absolute.[36] The regime also cultivated a personality cult around Bourguiba, who assumed a flamboyant lifestyle, living in palaces, accompanied by martial bands and salutes.[37] Bourguiba took the title *al-Mujahid al-Akbar* ("Supreme Combatant") and his birthday became a holiday, streets were named for him, statues built, and a grand golden-domed mausoleum for him was erected with the words "liberator of women, builder of modern Tunisia" above the door.[38] The strength of Bourguiba's autocratic powers and the ubiquity of Neo-Destour loyalists throughout the state deprived Tunisia of any significant opposition, a vacuum the Islamists later entered as the leading force.

For Tunisia's Islamists, the secular pro-Western Neo-Destour succeeded in ending the physical occupation of Tunisia, but the equally disturbing cultural and intellectual occupation continued unabated. Foreign customs, behaviour, language, even aesthetics, were imposed on Tunisia by Bourguiba and his political elites. As Ghannouchi would later write: "The independence achieved from the French in 1956 was not a real victory ... It turned out to be a continuation of the process of destruction in the form of an intensive campaign to culturally annex Tunisia to France as fast as possible."[39] Ghannouchi believed Bourguiba was "overwhelmed by French culture."[40] And, as Ennaifer would later note: "Those who joined the Islamists' ranks were those who found nothing to be attached to, Right or Left; they were uprooted."[41]

Socio-economic unrest was widespread in Tunisia throughout the 1970s. It began with university students and factory workers, but soon escalated into general uprisings in the cities. In October 1977, a workers' strike at a state-owned textile plant in Ksar Hellal – the birthplace of Bourguiba's Neo-Destour party – grew into a three-day uprising.[42] Three months later the first general strike since Tunisia's independence from France occurred. Thousands of workers took to the streets and attacked government institutions, until state security forces opened fire.[43] According to the regime, fifty-one protestors were killed and four hundred were injured, but a 1989 study of the incident claimed approximately two hundred were killed and at least one thousand were injured.[44]

The 1978 UGTT uprising shocked the Islamists and changed their relationship with the Left. As Ghannouchi later stated: "It was thanks to the Left that we realized that the socioeconomic conflict was no less important than the ideological conflict ... [The Left] opened our eyes to the conflict between the exploited, destitute, and impoverished majority and a small minority that in collaboration with the state exploited the entire population."[45] Turning to socio-economic conflict, Ghannouchi cited the Qur'an to explain how Islam supported the oppressed, exploited, and economically destitute.[46] As an Islamist, Ghannouchi saw the Qur'an as something that addressed every aspect of life. Thereafter, IG members were urged to join labour unions and mosques became centres for socio-economic activism. As Ghannouchi later recalled: "[We] supported and joined the workers and students and sought to restore the role of the mosque as a center of cultural and educational activities."[47]

In August 1979 the IG convened a major conference. Ghannouchi and his colleagues agreed on an Islamist platform to compete with the Leftists and established an organizational structure. During this "founding conference" the IG adopted the platform of Egypt's Muslim Brotherhood – led at the time by Umar al-Tilmisani – and agreed on an administrative structure, selecting Ghannouchi as the group's leader and Mourou as a member of the legislative council.[48] These decisions were not unanimously approved, though. Hmida Enneifer was critical of the Muslim Brotherhood and the direction Ghannouchi was taking. As a result, Enneifer was not selected for any leadership posts and resigned. He later formed an Islamist organization called al-Islamiyyun al-Taqadumiyyun ("The Progressive Islamists"), which Ghannouchi has described as "the rationalist trend."[49]

On 1 May 1980, International Workers' Day, Ghannouchi addressed a crowd outside a mosque using Leftist language that Islamists in Tunisia had not used before.[50] The speech was part of an effort to compete with the Leftists for control of the opposition. He stressed worker rights based on Islamic principles.[51] He also emphasized that the Islamic practice of *zakat* (alms) was designed to create greater economic balance in society and could be distributed by individuals, the community, or through state welfare programs.[52] None of these views were entirely surprising or unique, since the Islamic Left (*al-Yasar al-Islami*), or "Islamic socialism," was already an ideological trend in Egypt and elsewhere.[53]

Another notable shift occurred in 1979, when Ghannouchi travelled to the Sudan. Among Islamist figures such as the controversial and eccentric Muslim Brotherhood–affiliated ideologue Hassan al-Turabi, Ghannouchi reportedly observed that Sudanese women fully participated in the political and social programs of the group, interacted with male members, voiced their opinions, and had equal rights and responsibilities.[54] When he returned to Tunisia, Ghannouchi declared that his prior restrictive views on women were erroneous, and he called for equality between the sexes, the highest levels of education for women, and the training of female Islamic leaders for the Islamist movement.[55] Before this shift, Ghannouchi had opposed Tunisia's Code of Personal Status and its abolition of polygamy.[56] Now he accepted a radically different role for Tunisian women in society. Following this shift, the number of women in the Islamist association reportedly doubled within one year.[57]

In December 1980, the Bourguiba regime uncovered the existence of the newly organized IG. The state arrested and tortured two members of the executive bureau and managed to extract a great deal of information.[58] Thereafter, Ghannouchi decided to go public with the movement. In April 1981 a news conference was organized at Sousse, where they reorganized the administrative structure and chose to apply for legal registration as a political party.[59] Thereafter, they would be known as the *Harakat al-Ittijah al-Islami*, or the Islamic Tendency Movement (French acronym MTI).

By 1987, the health of the aging Bourguiba had waned, especially his mental stability. Bourguiba perceived enemies everywhere. Fears of Iranian-backed plots, in particular, grew (whether real or imagined). The Iranian embassy in Tunis was forcefully closed and the United States was assured that Tunisia would protect its secular "national achievements."[60] Ghannouchi, a key target of the crackdown (despite his having no ties to Shi'ite Iran), was arrested, tried in a "security court," and sentenced to life imprisonment for allegedly plotting against the state.[61]

Bourguiba was displeased by the sentence and sought a new trial to seek the death penalty. He would not get the chance.

In November, Bourguiba was removed from office for medical incompetence under article 57 of the Tunisian constitution. He was replaced by Prime Minister Zine El Abidine Ben Ali. Born in 1936, Ben Ali was a graduate of the French military academy in Saint-Cyr, and later studied at the French artillery school at Chalons, the US Army's artillery schools in Fort Bliss (TX) and Fort Holabird (MD).[62] When Ben Ali returned in 1958, he served as director of military security and later as head of national security. It was not until the 1980s that Ben Ali rose through the ranks of political power, ultimately becoming Bourguiba's autocratic successor.

The Ben Ali regime retained the secular single-party system, controlled by the Constitutional Democratic Rally or RCD (formerly the Neo-Destour). But there were shifts reminiscent of Sadat's reign after succeeding Nasser in Egypt. Liberalizing economic policies began in Tunisia, and Ben Ali's regime talked of "national reconciliation," making many optimistic about Tunisia's future as a multi-party, democratic republic.[63] Ben Ali issued concessions, including an *Eid al-Fitr* pardon for Ghannouchi and hundreds of other Islamists in May 1988, and even allowed Amnesty International to establish an office in Tunis.[64] Ben Ali's "National Pact," as it is known, was announced on the first anniversary of his ascent to the presidency. It acknowledged Tunisia's Arab and Islamic heritage and called for closer ties to the Arab world, especially the Maghreb states.[65] The cult of Habib Bourguiba was definitively ended, and Islamic symbols and language returned to the public sphere.[66] Ben Ali also performed *umra* (the lesser pilgrimage to Mecca), modernized al-Zaytouna on the model of al-Azhar in Cairo, and declared publicly at an RCD meeting: "It is incumbent for the state, and it alone, to ensure the vitality and influence of Islam."[67] It seemed that the secular state of the Arab Atatürk (i.e., Bourguiba) was over.

Eager to capitalize on the nominal spirit of reform, the MTI mobilized for a new era. However, two articles in the constitution, namely articles 2 and 3, prevented its participation. Ghannouchi and Mourou tried to overcome the barriers by re-emerging as *Harakat al-Nahda*, or Ennahda ("The Renaissance"). The constitution prohibited political parties from referencing religion in their names. Thus, the "Islamic Tendency Movement" would no longer work. Nor would any name with an explicit reference to Islam. Like Tilmisani's Muslim Brotherhood in Egypt, Ghannouchi's Ennahda would field candidates as "independents" for the time being. Political parties were required to have the formal approval of the regime. Ennahda had no such recognition due to dubious legal technicalities.[68] But soon the reality of Ben Ali's odes to political pluralism began to show. The facade fell at the polls in April 1989, when the outcome was rigged in favour of the RCD. Ben Ali's party won 80 per cent of the vote, including every seat in parliament, while Ennahda's candidates took 14.6 per cent overall (but no seats).[69] Despite the defeat, Ennahda nevertheless proved it was a legitimate challenger.[70]

The 1989 election outcome concerned the regime. It therefore rejected Ennahda's efforts to pursue legal democratic channels. The brief period of reconciliation was over. Ghannouchi fled into exile, first to Algeria and then London, where he remained for decades. Government crackdowns ensued and violence erupted. The most infamous incident was on 8 February 1991, when student protests escalated into an attack on an RCD office in Bab Souika. Protestors doused the office and two security guards with gasoline and set it ablaze. One guard died and the other was hospitalized. Meanwhile, the regime accused Ennahda of plotting a violent coup by infiltrating the military to create an "Islamic state." By June, several hundred Ennahda members were arrested and tortured. The RCD's war on Tunisia's Islamists now peaked, supported by neighbouring Algeria's own violent war against Islamists.

As a result of the Algerian military's cancellation of the 1991 elections, which an Islamist party – the Islamic Salvation Front (French acronym FIS) – was winning, civil war broke out. Extremist factions among the Islamists – once nominally restrained by the success of the FIS – and the state security forces set out to purge one another with violence. In 1994, groups of pro-FIS guerrillas united as the Islamic Salvation Army (French acronym AIS) to fight the state military. The strength of the AIS was concentrated in the borderlands of Algeria, away from the capital. But the region around Algiers was the home of a far more extreme Islamist faction. This group opposed the secular state regime *and* the FIS/AIS. They were known as the Armed Islamic Group (French acronym GIA).

In 1994 the GIA attacked and killed 140 pro-FIS Islamists, including important FIS leaders.[71] A year later, the GIA sent fighters into Tunisia and killed seven police officers. The GIA also launched attacks at France, including several bombings in Paris in 1995. But when Antar Zoubari (a.k.a. "Abou Talha") became leader (emir) of the GIA in 1996, a veritable epidemic of civilian massacres ensued, often carried out with machetes, swords, and knives. Some victims were even burned alive.[72] The GIA guerrillas, proponents of the Kharijite heresy of *takfir* (excommunication of other Muslims), quickly grew infamous for their sweeping indiscriminant violence, including beheadings. Algerian journalists who wrote in French and foreign nationals (e.g., French Trappist monks in Algeria) were among their targets. Zouabri explained: "In our war, there is no neutrality, except for those who are with us, all others are renegades."[73] The violence committed by the GIA horrified Algerians and the international community. Schoolgirls were killed simply for not covering their hair.[74] Popular Berber singers from the Kabylia region of Algeria, such as Cheb Hasni, were kidnapped and killed for being "enemies of God" and "symbols of deprivation and debauchery in the Kabylia region."[75] Seldom has there been anything akin to the GIA in all of Islamic history, save perhaps the "Islamic State" or IS movement in contemporary Iraq and Syria.

Meanwhile, speaking in October 1994, the military head of Algeria's High State Council declared that the government would achieve "total eradication" of the Islamist guerrillas.[76] The GIA was condemned by rival pro-FIS fighters too. As proponents of the most extreme form of Islamism – rooted in the writings of the fourteenth-century Hanbali scholar Ahmed ibn Taymiyyah (d. 1328) and Egypt's twentieth-century Islamist dissident Sayyid Qutb (e.g., his book *Milestones*) – the GIA considered democracy antithetical to Islam. Sovereignty (*al-hakimiyyah*), Qutb had argued, belonged to God *alone*, and a world that did not recognize that fact had relapsed into *jahiliyyah* – barbaric ignorance of God – and must be defeated, even if it claims to be Muslim. Therefore, anyone who supported or participated in democratic elections (e.g., the Islamist FIS) was declared a treasonous apostate or infidel of the worst kind ("hypocrites"), and an enemy in the struggle (*jihad*) against the godless forces of *jahiliyyah*. This reflects the heretical doctrine of *takfir* – the view that one Muslim can declare another Muslim an infidel (*kafir*) or renegade (*murtad*) based on perceived improprieties (i.e., doing something deemed "sinful," in this case voting in an election). This doctrine runs contrary to the teachings of both Sunni and Shia Islam, which have traditionally accepted that professing Islam is sufficient and judgment is left to God. Departing from this traditional view of belief (*iman*) and emboldened by militant revolutionary fervour engaged in statecraft, the GIA sought to destroy anyone tied to the secular regime (however tangentially) and the Islamist FIS and AIS too.[77] As a result, Algeria was torn apart in all directions by war. And amidst the violence, some exploited the conflict for economic gain, indulging in piracy and looting. Historian Luis Martinez has described the GIA's "*jihad*" in Algeria as a "lucrative business" willing to accept dubious fighters rejected elsewhere.[78] Indeed, the doctrine of *takfir* can serve as a licence for people to declare the property and wealth of other Muslims (now declared "infidels") permissible for plunder, conferring religious legitimacy (legality) on theft and banditry.

Away in London, Tunisia's Ghannouchi adapted to a quiet life as an ideologue in exile, denouncing Ben Ali and the RCD from abroad. Mourou, meanwhile, remained in Tunisia and distanced himself from politics and the violence. His break with Ennahda, however, was largely attributed to state pressure. Mourou was reportedly subjected to disturbing interrogations wherein state police threatened to rape his wife.[79] Subsequently, Mourou publicly broke with Ennahda and declared his intent to create his own party. Only months later, the regime accused Mourou of sexual indiscretions in his law office, and claimed to have them on video.[80] Thereafter, Mourou quietly lived out his years under Ben Ali as a private lawyer, until the Arab Spring.

Ghannouchi's role as an Islamist ideologue and political philosopher became more pronounced abroad. His Islamist vision for Tunisia was more of an intellectual enterprise than ever before. Ghannouchi now grappled on a deeper level with questions about the role of women in an "Islamic state," or the status of non-Muslims. These were no small matters. Rather, they are among the most contentious in Islamist thought, especially for outside observers. In Tunisia, where women have advanced farther than any other Arab state, the subject of women's rights is a pivotal benchmark for any viable political platform.

The role of women is arguably the most visible and embattled component of Islamist ideologies. As Nikki Keddie has noted, Islamists "see Western practices toward and views on women as part of a Western Christian and Jewish cultural offensive, accompanying political and economic offensives, and turn to their own traditions as a cultural alternative."[81] Women thus become a front or battleground for Islamists, because they are treated as referents for the society as a whole. Women become the symbol of the society's character or virtues, especially as they communicate a message to the West: *We are what you are not*. This was evident in the Iranian revolution, where Shia Muslim women donned black *hijabs*, *abayas*, or *chadors* in public, in defiance of the pro-Western Shah's secular laws against it, as an affirmation of a non-Western (or anti-Western) identity.

Tunisia is a Sunni Muslim country, but the preservation of the secular state has also served as a benchmark for political viability, similarly to the situation in Turkey. In this respect, Ghannouchi's thought followed the model set forth by the Turkish Justice and Development Party (AKP), which achieved success as a moderate pluralist Islamist party in the secular Kemalist state. Ghannouchi, referring to "Tunisian specificity," emphasizes that Islamism must adapt in each context. Indeed, the Tunisian populace, long living under a secular system, has little interest in new restrictions on society. The "Jasmine Revolution" and its martyrs had called for *more* freedoms and opportunities.

In a treatise written in the early 1990s, Ghannouchi related that "realism and flexibility are among the most important features of Islamic methodology," because Islam is "an eternal way of life suitable for all times and all places," and Muslims must do only what they can under the circumstances they face (e.g., in Tunisia) and can therefore fully participate in a secular democratic system.[82] To support his argument, Ghannouchi recalled several Islamic narratives, including the Prophet Yusuf's service to the infidel ruler of Egypt, the early Muslim migration to the Christian kingdom of Abyssinia, and the reign of the pious Caliph Umar ibn Abdul-Aziz within a corrupted Umayyad system. Even if a government is not based on *shari'a*, a system based on *shura* (community consultation) or the authority of the community (*ummah*) is sufficient in Ghannouchi's view, especially if it prevents "the evils of dictatorship, foreign domination, or local anarchy."[83] In another treatise published in 2000, Ghannouchi wrote that Ennahda accepts that "the popular will is the source of political legitimacy and believe[s] in pluralism and in the alternation of power through free elections."[84] But true to his Islamist views, he also noted that "a conflict between Islamic culture and aspects of the incoming Western culture does exist, whether in Tunisia or in other parts of the Arab and Muslim world."[85]

Tensions between the Western-oriented state and the Muslim populace of Tunisia, especially beyond the capital, remained readily apparent under Ben Ali. Beyond the regime-approved Islam with its state-appointed preachers and Friday sermons in official mosques, the private observance of Islam, study of the Qur'an and other Islamic literature, continued in homes and quiet meetings. Furthermore, Ben Ali's economic liberalization had fostered a materialistic consumer culture that pulled many back to religion, albeit outside of official regime-controlled settings. In one example, in 2007 six young men, in a suburb of Tunis, founded the Riadh Ennasr Qur'an Association, which had 1800 participants by 2010 (most of them women).[86] Thus, the sudden groundswell of support for Ennahda's platform after the revolution was not limited simply to Ennahda members or close sympathizers, but rather a broader spectrum of the population that identified with Ghannouchi's values and Islamic conception of Tunisian identity.

In the ensuing days after Mohamed Bouazizi's death, protests grew nationwide. Soon more national martyrs emerged. For example, twenty-two-year-old Houcine Falhi committed suicide by electrocuting himself after crying out "No to misery! No to employment!" and at least two protestors were killed by state security two days later.[87] Video clips of the protests, recorded on cellphones and posted online, spread across the region. They were shared via social media sites (e.g., YouTube, Facebook, Twitter) and broadcast by satellite news channels like *al-Jazeera*.[88] Meanwhile, the labour unions joined the uprising too, adding to the momentum. Hundreds of union members protested in Tunis, decrying widespread unemployment and economic injustices, especially the cronyism of the Ben Ali regime. Then the lawyers joined, condemning the brutality committed by security forces cracking down on the protests.

Seeking to intensify the crackdown, Ben Ali initiated fierce sweeps arresting bloggers, activists, and even artists. With countless arrests, dozens killed and protests still growing, the regime finally conceded that the crackdowns were unsuccessful. Ben Ali announced major concessions on 13 January. The following day, he and his wife fled the country for Saudi Arabia, which granted them political asylum.

In the absence of Ben Ali, the Tunisian military struggled to assert control. An interim unity government was established consisting of several Ben Ali loyalists. But this provoked further protests and clashes. There was no significant organized opposition under Ben Ali, and thus a void existed. Gradually, changes in the interim government met popular demands and won the support of the unions and other opposition groups. The interim government then recognized all banned political parties and granted amnesty for all exiles and political prisoners.[89] This amnesty law opened the door for Rachid Ghannouchi to return home and the public re-emergence of Ennahda.

On 30 January Ghannouchi left London and returned to Tunisia after more than two decades in exile. "When I return home today, I am returning to the Arab world as a whole," he said.[90] When Ghannouchi arrived in Tunis, a crowd of supporters awaited him, reportedly as many as five or six thousand people, and cheered in celebration.[91] Critics, warning of the "Islamist threat," immediately drew comparisons to Ayatollah Khomeini's return to Iran via plane from exile in Paris in 1979. Shortly after Ghannoushi's return, he responded directly to those comparisons by stating: "Some Western media portray me like [Ayatollah Ruhollah] Khomeini, but that is not me."[92]

When Tunisia's first free elections were held on 23 October 2011 to select the 217 members of the constituent assembly to draft a new constitution, Ennahda came in first with 40 per cent of seats. When the results were announced, a young female Ennahda supporter, Zeinab Omri, told *Reuters*: "This result shows very clearly that the Tunisian people is a people attached to its Islamic identity."[93] Nevertheless, eager to prove their support for democratic pluralism, Ennahda joined a ruling coalition with two secular parties, the Congress for the Republic (or Al-Mottamar) and Ettakatol. Together, the coalition was known as the "Troika." The secretary general of Ennahda, Hamadi Jebali, was subsequently appointed prime minister in December 2011. A former political prisoner under Ben Ali, Jebali was an engineer (another "layman") from Sousse.

The subsequent debate in Tunisia over the articles in the draft constitution revealed ongoing fault lines between the country's competing factions – secularists, Leftists, and Islamists. Opposition to Ennahda appeared on all sides, including hardline Salafis. These hardliners opposed democracy (i.e., will of the people) as an infidel Western concept that violates strict monotheism (*tawhid*) and divine sovereignty (*hakimiyyah*). Liberal secularists, by contrast, treated Ennahda with the utmost suspicion, suspecting them of stealthily moving to eliminate individual rights, especially those of women. Secularists feared Ennahda would implement strict *shari'a* laws criminalizing alcohol, immodest dress, free artistic expression, and other activities. However, the draft constitution – made public by the Arabic Tunisian daily *Alchourouk* in August of 2012 – contained no reference to *shari'a*. The document was markedly secular compared to the Islamist constitutions drafted elsewhere, such as the (now overturned) Muslim Brotherhood–backed constitution in Egypt. The prologue of the draft constitution made only references to the "values of the Arab-Islamic identity" and the "strengthening of our [Tunisia's] cultural and civilizational bonds to the worldwide Muslim community."[94]

Tunisia (loosely defined) was part of numerous Muslim empires from the seventh century to the nineteenth century, including the Umayyads, Abbasids, Fatimids, and Ottomans. Secularism was not part of this historical experience until the twentieth century. Governance and law were rooted in Islam. The advent of the modern era and the rise of Europe and America ("the West") led to a radical break with the past under Bourguiba. Tunisia's "theocratic" past was treated as a source of ignorance, backwardness, and weakness. But the state project to reshape Tunisia along a Western model failed to separate the majority of Tunisians from their cultural identity as Muslims. Rather, Islam has remained an essential part of how many Tunisians understood themselves and their society. Thus, sociologically, the step towards an "Islamic" system of governance by Ennahda after the historic Arab Spring demonstrates that notions of "theocracy" often have as much to do with matters of pre-nationalist cultural identities in the Muslim world as they do with any doctrine of Islam. Thus, Islamism is far more adaptive, dynamic, and contextually rooted than is often imagined. The rise of Ennahda in Tunisia illustrates well the wide spectrum of Islamists in the twenty-first century – a spectrum that will likely continue to expand rather than retract. And bearing this in mind, the participation of Islamist parties in North African politics, such as those affiliated with the Muslim Brotherhood, need not lead observers to the worst sort of prognostications, such as the horrific violence of the Algerian civil war.

NOTES

1 See, e.g., Hesham 'Awadi, *In Pursuit of Legitimacy: The Muslim Brothers and Mubarak, 1982–2000* (New York: Tauris Academic Studies, 2004); Christina Phelps Harris, *Nationalism and Revolution in Egypt* (The Hague: Mouton, 1964); Gilles Kepel, *The Prophet and Pharaoh*, trans. John Rothschild (London: Al-Saqi Books, 1985); Brynjar Lia, *The Society of the Muslim Brothers in Egypt: The Rise of an Islamic Mass Movement 1928–1942* (Reading, UK: Ithaca Press, 1998); Richard Mitchell, *The Society of the Muslim Brothers* (London: Oxford University Press, 1969).

2 Marshall G.S. Hodgson, *The Venture of Islam: Conscience and History in a World Civilization*, vol. 3 (Chicago: University of Chicago Press, 1974), 107.

3 Azzam Tamimi, *Rachid Ghannouchi: A Democrat within Islamism* (New York: Oxford University Press, 2001), 4.

4 Ibid., 6.

5 Ibid., 10.

6 Ibid.

7 Tarek Amara and Andrew Hammond, "Islamists Claim Win in Tunisia's Arab Spring Vote," http://www.reuters.com/article/2011/10/24/us-tunisia-election-idUSTRE79L28820111024.

8 Rachid Ghannouchi, "Secularism in the Arab Maghreb," in *Islam and Secularism in the Middle East*, ed. Azzam Tamimi and John L. Esposito (London: Hurst & Company, 2000), 98.

 9 Richard H. Curtiss, "Women's Rights: An Affair of State for Tunisia,"
    in *Arab Women: Between Defiance and Restraint*, ed. Suha Sabbagh
    (Northampton, MA: Olive Branch Press, 1998), 34–6.
10 Tamimi, *Rachid Ghannouchi*, 7.
11 Ibid., 8.
12 Ibid., 10.
13 Ibid., 15.
14 Ibid.
15 Ghannouchi, "Secularism in the Arab Maghreb," 101.
16 Tamimi, *Rachid Ghannouchi*, 17.
17 Mohammed Elihachmi Hamdi, *The Politicisation of Islam: A Case Study of
    Tunisia* (Boulder, CO: Westview Press, 1998), 18.
18 Tamimi, *Rachid Ghannouchi: A Democrat within Islamism*, 19.
19 Ibid.
20 Ibid., 21.
21 Qtd. ibid., 22.
22 Ibid., 22.
23 Qtd. in Jeffry R. Halverson, *Theology and Creed in Sunni Islam: The
    Muslim Brotherhood, Ash'arism, and Political Sunnism* (New York: Palgrave
    Macmillan, 2010), 98.
24 Qtd. in Montasser al-Zayyat, *The Road to al-Qaeda* (New York: Pluto Press,
    2004), 23.
25 Tamimi, *Rachid Ghannouchi*, 24.
26 Qtd. ibid., 25.
27 Ibid., 31.
28 See Halverson, *Theology and Creed in Sunni Islam*.
29 Tamimi, *Rachid Ghannouchi*, 31–2.
30 Ibid., 32–3.
31 Emad Eldin Shahin, *Political Ascent: Contemporary Islamic Movements in
    North Africa* (Boulder, CO: Westview Press, 1998), 68.
32 Hamdi, *The Politicisation of Islam*, 18.
33 Tamimi, *Rachid Ghannouchi*, 40–1.
34 Qtd. in Hamdi, *The Politicisation of Islam*, 27.
35 Ibid., 26.
36 Clement H. Moore, *Tunisia since Independence: The Dynamics of One-Party
    Government* (Berkeley: University of California Press, 1965), 81.
37 Ibid., 81.
38 Anonymous, "Habib Bourguiba," *The Economist* 355, no. 8166 (2000): 94.
39 Ghannouchi. "Secularism in the Arab Maghreb," 108.
40 Qtd. in Ayman Zammali, "Era of Exclusion Is Over," http://www.majalla
    .com/eng/2011/04/article1250 (2012).

146   Jeffry R. Halverson

41 Qtd. in Hamdi, *The Politicisation of Islam*, 10.
42 Christopher Alexander, *Tunisia: Stability and Reform in the Modern Maghreb* (New York: Routledge, 2010), 47.
43 Ibid., 47; Tamimi, *Rachid Ghannouchi*, 50.
44 Hamdi, *The Politicisation of Islam*, 31.
45 Qtd. in Tamimi, *Rachid Ghannouchi*, 51.
46 Ibid.
47 Ghannouchi, "Secularism in the Arab Maghreb," 109.
48 Hamdi, *The Politicisation of Islam*, 34–5.
49 Ibid., 36.
50 Tamimi, *Rachid Ghannouchi*, 52.
51 Ibid., 52–3.
52 Ibid., 53.
53 See, for example, the writings of Hasan al-Hanafi.
54 Tamimi, *Rachid Ghannouchi*, 57.
55 Ibid., 57.
56 Ibid., 58.
57 Ibid., 58.
58 Hamdi, *The Politicisation of Islam*, 36–7.
59 Ibid., 38–9.
60 Andrew Boroweic, *Modern Tunisia: A Democratic Apprenticeship* (Santa Barbara, CA: Praeger, 1998), 43.
61 Ibid., 43–4.
62 William Mark Habeeb, "Zine El Abidine Ben Ali," in *Political Leaders of the Contemporary Middle East and North Africa: A Biographical Dictionary*, ed. Bernard Reich (Westport, CT: Greenwood Press, 1990,) 79.
63 Borowiec, *Modern Tunisia*, 62.
64 Ibid., 64.
65 Kenneth Perkins, *A History of Modern Tunisia* (Cambridge: Cambridge University Press, 2004), 187.
66 François Burgat and William Dowell, *The Islamic Movement in North Africa* (Austin: University of Texas Press, 1993), 230.
67 Rémy Leveau, *Le sabre et le turban: L'avenir du Maghreb* (Paris: François Bourrin, 1993), 107.
68 Burgat and Dowell, *The Islamic Movement in North Africa*, 237.
69 Borowiec, *Modern Tunisia*, 45.
70 Tamimi, *Rachid Ghannouchi*, 70.
71 Quintan Wiktorowicz, "Centrifugal Tendencies in the Algerian Civil War," *Arab Studies Quarterly* 23.3 (Summer 2001): 68.
72 Ibid., 69.

73 Quoted in Lauren Vriens, "Armed Islamic Group (Algeria, Islamists)," *Council on Foreign Relations*, 27 May 2009; available at https://www.cfr.org/backgrounder/armed-islamic-group-ageria-islamists.

74 Wiktorowicz, "Centrifugal Tendencies in the Algerian Civil War," 70.

75 Ibid.

76 Luis Martinez, *The Algerian Civil War: 1990–1998*, trans. Jonathan Derrick (New York: Columbia University Press, 2000), 116.

77 Ibid., 116.

78 Ibid., 138.

79 Burgat and Dowell, *The Islamic Movement in North Africa*, 244.

80 Ibid.

81 Nikki R. Keddie and Beth Baron, *Women in Middle Eastern History: Shifting Boundaries in Sex and Gender* (Hartford, CT: Yale University Press, 1991), 2.

82 Rachid Ghannouchi, "The Participation of Islamists in a Non-Islamic Government," in *Islam in Transition, Muslim Perspectives*, 2nd edition, ed. J.J. Donohue and John L. Esposito (New York: Oxford University Press, 2007), 272.

83 Ibid., 273.

84 Ghannouchi, "Secularism in the Arab Maghreb," 101.

85 Ibid.

86 Franceso Cavatorta and Rikke Hostrup Haugbolle, "Beyond Ghannouchi: Islamism and Social Change in Tunisia," in *The Arab Revolts: Dispatches on Militant Democracy in the Middle East*, ed. David McMurray and Amanda Ufheil-Somers (Bloomington: Indiana University Press, 2013), 53.

87 Ryan Rifai, "Timeline: Tunisia's Uprising," 2011. http://www.aljazeera.com/indepth/spotlight/tunisia/2011/01/201114142223827361.html.

88 Robert Mackey, "Video That Set Off Tunisia's Uprising," 2011. http://thelede.blogs.nytimes.com/2011/01/22/video-that-triggered-tunisias-uprising/.

89 David D. Kirkpatrick, "Tunisia Takes Step toward Allowing Exiles to Return," 2011. http://www.nytimes.com/2011/01/21/world/africa/21tunis.html?pagewanted=all&m.

90 Qtd. in Anonymous, "Tunisia's Exiled Leader Returns to Rapturous Welcome," 2011. https://www.dawn.com/news/602760.

91 Cecily Hilleary, "Return of Islamic Leader Worries Some Tunisian Women," 2011. https://www.voanews.com/a/134523.html.

92 Qtd. in Molly Hennessy-Fiske, "Tunisia: Returned Exile Insists 'I'm No Khomeini,'" 2011. http://latimesblogs.latimes.com/babylonbeyond/2011/01/tunisia-returned-exile-insists-im-no-khomeini.html.

93 Amara and Hammond, "Islamists Claim Win in Tunisia's Arab Spring Vote."

94 Translation from the Arabic by Jeffry R. Halverson.

8 Theocratic Arguments in Judaism

ALAN MITTLEMAN

"If you say, I will set a king over me" (Deut. 17:14). As Scripture says, *"Put not your trust in the great ..."* (Psalms 146:3). Whenever one relies on flesh and blood, as he fails so does his word fail, as it is written: *"... in mortal man who cannot save"* (Psalm 146:3). What is written next? *"His breath departs; he returns to the dust; on that day his plans come to nothing"* (Psalm 146:4). The Holy One said: Though they know that flesh and blood is nothing, they abandon My glory and say "Set a king over us." Why do you seek a king? By your life, in the end you will experience what befalls you under your kings, as it is written, "all their kings have fallen – none of them calls to me" (Hosea 7:7).[1]

The citation above, an ancient rabbinic gloss on Deuteronomy's reference to the appointment of a king, calls attention to how contentious kingship was, both in ancient Israel and in rabbinic Judaism. In this chapter, I shall argue that the concept of theocracy, alluded to *avant la lettre* in the citation, represents a normative alternative to monarchy. Theocrats, in Judaism, intend to challenge the standard view that stable political rule requires strong governmental authority. They advocate a weak politics of direct divine governance, effectively relativizing the authority of any human political institution. That is, in the Jewish context, theocracy has often functioned as a critique of government, of politics as a whole, rather than as the program of a group (say, the rabbinic elite) to dominate politics. *Jewish theocracy is less a vision for the domination of Jewish society by Jewish law (halakha) and its rabbinic interpreters than it is an abiding counter-argument to political normality, whatever that might mean under the conditions of exile and loss of sovereignty that have characterized most of Jewish political history.*[2]

The Torah and subsequent rabbinic literature preserve conflicting assessments of human kingship. On the one hand, there is a clear royalist tradition in the Bible. After a shaky start with Saul, God (and the people) choose David, with whom God enters into an eternal covenant (2 Samuel 7:11–13). The geographic and conceptual focus of biblical religion, the Temple in Jerusalem, is intimately tied to the royalist project. Royal Psalms, such as Ps 2 and Ps 89, elevate the monarch to the status of God's son, a motif that is later taken with some literalness in Christianity. The Mishnah and Talmud accept monarchy and work to define the status of the king vis-à-vis other institutions of Jewish governance, such as the High Court or Sanhedrin. For some rabbinic thinkers, preeminently Maimonides, kingship is crucial to the functioning of Jewish society, in this case to the future, restored Jewish polity of messianic times. Indeed, the Messiah (*mashiaḥ*; Hebrew for "anointed") is a future Davidic king of Israel.

On the other hand, the arrival of kingship in Israel was clearly a contentious affair. When the elders came to Samuel to ask for a king, God told Samuel that it was not him, but God whom they were rejecting ("Heed the demand of the people in everything that they say to you. For it is not you that they have rejected; it is Me they have rejected as their king," 1 Samuel 8:7). Earlier figures, such as the warrior Gideon, when offered dynastic kingship by the grateful people, firmly spurned the offer: "I will not rule over you myself, nor shall my son rule over you; the LORD alone shall rule over you" (Judges 8:23). Even the verse in the Torah which (minimally) licenses or (maximally) requires a king, is ambiguous, giving rise to centuries of argument as to whether a king is commanded (*mitzvah*) or simply permitted (*reshut*). "If, after you have entered the land that the LORD your God has assigned to you, and taken possession of it and settled in it, you decide 'I will set a king over me as do the nations about me,' you shall be free to set a king over yourself, one chosen by the LORD your God" (Deut. 17:14–15). Authorities who affirm monarchy, such as Maimonides and Nachmanides, count this as one of the 613 commandments. Others such as Saadia Gaon and Abraham ibn Ezra see it merely as something permissible, a divine concession to human weakness.

If it is the case that theocracy is a critical, typically anti-monarchical stance, then it is not to be equated with just any religious intrusion into politics. The Royal Psalms, which elevate the Davidic king to the status of God's son and thereby provide a strong metaphysical basis for dynastic legitimacy, are not theocratic in the sense advanced here.

Theocracy, in the Jewish context, should not be conflated with a religious basis for or influence on government *simpliciter*. Nor would I say that the attempts of religious parties in the State of Israel to advance their agenda are theocratic. They are "normal" interest politics in a fractious modern democracy.

Does theocracy then, on this reading, carry into the modern Jewish world? I would argue that it does not, in pure form. Rather, there are merely distilled versions of a theocratic impulse. There are no serious projects, driven by organized interests, for a comprehensive theocratic constitution. The impulse towards theocracy was expressed in some theoretical proposals for a "Torah state" (*medinat ha-Torah*) or an "halakhic state" (*medinat ha-halakha*), advanced by some religious ideologues in the pre- and early state period. It might also be found in religious readings of contemporary Jewish history which are taken by religious ideologues to reveal God's providential purposes – with direct implications for Israeli policy. I refer here to the view that Israel's conquest of the West Bank and Gaza strip in the Six-Day War (1967) was part of a divine plan and that any merely political dealing with these territories would thwart the messianic dynamic of contemporary history. But the advocates of such views want a strong state, not a theocratic anti-politics of direct divine governance. Even a recent proposal, by the theologian Michael Wyschogrod to restore the Davidic monarchy – with an empty throne occupied by a regent until the messiah comes – assumes that Israel would remain a parliamentary democracy. The formal declaration of monarchy would be merely symbolic.[3]

In addition to the intra-mural Jewish argument about what form of constitution best represents biblical and Jewish ideals, the concept of theocracy was also turned outward, to the wider world, where it functions in an argument on behalf of the political virtues of the Jews. The leading advocate for theocracy – and the man who first coined the term, Josephus – addressed a non-Jewish audience. He defended the Jews against the first-century version of anti-Semitism using theocracy as an emblem of Jewish wisdom and nobility. Unlike the intra-mural Jewish argument, Josephus's critique is not of the Jewish monarchical tradition. It is of Hellenistic political theory, of the aspirations of the Greek philosophers for a good city. Spinoza also makes use of theocracy in an externally directed philosophical argument, which in some ways mirrors that of Josephus. But whereas Josephus argues to defend the Jews against calumnies, Spinoza endorses them. He uses theocracy to show the political fecklessness of the Jews and the hazards that await those who model modern politics on, in his telling, the failures of the *Respublica Hebraeorum*.

In this chapter, I shall first consider the argument of Josephus (d. 100 CE).[4] "Theocracy" appears in volume 2 of his mature work *Against Apion*. In context, Josephus was trying to describe the Mosaic "constitution" for his educated, Greek-speaking, non-Jewish audience. Josephus presented Judaism as a law (*nomos*), given by a venerable, sagacious legislator (*nomothetes*), who thereby simultaneously created a frame of government (*politeia*). He found the existing types of government in Greek theory – rule by one, rule by a few, and rule by many – inadequate to conceptualize the Jewish constitution and so, asking for his audience's pardon, introduced the new term. Josephus sought both to capture the uniqueness of Judaism for his uninformed audience and to render Judaism into intelligible Greek conceptual categories thus, ironically, scanting its uniqueness.

For the next thinker whom I consider, Isaac Abravanel (1437–1508), the argument, written in Hebrew, is directed inward to an exclusively Jewish audience. Abravanel wants to persuade his fellow Jews that direct governance by God is the Jewish ideal, the form of the future (messianic) Jewish polity, and the best interpretive reading of those biblical narratives and legal texts that deal with political institutions. In contrast to strong monarchists, such as Maimonides and Nissim Gerondi, Abravanel argues that monarchy was indeed a rejection of God's rule. Other nations may need kings but not the Jews. For Abravanel, the concept of theocracy allows him to contend not only with powerful arguments on behalf of monarchy but to reject incipiently secularizing trends within Jewish political thought. The latter, represented by Maimonides and Gerondi, diminished, in his view, the metaphysical holiness of the Jewish people. Theocracy is a way of emphasizing both radical Jewish difference and focusing messianic hope during the dark times of the Expulsion from Spain and Portugal.

Theocracy also serves as an argumentative tactic for Spinoza. Spinoza analyses the Hebrew commonwealth formed after the exodus from Egypt as a theocracy, in which each Israelite, now living in a functional state of nature, "decided to transfer their right to no human being, but only to God."[5] The terrifying power of God, however, soon persuaded them that they needed an intermediary. They transferred their natural right to Moses, abrogating their earlier covenant with God alone. By degrees, the purity of their theocracy, which entailed a desirable democratic equality of persons before God, was compromised. The theocracy collapsed into hierocracy and monarchy, an unstable, internally divided polity bound for destruction. There is something for Spinoza to admire in the theocracy (e.g., its equality, public spiritedness, and religiously incensed patriotism), but more for him to condemn.[6] The lesson of the failed Hebrew theocracy is that religion must be kept under the control of a civil sovereign. What Josephus and Abravanel find to be the greatest strength of theocracy, Spinoza diagnoses as it chief weakness. His criticism is directed outward to the Dutch public in the hope of constraining the power of the Calvinist clergy. By showing the deep flaws of Hebrew theocracy, Spinoza hoped to discourage those who sought to replicate it in modern times. For reasons of space, I will not further analyse Spinoza. He is, however, too important and too relevant a thinker – although his status as a "Jewish thinker" is contentious – to completely ignore.

The modern philosopher and social thinker Martin Buber (1878–1965) argues for theocracy as an actual social-political framework realized in the period of the biblical judges. Although the most scholarly and technical of Buber's books, *The Kingship of God* intends something more than just an arcane exegetical argument about how to interpret the biblical Book of Judges. Writing a decade after the publication of his *I and Thou*, Buber sought to find a political expression for the powerful experience of normative orientation captured by the "I-Thou encounter." Theocracy in politics is the counterpart to the spontaneity and normativity of the *Ich-Du Begegnung* in personal life. As such, the concept of theocracy can provide a critical perspective on the static, institutionalized forms of politics (and life) that dominate human interaction. Buber's work is directed outward to an audience of German biblical scholars, theologians, and social thinkers, as well as inward towards Jews searching for the renewal of Judaism. Theocracy is, for him, a way of both making sense of ancient Judaism and of advocating for a kind of weak, anarchic politics within the horizon of modern Judaism.

Finally, I briefly consider some other modern and contemporary manifestations of the theocratic impulse, arguing that the classic theocratic tropes have little resonance in the context of the Jewish return to sovereign statehood in Israel.

Josephus

Josephus, the scion of an aristocratic and priestly Jerusalem family, served as the leader of Jewish forces in the Galilee during the first Jewish revolt against the Romans (66–73 CE). He survived the defeat of his forces and the collective suicide of his remaining troops and surrendered to the Romans. Ingratiating himself with his captors, he eventually gained Roman citizenship and lived out his days in Rome on a pension, writing historically oriented works on various aspects of Judaism and the Jewish people. Towards the end of his life, he wrote a two-volume diatribe against an Egyptian anti-Semite, Apion. (The term "anti-Semite" is, of course, an anachronism but it nonetheless fits. Apion and others' hate-filled condemnations of the Jews go beyond criticisms of Judaism; they characterize the Jewish people as such.) Roman Alexandria, which housed a large Jewish diaspora, was a place of fierce ethnic and political tensions. Josephus in *Against Apion* meticulously refutes the arguments of Apion and others, often with an irony and humour that alleviate the otherwise depressing content of the work.[7]

Apion accuses the Jews of hating all of humanity, especially the Greeks, of practising human sacrifice, and of contributing nothing of value to mankind. Josephus must therefore argue that Moses belongs to the ranks of the most distinguished thinkers and statesmen of antiquity (thus highlighting the contribution of the Jews to humanity) and that his legislative legacy to the Jews imbued them with noble traits. Nothing in the Jewish way of life corresponds to the calumnies of Apion and other anti-Semites. Josephus writes:

> I desire to give, to the best of my ability, a brief account of our constitution as a whole and of its details. From this, I think, it will be apparent that we possess a code excellently designed to promote piety, friendly relations with each other, and humanity towards the world at large, besides justice, hardihood, and contempt of death … I consider that, in reply to the numerous false accusations which are brought against us, the fairest defence which we can offer is to be found in the laws which govern our daily life.[8]

Josephus argues that the civilized are distinguished from the barbarous by the acceptance of law and by life under law. The wise legislator sees what is best and wins his people over to the laws he frames for their benefit. The corresponding virtue of the people is to show loyalty to the laws and not to change them; their very antiquity attests to their excellence. Moses proved his greatness by leading his people out of Egypt and keeping them safe through the entire period of wilderness wandering. With Israel entirely dependent upon him he might have become a despot – an all-too-familiar scenario. He did not, however, accrue power for his own benefit but solely on behalf of his people and their "lasting welfare."[9] "With such noble aspirations and such a record of successful achievements, he had good reason for thinking that he had God for his guide and counsellor. Having first persuaded himself that God's will governed all his actions and all his thoughts, he regarded it as his primary duty to impress that idea upon the community."[10]

It is significant that Josephus does not invoke the biblical narrative of Sinaitic revelation. Rather than begin with the thunderous presence of a law-giving God, Josephus begins with the reflective piety of a states-man; Moses's conception of God rather than a God acting in history guides Moses's work. The emphasis on the inspired lawgiver is more Hellenic than Hebraic. Accordingly, Josephus notes that the Greeks attribute their laws to Zeus or Apollo, "either believing this to be fact or hoping in this way to facilitate their acceptance." His claim is not that this is all fiction and that Mosaic law just happens, as a matter of brute fact, to be divine. Rather, he claims that a fair minded, comparative evaluation of the laws as such will yield the conviction that Mosaic law reflects the "truest conception of God."[11] Josephus is not being espe-cially innovative here, as both the Letter of Aristeas and Philo frame Moses's activity in this way. But it is remarkable how much ground has been ceded to a fundamentally Greek, non-biblical characterization of the origins of the Torah and the founding of the Jewish polity.

Within this context, Josephus offers his theory of the Mosaic polity:

> Some people have entrusted the supreme political power to monarchies, others to oligarchies, yet others to the masses. Our lawgiver, however, was attracted by none of these forms of polity, but gave to his constitution the form of what – if a forced expression be permitted – may be termed a "the-ocracy," (θεοκρατίαν), placing all sovereignty and authority in the hands of God. To Him he persuaded all to look, as the author of all blessings ... He convinced them that no single action, no secret thought, could be hid from Him. He represented Him as One, uncreated and immutable to all eternity; in beauty surpassing all mortal thought, made known to us by His power, although the nature of His real being passes knowledge.[12]

Moses's achievement is both metaphysical and ethical-political. His conception of true divinity sponsors the legislation he enacts.

Josephus claims that the best of the Greeks – Pythagoras, Anaxago-ras, Plato, and the Stoics – reached views of the nature and majesty of God consonant with those of Moses (implying, as the Hellenistic Jewish motif had it, that the Greeks learned these teachings from the ancient Hebrews). But the Mosaic achievement is in fact superior to the Platonic one, for the philosophers were content to teach only their disciples and to let the masses wallow in their ignorance. Furthermore, the philosophers taught, in their overly cerebral way, only noble principles. Moses, however, both taught the masses and implicated his principles in practical precepts so that the Jews would learn by doing. Daily life would be permeated by an exalted conception of the divine; the logic of law would be internalized in the most profound way. Rather than see the law as distant and alien, Jews raised under Mosaic precepts would learn the animating principles of their law whenever they ate bread or rested on the seventh day from labour. There would be no ignorance of the law, as every week they would gather to recite it.

Unlike other systems, Moses did not make piety (*euseibeian*) a department of virtue, but the master virtue. The standard virtues: justice, temperance, courage, and (instead of *phronesis*) "mutual harmony in all things between the members of the community" were part of piety.[13] (For Josephus, Plato's Euthyphro problem could not have arisen as there can be no tension between goodness and piety; all the virtues are ordered to piety and piety seems to be constituted by the harmony of all the virtues.) The law inculcates piety and the classical virtues through a regimen of disciplined, daily life in which all Jews participate. In addition to the intrinsic benefits of this way of life, there is an instrumental one: the "admirable harmony" (*homonoian*) that prevails among the Jews.

> Unity and identity of religious belief, perfect uniformity in habits and customs, produce a very beautiful concord (*symphonian*) in human character. Among us alone will be heard no contradictory statements about God, such as are common among other nations ... Among us alone will be seen no difference in the conduct of our lives. With us all act alike, all profess the same doctrine about God, one which is in harmony with our Law and affirms that all things are under His eye. Even our womenfolk and dependents would tell you that piety must be the motive of all our occupations in life.[14]

In this (exaggerated) way, Josephus seeks to refute the canard that Jews are clannish or tribal. Rather, the mutuality that their common life displays comes from the excellence of their metaphysical insights and the practical wisdom of their law. So perfect is their law, in fact, that they do not change it to suit their circumstances. While others praise those who depart from tradition and contribute to mankind by inventing new things in crafts or literatures, the Jews show fidelity to the unsurpassable excellence of their inheritance. So much for Apion's charge that the Jews contribute nothing to humanity.

So far, theocracy functions more as an underlying justification for the Jewish way of life than as an actual frame of government. Josephus does not neglect that topic, however. For him, there is no "finer or more equitable polity than one which sets God at the head of the universe" and "which assigns the administration of its highest affairs to the whole body of priests, and entrusts to the supreme high priest the direction of all the other priests."[15] Moses first assigned the priests the conduct of public worship not on account of their wealth or other accidental advantages but because of their "persuasive eloquence and discretion." He expanded their charge to the supervision of daily life and to civil and criminal matters. Like Moses, the priests did not serve for reasons of self-aggrandizement but out of dedication to the common good. "Could there be a more saintly government than that? Could God be more honoured than by such a scheme, under which religion is the end and aim of the training of the entire community, the priests are entrusted with the special charge of it, and the whole administration of the state resembles some sacred ceremony?"[16]

In his earlier work, *Antiquities*, Josephus had advocated aristocracy, rule by the best, as the best regime. For him, the best were none other than the priests. To hold that position, he had to degrade the value of monarchy, arguing that Deuteronomy 17:14–15, the law regarding the appointment of a king, should be interpreted as an *option* rather than as a commandment. And not only was biblical kingship optional, it was unadvisable. "For God suffices as a ruler."[17] Josephus's demotion of kingship and its replacement by priests in *Antiquities* is continued in *Against Apion* under a new nomenclature. But in a deeper sense, Josephus is not just substituting "theocracy" for "aristocracy" and leaving rule by priests intact. Although priests play an administrative role, they cannot play a decisive, dominating one. That is because Josephus, like Plato, is searching for a genuine unity among the people and for that a part cannot rule over other parts. All must be ruled by one who transcends the polity, by the Platonic Good or by the monotheistic God.[18] The Mosaic constitution effects a weak government. Firm fidelity to the law obviates the need for strong hierocracy. Theocracy equals nomocracy – rule by God in the form of unwavering popular adherence to the law. What Plato sought to achieve through an imaginary Kallipolis, Moses achieved through an actual theocracy.

Isaac Abravanel

Abravanel likely knew more of the world of high politics than any other medieval Jewish thinker. The descendant of a leading Portuguese Jewish family, he served rulers in Portugal and Spain, as well in Naples, where he settled after the Expulsion. He worked to convince King Ferdinand and Queen Isabella to cancel the edict of expulsion, but was thwarted by Torquemada. Abravanel's extensive political experience brought him to a highly anti-political attitude.[19] Other medieval Jewish thinkers, such as Rabbi Solomon ben Abraham Adret (1235–1310) and Rabbi Nissim Gerondi (1320–76) approached a conception of politics recognizably like our own: politics as a worldly art which requires the use of rational judgment and practical action to facilitate group life under historical conditions. Politics in this sense may be licensed by a sacred script, but it doesn't follow one. It is utilitarian, discretionary, and pragmatic. These thinkers understood the tradition of monarchy, normatively grounded in Deuteronomy, chapter 17 and "historically" founded within the narrative frame of 1 Samuel, chapter 8 to sponsor a strong civil authority, whether royal or republican. Their framework for understanding politics is less the biblical world of kings than the medieval world of autonomous Jewish communities (*kehillot*). Within that world, politics was disenchanted and practical. As rabbinic authorities, Adret and Gerondi maximized the power of communal officials as functional successors to the ancient kings. Civic officers (*parnassim*) handle "non-religious" aspects of communal life; they have the authority to tax, punish, fine, coerce, and (when permitted by the gentile sovereign) to execute, even in excess of the standard civil and criminal law of the Talmud. The people stand to these elected, republican leaders as all Israel stood to the Sanhedrin or the king. This expansion and quasi-secularization of civil authority constitutes a strong challenge to the theocratic ideal. If the Jews can function, even allowing for the loss of sovereignty and the rigours of exile, in a "normal" political way, their metaphysical status as God's holy people may be compromised.

Abravanel argues against monarchy and, by implication, against strong versions of civic government. He argues in favour of direct rule by God, which will soon prevail in the coming Messianic age. He first attacks the medieval idea that a king is necessary for political society in order to guarantee its unity (*aḥdut*), continuity (*hatmadah*), and sovereignty (*y'kholet ha-muḥlat*).[20] Abravanel argues theoretically that concentration of power in a single individual can be ruinous, while dispersion of power among a group of leaders can be beneficial. He argues on empirical grounds that the Italian city republics are more dynamic and powerful than monarchies. By pointing to successful republican regimes, Abravanel undermines the claim that monarchy is necessary for or essential to political society (*ha-kibbutz ha-medini*) in general. Nonetheless, monarchy is widespread among the gentile nations. The Jews, however, are in a different category.[21] They should not need monarchy at all. The gentiles, where monarchy prevails, think that they need it because monarchs appear to be essential to conducting wars, to promulgating laws that improve the state of political society (*tikkun kibbutz ha-medini*) and for punishing criminals in extrajudicial ways when the law falls short.[22] The Gentiles do indeed need rulers to accomplish these tasks – although republican rulers would be better than kings – but they only need such rulers because they do not possess "a divine Torah and commandments" nor are they under the protection of "divine providence" (*ha-hashgaḥah ha-elohit*).[23]

Divine providence – effectively, direct divine rule – ensured the Israelite victories narrated in the Book of Joshua. No king other than the divine King was needed by Israel for the conduct of war. Nor is any law other than the Torah needed. The Torah is perfect and may not be added to or diminished. If additions to the law are needed, God Himself will provide them. Indeed, the law already makes provision for its own occasional suspension – extra-judicial punishments may be inflicted by the court at its discretion (BT Sanhedrin 46a).[24] Abravanel is arguing implicitly here against both Maimonides and R. Nissim Gerondi, who thought that kings were necessary to augment and complement the Torah's legal system. Gerondi, in particular, developed an extensive theory based on the ideality of Jewish law: it was so holy and elevated that a society that tried to run according to it would inevitably fail. Therefore, the Torah licensed kings or other forms of civil sovereignty that could function realistically in the world as it is.[25]

Abravanel does not yield any ground to the quasi-secularized conception of politics advanced by Gerondi. For Abravanel, the Jews, as a holy people, have constant direct access to God. They can cleave (*devekut*) to the divine providence that is with them and to the prophecy that is always within their midst.[26] Although Abravanel frames these views within the historical context of the people's reckless desire for a king, they have ongoing salience. Even though God acquiesced and chose a king (and then other kings) for them, God's own Kingship never separated from them. God is not envious of a human king – that would be absurd. God designates a righteous, God-fearing man, David, as Israel's human king, so that God's law might be preserved and strengthened among them. But in the absence of this form of governance, direct divine governance remains. God's rule orders and constrains any version of human rule, including the republican one which Abravanel prefers as a matter of general (i.e., non-Jewish) political theory.[27]

Martin Buber

Buber was a leading Jewish thinker and what we would today call a "public intellectual" in German-speaking central Europe and, after 1938, in Mandate Palestine and Israel. His expansive body of work is difficult to characterize, comprising scholarly studies, translations and reconstructions of the Bible and Hasidic stories, the spiritual classic *I and Thou* and related religious-philosophical works, essays on sociology and politics, and Zionist writings inter alia. Throughout Buber's entire oeuvre a focus on the nature of human interaction in society and state looms large. Like many modern European thinkers of an existentialist cast, Buber is concerned with alienation, the loss of the authenticity, the impersonal nature of the modern *Gesellschaft*, and redemptive potential of genuine, immediate human encounter. Such encounters cannot be coerced or institutionalized, but they can be facilitated by living in *Gemeinschaft*, in a face-to-face social world.[28] As a religious thinker, Buber grounds the truly human community in encounter with the divine Thou.[29]

There is no bright line between Buber's work as a historian of mysticism or philosophy or as an academic biblical scholar and his role as a religious thinker. His scholarly work tries to evoke the state of mind, the inner orientation, of the subjects it investigates. Thus, his work on Hasidism is not a pure historian's treatment of hasidic figures, texts, and ideas, but rather a reconstruction of hasidic life-worlds, such that his readers can enter into the mentality and vision of the hasidic masters. Buber practised *Verstehen*, the methodology of his teacher, Wilhelm Dilthey. This approach of seeking to understand from the inside out, as it were, the consciousness of persons who hold the views and attitudes under investigation is evident in *The Kingship of God*. Thus, Buber contends that historians, such as Julius Wellhausen, misunderstand biblical theocracy when they claim that it was merely "an ideal concept" or a retrojection from a later period of history.[30]

Against Wellhausen, Buber wants to locate a primitive "will to theocracy" among the Israelites in the post-conquest period described by the Book of Judges. Buber takes Judges to have historicity; the mentality of Gideon, in particular, he presents as an authentic attestation of the consciousness of God as King, appropriate to its time. Gideon – who rejects the elders' offer to be king of Israel – represents the pristine commitment to "naïve theocracy."[31] In the early period, God is thought of – more precisely, encountered – as a leader, a *melekh*, who walks in front of his people, fights for them in war, settles them in peace, and is ever present among them. He is the head, not of a state, with all the stability and institutionalization that concept implies, but of a "land-seeking confederation of tribes."[32] God is ever-present, palpably in the midst of the loosely organized people. At moments of urgency, the divine King endows human leaders with charisma, commissioning them to follow his lead and save his people as need arises. This arrangement is thought sufficient, indeed, ideal by the editor of Judges, chapters 1–12. On Buber's reading, the book is divided into an anti-monarchical section (chapters 1–12) and a diametrically opposed pro-monarchical one (chapters 17–21), which sees the theocratic phase as an anarchic failure. But for Buber, whose political thought favours inspired decisions on "the narrow ridge" over reliable norms deployed on firm ground, the theocracy expresses an abiding theo-political ideal.

Invoking the Sinai covenant as the establishment of a theo-political relationship between Israel and the divine King, Buber writes:

> He [the divine King] is not content to be "God" in the religious sense. He does not want to surrender to a man that which is not "God's," the rule over the entire actuality of worldly life; this very rule He lays claim to and enters upon it; for there is nothing which is not God's. He will apportion to the one, for ever and ever chosen by Him, his tasks, but naked power without a situationally related task He does not wish to bestow. He makes known His will first of all as constitution – not constitution of cult and custom only, also economy and society – He will proclaim it again and again to the changing generations, certainly but simply as reply to a question, institutionally through priestly mouth, above all, however, in the freedom of His surging spirit, through every one whom His spirit seizes. *The separation of religion and politics which stretches through history is here overcome in real paradox.*[33]

The immediate context is Buber's analysis of the covenant in Exodus chapters 15 and 19, but there is no doubt that Buber intends this description to apply normatively to all periods of Jewish history. Living by the "freedom of His surging spirit" – an abiding religious antinomianism – informs Buber's view of true biblical leadership and of its lessons for the contemporary world. Openness to the divine spirit, or in Buber's dialogical language, to the Divine *Du*, leads a person to seek the transformation of all social and political structures. The goal is utopia. And, as Buber puts it, "the sociological 'utopia' of voluntary community is nothing else but the immanent side of direct theocracy."[34]

Buber writes in *I and Thou* of the "sublime melancholy" of our fate: every I-Thou encounter turns quickly into a memory. The Thou becomes an It. The charismatic, spontaneous bond dissolves; embers take the place of fire.[35] This melancholy lot also infects the social-political form of the encounter. Theocracy is separated by a hair from anarchy, from social dissolution. Not in vain do the elders approach Samuel and call for a king to rule them "like all the other nations." For Buber, the true statesman lives not by a code of conduct but on a "narrow ridge." The concreteness of life demands unique decisions in every hour. Neither romantic-religious political idealism nor hard-bitten political realism captures Buber's stance. He believes that we must live within politics in order to be in relation with one another and with the world, and that politics will always have a share in evil. We cannot transcend that. But we must choose, moment by moment, what course entails the lowest cost in human blood and degradation. That assumption of risk and vulnerability, of choice without a safety net, is what lingers of "the will to theocracy" for political personae in our time.

Israeli Theocracy?

To an extent, the theocratic musings of the authors considered above are expressions of the moral imagination; they are theoretical constructs and critiques emerging from a condition of Jewish statelessness and powerlessness. The Jewish return to sovereignty in a modern state (a category not contemplated by halakha) in the land of Israel stirred a small revival of theocratic thought, albeit within the limits of modern conceptions of statehood, human rights, and citizenship. The acceptance of those limits by rabbinic authors such as Shimon Federbush, Hayim Hirschensohn, Isaac Herzog, and others conditioned their theocratic impulses. It is probably more correct to say that these early and mid-twentieth-century projects of constitution building on the basis of halakha simply aimed at synthesizing modern democratic culture with rabbinic culture more than substituting the latter for the former.[36]

The Israeli scholar Aviezer Ravitzky points to the paradoxes that infect the Jewish "will to theocracy." Politics as such is construed by Jewish sources, Ravitzky claims, as an instrument to restrain human wickedness. The paradigmatic expression is from the mishnaic ethical treatise *Pirke Avot*: "Rabbi Hananya says, Pray for the welfare of the government, for if it were not for fear of the government, men would eat one another alive" (*Pirke Avot* 3:2). This rather negative, Augustinian justification for politics assumes that government requires stability and duration to perform its central task, that is, what Augustine would later call *tranquillitas ordinis*. In order to achieve stability and duration, a regime must be accepted by the people as legitimate. Regimes are evaluated by how well they provide peaceful living conditions for their citizens. Ravitzky argues that this highly pragmatic approach to politics militates, on the grounds of the tradition per se, against theocracy. Under the conditions of Jewish modernity, when most Jews have abandoned the halakhic frame of reference both normatively and existentially, a halakhic state could only be imposed by force. That, however, would vitiate its legitimacy and hence its stability; it would fail to meet the task that the Jewish tradition itself sets for politics. Thus, proponents of a *medinat ha-Torah*, the rabbinic version of theocracy, acknowledge that the Jews would have to experience a sea change in normative orientation in order for a state governed by halakha to be possible.

Another factor contributing to the purely notional status of theocracy is that the halakha itself acknowledges the need for civil governance. Halakha developed under conditions of Jewish powerlessness (relatively speaking); it assumes that a gentile sovereign will address the overtly political dimensions of common life. Thus, even if a general will to live in a *medinat ha-Torah* existed, the Torah itself would not be up to the challenge. It would have to innovate whole bodies of public law that themselves would be thoroughly shot through with modern political values. One sees this in Shimon Federbush's attempt to revise and renew halakha in a way that would make it constitutionally and culturally compatible with a modern state.[37]

Since halakha as currently constituted is inadequate to ground a constitutional nomocracy-theocracy, its role at best is to serve as a cultural source for the development of Israeli law. As such, it is shorn of its presumed divine origin and import and becomes a Jewish version of Roman law, a "mere" civilizational heritage (*mishpat ivri*). The Basic Laws of Israel allow for the inclusion of halakha, in the secularized form of *mishpat ivri*, into Israeli law, but there is nothing theocratic about this. Nor is there any active "will to theocracy" in the lingering control that the Rabbinate has over personal status – marriage, divorce, etc. – in Israeli society. That is an inheritance of the Turkish millet system and a more or less intractable survival, given the nature of coalition politics. Religious parties, which are necessary for coalitions, will not surrender institutions over which they have some control. Jewish law, such as the cessation of work on the Sabbath, does apply in many municipalities and some secularists are aggrieved by the "religious coercion." But this hardly amounts to theocracy any more than does the restriction of alcohol sales to special "state stores" in the Commonwealth of Pennsylvania. Such institutions give lingering legal expression to traditional values still salient in civil society. A Tocquevillean case can be made for them that has nothing to do with theocracy.

Perhaps a will to theocracy may be found in the movement of religious settlers, after the Six-Day War, to the administered territory of the West Bank and, before the withdrawal of 2005, to the Gaza strip. The settlers' movement, Gush Emunim (the Bloc of the Faithful), was based on the teaching of Rabbi Zvi Yehuda Kook (1891–1981), the son of the first chief rabbi of Palestine, under the British Mandate, Rav Abraham Isaac Kook (1865–1935). The elder Kook, a mystical theologian, saw Zionism, in its majority a revolutionary, secular movement, as revelatory of the God's work in history. God was using those Jews who threw off the "yoke of the Torah" to accomplish His holy redemptive purposes. Unlike the elder Rav Kook, the son, Zvi Yehuda, lived to see the establishment of the State of Israel and its conquest of the historic Judean heartland in 1967. Zvi Yehuda went farther than his father in the definiteness of his claims: "Zionism is a heavenly matter. The State of Israel is a divine entity, our holy and exalted state."[38] He and his disciples found providential meaning in Israel's wars: "From the perspective of faith, we see the divine hand spread over us and especially over our wars. It leads us to recognize the righteousness of our actions and of our wars and of their indispensability, not only for us but for the nations!"[39] For followers of Kook, we are in a time of realized eschatology, of messianism (albeit without a personal messiah). The principal implication of this metaphysical reading of contemporary history is that the entire historic land of Israel must be settled and that there can be no compromise, no concession to merely rational politics that might diminish the holy work. Even though religious settlers who hold such views constitute a small minority of Israel's citizens, they have considerable political clout, as the inclusion of their most representative party, Jewish Home, in the current coalition (May 2015) indicates.

But is this theocracy? If the foregoing argument is correct, theocracy has largely functioned as a critique, as a way of relativizing reliance on politics. The messianism that impelled Kookean messianism absolutizes politics. It sees the divine hand in contemporary history in a definite, crystal-clear way and draws non-negotiable political conclusions from that "fact." Theocracy it may well be in the (toxic) contemporary sense, but it is a theocracy at odds with the tentative and critical spirit that informed earlier Jewish engagements.

NOTES

1 *Midrash Rabbah: Deuteronomy*, Shoftim 5:9, cited in *The Jewish Political Tradition*, vol. 1: *Authority*, ed. Michael Walzer, Menachem Lorberbaum, Yair Lorberbaum, and Noam Zohar (New Haven: Yale University Press, 2000). I have altered the translation slightly to improve readability.

2 My use of "theocracy" thus differs from the standard usage elsewhere in this volume, particularly that of Ronald Beiner. On my usage, a government may have strong religious legitimation, such as the Davidic dynasty, but not qualify as a theocracy. For a history of the semantic range of the term that casts light on its ancient use and substantiates the nuance that I give it, see the chapter by Yvonne Sherwood in this volume.

3 Michael Wyschogrod, "A King in Israel," *First Things*, May 2010. http[s]://www.firstthings.com/article/2010/05/a-king-in-israel.

4 For additional perspective on Josephus, see Yvonne Sherwood's chapter in this volume.

5 R.H.M. Elwes, ed., *The Chief Works of Benedict Spinoza* (New York: Dover, 1951), 219.

6 For a thorough study of Spinoza's political thought and attitudes toward theocracy, see Steven B. Smith, *Spinoza, Liberalism and the Question of Jewish Identity* (New Haven: Yale University Press, 1997), 147–56. Additional perspective on Spinoza, as a thinker within the civil religion tradition, may be found in Ronald Beiner's chapter in this volume.

7 Josephus, *Josephus*, trans. H. St. J. Thackeray, vol. 1 (London: William Heinemann, 1926). The relevant discussion takes place in book 2, lines 149–89.

8 *Josephus*, 351.

9 *Josephus*, 357.

10 Ibid.

11 Ibid.

12 *Josephus*, 359.

13 *Josephus*, 361.

14 *Josephus*, 365.

15 *Josephus*, 367.

16 *Josephus*, 369.

17 Yehoshua Amir, "Josephus on the Mosaic 'Constitution,'" in *Politics and Theo-Politics in the Bible and Postbiblical Literature*, ed. Yair Hoffman, Henning Graf Reventlow, and Benjamin Uffenheimer (Sheffield: Sheffield Academic Press, 1994), 16. Cf. *Antiquities* 4.223.

18 Amir, "Josephus on the Mosaic 'Constitution,'" 24.

19 For a comprehensive overview and analysis, see Urbach's classic study. Ephraim Urbach, "Die Staatsauffassung des Don Isaak Abravanel," *Monatsschrift für Geschichte und Wissenschaft des Judentums* 81.3 (1937): 257–70. See also Rochelle Millen, "Isaac Abravanel's Concept of Monarchy," *Shofar: An Interdisciplinary Journal of Jewish Studies* 10.3 (1992): 47–61.

20 Abravanel on 1 Samuel 8:6. See Yehudah Shaviv, ed., *Perush Ha-Neviim L'Rabbenu Yitzhaq Abravanel* (Jerusalem: Chorev Publishing House, 2010), 96. All references will be to this edition.

21 Benzion Netanyahu, *Don Isaac Abravanel: Statesman and Philosopher* (Philadelphia: Jewish Publication Society, 1972), 189–242.

22 *Perush Ha-Neviim*, 99.

23 Ibid.

24 Ibid.

25 For the relevant text of R. Nissim Gerondi, see Walzer, M. Lorberbaum, Y. Lorberbaum, and Zohar, eds, *The Jewish Political Tradition*, vol. 1, 156–61. For a book-length treatment of Maimonides and Gerondi on this topic, see Menachem Lorberbaum, *Politics and the Limits of Law: Secularizing the Political in Medieval Jewish Thought* (Stanford: Stanford University Press, 2001).

26 *Perush Ha-Neviim*, 102.

27 Abravanel thus treats Deut. 17:14–15 not as a commandment per se but as a normative framework for dealing with a weakness of human nature. In his analogy, appointing a king is like the law of the war captive (Deut. 21:10–14), which stipulates how an Israelite soldier is to treat a conquered woman whom he wants as his own. The Torah does not command that he wed a conquered gentile woman, but if he wants to do so, because of his "evil inclination," he does it in the Torah's stipulated way so as to avoid

sin. Similarly, the Torah does not command Israel to appoint a king, but if they want to do so, they must do it in a certain way. The commandment shifts from the appointment to the way in which it is carried out.

28 For a concise analysis of Buber's social and political thought, drawing on the considerable scholarly literature on this theme, see Alan Mittleman, *Hope in a Democratic Age* (Oxford: Oxford University Press, 2009), 220–9.

29 Buber's iconic book is entitled *Ich und Du* (1923); "du" being the German familiar form of "you." An unfortunate choice by the first English translator of the book, Ronald Gregor Smith, rendered "du" as "Thou." "Thou" captures the elevated prose and sublime spiritual vision of the text, but it also elides the intimacy and familiarity of a genuine "meeting" which Buber sought to convey. Even the later translator, Walter Kaufman, felt compelled, with regret, to stick with the title *I and Thou* since that is how the famous book became known to English speakers.

30 Martin Buber, *Kingship of God*, trans. Richard Scheimann (New York: Harper & Row, 1967), 64.

31 Ibid., 80.

32 Ibid., 107, 133.

33 Ibid., 119. Italics in the original.

34 Ibid., 139. For Buber's approach to biblical leadership, see the essay "Biblical Leadership," in Martin Buber, *Israel and the World: Essays in a Time of Crisis* (Syracuse: Syracuse University Press, 1997). For Buber's writing on utopia, see Martin Buber, *Paths in Utopia* (Syracuse: Syracuse University Press, 1996).

35 Martin Buber, *I and Thou*, trans. Walter Kaufmann (New York: Touchstone, 1970), 68.

36 For a comprehensive overview and analysis of the state of theocracy in modern Israeli political culture, see Aviezer Ravitzky, *Is a Halakhic State Possible? The Paradox of Jewish Theocracy* (Jerusalem: Israel Democracy Institute, 2004). For the compromises made by the contemporary theocratic imagination, see p. 29.

37 On Federbush, see Alan Mittleman, *The Scepter Shall Not Depart from Judah: Perspectives on the Persistence of the Political in Judaism.* (Lanham, MD: Lexington Books, 2000), 157–14.

38 Aviezer Ravitzky, *Messianism, Zionism and Jewish Religious Radicalism*, trans. Michael Swirsky and Jonathan Chipman (Chicago: University of Chicago Press, 1996), 82.

39 Ibid., 83.

9 Saving Miracles: Political Theology and Theocracy in the Schmitt-Benjamin Encounter

HERMÍNIO MEIRELES TEIXEIRA

The exception in jurisprudence is analogous to the miracle in theology. Only by being aware of this analogy can we appreciate the manner in which the philosophical ideas of the state developed in the last centuries.

Carl Schmitt

What other function have they [the "columns and pilasters" of Baroque architecture] than to emphasize the soaring miracle above, by drawing attention to the difficulties of supporting it from below.

Walter Benjamin

But He said to me, "My grace is sufficient for you, for my power is made perfect in weakness" ... For the sake of Christ, then, I am content with weaknesses, insults, hardships, persecutions, and calamities; for when I am weak, then I am strong.

St Paul[1]

In the images of the above quotations, in their hierarchical order and content, rests the architecture of the Western history of sovereign power and authority. From Schmitt's vantage point, jurisprudence is analogous to the miracle not simply as a secularized theological concept, but because it decides on the exceptional case.[2] Jurisprudence, like the miraculous, therefore, is the experience of the exceptional itself, so Schmitt contends. This "case" demands an exceptional decision because its image emerges, whether in perception or/and actuality, as an emergency, a threat, to the civil order of a society and state. Like the scriptural events of a divine intervention, Schmitt describes the legal decision as an act that "suspends" its own legal and institutional creations, so as to unleash the pure force of a political decision that can create, restore, and maintain legal-political orders as such.[3] This is his miracle, one always guarded and saved (redeemed) by the aesthetics and founding myths of the history of sovereign nation states.[4] This is what Schmitt means when he writes that sovereign is "he"[5] who decides on the exception.

Benjamin looks up from the lowest point of the "columns and pilasters" at the images of Baroque balconies, and engages the profound sense that the miracle "soaring above" is not the decision, but the weakness of both those supported by it, and especially those lives used as supports for it. Moreover, as we will demonstrate in what follows, Benjamin not only affirms this weakness, but reclaims it as the essence of theocratic rule.[6] Why weakness, and what exactly is it when used in a theocratic sense? More importantly, for our purposes at least, what then is this image of theocracy expressed in Benjamin's work, and why does he espouse it at a point of supposed historical progress when theocracy is most outmoded, at its weakest, and kept out of sight (at least in the West)?[7] This is the central concern of this study. It is not therefore a focus on the work of Schmitt, Benjamin, and/or the evidence of their encounter. Elements of all three, however, will factor into what follows. Instead, following Benjamin's brief writings on theocracy, this study contends that theocratic rule is the constitutive "end" of the history of all legal-political regimes hitherto known in the tradition of Western sovereignty (including today's secular, democratic regimes).[8] Following Giorgio Agamben's monograph on the concept of "the contemporary," we also suggest that Benjamin's untimely work on the outmoded figures of St Paul and theocracy may be the most contemporary and urgent of his political contributions.[9]

The Pauline Transfiguration and the Messianic Power of Transience

St Paul did not decide to write the words "for when I am weak, then I am strong." The decisiveness, the command, of these words befell him like a spiritual flash in a moment of danger. In the urgent immanence of a life of exile and wander, brought on by the flash of this exceptional moment, Paul was weakened not just physically but spiritually by the images of his vision. In a most precise way, he sensed that these words were not "his" own, but exclusively "His" words ("He said to me"). Importantly, in repeating these words, in the very experience of repetition that sustained them in the flashing moment, Paul encounters the sacrifice and annihilation of his own intentionality, of any sense of self as a source for the sudden realization that "a light from heaven flashed about him."[10] He fell to the ground, but rose again before the light. And when his eyes were opened, he could see nothing: "And for three days he was without sight, and neither ate nor drank."[11] A weakness no doubt that also left him bereft of a world, and into which he falls and rises with nothing but the transience of the moment – or, more precisely, Paul falls and rises in a moment of transience, but a moment which is nothing other than the experience of transience itself.[12] But how can this weakening movement of transience transfigure a life (and itself) into strength? The first step of an answer is the realization that for Paul, as we shall see, transience is never *mere* transience. It *is* an emptying out of a self and its world, but occurring in the full bloom of salvation.[13] In the moment of this transfiguring event, and before the invocation of any theological symbol, salvation is here nothing less, and inseparable from, the immanent experience of a passing away of the norms of one's previous life and world. Just note that Paul does not try to recollect the life and world he suddenly lost. He does not try to reconcile with, or renew, what he once was. Instead, Paul repeats the vanishing image of his transfiguring vision in the different form of letters, or epistles. And he addresses a key letter not to emperors or high priests, but to a people, a Christian collectivity in Rome, struggling to create itself as such, that is, a minor people of Jewish and gentile Christians living under the urgencies of imperial rule.

Thus, in *Romans* we read:

Besides this [stated just before, at 13:10: "Love is the fulfilling of the Law."] you know what hour it is, how it is full time now for you to wake from sleep. For salvation is nearer to us than we first believed; the night is far gone, the day is at hand. Let us then cast off the works of darkness and put on the armour of light; let us conduct ourselves becomingly as in the day, not in reveling and drunkenness, not in quarreling and jealousy.[14]

Paul's "full time now" is nothing less than the power of messianic time. More precisely, the weakening experienced in the event of Paul's vision, unleashes its opposite – the full messianic power of salvation, "nearer to us than we first believed." As the latter quote intends, the coinciding and indetermination of opposites only begins with the weakness of messianic power. Importantly, this indetermination is not a *mere* coincidence of opposites, but one where opposing powers co-extend into each other. More indeterminations proliferate from Paul's messianic vision: the nearness of the distant ("salvation is nearer to us than we first believed"), the casting off of works ("of darkness") in the putting on of armour ("of light"), living in the night so as to "conduct ourselves becomingly as in the day," and a full time now in which the night is "far gone" but the day is still only "at hand."[15] Lastly, one has to note the coinciding of a radical juxtaposition of opposites that co-extends and envelopes all the ones above: the transfigurations of transcendence occurring in, and indecipherable from, the immanence of the event. In the event of his vision Paul's will is transfigured into a command that now, in the "full time," he *must* carry through, in which he cannot do otherwise.

No doubt this is an expression of religious faith in messianic salvation, in the direct intervention of the divine in time. In its expression it is irrevocably situated in religious life, but at the exceptional moment of transfiguration Paul's experience is decidedly *non-religious*.[16] His life is commanded, and suspended, by the pure dissolution of an anomic condition (for three days until Anni'as arrives to save him). This anomic outside of religious experience is certainly *not* the early murmurings of the secular – nor can it be explained by some latter-day attempt to secularize and politically appropriate, as Schmitt claims to do with miracles, the potency of spiritual transfiguration. In fact, as the anomic void that is constitutive of religious experience itself, this anomic outside accomplishes the exact opposite: secularized concepts such as miracles, salvation, and sovereignty not only continue to depend on the religious irruption of the anomic, to recapitulate this *anomie* in the history of their secular institutions, but are even more susceptible to its theology (and therefore its theocracy, as we shall see shortly) precisely at the historical point where the latter is now ugly, deformed, and kept out of sight.[17]

If, in publications from 1938 on, Schmitt continues to recall and redress the secular "miracle" of sovereign decision in phrases such as "the assumption of emergency action," "the concrete situation," or especially "openings through which historical time irrupts into the time of the play" (in the case of seventeenth- century theatre, such as Shakespeare's *Hamlet*),[18] it is precisely this anomie that haunts him.[19] What will haunt him even more – personified in the image and death of Walter Benjamin (in 1940) – is the possibility that the anomic, the exceptional and the singular, cannot be excepted without consequence, because they themselves ground the rule of sovereign power and authority. Like

Paul's anomie, the theological heart of sovereign power may be the rule of the exception over sovereign decisions themselves. To repeat Samuel Weber's wonderful turn of phrase, Benjamin shows that the miracle of sovereignty is in fact a taking exception, a violent exception if necessary, to political decisions on the exceptional case.[20] This "taking exception to political decision" is, for Benjamin, as we shall expound in the next section, nothing less than the power of theocracy, of *the* regime upon which all historically manifested regimes rest and fall, *the* regime that is "the rhythm of this eternally transient worldly existence."[21]

Theocracy *in* Politics, or the Eternal Recurrence of Messianic Revolution

It is clear that as early as 1921 Schmitt and Benjamin not only were aware of each other's work, but were beginning an encounter in which each was a haunting spectre for the other's thought. By "haunting" we simply mean that images of the other's scholarship had a formative effect on the subsequent work of each. This is especially the case for Schmitt, for the simple reason that he lived forty-five more years and published at least seventeen more works after Benjamin's death in 1940. No doubt the encounter for Benjamin began in 1921, with his reading of Schmitt's work on dictatorship (when *Die Diktatur* was first published), as his laudatory letter to Schmitt in 1930 makes clear.[22] Moreover, it was in 1921, in the German journal *Archiv*, of which Schmitt was an avid reader and frequent contributor, that Benjamin published his first major work that questioned the politics of a state of "emergency" in light of the biblical allegories of "divine violence": namely, his "Critique of Violence."[23]

As important as this early published work is, its explanation of divine violence pales in comparison with a short, densely written fragment that Benjamin never published in his lifetime and which scholars can still only guess was written around the same time as the latter "Critique."[24] This is not a judging of one work against the other, but a pointing out of key differences between them that, paradoxically as it may seem, render them inseparable. This fragment is the "Theological-Political Fragment." They are inseparable because the public deposition of the question of divine violence in the published "Critique" is comprehensible as a form of life, as a regime and way of acting politically, only if referred to this fragment that Benjamin leaves for a time that remains. Why? Because a violence that is divine is always the coming form of life that can never be contained in any political or legal conceptual framework (especially secularized ones that claim to have overcome their religious origins). Or, to say the same thing, this violence is *impossibly* contained in all historically defined forms and institutions. And it is a coming form of life not in the sense of an anticipated goal, or a progressive historical achievement, but in the sense of the eternal becoming of life itself. This is what Benjamin means when, in scholarly fashion, he defines the theological core of divine violence in his "Critique" against the legal and state-founding violence he calls "mythical": "If mythical violence is lawmaking, divine violence is law-destroying; if the former sets boundaries, the latter boundlessly destroys them; if mythical violence brings at once guilt and retribution, divine power only expiates; if the former threatens, the latter strikes; if the former is bloody, the latter is lethal without spilling blood."

If, as Agamben contends, the "Critique" was intended for publication, was written respecting current scholarly form (for the journal *Archiv*), especially in the research areas of law and theology, and for the attention and response of established scholars like Schmitt, the "Fragment," by contrast, displays none of these concerns. As a fragment, and unlike scholarly publications, it insists on its incompleteness, as if it is destined to remain a repeatable work for us living today and those not yet present, whose "coming was expected on earth."[25] Its style contrasts greatly with the "Critique" in that it is indirect, allusive, and allegorical, and, with one exception (a brief praising of Bloch's *Spirit of Utopia*),[26] dispenses with the scholarly conventions of citation and reference. In it Benjamin repeats the wisdom of ancient Jewish and Christian sources (the Messiah, the coming Kingdom of God, the profane, the eternal), but does so knowing full well that in his secular present they can only appear outmoded, lapsed, and deformed, and be regularly kept out of sight. But as in Paul's transfiguring experience, the lapsed state of these sources, their growing anomie amidst the dominant secularism of the present, are precisely moments for the discovery of what we have called the *non-religious* core of experience that is always recapitulated in religious transfiguration (i.e., Paul's three days). More precisely, for Benjamin, these anomic moments are such an essential part of religious life that they can never be superseded by the secularism of political life (like Schmitt's claim that secular jurisprudence supersedes miracles). They will at best reside, like an alien force, within the familiarity of secular institutions.

Historically, however, this supersession is exactly what has been attempted by legal-political regimes in the West since at least the seventeenth century, and claimed by scholars of sovereign political rule such as Schmitt.[27] Benjamin not only admits this historical attempt, but, unlike Schmitt, reveals the extreme case upon which it depends: like an opposing force extending into its opposite, the anomie of religious experience irrupts into political life not in the decision on the exceptional case, but in the condition where the sovereign cannot decide, where the exception, and thus the emergency, has instead become the rule.[28] This condition, for Benjamin, is nothing less than the anomic emergence of a theocracy *in* political life, but one that is never *of* political life. Such a condition is unavoidably revolutionary, but with a difference that no political revolution in Western history, especially those committed to the progressive regeneration of legal-political regimes, has or can ever accommodate. Turning to the "Fragment," we will see that this theocratic rule of the exceptional is precisely what Benjamin calls "Messianic" time. And one must say here, somewhat paradoxically, that this theocracy is a regime whose time can, and will, appear only as profound anomic transfiguration.[29]

Unlike Benjamin's completed, scholarly writings (the "Critique" and *Origin of German Tragic Drama*, for example), the three paragraphs of the "Fragment" are written in a state of urgency. He understood the consequences of Schmitt's powerful state of exception thesis already in 1921, with the publication of *Die Diktatur*. The density of these insights, therefore, is not simply due to Benjamin's deference to the traditions of Jewish and Christian mysticism. They are not simply dense, but condensed. Why? In the "Fragment," Benjamin condenses, or crystalizes one might say, thousands of years of Jewish and Christian theology because he has sensed the flashing moments of danger in his time in the work of burgeoning fascists such as Schmitt. This sudden image of danger is not simply the emerging fascism of Benjamin's present, but the latter's appropriation of the constitutive anomie bequeathed by the histories of theological life. The "Fragment" (unlike the published "Critique"), therefore, is written with an indifference towards established exegeses and debates in the history and scholarship of theology and politics. Benjamin is not interested in the recollection of the truths of theological exegeses. He no doubt alludes to these exegeses, but this is certainly not his goal. Note that Benjamin at no point in the "Fragment" contends with *the* truth of these traditions, of these theological-political insights. His concern is instead entirely the means of their transmission, of their transience and transmissibility to the remaining time of those of us whose "coming was expected here on earth." Only the image of

Kafka's writing, the image most formative of Benjamin's, could capture this anomic power of temporal transmission and transience in theology.

In two of his most seminal works, "Franz Kafka: On the Tenth Anniversary of His Death" and "Some Reflections on Kafka," Benjamin uncovers the power of transient "transmissibility":

> Many had accommodated themselves to it [i.e. "the consistency of truth"], clinging to truth or whatever they happened to regard as truth and, with a more or less heavy heart, foregoing its transmissibility. Kafka's real genius was that he tried something entirely new: he sacrificed truth for the sake of clinging to its transmissibility, its haggadic element. Kafka's writings are by nature parables. But it is their misery and their beauty that they had to become *more* [italics Benjamin's] than parables. They do not modestly lie at the feet of the doctrine, as the Haggadah lies at the feet of the Halakah. Though apparently reduced to submission, they unexpectedly raise a mighty paw against it.[30]

Is not this reading of Kafka a clear repetition of the anomic dissolution so essential to Paul's transfiguration, but situated squarely in Kafka's uncovering of an anomic relation between the "haggadic element" (the non-legal storytelling from the Talmud and Exodus that occurs at a seder) and the Halakha (oral and written laws derived from the Torah), muted beneath the official histories of Jewish theology? This anomic indetermination that Kafka finds in the relation between the Haggadah and Halakha, is exactly what Benjamin is attempting in the "Fragment" with the four key allegorical terms he sees at work in both Jewish and Christian theology: the "Messianic," the coming "Kingdom of God," the "order of the profane," and the "eternity of downfall."

The messianic is the event, "the Messiah himself," issuing in a new time, a now time, in which all recognized history is taken up again, but repeated in the different remaining time of the event. For this very reason – that is, the difference of the time that remains – the temporality of the messianic ensures that "nothing historical can relate itself on its own account to anything Messianic."[31] In this sense the Messianic undoes all uncritical histories that, foregoing transmissibility in the urgencies of their present, proclaim to recollect the past as the "the way it really was." Warning us of this type of conformism in the "Theses," Benjamin writes: "Only that type of historian will have the gift of fanning the spark of hope in the past who is firmly convinced that *even the dead* [italics Benjamin's] will not be safe from the enemy. And this enemy has not ceased to be victorious."[32] This is why the Messiah is presented in the opening sentence as the consummation of all history. But how does its remaining time constitute the next key term: the coming "Kingdom of God"?

The key, we believe, is in realizing, as Benjamin does, that in all theological accounts of the Kingdom of God resides the power of an anomic regime – a power therefore that can never allow the "historical dynamic" to set up such a kingdom as a "goal," or a "telos," for its telos is in fact the literal *and* figurative "end" of the historical dynamic itself. As Paul's experience of transfiguration was not simply the transience of his life, or of some other thing such as his Jewish faith, but the experience of transience itself, so the "end" that is always coming as the recurrence of the Kingdom of God is *never* the accomplishments of historical and institutional orders, but the experience of their *ending as such*. And as *ending* the Kingdom of God moves all life forms to their limits, if these forms are fortunate enough not to be destroyed by the intervention of the historical dynamic in the profane order of life.

By "order of the profane" here, Benjamin means simply those mundane cycles of life that pass most often in meaninglessness and unattended silence, but in which history will find and/or impose its orders, and build its narratives. As Benjamin explains, the order of the profane, especially its absorption in the immediacy of life, should be erected on the idea of happiness, but is regularly submitted to the tragedies of historical and political dynamics.[33] Moreover, such a profane concern for happiness *does*, therefore, act in the opposite direction of Messianic time: the Messiah brings anomic dissolution and *ending* as such, while the profane quietly seeks its own happiness. The key to understanding this apparent contradiction is to realize that the opposing relationship between messianic time and the profane is radically different from the opposing relationship between the messianic and the historical. If the political power of the historical dynamic builds itself by submitting profane happiness to its institutional orders and historical tragedies, the Messianic event in fact irrupts from the muteness of the profane into the heart of these orders and their histories. No doubt that profane happiness suffers and is sacrificed to a degree by the Messiah, but only to restore, or let us say redeem, a profane order that is regularly submitted to the sovereign powers of the historical dynamic. This is why Benjamin emphasizes that unlike the anomic relationship between Messianic time and history, the opposing relationship between the Messiah and the profane is actually one of mutual enhancement. It is so, to be clear, because the Messianic event signifies the irruptions immanent to the otherwise quiet passing of the profane. Explaining how the profane order assists the coming of the Messianic Kingdom, Benjamin writes: "The profane, therefore, although not itself a category of this Kingdom, is a decisive category of its quietest approach."[34] As a last word on this profane order, it would be a grave mistake to interpret this "quietest approach," from whence the Messiah irrupts, as Benjamin's currying favour with the still venerated history and traditions of pacifism. Benjamin's quietism is far from the moral dissent of passive resistance, and further from state-sanctioned figures such as dissenters and conscientious objectors. His is instead an active, revolutionary even, indifference that unleashes anomic dissolution at the heart of sovereign institutions. We will return to this question soon, for it is best explained by Benjamin's last key theological expression (in the "Fragment"): "the eternity of downfall."

The theocratic regime that Benjamin calls the coming "Kingdom of God" is therefore a form-of-life, an anomic regime residing within the profane order of political life, which undoes any and all historical attempts to build up the Messianic Kingdom on the order of the profane. It is here, in the announcement of this insight, that Benjamin expresses one of the few, but clearest and profoundest, statements on his enigmatic sense of theocracy: "Therefore the order of the profane cannot be built up on the idea of the Divine Kingdom, and therefore theocracy has no political, but only a religious meaning."[35] To be clear, the profane cannot be built on the Divine Kingdom because the latter is itself an anomic irruption immanent to the profane itself. It is the institutions of the historical dynamic that claim to have built Kingdoms of God on the earthly orders of the profane, but they have done so only through the adoption of this fatal, recurring, and anomic irruption that is the Kingdom of God. Theocracy can only have a "religious meaning," therefore, *not* because in principle and substance it is religious, but because in the immanence of its religiosity it occurs as the dissolution of political orders.

With the above in mind, one should caution that it would be another grave mistake to read this theocracy of the Divine Kingdom as an *apolitical* relation to the profane order of life. The matter is quite the contrary. That the Kingdom has no political meaning, and only a religious one, drives home the radical insight that if Schmitt is right – that is, the politics of state sovereignty built its concepts through the historical appropriations of theological symbols (see Schmitt's opening quotation) – then at the heart of the political legitimations of sovereign power and institutions reside the ancient sources of their recurring undoing, their *ending*.[36] The question is then how does Benjamin envision the emergence of these religious sources into political actuality? Clearly, as messianic, they do not depend on self-conscious political revolutions, or on the political and social movements of history, though the anomic expression of these religious sources may irrupt in these latter histories. Moreover, it follows that this Messianic anomie is never reducible to the conscious religious doctrines that have housed them for thousands of years. Indeed, history shows that the Messiah can strike the institutions of both state and church with equal devastation. It is the last of Benjamin's theological expressions, "the eternity of downfall," that provides the best image of actual Messianic occurrences. An elucidation of two quotations from the last two paragraphs of the "Fragment" will illuminate this image.

Right after Benjamin makes the essential connection between Messianic irruption and profane happiness, he writes the following: "For in happiness all that is earthly seeks its downfall, and only in good fortune is its downfall destined to find it."[37] The first part of the phrase is a basic theological insight, one not too distant even from today's secular common sense. Profane, or "earthly," happiness is inseparable from the unavoidable encounter with our coming "downfall," our passing away. The realization of this encounter should actually enhance one's appreciation for the happiness of profane existence.

The second clause, however, states the profound struggle with political life *for* which the coming Messianic Kingdom exists. In it Benjamin expresses the critical insight that *only* in good fortune does the happiness of earthly life actually find its own "downfall." In a word, the *un*fortunate are those whose downfalls are taken from them, from the immanence of their own existence, and separated out for the decisions of sovereign power. Some first images, then, flit by: a human life, a people, acting not so much from an ethic of survival as from a simple withdrawing of their own downfall and passing from the decisions of a political authority, brings a sudden halt to the mundane (read profane) operations of a sovereign institution. The Messiah appears as this halting itself. The Divine Kingdom is the image of unfolding institutional disintegration. The profane is the silent, unattended recurrence of life from which the Messiah irrupts. And the image of the eternal can be nothing other than the Messianic restitution of "total passing" to the happiness of the profane order of life. These first images are helpful, but they still do not clarify how this theocracy actually occurs. For this we must turn to the end of the "Fragment," especially the last paragraph, where Benjamin's theocracy takes a sudden turn into the heart of political life.

Benjamin writes the following towards the end of the second paragraph:

> and the rhythm of this eternally transient worldly existence, transient in its totality, in its spatial but also in its temporal totality, the rhythm of messianic nature, is happiness. For nature is Messianic by reason of its eternal and total passing away.
>
>   To strive after such passing, even for those stages of man that are nature, is the task of world politics, whose method must be called nihilism.[38]

The first part of the quote sets up the overtly political call ("the task") of the third and last paragraph. For the first time in the "Fragment" nature is explicitly identified with the Messianic, because of its total passing away. But this "nature" is certainly not the cosmology of ancient Greek *physis* (i.e., nature). Benjamin does not deny the cyclical harmony of teleological completion in, for example, Aristotelian *physis*. He simply insists on thinking the co-extension of this harmony with the anomie of theology, of the "total passing away" of its natural destruction.[39] Before it settles into institutionalized religious doctrines (fallen nature, original sin, which are mainly Christian), and even when it does so, theocracy always occurs as this "eternal downfall." This becomes clear in the politically charged third paragraph.

We learn in the first sentence that to "strive after such passing" is a political task. But we learned before we came to this clause in the last sentence that such passing is religious and Messianic, and therefore has "no political meaning." What kind of politics can this be then? As the last clause of the last sentence makes clear, it is a politics that undoes its own powers, institutions, and histories. It is a politics that can always irrupt at moments when existing sovereign institutions, in the midst of perceived and promoted crises, proclaim the "eternal downfall" of life as *the* legitimating object and jurisdiction of *their* decisions on exceptional cases. And it is a politics not by name or identity (a movement, a raised consciousness, etc.), but only by the immense power of its indirect effect – recall, its meaning is theological, *never* political. What is this indirect effect? It is "nihilism" as such, but in what sense?

One should be careful not to conflate Benjamin's sense of nihilism here with Nietzsche's. Indeed, it retains the sense of active de-valuation and re-evaluation found in Nietzsche's writings. But as Benjamin carefully adds, this nihilism is "method." In other words, it is never goal or result, and is therefore the essential form-of-life, the way, of eternal downfall and passing. This is an important difference between Benjamin and Nietzsche, because Benjamin discovered in theology, and its religious life, what Nietzsche could only see as rancorous decadence. We must say that on the question of religious nihilism, it is Benjamin and not Nietzsche whose meditations are untimely. He saw how nihilism is not simply the historical culmination of theological *ressentiment*, of a nay-saying to life. As method, as pure means rather than goals, theological nihilism is rather a nay-saying to a specific historical form of life: the power over life that claims, especially in the emergency situation, to decide and dictate life's form and existence, namely, the institutions of sovereign decision.

As an ending to this section of our study, the point needs to be explicitly asserted that Benjamin was not a religious thinker, but in no way was he a secular scholar of the theological either, even though he was an assimilated Jew, and most likely an atheist. This for the simple reason that secularism (even in its most democratic forms) is precisely the way in which sovereignty retains its decisive power over life without being accountable to its religious origins. This was precisely how Schmitt could remain both a devoutly religious scholar (a Catholic) and a dominant legal theoretician of strong sovereign, secular government. Benjamin understood this about figures such as Schmitt, and, in a small but monumental gesture, he reveals that the power secular government appropriates from theological symbols is not just decisions on the exception, but the exceptional undoing of this power of decision itself.[40] But how does this ancient theological power to *undo* not only persist, but also recur through history, even and especially, in non-religious times? This explanation will be attempted in the concluding remarks that follow, through a return to the image of Paul's transfiguration. This return, however, will entail a repetition of this transfiguring image as accomplished by both Benjamin and Agamben, with a view to an obscure politics that is most contemporary, that is the contemporary itself *as* obscurity.

Katargein, or Living the *Anomie* of the Legal-Political

In the past decade and a half, no scholar has done more to uncover the repetition of Paul's Messianic transfiguration in Benjamin's work than Giorgio Agamben. More precisely, Agamben's work reveals the recurrence of Paul in Benjamin's encounter with Schmitt's state of exception thesis. He demonstrates persuasively that, in the last writings of his life, "Theses on the Philosophy of History," Thesis II, Benjamin repeats Paul's messianic announcement (see our opening quotation from Paul's 2 Corinthians) of the "now-time" by italicizing the word *"weak"* in the following last sentences of his second Thesis: "Our coming was expected on earth. Like every generation that preceded us, we have been endowed with a *weak* Messianic power, a power to which the past has a claim. That power cannot be settled cheaply. Historical materialists are aware of that."[41] Who are those of the past that have a claim to this weak Messianic power, who have expected our coming on earth? Is it those that history shows were unjustly made exceptions of, robbed of their eternal downfall, and today justified as victims of historical and political injustices? Is it those today to whom leaders and sovereign states offer apologies? It *is* also them no doubt that expected us, but "them" as remnants of those who never made, and will never make, the registers of historical-political dynamics. Why? Because these latter destroyed lives were not simply those excepted from human civility, they were and *are* the lives excluded, stripped bare of form to an anomic existence, but then included in this bare condition as the founding moments of the institutions of historical-political dynamics themselves. These lives were not simply silenced. Rather they *are* the obscure silence upon which the legal-political regimes of history are built. This is what it means to be an exceptional case, constituted as such for the power of sovereign decision. An example is in order.

At a dramatic moment of the *Origin of German Tragic Drama*, a moment recalled with a stark difference in 1956 by Schmitt in his *Hamlet or Hecuba: The Intrusion of the Time into Play*, Benjamin explores the anomic condition of perhaps, up to that time, *the* exceptional case upon which the history of sovereign power built its Kingdoms.[42] He sets it up, however, with a preceding discussion, with citations, of Schmitt's state of exception (he uses "emergency" as well) thesis in *Political Theology*. The exceptional case in which this discussion culminates is none other than the figure of woman, especially feminine character, in the Baroque Trauerspiels (German mourning plays). Women in these plays regularly appear as silenced victims in the tumults of states of emergency. In the political theology of their time, the politics of the patriarchal virtue of "chastity" is brought to bear on their bodies by legal-political regimes (including the family) deciding exceptional cases.[43] At best, the political recompense for feminine defences of chastity was martyrdom.

Let us remind ourselves that chastity, like martyrdom, is a theological symbol, but long appropriated by the legal-political regimes of history. That these symbols stay the same when transmitted from the first to the second is what Benjamin seriously questions. And as we have seen in this study, that sovereign concepts simply supersede the power of their theological origins is something that Benjamin questions even more seriously. This is why he demonstrates, at the heart of an elaboration of Schmitt's thesis, that the feminine image of the demise of these women in a "state of emergency" actually reveals an anomic difference not just in chastity, but in martyrdom as well. The chaste woman appears not as the purity and innocence of body and soul, not as a life born into the world to be protected (and therefore stamped with guilt) and justified, but as the stoic technique of "physical asceticism" in the midst of sovereign destruction. This is why Benjamin calls this theological chastity an "anti-historical creation."[44] Similarly, the martyring of this chastity cannot be contained in the built-up narratives of transcendent causes – nation, King/Queen, and God – as in the national myths of sovereign authority. Like chastity, martyrdom cannot be reduced to its religious conceptions, for both reflect those *non-religious* experiences upon which religions build their theologies, like Paul's three days. This is why, for Benjamin, the martyr, especially these feminine martyrs, evokes the immanent images of suffering and destruction against any narrative of transcendence.[45] The power of this image is precisely that in the immanence of their destroyed lives emerge the images of unjustifiable deaths – *not* deaths or lives, importantly, needing justification, but destroyed lives that did not, and should never have had to, live *for* historical and political justification. These are lives living for nothing more and nothing less than the happiness of their *own* downfall. They are the images of the living *anomie* in the historical dynamic.

In his *The Time That Remains*, Agamben returns to a recurring theological term in Paul's letters, whose theme he argues is repeated in Benjamin's Thesis II: *"weak"* Messianic power.[46] The term, which is repeated at least twenty-six times in Paul's letters, is "katargein."[47] It is the Greek verb Paul uses for a form-of-life, a living regime that ensues from the messianic event. It means to de-activate and/or un-work the works of the world ("cast off the works of darkness") after the halting experience of the Messianic event. This un-working is not direct destruction or subjective violence, but a far more potent, quiet withdrawal within the acts that sustain works. Such a politics is therefore not counter-action, or simply a refusal to act in accordance with institutional norms, but a purifying normative dissolution, an emptying from within acts. Agamben cites the ancient Greek term Paul uses in conjunction with *katargein*, *energeia*, which means the unity of being and act, to *be* in *act*. This is what withdraws in the most anomic moments of institutions, in the very repetitions of acts so essential to the norms of historical institutions.[48]

In a recent work Agamben engages in a genealogy of the concept of the contemporary, and, linking Paul and Benjamin, paints an image of contemporary politics *as* encounters with the obscure, lapsed, and anomic shadows of our present, but not to recollect the "true" lessons of our past. It is the obscure politics, rather, of a transmission of the images of the past, of its living anomie, in the faint, obscure light of the most illuminating moments of our present. Let us end with Agamben's thought-provoking account of what it means to be "contemporary" today: "To be contemporary signifies, in this sense, to return to a present in which we have never been."[49] Is this not what Benjamin meant when he wrote to us in his last days that we, those here today who have been expected on earth, are endowed with a *"weak* Messianic power,"* a power to which the past has a claim, and which we must never settle cheaply.

NOTES

1 Carl Schmitt, *Political Theology: Four Chapters on the Concept of Sovereignty*, trans. George Schwab (Cambridge, MA: MIT Press, 1985), 36. Walter Benjamin, *The Origin of German Tragic Drama*, trans. John Osborne (London: Verso, 1998), 235. H.G. May and B.M. Metzger, eds., *The Oxford Annotated Bible Revised Standard Version* (New York: Oxford University Press, 1962), 2 Corinthians 12:9–10. Referred to henceforth as *The Oxford Annotated Bible*, 1962. For an insightful account of St Paul's relation to theology and theocracy, see Frederick R. Dalmayer's important opening essay in this volume. Subsequent references will be made to these editions.

2 Schmitt, *Political Theology*, 6.

3 Ibid. 14. His exact expression here is that in the decision on the exception, the political-legal order "suspends-itself."

4 Schmitt devoted an entire book to what he viewed as the essential relation between sovereign decision and the governing myths of the state. Focusing on Hobbes's founding myth of the Leviathan, he describes it as "the zenith of sovereign power that brings about the unity of religion and politics." This unity is exactly what Benjamin called into question in his *Origin*

of German Tragic Drama. Carl Schmitt, *The Leviathan in the State Theory of Thomas Hobbes: Meaning and Failure of a Political Symbol,* trans. George Schwab and Erna Lifstein (London: Greenwood Press, 1996), 55. This book on the myth of the Leviathan is important not just because of its content. In his continuing research into the Schmitt-Benjamin encounter, Agamben has discovered that Schmitt considered it his direct response to Benjamin's *Origin of German Tragic Drama.* Schmitt published this text originally in 1938 and, as Agamben reveals through Schmitt's private letters, in 1973 was still lamenting that the "response to Benjamin remained unnoticed." Giorgio Agamben, *State of Exception,* trans. Kevin Attel (Chicago: University of Chicago Press, 2005), 52.

5 Ibid., 5. We quote only the gendered use of the pronoun "he" in the opening sentence of *Political Theology,* not simply to alert readers to his patriarchal account of sovereignty. As we will see towards the end of this study, when we examine Benjamin's careful engagement with Schmitt's thesis in the *Origins,* the predominance of the male voice – even when expressed by female sovereigns and/or representatives – is crucial to what Schmitt means by a decision on the "exceptional case."

6 Walter Benjamin, *Illuminations* (New York: Harcourt Brace Jovanovich, Inc., 1968), 254. For now, let us just point out that here, especially in the last chapter ("Theses on the Philosophy of History," generally considered his last writings before he took his life), *"weak"* [italics Benjamin's] is in fact defined as a "Messianic power." Ibid.

7 Ibid., 253. It is important to note here in the first of the "Theses," that it is "theology" and not "political theology" that is deformed like a "little hunchback," kept "hidden" below but secretly pulling the strings of the puppet master–chess player: the hunchback *is* theology, "which today, as we know, is wizened and has to be kept out of sight." Ibid.

8 Walter Benjamin, *Reflections,* trans. Edmund Jephcott (New York: Harcourt Brace Jovanovich, 1978), 312. One should keep in mind here the title of the short fragment in which Benjamin refers to this "end": "Theological-Political Fragment." In direct contrast to Schmitt's book title and expression, "Political Theology," these four paragraphs covering barely a page and a half (312–13) articulate, in a rare explicit reference to theocracy, a theological politics that brings about this "end."

9 Giorgio Agamben, *Qu'est-ce que le contemporain?* Translated from Italian to French by Maxime Rovere. Paris: Éditions Payot et Rivages, 2008), 40–1. Unless otherwise indicated, all English translations of French texts are the author's.

10 *Oxford Annotated Bible,* 1962, Acts 9:3–4.

11 Ibid., 9:8–9.

12 Let us recall that Paul remains in this anomic, transient state for three days, without seeing, speaking, or eating. It is only when the disciple Anni'as arrives, himself commanded by a vision of the Christ to go to Damascus to save Paul, and lays his hands upon him, that Paul emerges transfigured. It is clear that in these three anomic days, he is no longer the Jewish Saul nor yet the Christian Paul. Ibid., 9:10–19.

13 For this sense of the experience of transience, we are indebted to the work of Daniel C. Fredericks on the meaning(s) of transience in the Hebrew bible and Jewish theology. Focusing on Hebrew terms such as "Qotheleth" ("all is breath") and "hevel" ("the temporary"), especially in Ecclesiastes and in Psalms, Fredericks disputes the conventional view that these terms constitute an early crisis in Jewish theology: i.e., that this life is mere breath, and futile in its temporary endurance. Fredericks shows that these terms in fact affirm the opposite, especially "Hevel" – namely, it is precisely *in* the experience of "Hevel" that life gains meaning and value. Daniel C. Fredericks, *Coping with Transience: Ecclesiastes on Brevity in Life* (Sheffield: Sheffield Academic Press, 1993), 19–20, for the Hebrew meanings of "Qotheleth" and "Hevel"; p. 23, for "Hevel" as moments of meaningfulness and value.

14 *Oxford Annotated Bible*, 1962, Romans 13:11–13.

15 One should not overlook the fundamental indetermination of opposites that Paul uses to introduce the imperative of a "full time now": that the fulfilment of the law (in "love" for Jewish Christians) is in fact its completion, namely, the end of its rule. Ibid., 13:10.

16 In no way should the expression *non-religious* be conflated with the concept of the secular or its complex history in the West. In fact, as we shall see with Benjamin, the non-religious experience of anomie in religious life is exactly what cannot be secularized and politically appropriated by the sovereignty of the nation state.

17 Again, this is Benjamin's reference in the first thesis of "Theses on the Philosophy of History," to theology as a deformed hunchback, kept out of sight but "pulling the strings" of the "puppet chess-master" that is history. Moreover, let us add at this juncture, the hunchback "always wins." Why this is the case, we still need to explore. Benjamin, *Illuminations*, 253.

18 The reference is to a text of 1956 in which Schmitt explicitly addresses the importance of Benjamin's work on seventeenth-century sovereignty – i.e., *Hamlet or Hecuba: The Irruption of the Time into Play* (see the next endnote).

19 The 1938 text is again the book on the myth of the Leviathan in Hobbes, which, as Agamben has discovered (see endnote 4), Schmitt considered an "unnoticed" response to Benjamin's work on the crisis of sovereignty

in Baroque dramatic art. In this text he refines the concept of decision on the exceptional case into a "concrete situation "calling for the "assumption of emergency action" by sovereign government. Schmitt, *The Leviathan in the State Theory of Thomas* Hobbes, 83. In 1956, perhaps still haunted by this lack of notice and no doubt aware of the first publication of Benjamin's collected works in 1955, Schmitt publishes his most explicit response to Benjamin, mentioning the latter's *Origins of German Tragic Drama* as one of the few important works on the topics of aesthetics and sovereign rule. Here, arguing that the most important works of drama retain their brilliance because they reflect the crises and entry of their "time" into artistic creation, he defends, against Benjamin's *Origin*, the view that Hamlet is a new and most "un-Christian" character facing an unprecedented crisis of sovereign succession. And he includes, as a second appendix, an essay entitled "On the Barbaric Character of Shakespeare's Drama: Of *The Origin of the German Tragic Play* by Walter Benjamin," in Carl Schmitt, *Hamlet or Hecuba: The Irruption of the Time into Play*, trans. Simona Draghici (Corvalis, OR: Plutarch Press, 2006); 8, for the reference to the importance of Benjamin's *Origins*, 38, for the refinement of the decision into "historical time" that irrupts into play.

20 Weber shows that Benjamin takes exception to the decision from within Schmitt's own thesis on the exceptional case (to the latter's discomfort, no doubt), for the simple reason that they both share a "strong appreciation" for the extreme case. Samuel Weber, "Taking Exception to Decision: Walter Benjamin and Carl Schmitt," *Diacritics* 22.3/4 (1992): 6–8. In Weber's translation of Benjamin's carefully worded letter to Schmitt (of December 1930), alerting the latter to the arrival of his *Origin* and expressing "special admiration," Benjamin even presents his radically opposed thesis on the exception – shows its co-extension with Schmitt's thesis, we might say – in the form of a debt: "You will very quickly recognize how much my book is indebted to you for its presentation of the doctrine of sovereignty in the seventeenth century," 5.

21 Benjamin, *Reflections*, 313.

22 Weber, "Taking Exception to Decision," 5.

23 See Benjamin, "Critique of Violence," in *Reflections*, 282, for the first explicit reference in his work to the state's use of "emergency measures" when it consolidates the "mythical violence" of its law. For the insight that the encounter dates back to 1921, in the journal *Archiv*, and not 1930, as Benjamin's letter to Schmitt might lead some to believe, we rely on Agamben's original research. Agamben, *State of Exception*, 53. The point here is not simply to discern the accurate date of their encounter, but to

show, as Agamben makes clear, that Schmitt is engaged with Benjamin's critique just before and during the publication of his masterwork on the state of exception, his *Political Theology* of 1922. For an earlier work by the author of this study exploring the significance of this "divine violence," see Herminio Meireles Teixeira, "The State of Exception, Divine Violence, and Peace: Walter Benjamin's Lesson," in *The Question of Peace in Modern Political Thought*, ed. Toivo Koivukoski and David Edward Tabachnick (Waterloo, ON: Wilfrid Laurier University Press, 2015), 199–222.

24 Peter Demetz, for example, the author of the "Introduction," and editor of the collection assembled in *Reflections*, cannot confirm that the fragment was written in 1920–1. He only surmises that it is likely the case, and places the fragment in the fourth section of the book with the two writings that he can confirm were published in 1921: the "Critique of Violence" and "Fate and Character." As far as its publication goes, Demetz shows that it did not appear publicly until the posthumous appearance of Benjamin's first collected works in 1955. Benjamin, *Reflections*, 338.

25 Benjamin, *Illuminations*, 254. This phrase is in "Thesis II" of the "Theses on the Philosophy of History," and occurs just before the reference to a "*weak* Messianic power" [italics Benjamin's].

26 Benjamin, *Reflections*, 312.

27 Peter Simpson also argues (although with different objectives than Benjamin) that secular, liberal democracies are in fact "challenged" by the theological and theocratic traditions that secular liberalism claims to have overcome. Like Benjamin, Simpson is attuned to the theological claims of secularism. See his chapter in this volume.

28 Benjamin, *Illuminations*, 257, "Thesis XIII."

29 Although the literature on Benjamin, and on his encounter with Schmitt, is enormous, scholarly work that deals thematically with his notion of theocracy is at best implicit or altogether absent. The literature, especially since the appearance of a couple of publications by one of the editors of Benjamin's first collected works in 1955, Rolf Tiedemann, essentially divides into three interpretive options: Benjamin is either a scholar of theology seeking political redemption in the traditions of messianic scripture, or a historical materialist combatting the reduction of historical time into progress by recourse to the material histories of theology; or, both of these are operative in his work, but Benjamin failed to dialectically reconcile them into a revolutionary political ethic. This last option is Tiedemann's. Rolf Tiedemann, "Historical Materialism or Political Messianism: An Interpretation of the Theses 'On the Concept of History,'" in *Benjamin: Philosophy, Aesthetics, History*, ed. Gary Smith

(Chicago: University of Chicago Press, 1983). His argument concerning Benjamin's failure at dialectical mediation is most pronounced in an essay appended to his edited edition of Benjamin's *The Arcades Project*. Tiedemann expresses this failure in what he believes to be incontrovertible historical fact: Benjamin's puppet in thesis I, which he calls "historical materialism" and is always "supposed to win," has in fact hitherto never won – fascism ensued and the exploitations of technological capitalism have only expanded. Rolf Tiedemann, "Dialectics at a Standstill: Approaches to the *Passagen-Werk*," in *The Arcades Project*, trans. Howard Eiland and Kevin McLaughlin (Cambridge, MA: Harvard University Press, 1999), 945. As is evident by now in this study, we do not agree with this interpretation. Though it is easily the most erudite of the three options, it misses or simply ignores Benjamin's theocratic impetus indecipherably at work in any secular politics, including historical materialism. On this question, the French scholar Michael Lowy has contributed a far more persuasive reading of the first thesis than Tiedemann's. He interprets the phrase "the puppet called 'historical materialism' is to win all the time," not as Benjamin's hoped for victory of Marxian historical materialism, but as the immanent victory of messianic time itself, and its mute, deformed dwarf (hidden underneath but "pulling the strings"), as the theology of messianic time, *the* master chess player, upon which the puppet (which is history itself for Benjamin, and not just "historical materialism") rests and depends. The next phrase, which Lowy understood so well, is the crucial qualifier and caution to historical materialists and Marxists in general: "It [the puppet 'called historical materialism'] can be a match for anyone *if* [italics ours] it enlists the services of theology." Although it carries out the chess moves, the victory belongs not to the puppet ("historical materialism") but to the "wizened" dwarf (theology). Michael Lowy, *Walter Benjamin: Avertissement d'incendie: Une lecture des thèses "Sur le concept d'histoire"* (Paris: Éditions d'éclat, 2001), 39. Lowy adds, against Tiedemann, that theology may be deformed and out of sight, but this "dwarf is alive and active." Ibid.

But even Lowy misses Benjamin's appeal to theocratic power, to the messianic power of co-extension and indetermination, when he criticizes Agamben for situating Benjamin's idea of messianic time (the "jeitztzeit," the now time, of Thesis XIV) in a Christian source such as Paul's Letter to the Romans. In a footnote to his interpretation of Thesis XIV, Lowy simply contests Agamben's recourse to Christian theology by claiming that Benjamin's theological writings, even their references to Christian themes such as the "Antichrist," are informed above all by Jewish, messianic theology. Again, what is lost here, is the theocracy of Paul's immanent transfiguration, where, in the flashing moment, he is neither Jewish nor Christian, no longer Saul but not yet Paul (see endnote 12). Ibid., 129.

Concerning the first two interpretive options – the theology of messianic politics, or the historical materialism of messianic theology – a careful but by no means exhaustive review reveals admirable works exposing the admixture and importance of both theology and historical materialism in Benjamin's work. But this admixture as the anomic indetermination of both, what Benjamin calls theocracy, remains absent or implicit at best. Though their co-determination is generally recognized, studies still privilege one or the other. For example, McQuillan understands the significance of the "real state of emergency" (Thesis VIII), but, wrongly, cites Agamben as support for his view that such a state is essentially "a political concept." We will see shortly in one of Agamben's most recent publications on St Paul and Benjamin why this view is manifestly wrong. Colin McQuillan, "The Real State of Emergency: Agamben on Benjamin and Schmitt," *Studies in Social and Political Thought* 18 (2011): 97. In top journals with "special issues" on Benjamin, Schmitt, and/or the Schmitt-Benjamin encounter, we find a similar absence of Benjamin's theocracy: see the "Special Walter Benjamin Issue," *New German Critique* no. 17 (1979); and another "Special Issue on Walter Benjamin" twenty-two years later, *New German Critique* no. 83 (2001). For another special issue which focuses mainly on Schmitt with some attention to his encounter with Benjamin – dedicated largely to the impact of Schmitt's *Hamlet or Hecuba: The Irruption of the Time into Play*, which includes a critique of Benjamin's *Origin* in the second appendix – see the "Special Issue on Schmitt's *Hamlet or Hecuba*," *Telos* no. 153 (2010). The issue that comes closest to the theme of theocratic rule, because of its focus on Benjamin's theological allegory of the "angel of history" (Thesis IX on "Angelus Novus"), is "'Angelus Novus': Perspectives on Walter Benjamin," *Critical Inquiry* 25.2 (1999). But this issue, as Mennignhaus explains in the introduction, still only uses the theology of the allegorical angel as a way of shedding "indirect light on Benjamin's reflections on justice" (200). Here, it is Shoshana Felman's "Benjamin's Silence" that best points us in the direction of Benjamin's theocratic politics. She explains that Benjamin's work on historical struggle and political revolution is essentially about theological redemption in the experience of messianic time. They are both "materialist ..., and theological. Redemption is discontinuity, disruption" (211).

Lastly, works that focus on Benjamin as primarily a scholar of theology and scriptural life are mainly informed by at least three works of Gershom

Scholem – the great twentieth-century scholar of Jewish theology, and Benjamin's childhood friend and closest confidant: *Major Trends in Jewish Mysticism* (New York: Schocken Books, 1946); *The Messianic Idea in Judaism* (New York: Schocken Books, 1971); and *Jews and Judaism in Crisis* (New York: Schocken Books, 1976). As Habermas writes of these texts inspired by Benjamin: "Scholem assumes the role of non-polemical, preeminent, and completely uncompromising advocate of that dimension in Benjamin partial to the traditions of Jewish mysticism." Jürgen Habermas, "Consciousness Raising or Redemptive Criticism – The Contemporaneity of Walter Benjamin," *New German Critique* no. 17 (1979): 30. Brian Britt, in what amounts to an attack on Agamben's reading of the Pauline transfiguration in Benjamin, is squarely within Scholem's horizon. It is easy to miss this anomic void that Benjamin calls a "Messianic cessation of happening" (Thesis XVII, *Illuminations*, 262) if one fails to think outside, to think *the* constitutive outside (as Benjamin does), of pre-existing traditions such as the theology of scriptural life, or historical materialism. In what amounts to a dubious accusation, without foundation in Agamben's work, Britt ignores the anomic moments Agamben says recur in Paul and Benjamin, and instead accuses Agamben of elevating "the theory of secularization to a trans-historical, transcultural concept." Brian Britt, "The Schmittian Messiah in Agamben's *The Time That Remains*," *Critical Inquiry* 36.2 (2010): 273. But what best confirms the absence of scholarly attention to Benjamin's enigmatic view of theocracy, is a volume on the concept of political theology within the eminent Blackwell series *The Blackwell Companion to Political Theology*. A key chapter is reserved for the work of Schmitt, but Benjamin is absent, relegated, in a few lines in the Schmitt chapter, to the role of a Marxist leftist (like Kojève), "less concerned with the religious dimension of political theology." Our view of Benjamin's idea of theocracy, of course, argues the *exact* opposite. See Michael Hollerich, "Carl Schmitt," in *The Blackwell Companion to Political Theology*, ed. Peter Scott and William Cavanaugh (Oxford: Blackwell Publishing, 2004), 109. For important earlier work in the English language that examines Benjamin's turn to theology (especially in the figure of the "angel of history") for a different and more critical reading of historical materialism, see the work of Ronald Beiner: Biener, "Walter Benjamin's Philosophy of History," *Political Theory* 12 (1984): 423–34. See also his contribution to this volume dealing with Shaftesbury and the question of the "priestly class."

30 Benjamin, *Illuminations*, 143–4.
31 Benjamin, *Reflections*, 312.
32 Benjamin, *Illuminations*, 255. Thesis VI, for both quotations.

33 Benjamin, *Reflections*, 312. His idea of the "happiness of the profane order" is much akin to what Rousseau would describe as the *sweet sentiment of existence*.

34 Ibid.

35 Ibid.

36 Although he is dealing with Shi'a Islam, and an entirely different theological and historical situation, Houchang Hassan-Yari similarly shows that the theocratic traditions of the Shi'a in fact contest the theological and historical legitimacy of Iran's current "theocratic" regime. See his fascinating chapter in this volume.

37 *Reflections*, 312–13.

38 Ibid., 313.

39 This is why Benjamin includes in the second part of his *Origin of German Tragic Drama*, a short section proclaiming: "The Insignificance of the Influence of Aristotle," ibid., 60–2. The point is not to refute Aristotle; indeed, the German Baroque playwrights of the seventeenth century, as Benjamin shows, wrote within the horizon of Aristotelian tragedy. His point is simply that Aristotelian *physis*, and the tragedies derived from it, is not sufficient to explain the difference of the Christian *Trauerspiel*; namely, how they are not quite tragedies, but mourning plays driven by the image of the dissolution of sovereign powers in the urgencies of the Christian wars of religion.

40 Alan Mittleman gives us insight into a similar power to *undo* (though he does not use this word) the institutional power of sovereign decision in the theocratic traditions of Jewish theology – a power to hold the state of Israel accountable to its theology. See his key chapter in this volume.

41 Benjamin, *Illuminations*, 254. For Agamben's argument that one discovers a repetition of Paul's letters in Benjamin's "Theses on the Philosophy of History," especially the second thesis in the original *handexemplar*, calling us to the realization (with European Fascism in full bloom) that we have been endowed with a *"weak* Messianic Power," see: Giorgio Agamben, *Le temps qui reste: Un commentaire de l'Épître aux Romains* (in English, *The Time That Remains: A Commentary on Paul's Epistle to the Romans*), trans. to French by Judith Revel (Paris: Payot et Rivages, 2000), 232–6.

42 In the second appendix to his *Hamlet or Hecuba*, his only published work in which he deals (in just six pages) not only with Benjamin but with this section of the *Origin* in which Benjamin critiques the decision on the exceptional case by reference to these Baroque "feminine" characters, Schmitt directly ignores Benjamin's study of a feminine anomic form-of-life, and focuses on his defence of Hamlet as an emerging non-theological,

"un-Christian," figure who is trying to decide on the "emergency situation" of the crisis of sovereign succession. But feminine anomie is still very indirectly present, obscurely present even, in Schmitt's need to dispense with Benjamin's return to theological motifs. Ibid., 51–6.

43 See Benjamin, *The Origin of German Tragic Drama*, 65–74 for the engagement with Schmitt's state of exception thesis (see his endnote no. 14 as well); 73–4 for the discussion of martyrdom, chastity, and feminine character in Baroque Trauerspiels.

44 Ibid., 74.

45 Ibid., 73.

46 Again, see Dallmayr's opening essay on St Paul in this volume.

47 Agamben, *The Time That Remains*, 164.

48 Agamben explains it as the repetitions of works whereby katargein seeks no power to make or re-make, no *poieo*, but the power to weaken, to withdraw with the most ascetic discipline, the *energeo* of life. Ibid., 164–6.

49 Giorgio Agamben, *Qu'est-ce que le contemporain?* trans. into French by Maxime Roverre (Paris: Payot et Rivages, 2008), 36.

PART THREE

Responding to the Challenges
of Theocracy

10 Theocracy's Challenge

PETER L.P. SIMPSON

Liberalism's Rise and Fall

The phrase "challenging theocracy" may be taken in two ways, depending on whether "theocracy" is the object or subject of "challenging." When theocracy is taken as object, the phrase means the challenge made to theocracy; when it is taken as subject, the phrase means the challenge that theocracy itself makes. The first way typically connotes hostility to theocracy; the second way typically connotes hostility to modern liberalism. This chapter takes the phrase in the second way, and explores how theocracy is itself a challenge to modern politics. The proper sense and importance of this challenge must be taken largely from ancient thought, since it is not much present in modern.

A feature of ancient Greek and Latin thought, then, is that the divine is an integral part of politics. To begin with, political life and community are understood to be comprehensive. The point is expressly made by Aristotle at the beginning of his *Politics*, where he calls the city, or polis, the comprehensive community that embraces all others. The passage is well known but is worth quoting:

> When the community made up of several villages is complete it is then a city, possessing the limit of every self sufficiency, practically speaking, and though it originates for the sake of life it exists for the sake of good life. Consequently every city is by nature, if, that is, the first communities also are. For the city is the end of those communities and nature is an end, since we say that a thing's nature is the sort of thing it is when its generation has been completed (as in the case of a human being, a horse, or a house). Further, that for the sake of which something is, or its end, is best and self

sufficiency is both an end and best ... By nature, then, the drive towards such a community exists in everyone; but the first to set one up is responsible for very great goods. For as human beings are the best of all animals when perfected, so they are the worst when divorced from law and right.[1]

As this quotation makes clear, the city is comprehensive because it is directed to the comprehensive end of human life, the good or happy life. By contrast, the modern or liberal understanding of politics understands the political not to be comprehensive but to be a neutral space that stands aside from questions of happiness and the good life. Instead, it guarantees to all the pursuit of their own vision of happiness. It is neutral because it lays down no single view of happiness and because it uses its coercive power to prevent any individuals or groups from imposing on others a view of happiness they do not share.

Politics in the modern world, therefore, is fundamentally different from politics in the pre-modern world (and indeed in the modern non-liberal world). A key instance of this difference is the so-called separation of church and state in modern politics. There was no such separation in the ancient world, or now in the non-liberal world; otherwise, the political could not be the comprehensive community pursuing the comprehensive good.

That the ancient worlds of Greece and Rome understood politics as comprehensive is proved not only by Aristotle in the passage already quoted, but also by Plato in his *Republic* and *Laws* and by Cicero in his own works of the same names. St Augustine, often regarded as the last of the ancients and the first of the medievals, encapsulates the same idea in his description of the two cities: the city of man and the city of God. Both are created by a supreme love, a love focused on rival visions of happiness, each of which is universal and exclusive.[2] Each of them too is religious or theological, for each calls on its God or gods for guidance and help, and each has its worship and its sacrifices. One could as easily prove the same from Greek and Roman poetry and history, where the presence of the gods and their role in securing human happiness and punishing human wickedness is ubiquitous.

But we need not confine ourselves to the Greeks and Romans in illustration. What we know of the worlds of the ancient Persians and Egyptians and Germans and Gauls and Britons, or of the ancient Indians or Chinese or Scythians, or of the Incas and Aztecs and Mayas or other Pre-Columbian nations in the Americas, proves the same.[3] All had their public gods and their public worship and sacrifices, which to deny was to deny the being and life of the community. The still existing Aborigines in Australia or tribes in Africa or in the multifarious Pacific islands give further evidence, as do modern Islamic nations. Communist countries, past and present, are again examples, even if their "gods" are not supernatural beings but a comprehensive ideology and a "dear" leader who upholds it.

In the light of such facts the modern world, with its neutrality and separation of church and state, appears to be a rare and novel exception. Never was there a politics of this sort before. We pride ourselves, of course, on this achievement, and consider our modern and liberal world a remarkable advance in human civilization. It is the most signal proof of our superiority over previous ages and previous thought.

Or so we tell ourselves. But novelty is no guarantee of truth, and the rareness of a discovery may be as much a sign that we have gone wrong as that we have gone right. Let us therefore step back a little and reconsider the question that modern thought has so firmly settled in its own favour. Is a separation of state and church, or of state and visions of the good life and happiness, an advance and improvement or not?

A first clue here is that liberalism, in its own self-understanding, agrees with a key thesis of theocratic or non-liberal regimes. For it agrees with ancient Greek and Latin thinkers, and with just about every tradition of religious and philosophical reflection, that man's natural drive is towards comprehensive happiness, for self and family and friends. The formation of larger communities arises from this drive. The first objects of the drive may well be material security and comfort, but they are not the only objects or the ones most passionately pursued. The theft of whole countries and peoples by tyrants is worse than the theft of bread or clothes by the impoverished, and is undertaken by men who, in material terms, would seem to have all they want. Aristotle illustrates the point with Jason of Pherae, of whom he says, "That is perhaps why Jason said he was hungry when he was not being tyrant, because he did not know how to be a private citizen."[4] Stalin and Mao are striking modern examples, since neither was in material need, yet both seized and clung onto power with unrelenting grip. For them happiness and success was political mastery, such political mastery as would enable them, by sheer will and force, to destroy the old and establish the new and so win lasting fame as founders.

The phenomenon of tyranny tells us something important about mankind: a passion for more that seems to have no limit. The passion can be suppressed or rendered inoperative, at least for a time, by need and the necessity to make a living. But set a man loose from such impediments and he will devote himself to pursuit of unfettered happiness, which he will find, as all men have found, in wealth or pleasure or power or fame or, less often, virtue and wisdom. There is no sure way to control this passion for more. Once let loose, it will not stop. Liberalism, indeed, tries to stop it, but the liberal solution is a solution only by way of paradox: satisfy the human passion for more by not satisfying it; leave open to all the means to find their own way to satisfy it, but on one condition, which is to be imposed by force, that no one's pursuit interferes with or prevents the pursuit of anyone else. Tame the beast of infinite passion by the equal coercion of all. Make such coercion, and not infinite pursuit, the object and measure of politics. Overthrow the ancient tradition of political thought, which aimed politics at the comprehensive good of happiness. Replace it with the novelty of liberalism, which aims politics at securing for all the pursuit of their own vision of happiness in conditions of peace guaranteed by the power of the modern state.

Whether this liberal solution works, in theory or practice, is a disputed question. But what is beyond dispute is that this solution, even if it eschews concern with the comprehensive good, has to strive for comprehensiveness in another way. To secure freedom for all to pursue the comprehensive good that each prefers, the state must have, not just coercive force, but the monopoly of it.[5] There must be no other centres of coercion around that could oppose or deny the coercion of the state. If there were, and if these centres used their coercion to impose one comprehensive vision of the good, the liberal solution would collapse. Liberalism has to replace the politics of comprehensive good with the politics of comprehensive coercion.

Liberalism is paradoxical in a further way. The paradox concerns the so-called separation of church and state. Such a separation is said to be guaranteed by the First Amendment to the US Constitution, which forbids Congress to make an establishment of religion. We need not quarrel about whether this "disestablishment" clause is rightly described as a separation of church and state. Consider only that a separation of church and state is not a separation of church and society. The latter separation is not in the US Constitution or in US society, or indeed in society in any state, liberal or otherwise. Yet liberal theorists (one thinks naturally of Rawls and his notion of public reason)[6] want to enforce something like the latter separation by forbidding the introduction of religious beliefs into certain acts that seem clearly to belong to society. Particular instances would be voting and canvassing and political advocacy. Individuals are required by Rawlsian liberal theory to put their religious convictions aside when they enter the polling booth or canvass their neighbours or ascend the rostrum. Liberal theorists, to be sure, have grounds for making such a requirement, but the requirement itself enforces a separation of church and society, not a separation of church and state.

There is in liberal thought a sort of "separation-creep." Religion is to be separated, not just from the state, but from any activity of society that affects the state. One has visions of religious buildings and symbols being banished from cities and towns, and of religious devotees being forced to practise their religious rites in private dwellings or isolated communities. Indeed, one is at a loss here where to draw the line. There are few things that anyone does which will not in some way affect the larger community and which therefore may not, in some case or by some happenstance, affect the workings of the state too. Such "separation-creep" against religion threatens to become total banishment of religion.

The despotism here seems evident, and it has not, at least in recent times, been rare. China and the old Soviet Union engaged in outright suppression and banishment of religion, and North Korea, it seems, still does. But these communist countries had their own religion, the religion (or "anti-religious" religion if you will) of communism itself, to take the place of the religions they banished. They behaved not unlike ancient cities and medieval kingdoms, where those who openly opposed or threatened the public religion were marginalized or deprived of civil rights or, where necessary, imprisoned, exiled, or killed. But if liberal theory's "separation-creep" is going in the same direction, what can be said for liberalism and its separation of church and state that cannot be said for almost any political system at any time anywhere? All will suppress, when they can, the religion they oppose and enforce the religion they embrace. Here then is the other paradox. Liberalism asserts a separation of state and religion on the one hand, or asserts a universal opposition to theocracy, and yet on the other hand it drifts, by a creeping separation of society and religion, into the assertion of a like theocracy, a "liberal theocracy"[7] as it were, of its own.

Theocracy's Counter

Perhaps the gains here are greater than the losses. Perhaps, indeed, liberalism's monopoly of coercion is a gain for peace and freedom. Liberalism certainly claims so. But liberalism can only make this claim on the basis of a very particular, and historically very peculiar condition. Liberalism must deny that there is for all men a single comprehensive good or happiness that some could know and others not, or that the political authority could know and individuals not know, or that individuals could only or best know by instruction from some public authority. How can liberalism make this claim without claiming an authority to determine the true nature of happiness that it at the same time denies that it or anyone can have, or at least can publicly have?

Bear in mind that whether happiness is particular to the individual or something universally the same for all, knowable in principle at least to some, is one of the chief points of dispute about happiness, and was already a chief point of dispute in the pre-modern and pre-liberal world. An interesting example is found in the account of Protagoras given by Socrates in Plato's *Theaetetus*.

> For I maintain that the truth is as I have written; each one of us is the measure of the things that are and those that are not; but each person differs immeasurably from every other in just this, that to one person some things appear and are, and to another person other things. And I do not by any means say that wisdom and the wise man do not exist; on the contrary, I say that if bad things appear and are to any one of us, precisely that man is wise who causes a change and makes good things appear and be to him ... And yet, in fact, no one ever made anyone think truly who previously thought falsely, since it is impossible to think that which is not or to think any other things than those which one feels; and these are always true. But I believe that a man who, on account of a bad condition of soul, thinks thoughts akin to that condition, is made by a good condition of soul to think correspondingly good thoughts; and some men, through inexperience, call these appearances true, whereas I call them better than the others, but in no wise truer.[8]

The point, then, is that whatever anyone thinks is right or true is so for him when he thinks it. Socrates' Protagoras only claims the skill by rhetoric (as others do by medicine) to change a person's condition so that he thinks as right things that please or benefit him more than the things he thought before. Protagoras is a sort of political psychologist, as is amusingly illustrated by another image given in Plato's *Republic*.

> Each of these private teachers who work for pay, whom the politicians call sophists and regard as their rivals, inculcates nothing else than these

opinions of the multitude which they opine when they are assembled, and calls this knowledge wisdom. It is as if a man were acquiring the knowledge of the humors and desires of a great strong beast which he had in his keeping, how it is to be approached and touched, and when and by what things it is made most savage or gentle, yes, and the several sounds it is wont to utter on the occasion of each, and again what sounds uttered by another make it tame or fierce, and after mastering this knowledge by living with the creature and by lapse of time should call it wisdom, and should construct thereof a system and art and turn to the teaching of it, knowing nothing in reality about which of these opinions and desires is honorable or base, good or evil, just or unjust, but should apply all these terms to the judgments of the great beast, calling the things that pleased it good, and the things that vexed it bad, having no other account to render of them, but should call what is necessary just and honorable, never having observed how great is the real difference between the necessary and the good, and being incapable of explaining it to another.[9]

A central part of the dispute here is whether happiness is pleasure, the pleasure that each could only know and feel for himself and that another could not determine for him but could only provide him the means to secure. Liberal practice adopts the latter view in this dispute save for adding the qualification that, even were happiness an objective universal, determinable by some who know for others who do not know, yet at least it cannot be so determined by public authority. Only lesser authorities, authorities that are systematically denied by liberalism any possession of or right to coercive power, could make such a determination, and only for those who chose to subject themselves to it; not for those who did not.

But why make this assumption or any assumption like it? Indeed by what right or authority can liberalism make it? De facto it makes the claim by appeal to history, that where the political power takes up an official position on the comprehensive good or happiness and imposes it on the whole community, the result is war and misery. The main proof is the religious wars in Europe that followed the Protestant Reformation.[10] If the political power refrains from such practice, peaceful coexistence between everyone is secured, or at least the chances of it are vastly increased. Again, the main proof is what happened in Europe after the advance of liberal ideas induced political authorities to give up imposing a single vision of the good life.

Part of this appeal to history, and related to it, is the claim that, even if happiness or the comprehensive good is the same for all and knowable in principle, there is always an unavoidable difficulty involved in reaching a correct decision by means of reason and evidence (the so-called burdens of judgment)[11]. The result is that the correctness of the correct answer (if there is one) can never be made so clear to all that the forced imposition of it will not deny them their own use of reason, or will not deny them the opportunity to investigate further, or something else of the sort. In addition, the result of such imposition of the supposed correct answer will, as before, provoke opposition and hostility on the part of those who, despite using reason and evidence with as much care and rigour, have reached a different or no answer.

Now whatever may be true about the above interpretation of history, the claim that liberalism secures peace and lessens war and misery seems false. The twentieth century arguably saw the worst wars in human history, namely, total wars, which, as total, exceeded anything that went before. They exceeded anything in medieval times when wars were subject to a host of checks, as the peace and truce of God imposed by the Church, and not least the incapacity of the political authorities, because they lacked the power of universal coercion, to mobilize everyone and everything for the purpose of fighting the war. Liberalism's appeal to history in support of its claim to superiority as to war and peace is highly dubious, and certainly not strong enough to establish the claim with any compelling evidence. The appeal to the so-called burdens of judgment seems no less dubious. For whether there are such burdens is itself a matter of dispute. Proponents of the presumed correct answer have typically found those who disagreed with them to be unreasonable or prejudiced or invincibly ignorant or the like. Using reason to convince them is a hopeless task. Some people, observed Aristotle wryly, need force, not argument.[12] How is liberalism going to prove the opposite without this supposed proof itself falling foul of the burdens of judgment? The burdens-of-judgment argument is no less subject to the burdens of judgment than any argument about the comprehensive good. To insist on it against naysayers, as liberalism must if it is to make good its claim to rule, liberalism will have to be as dogmatic as, by the burdens-of-judgment argument, it accuses its opponents of being.

So the question remains: by what right does liberalism claim that happiness is not something knowable and universally the same for all, or that, even if it is so knowable and universal, political authority has no business trying to impose it but must leave each free to reach their own decision, and use force only to ensure that no one deprives anyone else of the same freedom? The answer seems to be: by no right at all.

Theocracy's Revenge

The liberal or non-theocratic solution to political life appears self-negating in theory and false in fact. What then about the opposing theocratic view, that political theory does have the right to discern, teach, and impose the truth about the happiness that is universally the same for all? How does it understand and defend itself?

Let us begin with some ancient sources expressive of a more theocratic view of political life and authority, and since right and law and how to understand them seem at the root of the liberalist answer, let us begin with sources about the nature and role of law.

A first source is Cicero:

> The light of reason from the nature of things ... incites to good actions and dissuades from evil ones, and ... does not begin for the first time to be a law when it is drawn up in writing, but from the first moment that it exists. And this existence of moral obligation is co-eternal with that of the divine mind ... Whatever is just is also at all times the true law; nor can this true law either be originated or abrogated by the written forms in which decrees are drawn up ... Let this, therefore, be a fundamental principle in all societies, that the gods are the supreme lords and governors of all things, that all events are directed by their influence, and wisdom, and Divine power; ... that they ... know what sort of person every one really is; that they observe his actions, whether good or bad; ... and that they are sure to make a difference between the good and the wicked ... For when once our minds are confirmed in these views, it will not be difficult to inspire them with true and useful sentiments ... Who will dispute the utility of these sentiments, when he reflects ... how much the sacred rites performed in making treaties tend to assure peace and tranquility; and what numbers of people the fear of divine punishment has reclaimed from a vicious course of life; and how sacred the social rights must be in a society where a firm persuasion obtains the immediate intervention of the immortal gods, both as witnesses and judges of our actions?[13]

> There is a true law, a right reason, conformable to nature, universal, unchangeable, eternal, whose commands urge us to duty, and whose prohibitions restrain us from evil. Whether it enjoins or forbids, the good respect its injunctions, and the wicked treat them with indifference.

This law cannot be contradicted by any other law, and is not liable either to derogation or abrogation ... It is not one thing at Rome and another at Athens; one thing to-day and another to-morrow; but in all times and nations this universal law must for ever reign, eternal and imperishable. It is the sovereign master and emperor of all beings. God himself is its author, – its promulgator, – its enforcer. He who obeys it not, flies from himself, and does violence to the very nature of man.[14]

Cicero stands near the beginnings of the long tradition of legal and political thinking that sets God and his authorship of the principles of right as the foundation of both law and government. William Blackstone stands near the end of the same tradition (and after the intervention of almost 2000 years of Christianity and 1400 of Islam). His celebrated *Commentaries on the Laws of England* were the standard textbook on law during the founding period of the United States and for many decades afterwards.

As God, when he created matter, and endued it with a principle of mobility, established certain rules for the perpetual direction of that motion, so, when he created man, and endued him with free-will to conduct himself in all parts of life, he laid down certain immutable laws of human nature ... These are the eternal immutable laws of good and evil, to which the Creator himself, in all his dispensations, conforms; and which he has enabled human reason to discover, so far as they are necessary for the conduct of human actions. Such, among others, are these principles: that we should live honestly, should hurt nobody, and should render to every one his due; to which three general precepts Justinian has reduced the whole doctrine of law ... The Creator ... has so intimately connected, so inseparably interwoven the laws of eternal justice with the happiness of each individual, that the latter cannot be attained but by observing the former ... The several articles into which [natural law] is branched ... amount to no more than demonstrating that this or that action tends to man's real happiness ... or ... that this or that action is destructive of man's real happiness ... This law of nature, being coeval with mankind, and dictated by God himself, is ... superior in obligation to any other ... No human laws are of any validity, if contrary to this ... But, in order to apply this to the particular exigencies of each individual, it is still necessary to have recourse to reason, whose office it is to discover ... what the law of nature directs in every circumstance of life, by considering what method will tend the most effectually to our own substantial happiness ... [But] divine

Providence … in compassion to the frailty, the imperfection, and the blind-
ness of human reason, hath been pleased, at sundry times and in divers
manners, to discover and enforce its laws by an immediate and direct revelation. The doctrines thus delivered we call the revealed or divine law …
[Its] precepts, when revealed, are found upon comparison to be really a
part of the original law of nature, as they tend in all their consequences to
man's felicity … Upon these two foundations, the law of nature and the
law of revelation, depend all human laws.[15]

Of chief importance here, express in Blackstone and implicit in Cicero,
is the connection between natural law and human perfection and happiness. Law, as well natural as divine, goes together with happiness;
the two are not different or opposed; they are one. To see the connection, one needs but to acknowledge the fundamental natural facts about
human existence and human community, namely, that the end of both
is the fullest realization of happiness possible. Liberal theory agrees on
this point (it would be odd if it did not – the fact is so evident), because
the idea that men pursue happiness, or what they judge to be happiness, as much as possible is part of liberal theory. It is the supposition
(derived from Hobbes and Machiavelli)[16] on which it bases its claim that
the state should have comprehensive coercion at its disposal to ensure
no one can pursue happiness at the expense of others.

Liberalism works by removing the pursuit of happiness from the
competence of the state. Non-liberalisms work by the opposite: putting
this pursuit at the very centre of the state's concern. What differences
thereby result?

The first and most determinative difference is the matter of the gods
or of religion. If the concern with happiness is the object of the state,
and if pursuit of happiness is marked by unquenchable desire to know
it and possess it, the divine comes to the centre of life. Abstracting for
the present from whether a god or gods exist, the idea of them necessarily arises. Human life is as much a story of failure to be happy as of
unwearied pursuit of it. We all want to be happy but few seem to attain
it or to think they have attained it. Even those whom the many admire
as plainly happy – the rich, the beautiful, the famous, the powerful, like
the fabled Sardanapalus[17] – seem often enough to prove they are not.
Their lives cannot be securely preserved from tragedy if only because
they cannot be securely preserved from the effects of chance. The rich
and fabulous lose loved ones as much as the poor and obscure do; they
lose country and fortune too in war and natural disasters; they suffer

disease and mental decay despite ready access to the best doctors and medicines; the years of their life are not longer than those of others; they too must die. Indeed, some of them hasten death by suicide, which is evidence enough that, contrary to popular opinion, wealth and fame and power are no guarantee of happiness.

Here is where the gods enter the picture. They are beings that have what we humans conspicuously lack. They are immune to the miseries and trials of life; they are ageless and remain always in the fullest bloom of health and youth; they are eternal and never die. Most of all, their knowledge and power vastly exceed our own. They know the future and the past, they understand the hidden secrets of nature, they ride the storms and calm the seas, they control earthquakes and volcanoes, they bestow gifts on their favourites, and they punish those they hate.

The crudity of some of these beliefs is plain. Homer's and Hesiod's gods are immortal and surrounded by material bliss, but they are liars, adulterers, and parricides, and they treat humans as playthings for personal and even cruel amusement. The Aztec gods notoriously delighted in human sacrifice. Such supernatural beings seem to be a projection into immortal and painless youth of the baser human passions and give imaginative life to the view that happiness is endless and unimpeded material prosperity and bodily pleasure. Yet if we abstract from the crudity we can form a fair picture of what everyone would call happiness: immortality, eternal health and youth, freedom, pleasure. The more refined would add wisdom and virtue to the mix. But what is clear is that no human life measures up to this standard. For us, happiness, to the extent we enjoy it, is a pale and temporary imitation of what we imagine for the gods.

We need not take the imagination seriously, but we should take seriously the projection of it. If we know anything about this life, we know that happiness in it is rare, fleeting, and ended by death. In fact, if reflection stops there it cannot fail to conclude, as *Ecclesiastes* concluded, and long after him the existentialists, that life is vain and absurd. "Vanity of vanities, saith the Preacher, vanity of vanities; all is vanity ... and striving after wind."[18] How possibly to make sense of the existence of beings whose longing is so in conflict with reality? Even our beloved modern theory of evolution seems silent before such a puzzle:

Move him into the sun –
Gently its touch awoke him once,
At home, whispering of fields half-sown.

Always it woke him, even in France.
Until this morning and this snow.
If anything might rouse him now
The kind old sun will know.
Think how it wakes the seeds –
Woke once the clays of a cold star.
Are limbs, so dear-achieved, are sides,
Full-nerved, still warm, too hard to stir?
Was it for this the clay grew tall?
– O what made fatuous sunbeams toil
To break earth's sleep at all?[19]

The image of deathless gods with youthful bodies and debauched lusts is an old poet's vanity. It does not answer the question of life; it mocks it. The new poet tears apart the mockery. If we were made for such a life, if such a life is happiness, how is it we and the world are so disposed that we can never have it? Life is indeed absurd if there is no better answer than pagan dreams.[20]

Is there a better answer? The philosophers tried to give one. They put virtue and wisdom above debauchery and worldly power. But even they could find no solution to pain, disease, and death.[21] Some, as the ancient Stoics, pretended the wise man could be happy on the rack.[22] But why should the world be such that wise men could end up on the rack at all? Is it too not absurd? Indeed, is this life, however considered, not absurd if death is the end and there is nothing more? But if there is more, what do we know of it? And if we wish to overcome our ignorance, where will we go to find out? Who has died and come back to tell us? And if someone has, how can we be sure he is telling the truth – unless perhaps he is sent by the God who cannot deceive or be deceived? As for the poets, who are full of stories about such things, we know that "poets tell many a lie."[23]

Our ignorance is our greatest misery. The questions we most want answered have no answer and, worse still, the question of how to go about finding an answer has no answer. The hectic life of the man struggling daily to survive, despite its lack of joy, is at least too busy to be wracked by the pain of the question.

We no longer live in a pagan world, whether Greek or Roman, Inca or Chinese. We live rather in a world of religions claiming to be divine revelations: Christianity, Islam, Judaism. A divine revelation professes to answer the questions we cannot answer because it professes to give us God's own knowledge. What man's mind cannot reach by itself, it can receive from God who, in very idea of God as such, knows everything and controls everything – or else he could not be God. These religions do give us answers to our questions, and answers that do in principle satisfy, because they speak of a life after death where, at least for the just, pain is removed, immortality bestowed, and perfect knowledge, with perfect joy in the knowledge, is received by direct vision of God.

Suspend, for a moment, the question of truth. Consider the hypothesis. The revealed religions promise the complete fulfilment of human longing: eternal life with eternal youth and health and beauty, justice and virtue as lauded by the philosophers (not the debased lusts of the poets), an infinite knowledge transcending, because divine, all humanly achieved philosophy and science. Would not such a life be happiness, a happiness beyond our comprehension perhaps, but not beyond our prayers? Without it we have the absurdity of the poets, where men, while wanting the life imagined for the gods, live wretched and mortal; or the absurdity of evolution, which produces creatures who may be fittest to survive but are far from fittest to be happy; or the absurdity of the existentialists, who paint life's grimness in garish colours and bid us embrace it.

The theological challenge is no less than this challenge. Who could prove it false? Who could with confidence assume it false? Who could honestly or sanely refuse it were it true? Why then does our world live as if it were not true, or not politically true? Why embrace a liberal system of politics, which banishes from the public square, as a matter of principle, even the question of its truth? Should this question not rather be the most important question of all in public and in private? What question could be greater? Economic prosperity? But we know prosperity cannot satisfy, because it cannot defeat death. War and world power? But wars bring death and empire as often brings tyranny that ends freedom and perverts morals. We know enough from our political leaders, professed liberals though they be, that they will not stop at lies or torture or war or abuse of science to obtain their goals.

The cure for the thirst after power and empire cannot be success in the attempt, for he who conquers one world will, like fabled Alexander, long to conquer another. Nor is the cure the suppression of the longing, or the coerced limiting of it within the bounds of liberalism's "as far only as you allow others an equal pursuit of their longing, and no further." The poor and weak may obey, because they have to. The great and the mighty will laugh, because they do not have to and scorn such debasing self-denial.[24] The cure is not suppression but transcendence. As Aristotle remarked, one can be happy and do noble and fine things without being lord of earth and sea;[25] and Socrates in Plato's *Republic* cures the temptation to tyranny in Glaucon and Adeimantus, if not also in Thrasymachus, by converting the lust to rule a city first into the desire for justice in founding a city and second into a longing for the philosophic vision of reality outside the cave of life that surpasses every city.[26]

The liberal solution is a failure precisely because it is a confessedly political solution. Liberalism would throw us back politically into ignorance, and of express and settled purpose too, because it forbids the presence in political life of the theological interest and so, by necessity, of any theological solution. But the solution, if there is one, can only be theological; it cannot be one that marginalizes or confines man's longing; it must be one that liberates it by raising it from the material and temporal to the spiritual and eternal. Forget the city of man; look to the city of God. Or rather, refashion the city of man so that it becomes at least the beginning of the city of God.

Do not be deterred by the liberal bogey that theocracy leads to war. The liberal state with its monopoly of coercive authority does not end war but, if anything, increases it by introducing total war. Only something transcendent to the political could tame the political and thereby too the lust for empire, because only something transcendent, or only the empire of the mind and heart, could satisfy human desire. Introduce the theological, therefore, directly into the political community. Do not do so arbitrarily but by concerted study of theological facts, especially the facts, if there are any, of divine revelation. And look seriously for such a revelation and do not assume, by spurious appeal to some burdens of judgment, that there can be no decisive evidence of its existence. Above all, seek what is good in the past moderating effects on politics by theology, and adapt it as possible to present conditions. Be humble too about modern beliefs and practices, and be just in assessing those that preceded modernity.

Consider, then, that modern liberal politics has introduced into communal life a division between state and society. The state is the public sphere and the seat of command and coercive authority over society; society is the private sphere and has no coercive authority; the state is the source and guarantor of civil peace; society is the source of disruption and subversion, needing always to be kept in check by the power of the state. This political theory derives from the state of nature doctrine devised by Hobbes and continued, with modifications, by Locke, Rousseau, Kant, and latterly Rawls.[27] It was in Hobbes already a tyrannical doctrine; it has remained in principle tyrannical ever since, if only because society and the individual are understood to be insatiable for personal gain and need always to be checked by the monopolizing coercion of the state.

The doctrine is false. Society and individuals are largely the source of peace and free activity. Criminality is always present and always a temptation (for men are naturally insatiable), but comparatively rare; most are too busy or too afraid or too morally disciplined to resort to crime and violence, or at least to great crime and violence. The state, by contrast, is largely the source of such crime and violence. It has exclusive access to coercion yet it is in the hands of men who, being men, are no less naturally insatiable than anyone else. The main difference is that these men have unlimited opportunity, because they have exclusive power, to commit crime: to lie, cheat, steal, debauch, kill, and war.

The main desideratum is to tame, not society as the state of nature doctrine supposes, but the state. The chief means to this end is to divide the state so that it is no longer the exclusive possessor of coercive power and public authority. The state exercises coercive power through professional armies and professional police forces; it exercises public authority through controlled means of propaganda and, increasingly, pervasive surveillance. Imitate ancient practice, therefore, and abolish professional armies (or standing armies as they used to be called) and professional police (or armed guards for state officers). Diffuse army and police functions through society, requiring all able-bodied adults to possess and be practised in the use of weapons, after the manner still followed by the Swiss. Make the keeping of the peace, the search and apprehension of the criminal (especially the criminal among state officers), a matter first and foremost of societal activity. Do the same again with educational, medical, economic, and charitable functions.

Society, nevertheless, should not be idolized, as if it was necessarily free of crime and corruption. State officers, after all, come from society, and bring their criminality or their proneness to it along with them. Social life may naturally tend to the just and the peaceful, but the tendency is neither invincible nor infallible. It can be corrupted if the base element in each man is not constantly guarded against and, especially during youth, not constantly corrected. Coercion is a weak and brute corrective and serves rather to restrain the already corrupt than to prevent their emergence in the first place. It can do little more than impose restraint; reform of mind and heart is largely beyond it.[28]

So society, besides a force of coercion over it (which is all the state of nature doctrine understands and all the liberal state provides), needs a force of moral teaching within it. The family is the first moral teacher and, at the beginning of life, always the strongest. But the family will not be moral if the parents are not, and the parents will not be moral if, after the training first provided by their parents, they have received no training in later years. Moral teaching needs a social and not just a familial teacher. In all previous ages, up to and still largely including our own, this teacher has been religion, and a religion that was as much a public as a private authority. The merely political, as the modern state, collapses into crude coercion unless it is supplemented by, even subordinated to, the religious. Or, to speak in older terms, communal life embraces a temporal authority and a spiritual authority. The two are different but, when in good condition, naturally function as one. The unity of the political sought and secured in modern thought and practice by the monopoly of coercion by the state is sought and secured in older thought and practice by diffusing coercion throughout society and by having a public and religious moral authority teaching spiritual truths in addition to a secular authority managing temporal concerns.

Consider Cicero again:

> We possess a certain consanguinity, and kindred, and fellowship with the heavenly powers. And among all the varieties of animals, there is not one except man which retains any idea of the Divinity. And among men themselves, there is no nation so savage and ferocious as not to admit the necessity of believing in a God, however ignorant they may be what sort of God they ought to believe in. From whence we conclude that every man must recognize a Deity, who has any recollection and knowledge of his own origin.
>
> Now, the law of virtue is the same in God and man, and in no other disposition besides them. This virtue is nothing else than a nature perfect in itself, and wrought up to the most consummate excellence. There exists, therefore, a similitude between God and man.[29]

The divine and human authorities, though different in idea, have often enough been in the hands of the same persons, especially in the case of kings, who were high priests for their people as well as temporal masters. But even then, the unity was incomplete. Lesser priests and religious ministers, while officially acknowledged, did not have temporal power. Lesser political functionaries, while religiously supported, did not have priestly power. The spiritual or religious power was always implicitly admitted to be different and differently instituted.[30] The reason is not far to seek. The spiritual power deals with the divine, which is not under human control. The temporal power deals with the material, which is under human control – or is so except as the divine may intervene in human affairs and assist or thwart human plans and actions.

The exception is significant. It determines the principle of priority between the two powers in case of overlap or conflict. The spiritual power is always superior and always has the final say. Pagan practice in the old and new worlds makes the point plain. The secular power cannot proceed to judgment or war or even agricultural management if the spiritual interposes its veto and declares the gods not pleased or propitious. The practice of the Muslim, Christian, and Jewish worlds has not been dissimilar. One need only cite the famous events at Canossa when the pope compelled the emperor to submit; or the occasions when the Muslim authorities declared a fetva or fatwah to depose a sultan; or the times too when the Hebrew prophets confronted and opposed the kings of Israel and Judah.

In medieval Christendom we have the doctrine of the two swords, where the temporal power of the emperor was one sword and the spiritual power of the Church another.[31] The temporal power supported the spiritual; the spiritual gave moral commands to and in support of the temporal; in cases of conflict the spiritual claimed superiority. But most of all, the very division of rule into temporal and spiritual, and the ultimate superiority of the spiritual, gave an orientation to the whole focused on the divine and eternal and not on the human and temporal. It was Machiavelli who, in Western thought, seems first to have directed political thinking against the very idea and existence of a spiritual power contrasted with the temporal one. Liberalism, or the doctrine that the spiritual has no special political rights and in particular no rights of coercion, takes its main inspiration from Machiavelli.[32] The demotion of the spiritual to the private sphere and the glorification of the secular and temporal as alone necessary and legitimate are integral to the vision of political power that emerges from Machiavelli or is stimulated by his thought.

Machiavelli is notorious for giving unlimited final authority to the secular power and even for saying that, in the service of temporal success, the secular power may commit any crime, or rather that crime committed by the secular power for the preservation of secular power is no crime. The modern world in all its political forms, liberal, social-ist, communist, or fascist, apotheosizes the secular power and makes it absolute, especially over against the spiritual. Gone are the checks and balances that the division between a power spiritual and a power temporal imposed on communal life. The spiritual authority has lost all power of veto or command over the temporal, and not only coercive power but also, no less significantly, moral power. The truce and peace of God formerly imposed by the Church on armed antagonists no lon-ger exist; the right of the community to resist or depose unjust rulers is observed only in the breach; the authority to absolve peoples of obe-dience to tyrannical or impious governments, always claimed by the spiritual power if seldom exercised or followed even when exercised, is barely now a memory.

No doubt the spiritual power sometimes overreached itself, but the very existence of it imposed an independent check on secular rule. Such check has long been removed and nothing has taken its place, for the proclaimed right of the people to vote out a government is more fanci-ful than real, and is manipulated by gerrymandering and propaganda[33] and, where necessary or even where not necessary, by bribery and fraud. The fear of ancient thinkers, philosophers and theologians, that a political rule merely temporal and without orientation to something higher than this world's goods would inevitably become a tyranny,[34] is no longer understood let alone shared. Yet who can look at political rule in its concrete reality in the modern world and not suspect that the fear was sane and genuine and that returning to the means to counter the fear, especially the division of power into temporal and spiritual, is as needed now as before?

The modern world has prided itself on getting rid of a theological power capable of commanding and restraining the political. Its much-touted claim is that we have thereby secured for ourselves a freedom unknown and inconceivable by a past under the deadening thrall of priests. But pride, as they say, goeth before a fall.[35] Few things in human life can be trusted pure and left alone without external check and restraint. Most men are no more angels than they are devils; they oscillate between the two. To ensure that none become devils, or that any who do can never hold power unchecked, the universal practice of the pre-modern world, pagan or Christian or something else, where the temporal power exercised political authority in necessary concert, peaceful or conflicted, with the spiritual power, needs to be revived. One way or another theocracy will have its revenge.

NOTES

1 *Politics*, 1252b27–1253a1, 29–33. *The Politics of Aristotle*, trans. Peter Simpson (Chapel Hill: University of North Carolina Press, 1997).
2 Augustine, *City of God*, 14.28.
3 For sources see, for example, Herodotus's *Histories*; Caesar's *Gallic War*; Tacitus's *Germania* and *Agricola*; Joseph Needham, *Science and Civilization in China*, vol. 1 (Cambridge: Cambridge University Press, 1954); Joseph de Acosta, *Historia Natural y Moral de las Indias* (Mexico: Fondo de Cultura Economica, 2006); Bartolomé de las Casas, *Historia de las Indias* (Mexico: Fondo de Cultura Economica, 1986).
4 *Politics*, 3.4.1277a23–5. Translation in Simpson, *Politics of Aristotle*.
5 The point is first made by Weber. Max Weber, *Politics as a Vocation*, trans. H.H. Gerth and C. Wright Mills (Philadelphia: Fortress Press, 1965), 2.
6 John Rawls, *Political Liberalism* (New York: Columbia University Press, 1996), lecture VI.
7 The invented term of "liberal theocracy" here is used provocatively, to highlight the self-contradictory and despotic character of modern liberalism, namely, that, despite protestations to the contrary, liberalism seeks to impose its own comprehensive vision on society and, to this extent, to do what theocracies do. The term is not adapted from the term political theology or the thinkers associated with that title. Their project is of a specific kind to which the distinction between spiritual and temporal power, discussed and endorsed later in this chapter, seems opposed. See, for example, Peter Scott and William T. Cavanaugh, eds, *The Blackwell Companion to Political Theology* (Oxford, UK: Blackwell, 2004).
8 Plato, *Theaetetus*, 166–7. Harold N. Fowler, *Plato in Twelve Volumes*, vol. 12 (Cambridge, MA: Harvard University Press, 1921).
9 Plato, *Republic*, 6.493. Paul Shorey, *Plato in Twelve Volumes*, vols. 5 and 6 (Cambridge, MA: Harvard University Press, 1969). Compare the rather different view expressed by Whately, "If anyone really holds that it can ever be expedient to violate the injunctions of duty, – that he who does so is not sacrificing a greater good to a less (which all would admit to be inexpedient), – that it can be really advantageous to do what is morally wrong, – and will come forward and acknowledge that to be his belief, I have only to protest, for my part, with the deepest abhorrence, against what I conceive to be so profligate a principle." Richard Whately, *Elements of Rhetoric* (London: Longmans, 1877), 316.
10 Rawls, *Political Liberalism*, xxiv–xxvii.
11 Ibid., 54–8.

12 Aristotle, *Metaphysics*, 1009a16–18; *Nicomachean Ethics*, 1179b10–16, 1180a4–
    10; *Eudemian Ethics*, 1215a2–3. Contrast the view of John Locke in his *Letter
    concerning Toleration* favoured by Scott Hibbard in his "Religion, Tolerance,
    and American Theocratic Politics: Lessons for the Contemporary Era" in
    this volume. The facts, however, seem to favour Aristotle over Locke. See
    Richard Sorabji, *Moral Conscience through the Ages* (Chicago: University of
    Chicago Press, 2014).
13 *Laws* 2.5 (11)–7 (16). C.D. Yonge, trans., *The Treatises of Cicero: On the Nature
    of the Gods; On Divination; On Fate; On the Republic; On the Laws; and On
    Standing for the Consulship* (London: G. Bell, 1878).
14 *Republic*, quoted from Lactantius, *Div. Inst.* 6.8.6, trans. Yonge, ibid.
15 William Blackstone, *Commentaries on the Laws of England*, vol. 1,
    Introduction, section 2, "Of the Nature of Laws in General." Philadelphia,
    1893. The marginalizing of Blackstone and natural law jurisprudence in
    US legal teaching and practice no doubt had many sources, but one often
    referred to is Oliver Wendell Holmes, Jr, sometime associate justice of the
    US Supreme Court. See Oliver Wendell Holmes, Jr, "The Path of the Law,"
    Harvard Law Review 10.8 (1897): 457–78. Francis Biddle, *Justice Holmes,
    Natural Law, and the Supreme Court* (New York: Macmillan, 1961).
16 See the supplement in Peter L.P. Simpson, *Goodness and Nature* (New York:
    Lucairos Occasio Press, 2011).
17 Aristotle, *Eudemian Ethics*, 1216a15–19.
18 *Ecclesiastes* 1:2, 14.
19 "Futility," in Wilfred Owen, *Collected Poems*, ed. C. Day Lewis (New York:
    New Directions, 1965).
20 Aristotle, *Eudemian Ethics*, 1215b15–1216a10.
21 The article by Mark Lutz in this volume, "The Confrontation between
    Classical Political Philosophy and the Gods of the City," nicely illustrates
    how the philosopher's answer, as presented by Plato in the character of
    Socrates, is a failure. Socrates does indeed expose the incoherence and
    hypocrisy in prevailing religious belief and practice, and does point to
    something plainly better because to something plainly more intelligent. But
    Socrates' wisdom is confessedly knowledge of ignorance, and when it does
    dare to teach rather than merely to question it teaches theology. The Platonic
    Ideas are, after all, children of the gods, and Platonic myths repeat, if in
    sophisticated fashion, what the pagan myths taught: a life after death where
    the just are rewarded and the unjust punished. Philosophy needs theology, a
    theology it can point to on its own but cannot substantiate on its own.
22 Plutarch, "Abstract of a Discourse Showing that the Stoics Speak Greater
    Improbabilities than the Poets," *Moralia*, 13.73.

216 Peter L.P. Simpson

23 Aristotle, *Metaphysics*, 983a3–4, ironically quoting the poet Solon.

24 Nietzsche, perhaps, gives us the most untamable answer to socialist and liberalist equality. Friedrich Nietzsche, *Jenseits von Gut und Böse* and *Zur Genealogie der Moral*, ed. Giorgio Colli and Mazzino Montinari (Munich: Deutscher Taschenbuch Verlag, 2002).

25 Aristotle, *Nicomachean Ethics* 1178b28–1179a6.

26 Plato, *Republic*, books 1–7. Cicero, *Somnium Scipionis*.

27 Simpson, *Goodness and Nature*, supplement.

28 This point is well made by Neill in his "The Aristotelian Roots of Religious Governance Approaches" in this volume.

29 *Laws*, 1.8 (24), trans. Yonge. See also Plato, *Laws*, book 10.

30 The difference between the temporal and spiritual powers, and the need for both in traditional religious understandings of communal life, is obscured by our practice today of speaking of the "government" as if it were a single entity with undivided authority. The unifying of political authority is of the essence of the liberal state. The division of political authority into the temporal and spiritual is of the essence of religion. Neill, in his essay "The Aristotelian Roots of Religious Governance Approaches" in this volume, follows today's way of speaking, and weakens as a result an otherwise forceful argument. Note too, a propos his appeal to Aristotle, that priests are a separate part in Aristotle's city, different from the rulers who judge and deliberate, *Politics*, 4(7).8–9, 12, especially 1331b4.

31 The classic expression of the idea is found in Pope Gelasius's letter *Duo Sunt* of 494 to the emperor Athanasius, although the phrase "two swords" (from Luke 22:38, "Behold, here are two swords") is first used for this purpose by Pope Boniface VIII (following St Bernard's *De Consideratione*) in his bull *Unam Sanctam* of 1302.

32 Simpson, *Goodness and Nature*, supplement. Paul. A. Rahe, ed., *Machiavelli's Liberal Republican Legacy* (Cambridge: Cambridge University Press, 2006).

33 See especially chapter 2 of Peter L.P. Simpson, *Political Illiberalism: A Defense of Freedom* (New Brunswick, NJ: Transaction Publishers, 2015).

34 Aristotle, *Politics* 1324a25–1325b32.

35 Proverbs 16:18.

11 The Impossibility of Theocracy: The Weakness of the Gods

YVONNE SHERWOOD

The Secularization Narrative: Aggrandizing Religion's Powers

In order to justify acts of aggression or self-defence – military, political, and conceptual – we name the enemy and talk up the enemy's powers. This was the case, famously, with the invasion of Iraq in 2003. It is also the case with the story of secularization, which inflates the divine enemy's powers.

In the case of Operation Iraqi Freedom, the official rationale was disarmament. Saddam Hussein was gathering nuclear and biological capabilities and therefore needed to be contained. The story of secularization also functions as a war story, a containment narrative. For the sake of our emergent freedoms, the old gods needed to be restrained.

Saddam's nuclear capabilities turned out to be much exaggerated. In contrast, God/the gods stand tautologically (as a consequence of the very idea of divinity) for perfectly realized, permanent-eternal power. In Western/Christian metaphysics, the name of God is synonymous with omnipotence, omniscience, omnipotence – and transcendence. This gives divinity a unique capability and a unique place in politics, the discourse of power. His is the kingdom, the power, and the glory – and the absolute coverage (so the truisms go). "He holds the depths of the earth in his hands; the mountain peaks too belong to him" (Psalm 95:4). He has a unique hold on sovereignty, from the alpha to the omega, the origin to the *telos*. With no need for consultation or election, a god reigns for a fixed term of eternity. A god, by definition, is always in power.

Unless we do something about it. The secularization story is narrated as a coup against divine autocracies. The oft-rehearsed notion of the *separation* of "church" and "state" singles out religion as a source of particular danger.[1] The implication is that the gods were everywhere and had taken over everything – for a long time, and maybe since the beginning of time. Because they had complete (omnipresent) coverage, we had to restrain the gods to make space for quintessential modern goods such as politics and parliaments and constitutions and states and selves. Selves were released, "having stumbled in the dark and under the thumb of powers dead set against human beings standing up for themselves"[2] The time of "primitive fusion,"[3] the primal swamp when all was religion, burst into life through creative differentiation. The God of Genesis 1 created form by division and distinction, separating the sea from the dry land, the earth from the heavens. Similarly, modernity created "religion" by imagining the restraint of religion, and the opposites released by divine confinement, like politics and selves.[4]

As Mark Goldie confesses, historians of ideas have been obsessed with identifying that special point in time that marks the "disjunction between the civil and the religious" and the birth of "politics" proper. "To discover the moment in which politics became 'autonomous' and 'rational' is a constant endeavour for a profession still deeply imbued with the Enlightenment presumption that the maturity of the species consists in its ability to conduct civil life without recourse to superstition … The positivist mode in the history of political thought eagerly searches the era of human adolescence, and rewards philosophers for signs of 'science,' 'the modern,' 'the secular' attributed to prophetic landmark names like Machiavelli and Hobbes."[5] Varied iconic birthdays have been proposed, ranging from the mid- or late-seventeenth century (the English Civil War, Locke, Westphalia); to the decapitations of Charles I and Louis XVI as divine right kings; to the French and American Revolutions; to the "Enlightenment(s)" in a more vague and general sense. The *casus belli* for the necessary wars against religion include all-controlling dogmatism, overreaching divine-monarchic power, and, above all, religious violence and exhaustion from endless wars of religion. But note how automatically we speak of wars of religion or religious violence, while finding it far less natural to speak of economic violence or wars of economy. Religion has a privileged relation to war and violence, it seems.

Arguably, "modernity" found its dominant emblem in the death of the theocratic god-dictator; the decapitation of the divine right king. The king-god underwent the first of many modern deaths in the political sphere, and through his (sacrificial and productive) death gave birth to politics as a secular sphere. And this had to be. In a historical cautionary tale, "Divine Right [manifestly] Went Wrong."[6] The gods, chastised by history, were forced to repent. They were chased (or went of their own accord) into the confinement of the space marked "church." The modern notion of the state, evolving from the *status rei publicae* "condition (or existence) of the republic," took as its primary condition the sequestering of the gods.

The epiphany of the secular is dated to centuries ago, and yet "secularism remains as much a boast as a fact."[7] The tenses and times in the stories of secularization are uncertain, split. The separation of religion from politics is narrated as past preterite: a watershed that has been crossed, once and for all. The pastness of the religious past is accomplished and this pastness (this sense of *history*, and this sense of religion *as history*) grounds what is distinctive about "Western" identity and Western democratic states. In this sense, the separation of church and state serves as one of those "historical Rubicons" seen as "the hinges on which the door of history [and identity] swings."[8] And yet at the same time we still seem to feel that this pastness is far from accomplished. Many feel – now more than ever – that we must hold the temporal lines of progress against forces that might yet push us back into the anachronistic time of "theocracy" (vaguely defined, just like religion). Secularization functions as an inevitable, inexorable process that had to take place, and therefore has taken place. How could it be otherwise in the history of progress? But secularization is also narrated as an insecure process, beset by setbacks and fears.

The Revival of Theocracy

So why are the old gods, and the old idea of theocracy, still thriving, and even undergoing a revival? The first answer is that religion's resurgence is built into the very idea of the secular, and so the resurgence of religion is something that we do to ourselves. As Hans Blumenberg puts it, the logic of the secular states that "something was absent, which is supposed to have been present before," and without reference to that something, "one would cease to understand the term 'secularization.'"[9] It is extraordinarily difficult to tell the story of becoming modern without talking about religion and this or that overcoming of religion; without reporting how this or that old power of religion was attenuated, limited, cut up, shared. Narratives of secularization are by definition haunted by religion. If secular politics comes into being by being defined against religion, then religion is always hovering in the wings. Not only is a comeback always possible (we must be vigilant), but our own ways of speaking ensure that religion never goes away. Every time we talk of secularization we keep the old gods plugged into the conceptual life-support machine. We also – as I will explore more fully in a moment – ascribe to them powers of which they themselves could only dream.

The very structure of the secularization narrative leads to a perpetual renascence or resurgence of religion. One of the reasons why religion seems "resurgent" (or, in a more threatening inflection, "insurgent") is because we keep summoning "it" as we narrate the coming-into-being of modern selves and states. But modernity has also led us to conceptualize and intensify the idea of religion in particularly concentrated and extreme ways. Modernity patented the concept "religion." It also invented ways of talking about religion that turned religion into an omnipotent looming threat. For example, as I have argued more fully elsewhere,[10] Enlightenment philosophers like Kant invented the notions of "belief" and the "believer," imagining the believer as totally unanswerable to reason and totally enthralled by her belief. The gods and religion are assumed to have the power to overwhelm the individual and command complete allegiance, every time we refer to this strange mystical conviction: belief.

We no longer all "believe in" the old gods (as we say in that distinctly modern phrase). But the deaths of god have resulted in the birth of the believer: divine power at one remove. The gods are still present in the belief of the believer, assumed to feel a force of influence or inspiration that we would not attribute to, say, politics. We believe, above all, in the power of belief. Secular and religious observers alike all join in the assumption that belief is unqualified, or only ever to be partnered with unqualified qualifiers like "fervent" and "deep."[11] The gods survive and flourish more than they have ever done before in the idea of religion as the ultimate ideology, the one that transcends all evidence and reason and persists despite all evidence and reason. The possibility of fanaticism does not (just) come from the outside. It is built into our homegrown modern understanding of religion centred on belief.

Religion arguably becomes even more powerful when it is demystified as a human projection and transformed into a potentially fanatical belief. Mark D. Lilla's *The Stillborn God* is one of many contemporary warnings exhorting us to preserve the "great separation": the prising apart of church and state that constitutes the unique soul (and unique Christian legacy) of the West. This separation did not take place as a

natural progression, Lilla warns, like the overturning of Ptolomaic cosmology by Copernicus, Galileo, and Kepler. We must strive to hold the
distinction between religion and politics opened up by trailblazers like
Hobbes, Spinoza, and Locke. And this is because the opening had to
be forced. The default setting of the human brain is for "theocratic political theology." The *"unconstrained mind* seems compelled to travel up
and out" in the quest for transcendence.[12] We therefore must discipline
this *unconstrained mind*, the modern update of the unconstrained gods,
as we once disciplined and secularized the gods, so that the powers
wrested from the gods by Promethean humanity are not rashly given
back. Lilla's exhortation to stay vigilant, guarding against the resurgence of political theology, reads like a strange reversal of Jesus's sayings in the gospels, where he exhorts the bridesmaids and followers to
stay awake watching for the return of the messiah.[13] There is a tendency
for theocracies to be chiliastic, millenarian, apocalyptic, eschatological.
Lilla acts as a reverse prophet, or secular *katechon*/restrainer.[14] The task
of secularization is to hold back the "unrestrained" mind and to guard
against the second coming of the gods.

The Management of Scripturocracy: The Strategic
Invention of a Christian Foundation

Repeatedly, we hear the warning that "theocracy, a subject once confined to the history books," is bursting out of its confinement.[15] This
sensational drama masks the fact that "theocracy" is in fact a new-ish
word – even a neologism. The paradoxes of secularization have arguably led us to talk *more* about religion. Similarly, we are talking *more*
about theocracies, and finding new purposes for a term that was left
to languish in obscurity after being coined (with some hesitation) by
the Jewish historian Titus Flavius Josephus (37–ca. 100 CE) in the first
century CE.

The English term "theocracy," first coined as "theocraty" in the 1620s,
was originally used in a neutral and technical sense. Confined to the same
sphere of reference established by Josephus, it was used to describe the
unique form of pre-monarchic government in ancient Israel between
the Exodus and the reign of Saul, the first king. In *Against Apion*, Josephus (who had elsewhere described the pre-monarchical biblical rule of
Moses, Joshua, and the so-called judges as an "aristocracy" describing
aristocracy as the most "divine" form of government)[16] departed from
his own previous terminology and described the ancient constitution

in the books of Exodus, Joshua, and Judges as a theocracy, meaning direct rule by divinity, without the mediation of kings or priests. Key biblical texts inspiring this theo-political neologism included 1 Samuel 8:7, where the people's request for a king is interpreted by God as a rejection of direct rule by God alone (cf. Josephus, *Antiquities*, 6.38) and several passages in the book of Judges, particularly the repeated statement that "there is/was no king over Israel" (Judges 17:6; 21:25); Judges 8:22–3, and the sequel in Judges 9 – Jotham's parable of the trees. In Judges 8:22–3, Gideon the "judge" ("judge" in the sense of a temporarily appointed charismatic leader) refuses the people's petition that he, his son, and his grandson rule over them in a hereditary monarchy. "I will not rule over you, and my son will not rule over you; the Lord will rule over you," proclaims Gideon, in a statement begging to become a founding prooftext for "theocracy." In Judges 9, when Gideon's son Abimelech has killed all his 69 (!) brothers (or so he thinks) to seize the kingship, the secretly surviving son, Jotham, recites a cryptic poem-parable that the Jewish philosopher Martin Buber terms "the strongest anti-monarchical poem in world literature": the strange, cryptic parable of the trees.[17] The trees want to anoint a king over themselves and so approach the good trees: the olive, the fig, and the vine. All demur, choosing instead to continue with their age-old tasks of producing oil, figs, and wine for the community. Finally, the bramble is approached. The king-bramble is only elected as a last resort (without legitimacy?) and ominously offers the people the promise-threat of burning, the bramble's only skill.

Nineteenth-century historical critics, like Julius Wellhausen, would understand theocracy in the Hebrew Bible as an "ideal concept," a nostalgic retrojection by later writers.[18] Josephus takes it literally:

There are infinite varieties in individual customs and laws among humanity as a whole, but in summary one may say: some have entrusted the power of government to monarchies, others to the rule of the few, others again to the masses. But our legislator took no notice of any of these, but instituted the government as one might call – to force an expression [literally to "violently strongarm a word," βιασάμενος τὸν λόγον] – a "theocracy," ascribing to God the rule and power.[19]

Note that strange expression βιασάμενος τὸν λόγον which I have translated (perhaps too gently) as "to strongarm a word." The verb *biázō* has a range of meanings from "to act forceably," "constrain," "compel" or "force one's way," "force unjustly," even "rape."[20] Josephus uses the term metaphorically to present θεοκρατίαν in the equivalent of ancient scare quotes.

Translated into Latin by Cassiodorus (d. after 580 CE), *Against Apion* and the neologism "theocracy" was accessible to early modern Europeans – but the term was understood to refer to the exceptional government of the Hebrews. Josephus's implied scare quotes were retained in the sense that theocracy was seen as a special term, and an untranslatable one. A "theocracy" was understood as something like the political equivalent of the Edenic language. It was doubly sealed off from the political present in the uniqueness of biblical revelation and in antiquity, the deep past. When sixteenth- and seventeenth-century Europeans started imagining themselves as the inheritors of Israel, and revivers of the ancient Hebrew republic,[21] they never used the term "theocraty" or "theocracy" to describe the political futures that they sought to bring to earth. Modern commentators on Calvin and the Puritans use terms like "theocratic oligarchy."[22] Calvin doesn't. Oliver Cromwell never used the word theocracy. This would have been tantamount to political suicide for a parliamentarian who spoke, in the idioms of the time, about true government's double legitimation, by divine appointment and *by the election of the people*.[23]

The many ways in which the "forced" and ill-defined term theocracy has been understood and implemented include theonomy, the rule of the divine law, and what we might call scripturocracy, the rule of scripture. But divine law, or divine scripture, proves a fragile foundation for theocracy. The Protestant Reformers knew as surely as Hobbes that a doctrine of *solo scriptura* unleashed the terrifying prospect of freewheeling free-reading; a state in which (in Hobbes's nightmare vision) "every man, nay every boy and wench, that could read English, thought they spoke with God Almighty, and understood what he said."[24] As many in the sixteenth and seventeenth centuries sought political templates in a sprawling corpus of 774,776 words (or thereabouts, depending on how you count), the loosely syncretized collection appropriately named the Bible/*ta biblia* ("the library") proved unhelpfully undecided as to whether it was going to support absolute monarchy or agrarian communism, radical antinomianism, and the dissolution of property and the family. The quest for a biblical polity accommodated visions of the *civitas dei* as a *republic* (e.g., in the writings of James Harrington or John Milton), but was equally fervent in its support for divine right monarchy (as in Sir Robert Filmer's *Patriarcha*, or the *Politics Drawn from the Very Words of Holy Scripture* by Jacques-Bénigne Bossuet). Contemporary political "catechisms" and treatises created strange amalgams of the biblical and the Greco-Roman. This gave new political models the aura of double antiquity: support from the "ancient constitution" at once classical and biblical, historical/human and divine. No one spoke of "theocraty" any more than they advocated democracy (understood as a synonym for anarchy as in Aristotle). The limits of the thinkable are easily discernible because the political visions range so widely and wildly – and yet so many terms and options are off the page. Models of politics were expressed as wise and balanced *mixtures* of the basic constitutional categories found in Plato, Cicero, and Aristotle. The wonderfully titled *Political Catechism* of 1643 attributed to Henry Parker, secretary to Oliver Cromwell, offers the following political credo:

Qu. 1: How many simple kinds are there of Civil Government of States and
   Commonwealths?
Ans. There are three kinds of Government among Men; Absolute Monarchy,
   Aristocracy and Democracy,
Qu. 2: Are there any of these simple Forms perfect?
Ans. All these have their particular Conveniences and Inconveniences.
Qu. 3: Is the State of England governed by any one of these kinds simply?
Ans. The Experience and Wisdom of your Ancestors hath maintained this
   [Government] out of a mixture of these.[25]

By some very careful and strategic manoeuvring, the plural and chaotic field of biblical politics was streamlined into what I have termed the Liberal/Whig Bible, advocated by figures like John Locke.[26] It turned out (thanks be to God for all his mercies) that the Christian God was and always had been in favour of a modest and carefully managed pluralization of the powers, but was also firmly committed to keeping land and property ownership and the recently formed "family" intact. Fortunately for the ongoing alliance between Christianity and modern polities, the Christian god did not have to be forced to renounce the once omnipotent powers of religion over politics. According to the powerful cultural mythology of the Liberal Bible, the regnant deity of Christianity had never wanted such powers in the first place. He had always wanted "politics" as a domain distinct from "religion." The true Christian God and the true Christian Bible were kenotic, self-sacrificial. Of their own volition they granted autonomy to politics by renouncing and disavowing god-like powers. In other words, the true God and the true Bible were completely in support of the rise of that political force, the people/*demos*; that force that would eventually prove as numinous, invisible, and at least as powerful as a god.[27] As democracy was rehabilitated from political swear word to a word synonymous with good government (eventually reaching such an institutionalized status that all alternatives would look like bad government), the Christian Bible would turn out to be emphatically and progressively on the side of the *demos*. As one of Locke's contemporaries put the new and hugely influential formulation: "The laws of England (as all just and righteous laws) are grounded originally upon the divine law, as their foundation or fountain. The supreme and sovereign God among the heathen is supposed to have the name of Jupiter, quasi 'Juris Pater' – But more immediately human laws have their force and authority from the consent and agreement of men."[28]

Foreign, heathen gods (meaning, in this context, the gods of the Turks, Moors, and Catholics) misunderstand themselves as God-Fathers. They see themselves as Jupiters, which by dubious etymology is understood as the literal "father of the law." In contrast – defined by the force of contrast – *we* are uniquely freed by a particularly Christian dispensation to see our laws as "grounded *originally* upon the divine law, as their *foundation or fountain*."[29]

The hugely influential mythology of the Liberal Bible turned the Bible into the ancient venerated foundation. Potential theonomy and scripturocracy was managed by transforming scripture into the nominal foundation. The Bible or Christian foundation became a symbol or icon, separated from the confusing 774,776 words between the covers. Veneration of the foundation could be combined with helpfully anodyne and politically neutered stereotypes of what that foundation entailed. It turned out (very usefully) that not only did the Christian foundation sponsor "democracy," shorn of its negative Aristotelian connotations and transformed into the global political good. It also sponsored twentieth-century articulations of democracy in terms of human rights. These mythologies are widespread. They are believed by those who claim a particular affiliation to the "Judeo-Christian" tradition, and those who don't. (Compare the way in which we all tend to believe in the mythology of "belief.") Few find it strange for "Readers in Human Rights" to carry subtitles such as "Major Speeches, Essays and Documents *from the Bible* to the Present" (my italics).[30] Genealogies of democracy automatically pay lip service to unique factors in the Christian tradition – be it the Hebrew/Christian God's hands-off transcendentalism (understood as the divine desire to devolve earthly-secular political power); or universal priesthood (a prototype of democracy); or God's declaration in Genesis 1:26–7 that human beings were all created in God's image, and so destined for autonomy and rights.[31]

The specific "secularization" of Euro-America was strangely indebted to the unique virtues of Christianity. The idea of "the Christian foundation" is productively empty and vague. But it becomes insistent and concrete through the force of contrast: in particular, contrasts made with encroaching Islam. Most citizens of Western democracies are convinced that the Bible accommodates a potential for democracy that is not present in the Qur'an. This seems to be a cultural mythologeme that we simply inherit on faith, given that a very small minority of the citizens of Western democracies have read either the Bible or the Qur'an, or assessed the democratic potential of the Bible and the Qur'an.

In this respect, the moderate assumptions of liberal society are very close to the strong "beliefs" of those whom some are now calling the new "theocrats." According to the American judge Roy Moore, whose most famous act until recently was to attempt to erect a monument to the ten commandments in his Alabama courthouse:

> The god [sic] of Islam commands that no other faiths are to be tolerated by the government. In contrast, the God of the Christian faith prohibits government from interfering in that relationship which lies solely between God and his creation. Our forefathers recognized that essential truth and adopted the First Amendment to protect freedom of conscience from government interference.[32]

Roy Moore believes that the God of Christianity should reign over the United States because Christianity is tolerant, and Christianity is against government interference. The legacy of the "Liberal Bible" is so persuasive that, even in the hands of the most ardent literalists/fundamentalists, the Bible speaks in distinctly modern tones of liberalism and rights.

Theocracy as a Pejorative (like Body Odour or Oligarchy)

According to the evidence of the *Oxford English Dictionary*, in the seventeenth and eighteenth centuries the term theocracy had the same narrow referential remit that it had in Josephus, referring exclusively to the governance of Israel. In the nineteenth century the term began to be applied (cautiously), by analogy, to other theological-political structures. Interestingly, for a short period the connotative power of the term was undecided. In the early nineteenth century John Henry Newman could still refer approvingly to "the old Christian theocracy," which "took a wrong turn" when it clothed itself with the "the purple robe" of Caesar.[33] Here "theocracy" functions (a) technically and (b) *positively*, as it does in Josephus's description of the ancient theocracy of the Hebrews. But by the latter half of the century, we find the term developing the now familiar pejorative meanings of the *wrong kind of governance by a god (or his representatives)* or passive and dangerous thraldom to a god, priests, or a sacred text, and settling into its new role of describing the theological politics of the other, not ourselves. Far from accidentally, this shift in connotation coincided with the emergence of "the secular" as a newly coined concept and campaign.[34] In the nineteenth-century examples listed in the *Oxford English Dictionary*, theocracy is applied to the Incas, the Druids, the church of Calvin (but not by Calvinists), and Catholics (but not by Catholics). Like body odour or Aristotelian "oligarchy," theocracy became a term that no political body ever claims for itself.

Dictionary definitions can be grossly misleading. Theocracy is not simply "a form of government in which God (or a deity) is recognized as the king or immediate ruler, and his laws are taken as the statute-book of the kingdom, these laws being usually administered by a priestly order as his ministers and agents; hence (loosely) a system of government by a sacerdotal order, claiming a divine commission" (*OED*). Dictionary neutrality obscures how the term has absorbed all the opprobrium attached to anti-clericalism and *priestcraft*. "Theocracy" now clearly signals a betrayal of the call to secularization and progress, and the manipulation of politics by the wrong kind of authorities, emblematized in the old gods and *the priests*. Even more than "religion," "theocracy" has come to stand for the elsewhere, the other and the (always potentially resurgent) past: the bad old days when, as Tom Paine put it, "a set of artful men pretended, through the medium of oracles, to hold intercourse with the Deity, as familiarly as they now march up the back stairs in European courts."[35] Theocracy has evolved into the term for a polity at the mercy of the wrong kind of heavenly voices and their manipulative representatives, who lead their docile subject-citizens by the ear.

The Isolation of Theocracy in Time and Space

Through the force of habit and repetition, certain points in the past and the present have become hotspots of "theocracy." Massive swathes of time and space are left in the clear. Theocracy is never applied to those

American, Canadian, or European constitutions that openly declare a foundation in "god," or even a subjection "under god" – though theocracy has been used, especially since the rise of the American religious right in the 1970s, as a pejorative term for those who interpret this link too strongly. It is never used to refer those European states that talk repeatedly of an indispensable Christian foundation or Christian heritage, presumably because these foundations are seen as appropriately mediated, managed, distanced, or recently and hastily pluralized to religions and gods in general. (Maybe it no longer counts as theocracy when the gods are pluralized, even though there is a strong pressure for the gods to conform to the same basic theological grammar, in a loose ecumenism of the one.) Ran Hirschl defines a constitutional theocracy as a state in which "the designated state religion is often viewed as constituting the foundation of the modern state: as such, it is an integral part, or even the metaphorical pillar, of the national metanarrative."[36] Many Euro-American states seem to fit these criteria in their frequent appeals to an indispensable Christian foundation.[37] It could even be argued that they fit Hirschl's additional criteria, where laws conform to the idea of "a" or "the" religious source, and "no statute may be enacted" that is "repugnant" to the fundamental principles of the state religion. In modern Christian-secular democracies, this is expressed loosely and negatively. The state will not admit any overt conflict between mainstream religions – that is, their *true* expressions, which by definition (and coercion) are in harmony with the state. Paradoxically, the illusion of an alliance between the fundamental principles of secular law and religious law is supported by the invention of a (distant) Christian foundation, and the separation of religious discourse from law as the shared desire of that true Christian foundation and the secular state. I'm deliberately courting offence by suggesting that our states, our pasts, might qualify as theocracy. The charge seems rude, grossly inappropriate. It makes us want to create distinctions: for example, between "immediate" rule by God (the mark of the truly theocratic) as opposed to distant rule by God. But how secure is this distinction? How can any theocracy actualize or implement the immediate rule of a deity? Can gods and religions rule more effectively, perhaps, when they rule at an (untouchable) distance and have a deep and amorphous alliance with the state?

Our own local histories seem suspiciously free of theocracy. Theocracy is not a term used to name pre-Reformation Christendom or Reformation Christendom – though it is applied to short-lived aberrations, such as Cromwell's parliament. This seems strange, since the secularization narrative reports the separation of church and state and implies a time when all was theocracy: divine rule over the state. *Our pasts double as our other and our foundation.* We are loath to name our own pasts as theocratic, as if we want those pasts to have always been on the way to this future, and to have always been better than *that*.

Surely pre-Reformation Christendom or nascent European states are candidates for what are often vague definitions of theocracy as "some degree of rule by religion"[38] or rule or partial rule by ecclesiastical authorities. In England, bishops or spiritual lords still sit in the House of Lords, as more than relics of the days when the House of Lords or Upper House was comprised of spiritual lords and temporal lords (the landed gentry). Until they were repealed in the nineteenth century, test acts and corporation acts made access to public office and university degrees dependent on taking the Christian sacraments according to the only appropriate rite of the Church of England. Free-thought was punished with imprisonment and hard labour even in the early twentieth century, and blasphemy remained on the "secular" statute books till 2008. Not naming Catholicism as a "theocracy" is a recent politesse that postdates Vatican II, the election of JFK, and the rehabilitation of the Jew and the Catholic as co-founders of the "common faith" called democracy, the "religion of religions."[39] The pope (father-papa, heir to St Peter) must be one of the strongest candidates for the human incarnation of religious authority. He never stands for purely "spiritual" authority divorced from "temporal" (secular) authority; hence the notorious power struggles between popes and emperors and kings. It seems to be an unwritten rule that the now pejorative term "theocracy" is not to be applied to mainstream Protestant, Catholic, or Jewish groups, or annexes of the "Western" such as the modern state of Israel.[40] Mainstream Islam has not (yet?) been thus rehabilitated as one of the founding faiths of democracy. On the contrary, there still seems to be a widespread belief in the old mythology of the "Turks and Moors" who fervently believe in the old idea of God as literal *Juris Pater* or Father of the Law.

In general, we seem coy about applying the term theocracy, retrospectively, to powers that we regard as having made an important contribution to the foundational values of "the West." The Roman emperor was the adopted son of God, and Jesus, the adopted or birth son of God, was made partly in his image. Still, images of Caesar or Jesus Pantocrator notwithstanding, describing the Roman empire or Constantinian Christianity as theocracies seems like an offensive category mistake. We are much more inclined to apply the term theocracy to ancient Egypt, which has never qualified as the precursor of the West. In general, the Greco-Roman tradition is widely seen as the forerunner of secular "reason" and tolerance, not the bastion of "fanatical" or manipulative or bad religion, hence not theocratic.[41] As Peter Simpson argues in his essay "Theocracy's Challenge" in this volume, there is no ostensible reason why we should draw such a firm line between "theocracy" and Cicero's conflation of the pre-existent, unwritten law with the divine mind. Instead, we prefer to single out aberrations, like the second king of Rome, Numa Pompilius (753–673 BCE), who strategically manufactured a fiction of a personal audience with the gods and the nymph Egeria. This might just qualify as a momentary theocratic lapse.

Theocracy is only used to name small islands of space and time in the massive history and global coverage of Christianity. The Wikipedia entry on theocracy is typical in isolating Vatican City, the Jesuits in Paraguay, and Mount Athos. It seems that Christian theocracy does not reach across many square kilometres. Historically, theocracy seems similarly confined. With the exception of Calvin's Geneva and the Puritans in New England (and, more marginally, the Mormons in Salt Lake City, Utah), theocracy seems confined to "sectarian," "extreme," or heretical interpretations of Christianity that burnt bright and briefly. Theocracy flared up briefly in Savonarola's Florence (1490–7); the Anabaptists' Münster (1534–5); and Jonestown, Guyana (1977). What these movements have in common is non-recognition as a legitimate power; (brief) military successes against the ruling authorities; and the seeming connection to fanatical (illegitimate) beliefs: that is, beliefs for which one is prepared to die. No theocracy without a body count. Strong indicators of theocracy are death, insurrection, and illegitimacy.

Theocracy would be far more historically and globally widespread if it served as nothing but a technical term referencing governance, or part governance, by the gods or their representatives. The true meaning of theocracy is affective-connotative-pejorative: akin to that of a "rogue state." In modernity, theocracy becomes a synonym for illegitimate governance. To label a regime a "theocracy" is to identify it with the gods, the powers that do not exist. Thus we imply that a theocratic regime does not (really) and should not exist. Theocracy is a word identified with the illegitimate theft of state power and particularly the theft of the state monopoly on violence. It is in this specific sense that theocracy is undergoing a revival. The question of theocracy seems so pressing and insistent because theocracy connotes *threat* and implies an illegitimate, divinely inspired power grab over the powers of the state. The state is

the political body that has "the monopoly of legitimate physical violence within a particular territory" in the famous formulation of Max
Weber.[42] Encroachment on the terrain of the state and the terrain of "the
secular" is emblematized, above all, in the fearful spectacle of the old
gods coming back to judge, wage war, and steal back powers over life
and death.

Theocracy as a Neologism: The Rise of Theocracy post-1970 and 9/11

A series applying ancient categories to modern politics written before
the 1970s arguably would not have felt the need to add a whole volume
dealing with Josephus's strange little supplement, "theocracy." A series
published in the twenty-first century cannot ignore the revivification
and insurgence of the term that began in the 1970s and was intensified
even further post-9/11. Although this intensification has been related to
the "global" rise of religious fundamentalisms (a dubiously generalized
category),[43] the focus has not been the rise of the Bharatiya Janata Party
and Hinduvata in the 1970s or the 1980s; or Buddhist "theocracies" that
have led to the persecution of the Muslim Rohinga in Indonesia (is it
possible to have a theocracy in a "religion" without theism?); or indeed
the spread of mainstream Catholicism and Pentecostalism in the global
South. In the concern over theocracy, what matters is not the "East" or
the "Far East" but the "Near East": the East that impinges on the West
and the narcissistically focused battle for the soul of the "West." The
rise of theocracy is bound up with the perceived struggle to preserve
the separation of church and state. In a simple parable of politics, this
is understood as being under siege on two fronts: from the inside, by
the aggressive return of religion within the United States; and from the
encroaching East, in "radical" or "militant" Islam. The rise of theocracy
as a live question for politics has centred obsessively on the perceived
imitation and antagonism between Christianity and Islam. Theocracy is
seen to inhabit maverick (non-mainstream) forms of Christianity, while
being programmed into the very core of Islam.

The story of the recent rise of theocracy seems to strangely mirror
end-time theologies. The sequence of events seems to be providen-
tially pre-programmed. It runs like coded clockwork. North American
Christianity and "Islam" are perceived as having become increasingly
theocratic in a strangely synchronized timeline that began in the 1970s
and intensified post-9/11. Islamic theocracy rose to public visibility

with the 1979 Iranian Revolution led by the Ayatollah Homenei and Shi'ite clerics against the US-backed Pahlavi dynasty. In the same decade, the spokespeople and presidents of the United States – by then the only remaining global superpower – began to proclaim an increasingly explicit alliance with the divine superpower. In the 1950s and 1960s, the United States became more publicly attached to "Judeo-Christian" values in order to secure a firmer contrast with the atheistic Soviet Union. In the 1950s Dwight Eisenhower added the phrase "Under God" to the Pledge of Allegiance and invoked the "Judeo-Christian concept" of "all men created equal" against the threefold public enemy: "Communism, Korea, and corruption."[44] Officially, the United States backed a moderate secularism (to be clearly distinguished from the bleak, atheist secularism of the Soviet Union), a secularism supported by strong but distanced Christian foundations. But then, for many citizens of the United States, the strong background came to the foreground in ways that many of their compatriots found terrifying.

In his widely acclaimed *American Theocracy: The Peril and Politics of Radical Religion, Oil and Borrowed Money in the 21st Century*, former Republican adviser and member of the Nixon administration, Kevin Phillips, documents the growing influence of the religious right and the "theocrats" and the "theocons" on the Republican party since the 1970s. The playful compound "theocon" was first used in 1996, in an article for *The New Republic*,[45] but in the early years of the twenty-first century neologisms like "theocrat" and "theocon" came thick and fast.[46] For Phillips, the rise of fundamentalist religion constitutes a national Disenlightenment,[47] culminating in the now terrifying end-of-secular-times statistics that between 43 and 46 per cent of Americans affirm biblical inerrancy and identify themselves as "born again." The controversial rise of theocracy is framed as a political-theological Civil War. Following writers like John Egerton in his *The Americanisation of Dixie: The Southernization of America*, Phillips recounts how New England theocracies relocated to the south, then crept back north, moving in on the White House. Phillips points to "Bibles being brandished as public policy guides, pompous sermons proclaiming a chosen nation obliged to redeem the world, and fire-eyed preachers counting down to Armageddon" and "the world's leading Bible-reading crusader state, immersed in an Old Testament of stern prophets and bloody Middle Eastern Battlefields."[48] The end-of-secular-times warning mimics the apocalyptic end-times language so popular with the so-called theocrats in America: for example, in the crazily popular *Left Behind* rapture novels by Tim

La Haye and Jerry B. Jenkins, where the Antichrist Nicolae Carpathia is taken on by the Christian Tribulation Force.

I began this chapter with an analogy between Saddam Hussein and the massively inflated gods of the secularization narrative. But the contribution of the 2003 Iraq War to the question of theocracy far exceeds the metaphorical. 9/11 and the Iraq War played a crucial role at the pedestrian level of cause and effect – and retrojected cause. Concurrent with the rise of the religious right between the 1970s to 2000, at least two dozen predominantly Muslim countries, from Egypt to Pakistan, declared Shar'ia to be "a" or "the" source of legislation.[49] Islamic "theocracies" became even more visible, post-9/11, when shar'ia law was adopted in Afghanistan (2004) and Iraq (2005). Fighters for ISIS/ISIL/Daesh – the most recent embodiment of "theocracy" – were trained by officers left unemployed after the violent restructuring of the Iraqi army. Their captured weapons, including armour, guns, surface-to-air missiles, and even some aircraft, come from weapons recaptured during the Iraqi "insurgency" as well as weapons from government and opposition forces fighting in the Syrian Civil War.

The rise of theocracy – and the mirroring between US and Islamic theocracy – became the dominant way of reading the signs of the times in the run up to, and the aftermath of, the Iraq War. George Bush's 2001 speech to the nation and statements by Osama bin Laden established what many saw as a strange synchronicity between American Christianities and Al Qaeda. In the words of Bruce Lincoln, "Both men [Bush and bin Laden] constructed a Manichean struggle, where Sons of Light confront Sons of Darkness, and all must enlist on one side or the other, without possibility of neutrality, hesitation or middle ground."[50] The analogy underplays the differences. Unlike Osama bin Laden's speeches, Bush's words were "double-coded," with a secret meaning for Christian supporters. They referenced Bible-lite, or the Bible as symbol, and were shaped by the long-standing mythology of the Liberal Bible.[51] Phillips and other commentators on the US theocons and theocrats in a way concede these differences. They qualify the idea of theocracy in revealing ways. As we will explore in a moment, the place of full theocracy is always in the past or the future, as it is impossible to actualize theocracy in the present. But Phillips and other observers make a self-conscious point of this fact. They use terms like "incipient theocracy" or "virtual theocracy,"[52] terms with double connotations of qualification and threat. In an "incipient theocracy" or "virtual theocracy," theocracy is embryonic. It is not yet or not really theocracy; not yet fully itself. A virtual theocracy also has an element of confession. It is at most a pale simulation of full theocracy. It is not really theocracy, we admit. But heed the warning (and here we are reminded of Lilla): full theocracy may follow – and herein lies the threat.

Phillips describes the mechanisms of theocracy in distinctly nuanced ways. God becomes incarnate in American politics in

> an elected leader who believes himself in some way to speak for God, a ruling political party that represents religious true believers and seeks to mobilize the churches, the conviction that government should be guided by religion, and on top of it all, White House implementation of domestic and international political agendas that seem to be driven by religious motivations and biblical worldviews.[53]

The controlling force is imagined as belief, conviction, ideology; not god as such, but god as an incontrovertible force actualized in the fervent belief of the believers. This is a very modern scene of theocracy. The old gods have had to fit in with the structures of modern politics. Theocracy mixes with constitutionalism and the mechanisms of representational democracy. God becomes the one who is represented by the "religious true believers" who are "represented" by the political party. This is a circle of mutually reinforcing representation. Bush is not imagined for a moment to be a Caesar, Pantocrator, or God incarnate. Such a vision would be entirely at odds with the iconography of democracy.[54] But his policy is seen to become incarnate in the will of the believers, who in turn see themselves as strategizing and lobbying for the sake of the divine will. *In the distinctly modern "theocracy" of the USA, God is perceived as kind of lobbyist at one remove.* He actualizes his will in a complex process that involves recruiting believers and putting pressure on believers to put pressure on the White House. The more correct term for this kind of governance should perhaps be (and now I empathize with the awkwardness Josephus felt when proposing his forced neologism) something like pistisarchy, crederecracy, or religiocracy (with apologies for the crudely improvised Latin and Greek!).

Nor should we assume that only modern "Western" theocracies are strange amalgams of the ancient and the modern. In both "Christian" and "Islamic" theocracies, the gods, or their representatives, are for the most part in complex negotiations with modern constitutions. And in both, one of the dominant signs or symptoms of theocracy is a distinctive position on family, sexuality, and reproductive rights. Every regime has its distinctive signs and symbols – or iconography. The most obvious signs or icons of "theocracy" are restrictions of sexuality and the enforcement of monogamy, or more accurately, monoandry for women. We see signs of theocracy in the newly implemented curfew for women in Banda Aceh, Indonesia: the enforcement of the hijab in the aftermath of the Iranian Revolution; and the emergent identity of the religious right in America consolidated around a distinctive position on sexuality and the politics of the "family," formulated in a concerted backlash against the landmark 1970s case of *Roe v. Wade*. One could be forgiven for thinking that the old gods have always been obsessed, above all, with the family. But "the family" is a recent obsession for the gods, and a recent creation. In Egypt, the word *aila* (designating the nuclear family) only came into circulation in the mid-nineteenth century. The term emerged to reflect the conceptual and actual restructuring of domestic life under colonization. Very different rules applied under the old concepts and structures of the *usra* (extended family) and the people of the house: the *ahl al-bait*.[55] The illusion of antiquity, even eternity, that opponents and advocates ascribe to Islamic family law masks the compromise between ancient texts and distinctly modern structures. "Traditions" are constantly being remade. The family law codified in the Muslim Personal Status Code in Egypt in 1920 is a combination of selected readings of fiqh by committees of jurists, the Napoleonic Code, and the legal systems of the colonial state. The dominance of Christian Catholic law on contraception in the Philippines (which has never led to any labelling of the Catholic Philippines as a theocracy) has been recently forced to renegotiate with the force of "rights" to produce a new bill on reproductive health.

As Ran Hirschl argues, the rise of "theocracy" has coincided with the widespread export of constitutionalism and judicial review, now shared by over 150 countries. This has created new, distinctly modern mixed theocracies (or as Beiner has it, examples of "Islamic Erastianism")[56] as the gods and their representatives negotiate with bills of rights, judicial review, and, above all, the force of economy and international trade. Divinities and traditions must negotiate with the force of economy, and they do so very successfully in wealthy states such as Qatar, Saudi Arabia, or Kuwait. No Iranian woman can claim exemption from wearing the hijab, but the Iranian Free Zones Act does make special zones for exemption from the economic regulations imposed by Islamic law. On Kish Island, Qeshm Island, and the Port of Chabahar, the Qur'an and Sunna do not reign in quite the same way as across the

rest of the state. The meaning of theocracy lies in its connotative powers, as we have seen. And Western commentators and politicians often
use "theocracy" as a term of concern, exhortation, and also threat. The
lesson that theocracy (or too strong, "radical" religion) is bad for the
economy is constantly being made, for example, in Tony Blair's "Faith
and Globalization" lectures co-sponsored by the Divinity and Business Schools at Yale.[57] The wrong kinds of gods demand the sacrifice
of tourism and business. To become theocractic is to risk becoming the
dissident from economy, according to this cautionary tale. Needless to
say, the theocracies that make observers most anxious are those where
the gods have their numinous non-anthropomorphized sticky hands on
precious commodities, such as oil. Maybe only the gods (or the believers) seem strong and stubborn and fanatical enough to resist the pull of
"the economy." Theocracy is one of the few terms available to describe
a mode of politics that is not primarily subject to global trade.

As Hirschl points out, negotiations between tradition and constitutionalism can take the form of a negotiation between two hypergoods or
ultimate commitments. Genuinely pious investment in religious truth
must negotiate with equally passionate and pious faith in constitutionalism, the rule of law, and human rights. But negotiations between tradition and constitutionalism can also take the form of an "irreverent
constitutionalism": a "strategic, instrumentalist" use of the constitution
to make political theologies line up with the demands of realpolitik,
GDP, and international relations. As Hirschl writes: "Granting religion
formal constitutional status is not only a legitimacy-enhancing move
that appeases popular pressures; it also neutralizes religion's revolutionary sting, co-opts its leaders, ensures state input in the translation
of religious precepts into guidelines for public life, helps mutate sacred
law and manipulate religious discourse to serve powerful interests, and,
above all, brings an alternative, even rival order of authority under state
control and supervision."[58] In theocratic states that are regarded as successful states, the gods reign in certain zones more clearly than in others. They dominate the "family," but not the economy. They show that
there is no inevitable disharmony between the Muezzin's call and the
Dow-Jones bell. Our fears – and the term theocracy – are not concentrated on states which are not seen to constitute a military or economic
threat.

Republican commentator Kevin Phillips is concerned, above all, that
"incipient theocracy" is bad for the *American* economy. Having God on
your side looks like a major economic advantage, but gods go on the

defecit rather than the credit side of the national ledger. In his interpretation of the signs of the end times, he sees the Iraq War as the moment when the United States sowed the seeds of its own downfall in "a fusion of petroleum-defined national security; a crusading simplistic Christianity" and "a reckless credit-feeding financial complex" – but above all a crusading, simplistic Christianity and the "pre-emptive righteousness of a biblical nation become a high-technology, gospel-spreading power."[59] In a stark (and forced) historical allegory, he points prophetically to the former collapse of the Roman, Spanish, and British empires, which, he claims, were similarly destroyed by "religious hawkishness, the substitution of faith for reason," missionary hubris, and what he punningly terms Western "fuelishness."[60] Divine right always goes wrong. As he points out, in the Iraq War troops were immediately posted around the Iraqi Oil Ministry, which held the maps and charts that were the key to effective oil production. According to Phillips's oracle, the American empire was (or will be) destroyed by a fervent belief in divine election and the quest for oil, just as the high Victorian British empire was undone (in Phillips's idiosyncratic diagnosis) by the fervent belief in divine election and an overdependence on coal.

Old Gods Fuelled by Modern Technologies and Distinctly Modern Ways of Conceptualizing "Power"

Phillips's historical allegory seems to have about the same regard for historical fact as the old Christian typologies – but it accidentally makes an important point about the relationship between gods and powers. Our projections of the old gods and empires are automatically combined with modern notions of automaticity, and all the powers of modern media and technologies and weaponry and bureaucracy that structure the ways we think about power. When combined with the divinity-amplifying forces of the secularization narrative and all the omni's of Western metaphysics, these forces massively amplify the old gods' powers. We imagine the Christian deity charging ahead with all the fuel and force of the steam and electricity that powered the high Victorian empire. We imagine the gods of the old crusades operating as if they had access to the military force behind Bush's "crusade," hastily renamed Operation Iraqi Freedom. In fact, these old crusades were carried out by tiny armies. Henry II (1154–89), considered one of the most powerful kings of his time, had a tiny civil service and an annual revenue of just 22,000 pounds. The largest army defending Jerusalem had less than 15,000 soldiers. Most died in transit to the Holy Land. Eighty per cent of those who embarked on the first Crusade between 1096 and 1097 did not survive.

Divine transcendence and global-universal coverage becomes more conceivable in the age of fuel, petrol, electricity, digital communication – which is also, paradoxically, the age of secularization. The old gods who were beefed up, retrospectively, by the secularization narrative, also attained more convincing omnicapacities as nineteenth- and twentieth-century technologies gave us new ways of conceptualizing power. There is a heaven and hell of a difference between ancient deities and the modern reinventions of the old gods that have access to nuclear weapons – some of them bearing strange old biblicized names like "Gabriel," "Amos," "Hellfire," "Acrid," "Fireflash," "Goblet," "Satan," and "Savage" (as well as "Peacekeeper" and "Robust Nuclear Earth Penetrator"), as if recalling strange old theological fantasies of absolute divine/demonic apocalyptic power.

We imagine the old gods as if they were fuelled with oil, gas, and nuclear energy – not to mention the particular ideological compulsion of "belief," the idea that we have invented. We also imagine that in the times before modernity (or in other parts of the world that are at a different stage in the inexorable progress towards modernity), gods and sacred texts were protected from questions or critique.[61] The complex sediment of "tradition" is now seen, from a distance, as a single force that has got its story together and that imposes its will on its passive believer-servants without resistance or qualification. In modernity, ironically, the gods seem to have achieved what eluded them in pious eras: unity of purpose, complete obedience, and a single monotheistic will that knows what it wants and can project what it wants across time and space. We can believe in an effective theocracy far more than our pre-modern predecessors ever could. We can now really believe in divine omnipotence and the prospect of the gods really getting the power and the glory and the kingdom (and the state). We are more traditional theists than our pre-critical ancestors, insofar as we find the idea of divine weakness hard to think.[62]

Modern theocracies are qualified, virtual, mixed – but also (and for that reason) incredibly strong. The virtual theocracy of the United States can draw on the mass resources of vast megachurches and the resources of the richest people in the richest country in the world. This is the modern paradox of theocracy. Theocracy has changed, so that it is no longer faithful to the old definitions (if it ever was). In this sense it is weakened, "virtual." But theocracy has new tools and prostheses that make it newly believable, and newly (incredibly) strong. The Islamic State of Caliph Ibrahim or Abu Bakr al-Baghdadi is supported by howitzers, grenade launchers, armoured personnel carriers, tanks, artillery, resources of around 200 million dollars per year, and an aggressive media campaign that rivals the media output of most major international corporations, led by the Al-Furqan Foundation for Media Production and the Al-I'tisam Media Foundation, which distributes through the Global Islamic Media Front.[63] Modern corporate-sounding acronyms mix strangely with attempts to rebuild, and reference, that original "state-building" period of Islam (622–32 CE). Acts of atavistic primal violence – gory beheadings – are tweeted and posted on YouTube. Oxymoronic synchronies of ancient script and modern technology have become all too familiar since the choreographed "sacred drama" of 9/11.[64]

The affective sense of theocracy lies in threat – in particular, the threat of insurgent anachronism. This particular peril is harnessed quite specifically in the recent rebranding for an English-speaking audience: "Islamic State" (Islamic State of Iraq and Syria) or ISIL (Islamic State of Iraq and the Levant). At first the faction of Sunni fighters called itself *Jama'at al-Tawhid wal-Jihad*: the Group for Monotheism (*tawhid*) and Struggle (the literal meaning of *jihad*). The term was local and referred to the first years of Islam, when the monotheists first defined themselves against the polytheists/pagans. Later, new names were devised, to locate the group geographically, first in *bilad al-rafidayn* (land of the two rivers: Mesopotamia) and later in Iraq and al-Sham (a province in the earliest Muslim empire). Both names were "romantically archaic," and localized, unlike the recent rebranding, Islamic *State*.[65] "Islamic State" clearly references the ancient caliphate as a parallel and rival to the modern nation state. ISIS can now lay claim to vast areas of Iraq and Syria: a localized "theocracy," but still a far greater area than Jonestown or Münster or Florence. But what is designed to really terrify the "Rome" on which Caliph Ibrahim marches is the spectre of a violent Islamic faction laying claim to all the powers and recognition given to the modern nation state. The terror is perfectly pitched. What shocks and awes above all is the notion of the old retro violent gods gaining the defined territory, permanent population, military force, and sovereignty that we associate with the modern nation state. These days the "powers that be" (cf. Romans 13:1) lie in states and transnational (transcendent) multinational corporations and transnational alliances like the WTO and the UN led by a modest plenipotentiary of the strongest (permanent member) states. Gods and their believers must be represented: this is part of the iconography of democracy. But they must know their place. Gods (as represented in "religions" and "believers") are lower than states. Nothing seems more threatening than a divine takeover of the secular state. The secularization narrative presents the modern secular state as having "the monopoly of legitimate physical violence within a particular territory" (so Weber).[66] Insurgent theocracy appears as a theft of the now secular prerogative over life and death.

The modern state and the old gods are seen as political antitheses; mutually allergic terms. And yet we cannot help but anachronistically imagine the gods as possessing all the powers of the modern state. Perhaps this is because we are now so accustomed to all the political prostheses of modernity that we find it impossible to imagine politics without them. Perhaps it is because we attribute state-like powers to the powers still seen (according to a now old story) as the modern state's arch-rival and threat. Or perhaps it is because the traditional role of the gods (and their death-dealing powers) in our political mythologies has been to allow us to understate the potentially terrifying powers of the modern state.

The old gods would give their eye teeth to be a "pre-eminent bordered power container"[67] or to have "the monopoly of legitimate physical violence within a particular territory" (according to Giddens's and Weber's famous definitions of the state). The old jealous gods would look enviously at the borders, bureaucracies (particularly infrastructures of taxation, automatic revenue), militaries, artilleries, and powers (nuclear, oil-fuelled, digital, and electric) that can be taken for granted by the modern state. The priests who instituted tithes and the fat portions of sacrifice for the priesthood (a variable income, depending on famine and harvest) would surely covet the massive infrastructure of the IRS. The kinds of gods who populate the classical tradition and the Bible are no Constantine, no Aristotelian prime mover. The old gods wish – though in fact monotheism, let alone complete global coverage, is not something to which they even aspire. The old gods can often be heard complaining that they do not have coverage and coordination or control.[68] The god of the Hebrew Bible/Old Testament feels acutely the restrictions of ancient media and technology, through which his will is actualized (but mostly not). Not surprisingly, given the limitations of ancient cultures, the Bible is full of stories about how God did not get what he wanted; how his promises were not fulfilled; how he and his people were defeated by rival, local, neighbouring gods who proved more powerful on the day; how he was misrecognized, confused with other gods. In ancient texts, the powers of gods go up and down, like the Dow-Jones index, according to how well they have performed in this or that harvest or battle. Contra the truism that monotheistic gods are stable, unlike their polytheistic counterparts, history and contingency leaves the god(s?) of the Hebrew Bible/Old Testament with conflicting characteristics and highly variable powers. The old gods cannot dream of docile obedient believers. The old prophets, whose writings rehearse their rejection and the rejection of the word, have far less faith than moderns in the automatic success of the divine command. Those who actually sacrifice to and depend on the powers of the gods are powerfully aware of divine inability. They are particularly aware of the lack of divine muscle to secure land, and the line of supply in the goods of the land.

No effective governance without *territory* – but the old gods have far more trouble than modern nation states in gaining control and deciding the future of a particular piece of land. This is particularly true of the God of the Hebrew Bible, the God named by Josephus and others as the founding godfather of theocracy, a totalizing divine power. The kingdom of Saul and David was a very small piece of territory, held for just a few (mythologized) years before it was annexed by Assyria and then Babylon. Though technically a monarchy led by God, it was barely larger than the isolated theocracies of Savonarola's Florence or Münster or Jonestown: a tiny piece of time and space. The Bible tells a paradoxical story of the occupation of the promised land, which is always promised, but never quite actualized, or securitized. "God did not give any of it as a heritage, not even a foot's length" (Acts 7:5). The secure possession of the land is always in the future – or the past. Earlier I argued that there is something polemical, and suspicious, about the way we isolate and contain "theocracy," so that "theocracy" is only used to describe sectarian religion, or very small slivers of time and space. But these little pins on the world map and the timeline inadvertently point to an important revelation. *It has proved very difficult for the old gods to reign.* In practice, instead of reigning eternally, they reigned for a short time, before the new gods and new armies came; before they died, or passed their worship-by-date.

Theocracy as an Apologetic, Aspirational Term
That Can Never Live Up to Its Name

The grand aspirations of the word "theocracy" are undermined by the context in which the term was coined. The life of the author is a significant clue. The condition of being subject to the Roman empire gave birth to the metaphysical fantasy of the pure empire of God. Titus (?) Flavius Josephus (and note the name, compounded with the names of the ruling Roman dynasty) was born Joseph, son of Matthayahu, a priestly aristocrat with connections to the ruling Hasmonean family in what was then the Roman province of Judaea. Though he later harshly criticized the rebels, he was one of the leaders of the defence in Galilee during the war against Rome (66–74 CE). He surrendered after the siege of Jotapata (67 CE) and survived when everyone else was killed. His survival not surprisingly led to endless accusations – but his own version of the story was that he was saved and granted Roman citizenship because he had successfully predicted that Vespasian would become emperor. His Flavian conquerors took him to Rome, where he became a historian and propagandist for Jewish history and culture, and for his own career. At the same time that John of Patmos was creating his revenge-fantasy against Rome, led by a God who out-emperored the Roman emperor and was constructed in his image (we now call it the book of Revelation, the book that has been so beloved by millenarian Christian "theocrats"), Josephus was negotiating with empire in a very different tone.[69] He created a new hybridized Jewish identity for a Greco-Roman context, aiming for a form of Jewishness that was consummately Greco-Roman but in important respects unassimilated, distinct.

In *Against Apion*, 2.164–8, Josephus presents a Jewish Moses (and a Jewish Josephus) who are *au fait* with the basic constitutional forms rehearsed from Herodotus, Plato, and Aristotle to Plutarch and Cicero. Moses and Josephus can hold their own with the political and philosophical elites. They also contribute their own distinctly Jewish political category: theocracy. Even theocracy, arguably, is not completely independent of Greco-Roman precedent. Plato had tried out neologisms like *timokratia* (*Republic*, 545b), and suggested that "the state should be named after the God who rules over those who possess reason" (*Laws*, 713a–14a). Something rather like theocracy is anticipated in the Greek philosophical dream of a mode of governance that does not require human institutions, but operates through the force of immortality, reason, law, and the law within.[70] Josephus also claims that through his daring innovation, Moses laid the foundation for the very best of the Greco-Roman theology. In instituting theocracy, Moses intuited that God is One, uncreated, immutable, and transcendent. In this way he set the precedent for the later teachings of Pythagoras, Anaxagoras, Plato, and the Stoics, the "wisest of the Greeks."[71]

The neologism "theocracy" was devised as a riposte to Apion's scurrilous anti-Jewish polemic. Apion had claimed that the Jewish god and Jewish forms of worship must be completely impotent because the temple had been destroyed and the Jews lived in subjection to the gentiles in "their" land. Josephus responds by recounting the destruction of holy sites at Alexandria, Athens, Ephesus, and Delphi and by pointing out that no shrine has existed eternally and that every nation has its share of subjection in the mutations in human affairs. But Josephus's riposte masks the fact that the Jews have a particularly strange relationship to governance and land.

To deal with this strange history, Josephus coins the exceptional category theocracy. But instantly he is faced with the practical question of describing how God rules. Josephus is no modern demystifier, no Feuerbach. But he sees theocracy as a human creation: the rule of God implemented on the ground. He calls theocracy a strong-armed word; a word in scare quotes; a term wrested by force. Perhaps this is because it is a strained form of ruling: an impossibility. He creates this forced word from a compound of *theos* ("god") and *kratia* ("power"). Given that he talks of God's *arche* and his *kratos* in this passage, it is interesting that Josephus does not force a *theos-arche*. Aristotelian powers come as *archy*s and *cracy*s (aristocracy and democracy; monarchy and oligarchy). *Arche* carries the sense of origin, command, source. *Kratia* implies regime, strength; rule through the appropriation and actualization of power. *Arche* might therefore be considered the more natural term for divine rule. But *kratia* is more in line with what Josephus describes. His concern is with the paradox of theocracy as a human constitution and the question of how the reign of God gets made (fabricated?) on earth.

John Barclay is right, I think, to argue that Josephus does not simply use theocracy as a tautology for hierocracy. Josephus has other terms for the rule of the priests. For him "theocracy" means (and this is why the term and the regime seems forced) a pure metaphysical divine rule. But there is no divine rule without actualization and implementation.

So, theocracy is made through and by Moses, and the teaching/Torah of Moses. Theocracy comes to pass through Moses

> ascribing to God the rule [*arche*] and power [*kratos*] and persuading everyone to look to him as the cause of all good things, both those that are common to all humanity and those that they themselves received when they prayed in difficulties, and that neither any deed nor anything that anyone thought in private could escape his attention, he represented him as single and uncreated and immutable through all eternity, more beautiful than any mortal form.[72]

Yehoshua Amir rightly feels that there is something "secular" about this passage.[73] I agree, though the statement needs to be nuanced. This is not secularity understood anachronistically as a self-conscious decision, as if Josephus lived in nineteenth- or twentieth-century Europe. This is a secularism *avant la lettre* emerging from the impossibility of actualizing theocracy as purely "religious," as if God could auto-institute divine rule. The divine rule is dependent on Moses, on his teaching and persuasion. No Moses, no God for the people, and no theocracy as divine rule.

For Josephus, Moses is superhuman, a God on earth – as he is in Exodus in fact.[74] Compared to our ancient legislator, the Greek Lycurguses and Solons are nothing. In the light of his most ancient written constitution, the Greeks appear to have been born but yesterday, or the day before.[75] Moses is the ancient one, the founder, who "made the whole mass of people dependent on himself" and "won their consent on all things," but did not use his all-powerful position for "personal aggrandizement." As Cromwell became a king in all but name, so Moses, who should represent the exclusive rule of God without human mediation, somewhat ironically became a figure of God incarnate, monotheism on earth:

> In precisely that situation where leaders assume powers and tyrannies, and accustom the masses to a life of complete lawlessness, [Moses] exemplified piety and provided a complete system of good laws so providing the safest form of security for those who had made him their leader ... Having first come to the conviction that everything he did and thought was in accordance with God's will, he considered it his prime duty to impress this notion upon the masses; for those who believe that God watches over their lives do not allow themselves to commit any sin.[76]

This encomium to Moses immediately precedes the invention of theocracy, as the creation of Josephus. Josephus's Moses makes theocracy, by persuading the people that everything comes from God and that Moses is the one ruler in the image of God.

Josephus's description of theocracy turns out to be quite bathetic for those expecting the imposition of divine rule, direct from the skies. This seems to be an occupational hazard for theocracy. High claims to "theocracy" are soon followed by qualifying statements or highly pedestrian visions of how this actually works out on the ground. As soon as a dictionary or encyclopedia entry proclaims "rule by God or some god(s)," it begins to pile up caveats such as "usually it refers to some form of divine rule through some human agent or lieutenant."[77] The Merriam-Webster dictionary suggests "government of a state by immediate divine guidance or by officials who are regarded as divinely guided." The first definition – immediate divine guidance without an intermediary – is offset by a second, more realistic clause: "alternatively, the opposite, rule through intermediaries." The term theocracy never appears without qualifications and strange accompanying statements about the term's inability to live up to its etymology.

The problem for theocracy is excruciatingly simple. How does an invisible god become visible, palpable? How does he actualize his power? Elaine Scarry is one of the few to pose this deliciously simple question and to explore the Bible's answer. The God of the Hebrew Bible becomes present through bodies, institutions, sacrifices, tabernacles, temples, tablets, sacred texts – and massive changes wrought in bodies, peoples, temples, texts.[78] Similarly, Josephus represents theocracy as *represented* through Moses and his persuasions, ascriptions, convictions, and representations. Moses "persuades," "ascribes," "convinces," "represents." The rule of God becomes manifest as a sociopolitical-discursive formation implemented by Moses and the Torah.

And Josephus (for his own polemical purposes) presents an extremely rosy picture of how this actually works. His Moses (and hence his God) secure absolute obedience and dependence on the one leader and the one God. The Torah/Pentateuch tells a far more bathetic and turbulent story: a story of theocracy torn "between actualization and contradiction";[79] theocracy *inachevé*. The people make a golden calf, a rival god. The ten commandments are smashed (and rewritten). The ever-recalcitrant people are punished by forty years of wandering and a deferred entrance to the promised land. Moses himself dies on the edge of the promised land, and before he dies writes the second law or

Deutero-nomos, to go into the land in his place (Deuteronomy 31:9 and 25ff.). But scripts and words and books are not very powerful, or very trustworthy, particularly in ancient media settings. The book called Deuteronomy records its ineffectiveness; it remembers in advance its forgetting. The people will prostitute themselves to foreign gods. They will "eat and grow fat" in the land of milk and honey. They will despise God and his law. In short, they will forget (Deuteronomy 31:16–17; 32:15–16).

Theocracy, Holy War, and the Struggle for Land

With the long-delayed entrance into the promised land comes the genocidal Holy War against the Canaanites. Josephus ascribes the exceptional state of theocracy to the Jews of the Hebrew Bible. Max Weber similarly sees "war in the name of god, for the special purpose of avenging a sacrilege" as initiated under Jewish monotheism, as "the people of Yahweh, as his special community, demonstrated ... their god's prestige against their foes."[80] In modernity, theocracy and holy wars go together as the spectre of the particular threat of religion. *Holy* wars are fought more intensely, so we believe, because they are fought by believers, acting on behalf of nothing less than absolute truth and the divine will.

The divinely ordained decimation of the Canaanites from the "theocratic" period before the kings, stands as the classical example of holy war. The bloody and potent history of the Canaan mandate (god's gift of the land of Canaan, inhabited by Canaanites, to Israel) is infamous. The biblical mandate was used by the Puritans in New England; Oliver Cromwell in Ireland; the Boers in South Africa; the British putting down the 1857 Indian "Mutiny"; settlers in the West Bank, a.k.a. "Judaea" and "Samaria"; and the US judge justifying the bloody annihilation of civilians in My Lai in the war in Vietnam.[81] We can easily rehearse the litany of examples. But we forget that the successful implementations of the biblical text began at the same time as the rise of the state and the military machinery of the modern state. These violent successes have then been retroactively mapped onto the ancient text, as if the ancient god could marshall modern military and technological powers. Ironically, the original text about Joshua's much-exaggerated "conquest" was in all likelihood the fantasy of a group living in the Persian or Babylonian empires. The scenario is completely fantastic. It projects a "god of war" in far more than the fairly pedestrian sense of the god who fights on our side. This god fights alone, and without assistance. In a vision as close as possible to a pure military theocracy, there are no soldiers, only priests. The city is "devoted to destruction." They don't have to fight, because the land has been given by divine decree. The "war" is led by the priests carrying the ark of the covenant. The Canaanite city walls are reduced to rubble by the force of worship (Joshua 6). The walls fall down at the sound of the ram's horns blown by the priests.

This fantastic projection of purely theocratic or hierocratic warfare is a compensatory gesture. Divine power stands in where there is a complete lack of military power. The syncretized books of Joshua and Judges tell other stories that undercut the (rare) dream of absolute divine power. The genocidal invasion fantasy coexists with far more realistic accounts of living in the midst of other peoples, with whom Israel is uncertainly mixed. The Bible tells humdrum, interminable, and thoroughly believable sagas of fighting for, and losing, and gaining, and losing, wells, gravesites, and other small pieces of land.

Only modern armies operating under the auspices of states, or nascent states, had the clout to turn these strange biblical texts into an *ideology*: an idea with force, capable of becoming facts on the ground. The old words really began to *do* things when taken up by Oliver Cromwell, who, with other deeply religious protestant generals (such as Maurice of Nassau or Gustavus Adolphus), was one of the first leaders of a truly modern military. The military revolution of the sixteenth and seventeenth centuries pushed warfare beyond the old rituals of a "narrow circle of aristocrats engaging in quasi-ritualistic skirmishes."[82] Gunpowder; the mass use of cannon in siege and naval artillery; the gradual spread of handguns such as the harquebus and matchlock musket; multidecked galleons; virtually impregnable fortifications; cheap and easy-to-operate handguns; and above all the bureaucratization and professionalization of the military with the first military academies were far more effective than the old gods in drilling and instilling ritualized murder by command. The exceptional powers and commands of ancient gods are as nothing compared to command structures within a military system run by highly specialized professionals who undergo long, institutionalized training, who are separated from the rest of society, obey an impersonal hierarchical order, and follow a highly ordered system of technical rules.

The divine mandate to take the given land of Canaan and deal appropriately with the inhabitants became far more toxic in the hands of the Boers in South Africa and the British in India, who had access to telegraphs, rifles, and machine guns. The mandate became even more effective in

the twentieth century, when the United States had access to B52 bomb-
ers, artillery, helicopters, napalm, and defoliants (Agent Orange), and
when politicians were able to justify their actions not through the
(naive) force of the Bible and "theocracy" *simplicitas*, but through the
vague distant force of biblical principle combined with the force of law.
Max Weber himself notes how "the sober and rational Puritan discipline made Cromwell's victories possible ... Gunpowder and all the
war techniques ... became significant only with the existence of discipline ... The varying impact of discipline on the conduct of war has
had even greater effects upon the political and social order."[83] Such military discipline and statecraft were hardly available to Joshua, or to the
Crusaders. According to Bernard of Clairvaux's 1126 account, crusaders
and "monks of war" read in silence, at meals, "from a French translation of the Bible" with "special emphasis being placed on the books
of Joshua and the Maccabees," and "all found inspiration in the ferocious exploits of the war-bands in reconquering the Holy Land from the
cruel infidels."[84] But inspiration is a vague driving force compared to
the force of petrol, oil, tanks, and drones and a Department of Defense
able to draw on over six hundred billion tax dollars every year.

Throughout the centuries, the gods and their representatives vastly
improved their techniques for getting land. In pre-modern England,
land came into the ownership of the Church not through direct divine
command, but techniques that were far more pedestrian and effective.
(The lesson of the Liberal Bible is that weakness is strength. "Divine
power" is more effective and tenacious when it does not manifest itself
as "theocracy" or absolute divine power.) Lands were endowed for
the maintenance of the monasteries or passed into Church hands in
exchange for perpetual prayers or masses for donors and their families. Institutionalized tithes and feudal management systems gave
property and land to the Church and bishops, and Church dignitaries
were granted hereditary land. Between the beginning of Henry VIII's
"secularization" program in 1536 and the end of the century, probably
as much as a quarter of all England changed hands. Such exchange of
property is the root metaphor of the secularization narrative: at heart,
the story of the transfer of *ownership* of central goods and concepts,
passing from church to "state." But given that the Church held, at most,
a quarter of all England before the (wrong) gods were forced to give it
back, it is clearly an exaggeration to say that the gods ever had complete
hold of the land – or that the gods were forced to return it. Gods are
plural. The "secularization" of Henry VIII stole from the repudiated

god, the god of the pope and institutionalized Catholicism, for the god of the new state church.

Earlier I noted how, symptomatically, we refuse to talk about pre-Reformation or Reformation Europe as theocratic, even as we imagine a quasi-totalitarian reign of Christendom in our pasts. We like to confine theocracy, and keep its pejorative and affective power for the politics of the other. But at the same time, the limited application of the term theocracy may inadvertently point to an important truth. There never has been theocracy as such. The (true) god has always been weaker than we assume. Effortless control by divinity is far easier to imagine from the vantage point of the future. It is far harder to believe in the present, even at the high water mark of Christendom's power. Accounts of the progress of Christendom from the sixteenth and seventeenth centuries (the time of Christianity's peak success, and new empires) are often unexpectedly mournful. They present the true god and his followers as beleaguered, while the false gods, the devil, or the Antichrist run rampant. The kingdom, the glory, and the coverage always seems to belong to the wrong gods; the wrong kind of power. Speaking from the midst of the Spanish Golden Age and the Christianization of the "New World" (on the surface hardly a bad time for Roman Catholicism), the Franciscan friar Bernardino de Sahagún gives a bleak report of the progress of the true Church:

> The Church left Palestine and now the infidels live, reign, and hold dominion in Palestine. From there it went to Asia in which there are now nothing but Turks and Moors. It went to Africa where, now, there are no Christians. It went to Germany where, now, there are none but heretics. It went to Europe where, in the greater part thereof, the Church is not obeyed.[85]

The progress of the true Church is not a *translatio imperii* but a *translatio stultitiae*. The true Church moves, hounded, across the globe. The collective that we imagine as "the Church" or "Christianity" is always composite, fragmented. It seems to be a defining criterion of the true god that he does not reign fully (yet); that his reign is always to come. At the other end of the theological spectrum (and representing the true Church's arch-enemy, for a figure like Sahagún), John Calvin struggled with local Erastians and did not see himself as having successfully established a gospel-based society in Geneva – despite later idealizations of a "city of divine light set upon a hill." In his *Political History of the Devil* of 1726, Daniel Defoe reports that the devil holds "most parts of the world to this day; he holds still all the eastern parts of Asia, and the southern parts of Africa, and the northern parts of Europe, and in them the vast countries of China and Tartary, Persia and India, Guinea, Ethiopia, Zanquebar, Congo, Angola, Monomotapa &c."[86]

Cuius region, eius religio. The gods are local – though not in the same way as they were in the Old Testament/Hebrew Bible. Geographical expansion only reveals the massive holdings of paganism, "Mahomedism," and what we (but not citizens of early modernity) would think of as other Christianities – as well as Christianity's stubbornly persistent others, the Jews.

Theocracy as the Most Unstable Political Order, Perilously Close to Anarchy

Theocracy is the political category that makes us think of the unthinking ones, the ones who are puppets in the hands of the gods and their credulous/manipulative representatives. It is also (somewhat ironically) the category that is the least thought through. It appears as the most simple and stable of regimes: a monistic political force. But in fact it proves the most unstable, as it fractures on the way down to the ground. More than any other regime, rule by divinity raises the immediate question of the representatives, delegates, or plenipotentiaries: those who are conferred with "full powers" at one remove. But who or what is to be designated as the plenipotentiary, the ambassador for full divine powers?: the priest(s), pope, archbishop, emperor, mullah, ayatollah, imam, or caliph, or sacred text (and which version, which tradition, in what language?), and by what authority, with what ceremony, and by whom?

As a quasi-Aristotelian category, theocracy adds an interesting twist to Aristotle's categorization of polities by numbers: the politics of the one, the many, and the few. The regime that seems the most stable and the most singular (in both senses) turns out to be the most disputed, the most plural. The "forced term" theocracy splits into subcategories: hierocratic theocracy; papal theocracy; royal theocracy; imperial theocracy; theonomy, the rule of the divine law; and scripturocracy, the rule of scripture. And this is only the first stage of the fracturing of the full powers. As soon as we put it under the historical microscope, a single category fissures into diversity and competition. To take "hierocratic theocracy" as an example, different chronological strata in the Bible have different understandings of the priests. Deuteronomy speaks of the "levitical priests" as a single category. But the later book Chronicles separates the two categories and sees the Levites as non-priests.[87] Though the term priestcraft originates with James Harrington (as Ronald Beiner shows in his essay in this volume), the diatribe against the priests and their antics can be traced back to the Bible. It originates in micro civil wars between different visions of true religious worship and politics: priests versus other priests; or priests versus those who deliberately do not call themselves priests and take exception to the dominant group. Josephus documents three major Jewish factions in the first century: the Sadducees (representing the elite priestly class); the Pharisees; and the "Essenes," the desert community who produced the Dead Sea scrolls. Some have connected the Essenes to another priestly faction known as the Zadokites, who were training alternative priests to purify the corrupted temple in preparation for the coming of the messiah. Many opposed the high priests appointed from the Sadducean aristocracy by the Roman empire. They were widely regarded as the assimilated puppets of the empire. At the other end of the political spectrum were the Jewish "zealots" or revolutionaries, who, according to Josephus "undertook to dispose of the high priesthood by casting lots for it." Josephus argues that Torah clearly supports hereditary priesthood and condemns the Zealots' attempts to pass off this innovation as "an ancient practice." In his strong refutation of the Zealots, Josephus makes the deep controversies over the priesthood visible. The Zealots' abolition of the priesthood was "no better than a dissolution of an undeniable law, and a cunning contrivance to seize upon the government, derived from those that presumed to appoint governors as they themselves pleased."[88]

Nor is hierocratic theocracy an exceptionally unstable brand of theocracy. We have already touched on the fragility of theonomy or scripturocracy. Appointing a single divine representative (like Josephus's Moses or the divine-right monarch) seems like the obvious way of stabilizing theocracy – but in practice the relation between electing divinities and their representatives can be profoundly volatile, and plenipotentiary divine powers prove too much for any human (or indeed deity) to actualize or bear. Though Josephus sagely ignores the fact, the biblical Moses "wears himself out" with the task of representing divinity on earth, even among a fairly small group of people (Exodus 18). Unlike Josephus, Exodus clearly tells a story of how Moses is unable to actualize, or incarnate, theocracy. Maybe this is why Josephus feels the term and practice of theocracy is "forced." In a story that Josephus judiciously forgets to mention, the biblical Moses appoints a hierarchy of delegates because the one cannot bear the full weight of centralized power (Exodus 18). The difficulty of actualizing and incarnating divine power appears, in different ways, in the stories about the monotheistic deity and his human representative, the king. The relationship between kings and electing divinities is profoundly volatile. As if to insist on the point, the biblical deity proclaims himself for and against kings. He sometimes has more than one king on the go at the same time. He rather unhelpfully chooses a new king (David) while another (Saul) is still reigning, unleashing dynastic wars. Finally, God seems to abandon the idea of the human anointed one (the king-*mashiach*) altogether, instead opting to sponsor the reign of a messiah to come. This leads to endless conflict over which messiah, and when and where and whether he has / will come.

The reigns of God, like the reigns of kings, are, counter-intuitively, the least simple, because powers represented as complete and self-sufficient make the others nervous. Pre-modern polities devised subtle ways of reining in sovereigns – even, especially, divine-right or absolute sovereigns. The kingship was carefully conceptually regulated and held hostage to the scrutiny of monitoring concepts such as "tyranny," "sovereignty," and the king's two bodies: one public and eternal and one private and mortal. Pre-modern economies were such that the king had to ask and pray and negotiate and threaten (far more than modern democratic governments) for money and land and soldiers and arms. In the same way, the king was held conceptually hostage to monitoring concepts such as the distinction between the sovereign and the tyrant, or the ingenious concept of the sovereignty as an eternal condition that could transcend, and even on occasion turn against, the king. The mythology of the king's two bodies made it possible to kill the sovereign to protect the sovereignty, or decapitate Charles I to protect the king.

The largest corporations and would-be monopolies attract the most regulation, even as they can also transcend it. The same logic applies to gods. Careful theological mechanisms had to be devised for respectfully regulating the most monotheistic gods, those who had been amplified with all the powers of the terrifying "omnis" of Western metaphysics. Such gods were respectfully told what they could do by the theologians, who have functioned like court advisers or PR representatives of the divine king. Technically, the Christian God had the *potentia absoluta* to do whatever he willed. But in practice (thanks be to God – and so we told him) he had decided (with a gentle nudge) to restrict himself to the *potentia ordinata*, and keep within the regulative normality of moral, criminal, and "natural" law. Of all terms, "God" must be the most regulated in the kinds of behaviours and social forms that he is prepared to approve – while also being (technically) the most transcendent, the most free.

But the freedom of God has always threatened to be more than technical. It threatens/promises to militate against established government in more or less moderate or managed ways. The Christian fundamentalist Roy Moore sees the true god as being against government (by definition).[89] Yet presumably, Moore is able to direct this anti-governmental divine force into support for the Republican party, the political party that represents itself as against strong government (according to the logic of the politicians against politics or the priests against the priests). But the paradox of theocracy is potentially far less amenable to mainstream politics and two-party representational systems. As Martin Buber put it in 1932, theocracy expresses the "intractableness of the human person, the drive of man to be independent of man, but for the sake of the highest commitment."[90] We assume that theocracy is the most passive form of government, in which everything is ordained from above. But theocracy can be paradoxically passive-active: a structure of *obedience as freedom from all submission*. Unlike some historical democracies and aristocracies, theocracy has never been and can never be "an institution of fixity and unequivocality" – and this is the point.[91] "The kingship of God is a paradox"[92] because theocracy is always perilously (and redemptively) close to institutionalized anarchy. In a sense, our institutionalized histories of theocracy admit that theocracy is close to anarchy. We acknowledge this surreptitiously (maybe even unconsciously) when we reserve the term theocrat for the self-appointed messiahs and "sectarians" who have posed the most severe challenge to state authority and religious orthodoxy.

Writing in response to the rise of Nazi totalitarianism and Zionism,[93] Martin Buber treats theocracy as far more than a political exhibit from the old Bible world or a museum of the Ancient Near East. He reads the old book of Judges as "a real, struggling, religious-political will to fulfilment, of the times a fragment of realisation, however altered." For Buber, the book of Judges is a battle between "tearing-asunder multiplicity" and "completion-desiring unity": a record of theocracy *inachevé*.[94] In Buber's politicized historical criticism, Judges is a composite work with two main strata: the "naive-theocratic" and the "reflective-monarchical."[95] A manifesto for theocracy was overwritten with an editorial overlay from a pro-monarchical group who claimed, polemically, "That which you pass off as theocracy has become anarchy."[96] The celebration of anti-monarchy or pre-monarchy sits awkwardly alongside another theologico-political position statement from a rival group who write from a different moment in the chronological saga of realpolitik and offer the repeated censorial caveat: "In those days there was no king in Israel, and everyone did what was right in his own eyes" (Judges 17:6, 21:25). The positive model of rule by God is transformed, by a strong editorial hand, into a warning – which coexists with the original template for anti-monarchy/pre-monarchy, or (for Josephus), "theocracy," which is still legible (though countered). No wonder that these syncretized, composite old archives went on to productively confuse and inspire competing theologico-political groups.

Concluding Comments

This essay has uncovered at least three surprising truths about theocracy. The first is Buber's paradox that I have expanded on in different ways throughout this essay. Theocracy is strangely close to anarchy. The regime that we think of as the most monistic is perhaps the most plural; the regime that we think of as the strongest and most centralized may in practice be the most transient and weak. The second, related, truth is that "the gods" rule most effectively in "incipient" or "virtual" theocracies, where the power of divinity is mixed with and backed up by distinctly modern powers, such as constitutionalism, taxation, a permanent and disciplined military, and the modern technologies and machineries of transcendence (such as digital technology). The third is that theocracy, for all the aura of dusty antiquity, is a new term, and a new fear. The 1970s is when we really began to worry about theocracy. The gods we fear are not the old gods, or those with poor or isolated supporters. They are those with access to precious natural resources and the weapons that give them powers and identities analogous to those of the modern state.

The old secularization narrative (with which we began this chapter) sets the old reign of religion firmly against the modern secular state. It defines – and perhaps amplifies – our freedoms through contrast to the obedience and thraldom attributed to the old gods and their regimes. Emancipation from the control of religion (even if not named as theocracy, insofar as it applies to our own Euro-American histories) allows us to exaggerate our own freedoms. The axiomatic contrast with religion makes modern politics feel truly free. The imagined totalizing force and compulsion of theocracies helps us to forget the operations of power that do not wait around for citizens to reason and concur that "this is justice."[97] Without undermining the importance of the kinds of freedoms that improve a country's rankings in the international freedom index (freedom of the press; freedom to demonstrate), many citizens of democracy feel very sceptical about the actual impact of these freedoms, or the powers of "the people"/*demos*. The people and the sovereignty of the people operates rather like the king's two bodies: the transcendent force "the people" can be completely detached from individual persons, or even the collective of democracy. The demos has become a numinous, invisible, transcendent power – the spectre of virtue – that can be detached from the crowd. Edmund Morgan describes the people as a force that "could not be seen or heard at any given time or place," but that might "nevertheless give proof of its existence, like the existence of God."[98] The very belated extension of the *demos* to "all the people" (and always with caveats) reveals the primary function of this term as representation, iconography. And because "demos" and "freedom" function as self-affirming words, tautologies for virtue (unlike the now much maligned word "god" or "theos"), they can function as the old gods were presumed to do: bestowing the aura of automatic virtue on political decisions. The spectre of the old gods and their imminent takeover deflects attention away from those new transcendent forces that are more like the imagined gods than the old gods could ever be. Are gods and the believers really where the power is these days? Or are other transcendent invisible forces afoot, ones in which we all believe, such as law, economy, and the "demos" as the transcendent (unquestionable) virtues of democracy? Law really gets around, more than the old gods ever did. Far more effectively than Moses's Yahweh or Zeus, law regulates citizens' bodies, cities, and speech. And what of the mysterious numerology of "the economy" – that newly made noun of the twentieth century – with all its kabbalistic secrets and acronyms such as GDP? Transnational balance sheets and the desires of "the economy" are, like the ancient scriptures and the wills of the gods, known only to a few elites. But their pronouncements can effectively demand/command fasting – or austerity – far more successfully than the old priesthoods ever could. We have seen this recently in the supposed birthplace of democracy: Greece. Perhaps, counter-intuitively, the recent concentration on the old gods is comforting. It's an old frisson we can manage, and that we know what to do with. We can identify and resist old deities, fanatics, priests. We don't know what to do with these modern forms of divinity, or how to approach them. The focus on theocracy, and the old gods, gives us an identifiable target and reassures us that, in contrast, we are (relatively) free.

NOTES

1 Charles Taylor, "The Meaning of Secularism," *Hedgehog Review* 12.3 (2010): 23–4.
2 Jean Bethke Elshtain, *Sovereignty: God, State and Self* (New York: Basic Books, 2008), 57.
3 Thomas Luckmann, *The Invisible Religion: The Problem of Religion in Modern Society* (New York: Macmillan, 1967), 61.
4 Compare Timothy Fitzgerald's argument that "religion" and "politics" were created "as part of the same rhetorical movement." Timothy Fitzgerald, *Discourse on Civility and Barbarity: A Critical History of Religion and Related Categories* (Oxford and New York: Oxford University Press, 2007), 16.
5 Mark Goldie, "The Civil Religion of James Harrington," in *The Languages of Political Theory in Early Modern Europe*, ed. Anthony Pagden (Cambridge: Cambridge University Press, 1987), 198.
6 John Mullan, in *The Guardian Review*, reviewing Tim Harris, *Revolution: The Great Crisis of the British Monarchy 1685–1720* (London: Penguin, 2006), and Edward Vallance, *The Glorious Revolution: Britain's Fight for Liberty* (Boston: Little, Brown, 2006). https://www.theguardian.com/books/2006/feb/25/featuresreviews.guardianreview4.
7 Goldie, "The Civil Religion of James Harrington," 198.
8 Eviatar Zerubavel, *Time Maps: Collective Memory and the Social Shape of the Past* (Chicago: University of Chicago Press, 2004), 88.
9 Hans Blumenberg, *The Legitimacy of the Modern Age*, trans. Robert M. Wallace (Cambridge, MA: MIT Press, 1985), 4.
10 See, for example, Yvonne Sherwood, "On the Freedom of the *Concepts* of Religion and Belief," in *Politics of Religious Freedom*, ed. Winnifred Fallers Sullivan, Elizabeth Shakman Hurd, Saba Mahmood, and Peter G. Danchin (Chicago: University of Chicago Press, 2015), 29–44; and Yvonne Sherwood, "The Problem of 'Belief,'" in *The Social Equality of Religion or Belief: A New View of Religion's Place in Society*, ed. Alan Carling (New York: Palgrave Macmillan, 2016), 74–93.
11 Even professional atheists such as Christopher Hitchens or Richard Dawkins regularly recite the modern mantra that beliefs are "deeply held." See Yvonne Sherwood, *Biblical Blaspheming: Trials of the Sacred for a Secular Age* (Cambridge: Cambridge University Press, 2012), 57.

12 Mark D. Lilla, *The Stillborn God: Religion, Politics and the Modern West* (New York: Knopf, 2007), 307.

13 Matthew 25:1–13.

14 The elusive idea of the *katechon* – the restrainer, or the restraining force in history – is found in 2 Thessalonians 2:6–7 and was introduced to twentieth-century discussions of political theology by Carl Schmitt.

15 Kevin Phillips, *American Theocracy: The Peril and Politics of Radical Religion, Oil, and Borrowed Money in the 21st Century* (New York: Viking, 2006), 172.

16 Josephus, *Antiquities* 4.223–4, 6.36. See John Barclay's commentary on Josephus, *Against Apion*, trans. and commentary John Barclay (Leiden: Brill, 2003), 261. As Barclay notes: "At least on the surface, the depiction of the Judean constitution is quite different from the descriptions in Josephus's earlier works. There, despite references to the rule of God … Josephus applied the normal labels to the fluctuating forms of constitution. In his fullest survey (*Ant.* 20.224–51), the original constitution was an 'aristocracy' (under Moses and Joshua), followed by a period of monarchy (the judges), then the rule of kings; after the captivity, the high-priests governed 'democratically' before a period of Hasmonean and Herodian kings, whose dismissal led to the restoration of 'aristocracy.'" (The terminology is not always consistent; cf. *Ant.* 11.111–12 with 20.234.)

17 Martin Buber, *Kingship of God*, trans. Richard Scheimann (London: Allen and Unwin, 1967 [1932]), 75.

18 Julius Wellhausen, *Prolegomena zur Geschichte Israels* (1905), 417; cf. the discussion in Buber, *Kingship of God*, 64.

19 *Against Apion*, 2.164–5, trans. Barclay. I have used this translation in preference to the translation by Henry St John Thackeray in Josephus, *The Life and Against Apion*, Loeb Classical Library (Cambridge, MA: Harvard University Press, 1997). Placing the emphasis on idiomatic English, the Loeb translation uses phrases that Josephus would never use – for example, in this passage, the "hands of God"!

20 I am grateful to Ward Blanton for his assistance with translation.

21 See, for example, Eric Nelson, *The Hebrew Republic: Jewish Sources and the Transformation of European Political Thought* (Cambridge, MA: Harvard University Press, 2010).

22 See, for example, Milan Zafirovski, *The Destiny of Modern Societies: The Calvinist Predestination of a New Society* (Leiden: Brill, 2009), 281.

23 The double appointment of the biblical King David, by God and then by the people, was a key biblical proof for the double legitimation of kingship and government. William Allen (a pseudonym for Edward Sexby), was one of many who pointed to the fact that "David was appointed king by

[Samuel], but was afterwards, after Saul's death, confirmed by the people of Judah, and seven years after by the Elders of Israel, the people's deputies." William Allen, *Killing Noe Murder. Briefly Discourst in Three Quaestions* in *Divine Right and Democracy: An Anthology of Political Writing in Stuart England*, ed. David Wootton (Indianapolis: Hackett, 2003 [1657]), 365.

24 Thomas Hobbes, *Behemoth, or the Long Parliament*, ed. Ferdinand Tönnies (London: Frank Cass, 1969 [1682]), 21.

25 Anon., *A Political Catechism, or Certain Questions concerning the Government of this Land, Answered in his Majestie's own Words, taken out of his Answers to the Nineteen Propositions* (London, 1643). Compare the wise mixtures advocated, for example, by Plato, *Laws*, 712d; and Cicero, *Republic*, 1.69–70.

26 See Yvonne Sherwood, "The God of Abraham and Exceptional States: The Early Modern Rise of the Whig/Liberal Bible," *Journal of the American Academy of Religion* 76.2 (2008): 312–43; and Yvonne Sherwood, "The Genesis of the Alliance between the Bible and Rights," in Sherwood, *Biblical Blaspheming*.

27 The people and the sovereignty of the people operate rather like the king's two bodies: the transcendent force "the people" can be completely detached from individual persons, or even the collective of democracy. Edmund Morgan describes the people as a force that "could not be seen or heard at any given time or place," but that might "nevertheless give proof of its existence, like the existence of God." See Edmund S. Morgan, *Inventing the People: The Rise of Popular Sovereignty in England and America* (London: W.W. Norton, 1988).

28 Robert Atkyns, *An Enquiry into the Power of Dispensing with the Penal Statutes*, in *Complete Collection of State Trials and Proceedings for High Treason and Other Crimes and Misdemeanours, from the Earliest Period to the Year 1783*, ed. T.B. Howell (London: T.C. Hansard, 1816 [1686]), 34 vols., vol. 9 (32 Charles II to 4 James II, 1680–8), col. 1200–47.

29 Sir Robert Atkyns, "An Enquiry into the Power of Dispensing with the Penal Statutes," in *State Trials*, ed. T.B. Howell, 11, col. 1200–47 (Hansard, 1816).

30 Micheline R. Ishay, *The Human Rights Reader: Major Political Essays, Speeches, and Documents from Ancient Times to the Present* (New York and London: Routledge, 2007).

31 Robert Bellah, *Beyond Belief: Essays on Religion in a Post-Traditional World* (New York: Harper and Row, 1976), 68; Francis Fukuyama, *The End of History and the Last Man* (New York: Free Press, 2006); Peter Berger, *The Sacred Canopy: Elements of a Sociological Theory of Religion* (Garden City, NY: Doubleday, 1967), 127; Marcel Gauchet, *The Disenchantment of the World: A Political History of Religion* (Princeton: Princeton University Press, 1997), 80.

32 Roy Moore, *So Help Me God: The Ten Commandments, Judicial Tyranny and the Battle for Religious Freedom* (Nashville: Broadman & Holman, 2005), 109.

33 John Henry Newman, *Parochial Sermons*, 2nd ed. (1836), 2.21.283 (as referenced in the *OED*).

34 The first use of the term "secular" is usually attributed to George Jacob Holyoake in 1851, though it rose to prominence through institutions such as the National Secular Society, founded in 1866.

35 Thomas Paine, *Rights of Man*, in *The Complete Writings of Thomas Paine*, ed. Philip S. Foner, 2 vols. (New York: Citadel, 1945), 1: 277.

36 Ran Hirschl, *Constitutional Theocracy* (Cambridge, MA: Harvard University Press, 2010), 3

37 Working completely independently (until we read one another's essays at the end of the process), Peter Simpson and I both explored the provocative oxymoron "theocratic liberalism."

38 Phillips, *American Theocracy*, 208.

39 See, for example, Will Herberg, *Protestant-Catholic-Jew: An Essay in American Religious Sociology* (New York: Doubleday, 1955).

40 The state of Israel provides its own challenges to "theocracy." "Judaism" is a modern invention and is not necessarily "theistic," or even religious. The state of Israel is founded on profoundly modernized Jewish forms: Torah as a mandate and a book of historical foundation; and Zionism as a political cause.

41 For a recent statement of this position, positioning the Greeks and Romans on the side of reason and the proto-secular, see Charles Freeman, *The Closing of the Western Mind: The Rise of Faith and the Fall of Reason* (London: Pimlico, 2002).

42 Max Weber, "Politics as a Vocation" (1919), in Weber, *The Vocation Lectures* (Indianapolis: Hackett, 2004), 33.

43 See, for example, Bruce Lincoln, *Holy Terrors: Thinking about Religion after September 11* (Chicago: University of Chicago Press, 2006); Bruce B. Lawrence, *Defenders of God: The Fundamentalist Revolt against the Modern Age* (Columbia: University of South Carolina Press, 2006).

44 Douglas Hartmann, Xuefeng Zhang, and William Wischstadt, "One (Multicultural) Nation Under God? Changing Uses and Meanings of the Term 'Judeo-Christian' in the American Media," *Journal of Media and Religion* 4 (2005): 207–34.

45 Jacob Heilbrunn, "Neocon v. Theocon: The New Faultline on the Right," *The New Republic*, 30 December 1996.

46 Phillips, *American Theocracy*, 218. In 2005, *The Economist* reported that "liberals regularly contend that one of America's two great parties is bent on creating a theocracy – backed by a solid core of somewhere between

a quarter and one third of the population." In an article in the *New York Times* in the same year, Congressman Christopher Shays lamented that "the Republican Party of Lincoln has become a party of theocracy."

47 Phillips, *American Theocracy*, 99, 103.

48 Ibid., 103.

49 Hirschl, *The Rise of Constitutional Theocracy*, 4; Said A. Arjomand, "Islamic Constitutionalism," *Annual Review of Law and Social Science* 3 (2007): 115–40.

50 Lincoln, *Holy Terrors*, 20.

51 See further Yvonne Sherwood, ed., "Bush's Bible," *Postscripts* 2.1 (2006), including my own contribution, "Bush's Bible as a Liberal Bible (Strange Though That Might Seem)," 47–58.

52 Phillips, *American Theocracy*, 209.

53 Ibid., viii–ix. The term "virtual theocracy" is borrowed from Paul Kurz in an article in the *New Humanist*, "The New American Theocracy" (31 May 2007): "Today the USA has become a virtual theocracy (de facto if not de jure)."

54 For some first attempts to think through what I'm calling the iconography of democracy see Sherwood, *Biblical Blaspheming*, 53–61; and Sherwood, "Iconographies of Modernity: Figures of Religion, Authority, and Gender in the 'Secular' State," in Naomi Goldenberg and Kathleen McPhillips, eds., *The End of Religion: Toward a Feminist Reinvention of the State* (Farnham, UK: Ashgate, 2018).

55 Margot Badran, "Gendering the Secular and the Religious in Modern Egypt: Woman, Family and Nation," in *Religion, the Secular, and the Politics of Sexual Difference*, ed. Linnell E. Cady and Tracy Fassenden (New York: Columbia University Press, 2013), 114.

56 See Beiner, "Shaftesbury's *Characteristics* and the Problem of Priestcraft" in this volume. I was rather surprised by Ronald Beiner's statement that I argue that "the spectre of theocratic oppression is merely an invention of religion-despising Western liberals" (n. 7). In fact, I argue that "theocracy" became *much more powerful* in the modern period, when the gods and their representatives could use modern governmental infrastructures and military technologies. The weakness in my title refers to the weakness of the idea of divinity *simplicitas* as a mode of government, a weakness that is very clearly articulated in ancient sources like Josephus and the Bible. Following Hirschl, I explore the complex negotiations between tradition, the economy, and modern constitutional forms, resulting in an unseemly (unholy?) mixing of times and expectations – as in Beiner's "Islamic Erastianism" or Peter Simpson's oxymoronic "theocratic liberalism." I do not in any way deny the rise of "clericalism" in Iran or Afghanistan, but I would caution against the elision of complex international political

histories into Manichean narratives of the rise of "cruelty," "hatred," and "fear" that come, primarily, from the new powers given to the old gods.

57 "Globalization is basically a force that pushes people together. And if religion is a force that pulls people apart, it becomes actually a threat to the way the 21st century works." See "Tony Blair: A Conversation at Yale University," at minute 2:50, https://www.youtube.com/watch?v=hf1e-pf1irI.

58 Hirschl, *Constitutional Theocracy*, 13

59 Phillips, *American Theocracy*, 103.

60 Ibid., 6.

61 For a discussion of pre-modern critique see Sherwood, "Binding-Unbinding: Pre-critical 'Critique' in Pre-modern Jewish, Christian and Islamic responses to the 'sacrifice' of Abraham/Ibrahim's Son," in Sherwood, *Biblical Blaspheming*, 333–74.

62 I am intrigued by the way in which Peter Simpson presents the gods in his excellent essay "Theocracy's Challenge." He begins by stating the commonplace: the gods are "immune to the miseries and trials of life." He then challenges the crudity of these beliefs. But finally, he "abstracts" from the crude picture to return to a more traditional idea of divinity (as a standard that dwarfs humanity). Is this a symptom of the potency of the clichés and powers that we automatically attribute to the gods (despite counter-evidence)? I would contend that the anthropomorphism and the weakness of the gods can be pushed much further, and that the Hebrew Bible, and the classical tradition, are far less secure in the distinction between the human and the divine.

63 ISIS has issued annual reports, outlining in numerical and geographical detail its operations – the number of bombings, assassinations, checkpoints, suicide missions, cities taken over, and even "apostates" converted to the ISIS cause – as if mimicking the detailed public accounting of a corporation. See Roula Khalaf and Sam Jones, "Selling Terror: How Isis Details Its Brutality," *Financial Times*, 17 June 2014.

64 Kanan Makiya and Hassan Mneimneh, "Manual for a 'Raid,'" *New York Review of Books*, 17 January 2002, 18–21.

65 David Shariatmadari, "Why There's No Such Thing as Islamic State," *The Guardian*, 1 October 2014. http://www.theguardian.com/commentisfree/2014/oct/01/islamic-state-language-isis.

66 Weber, "Politics as a Vocation," 33.

67 Anthony Giddens, *The Nation-State and Violence* (London: Routledge, 1985), 119, 172.

68 The god of the Hebrew Bible is regularly presented as outraged because the people follow other gods who seem more potent and capable. He

is accused by his people of sleeping, or having abandoned them. He is urged by his people to act in order to *save his name*: that is, to prevent rival groups and gods from humiliating and abusing his name and the people identified with that name.

69 For discussions of Josephus's complex relationship to the Roman empire, see Jonathan Edmondson, Steve Mason, and James Reeves, *Flavius Josephus and Flavian Rome* (Oxford: Oxford University Press, 2005); James S. McLaren, "A Reluctant Provincial: Josephus and the Roman Empire in *Jewish War*," *The Gospel of Matthew in Its Roman Imperial Context*, ed. John Riches and David C. Sim (London: T&T Clark, 2005); Erin Runions, "From Babel to Biopolitics: Josephus, Theodemocracy and the Regulation of Pleasure," in *The Babylon Complex: Theological Fantasies of War, Sex and Sovereignty* (Fordham: Fordham University Press, 2014), 46–85.

70 Here I am inspired by John Barclay's comments in his notes to *Against Apion*, 2.165 (262).

71 Josephus, *Against Apion*, 2.168.

72 Ibid., 2.165–7.

73 Yehoshua Amir, "Theokratia as a Concept of Political Philosophy: Josephus's Presentation of Moses," *Politeia. Scripta Classica Israelica* 8–9 (1985–8): 83–105 (97). See the discussion in Barclay, 263.

74 In the book of Exodus, Moses is a deeply elusive character. He is portrayed as unable to speak, lacking the abilities of the average human, but he is *also* presented as a superhuman divinity on earth.

75 *Against Apion*, 2.154.

76 Ibid., 2.158–61.

77 Andrew J. Waskey, "The Political Theory of Theocracy," National Social Science Association, 2007. http://www.nssa.us/journals/2007-28-1/2007-28-1-16.htm.

78 Elaine Scarry, *The Body in Pain: The Making and Unmaking of the World* (Oxford: Oxford University Press, 1985).

79 Buber, *The Kingship of God*, 139.

80 Max Weber, *The Sociology of Religion* (Boston: Beacon Press, 1993), 86–7.

81 For the now widely familiar litany of examples, see for example Michael Prior, *The Bible and Colonialism: A Moral Critique* (New York: Continuum, 1997). On the use of the precedent of Joshua in the murder trial of William Calley for the massacre at My Lai, see Harold C. Washington, "Violence and the Construction of Gender in the Hebrew Bible: A New Historicist Approach," *Biblical Interpretation* 5 (1997): 324–63.

82 Sinisa Malesevic, *The Sociology of War and Violence* (Cambridge: Cambridge University Press, 2010), 109.

83 Quoted ibid., 25.

84 Desmond Seward, *The Monks of War: The Military Religious Orders* (New York: Penguin Books, 1995), 31–2.

85 Bernardino de Sahagún, *General History of the Things of New Spain: Florentine Codex*, vol. 11, trans. Arthur J.O. Anderson and Charles E. Dibble (Salt Lake City: University of Utah, 1950–82 [ca. 1570]), 93.

86 Daniel Defoe, *The Political History of the Devil, as well ancient as modern* (London: T. Warner, 1726), 143–4.

87 Cf. Karel Van der Toorn, *Scribal Culture and the Making of the Hebrew Bible* (Cambridge, MA: Harvard University Press, 2007), 92–6.

88 Josephus, *The Jewish War*, 4.151–8.

89 Roy Moore is the judge who erected a monument to the ten commandments on the grounds of his Alabama courthouse. See the earlier discussion in this chapter.

90 Buber, *The Kingship of God*, 138.

91 Ibid., 64.

92 Ibid.

93 The 3rd (1955) edition of *The Kingship of God* has three prefaces: from 1932, 1936, and 1955.

94 Buber, *The Kingship of God* (1932), 68.

95 Ibid., 80

96 Ibid., 78.

97 Slavoj Žižek, *The Sublime Object of Ideology* (London and New York: Verso, 1995), 37.

98 Morgan, *Inventing the People*.

12 Understanding Our Adversaries: Ancient vs. Modern Political Thought

JAMES FRANKE AND LAURIE M. JOHNSON

While over half of the world's Muslims live in non-theocratic systems, tensions which exist between the West and the Muslim world derive in part from a perceived conflict between relatively secular Western regimes and those elements in the Muslim world, often at odds with their own governments, who long for some sort of theocracy. On the one hand, the stated long-term goal of US foreign policy has been, for quite some time and across Republican and Democratic presidencies, the implementation of democratic reforms and the development of capitalist commerce in Muslim countries that are perceived as sponsors or potential sponsors of terrorist movements.[1] To the contrary, theocratic factions within various Muslim societies desire in the short term the triumph of their view of Islamic governance in Muslim majority countries. The longer term goal of some Islamic extremists like those in ISIS seems to be the conquest of additional territory for the Caliphate. In fact, some believe that peace will reign only once the world submits to the true religion. While much of the Western world has embraced secularism and religious toleration, some in the Islamic world have articulated a theocratic position. In turn, where the West is perceived by Islamic critics as being too worldly and materialistic, Islamic fundamentalists see their position as otherworldly and anti-materialistic, and therefore morally and spiritually superior.

Both sides accuse one another of sinister motives. Rather than taking the otherworldly focus of Islamic extremist movements seriously, Western political leaders have argued that religion is being used as a ruse designed to cover up the true ambitions of radical leaders for political power and wealth. Likewise, Islamic critics of Westernization argue that the real goal of the West is to dominate Islamic territory for access to oil and domination of markets, to conquer Islam with liberal and capitalistic ideology, or, worse yet, to destroy Islam and replace it with Christianity. These misunderstandings continue to obstruct the ability of the international community to address instability in the Middle East properly and have undoubtedly led to even greater violence and unrest globally. In truth, until we understand why liberal ideology and theocratic ideologies are so opposed, we will never comprehend why their opposition seems so intractable.

We will argue that this ideological conflict can be at least partly understood by recognizing that contemporary liberalism developed as a rejection of the tenets of religious fundamentalism. The work of political theorist Martin Diamond is especially helpful here because he clearly articulated the American founding as a distinctive response to the existent "pre-modern" religious world view that dominated politics and government at the time.[2] That is to say, because the separation of church and state was a specific liberal response to a dangerous conjoining of religion and politics, contemporary liberalism still necessarily rejects the theocratic position of many of today's Islamic fundamentalists.[3] Through a discussion of the differences between pre-modern and modern political thought inspired in part by Diamond's essay "Ethics and Politics: The American Way," we challenge the common and erroneous view that both sides' arguments are *mere* rhetorical window-dressing towards an explanation for why these two world views inevitably clash.

The Pre-Modern View

Diamond offers a thoroughgoing explanation of the pre-modern idea of ethics, politics, and their connection to one another. He does so by turning appropriately to Aristotle, whose thought has impacted both Western liberal and Islamic societies. Aristotle's notion of human excellence goes beyond what we normally think of as ethics, and encompasses the virtues that lead to the full development of the human being, ending in the twin ideals of citizenship/statesmanship and the life of contemplation in action. The Greek idea of the relationship between this type of ethics and politics was very different from the liberal viewpoint. For liberals, character formation is left up to individuals and families in private life. But, the pre-modern way was to see character formation as the chief occupation of the state. Each regime, in this way of thinking, produced a "distinctive human type."[4] Human beings make the laws and institutions of regimes over time, and they decide what they will value and promote through them.

Aristotle understood that most real regimes would fall short of the ideal, but all of them would aim at some sort of character formation. All had different views about the "best life" that could be measured against the polity as the ideal. While these regimes might not produce Aristotle's absolutely best human character, each strove to make human beings better than they were. But the best regime, according to Aristotle, is one in which a good citizen and good man are one and the same.[5] The "best life, both for individuals and states, is the life of excellence, when excellence has external goods enough for the performance of good actions."[6]

All regimes that aim at forming character in a particular way require a lot from their citizens. The natural inclination to be virtuous is usually believed to be in short supply. What's to be done? For pre-modern philosophers such as Aristotle, the solution was to promote virtue through laws in a way that today would be considered indoctrination. Pre-modern philosophers thought that the character of citizens could only be reformed in governments able to enforce such laws. Such governments had to set high standards and then enforce them. "An unceasingly demanding and powerful political art was required if men were to be raised so high against the downward pulls of ease, creature comfort, and the lower pleasures," according to Diamond.[7] In particular, they sought to allow those who could achieve true excellence to rise to the surface.

The consequence of this strategy is inevitably inegalitarian and authoritarian. Even within Aristotle's ideal polity some citizens would emerge as better than others. For example, within the Spartan regime, some warriors would prove more courageous than others, and therefore obtain more power. In order to produce some of the best human beings as defined by a particular regime, all must be ruled by what Westerners would deem inegalitarian and oppressive government: "the emphasis placed on rigorous and comprehensive programs of education; the strict regulation of much of what we now deem 'private'; the necessity of civic piety; the extremely limited size of the polis; and the severe restrictions on private economic activity."[8] The aim, and hopefully the result, was a higher quality of life, a life with meaning, defined and guided by the elites. By contrast, the modern way would been seen by these ancients as promoting a sort of aimlessness, in which each individual thinks and does as he wants, and very few if any come close to the ideal because they receive no guidance, and so most live without a higher meaning or purpose, a life that is mediocre at best. Plato's description of the democratic man in *The Republic* is also instructive here for glimpsing what would be the ancient opinion of modern liberal democracy, which leaves too much to the individual to decide. Discussing democratic man, Socrates says:

> And he lives on, yielding day by day to the desire at hand. Sometimes he drinks heavily while listening to the flute; at other times, he drinks only water and is on a diet; sometimes he goes in for physical training; at other times, he's idle and neglects everything; and sometimes he even occupies himself with what he takes to be philosophy. He often engages in politics, leaping up from his seat and saying and doing whatever comes into his mind.[9]

For Plato, pure democracy was not really a regime at all, or at least the worst regime (except for tyranny), because it did not aim to produce any particular kind of human excellence. Today, Islamic theocracy does the opposite – it aims to produce good Muslims and an ideal Muslim society and economy, because that is the idea of the best life as revealed in the Islamic religion. For the theocrat, it seems extremely irresponsible to do anything less, because people's souls, and the nation's relationship to God, hang in the balance. In this way, the Islamic theocratic point of view is close to Diamond's "ancient" view of the relationship between ethics and politics.[10]

The Modern Way

During the feudal era in Europe, theologians and intellectuals sought to support theocracy, monarchy, and feudal hierarchy via the combination of Aristotelian thought and Christianity. "But the great traditions of classical and Christian political philosophy came under trenchant attack during the sixteenth and seventeenth centuries by such political philosophers as Machiavelli, Bacon, Hobbes, and Locke."[11]

According to these modern philosophers, the standards of the ancient philosophers and medieval theologians were deemed too idealistic, even utopian. Machiavelli put it this way:

> My hope is to write a book that will be useful, at least to those who read it intelligently, and so I thought it sensible to go straight to a discussion of

how things are in real life and not waste time with a discussion of an imaginary world. For many authors have constructed imaginary republics and principalities that have never existed in practice and never could; for the gap between how people actually behave and how they ought to behave is so great that anyone who ignores everyday reality in order to live up to an ideal will soon discover he has been taught how to destroy himself, not how to preserve himself.[12]

Thus, modern thinkers like Machiavelli and Hobbes began to examine what they considered actual human behaviour – "what is" – versus the ancient and Christian idealists' focus on "what ought" to be. The moderns accepted aspects of human nature that were previously discouraged – self-interest, desire for glory, fearfulness – as normal, predictable, and therefore useful. Hobbes taught, for instance, that fear and rational self-interest would lead people to the social contract, which would lead to peace and prosperity. He did not aim at saving men's souls or leading them to higher virtues.

From the modern perspective these low aims were still very good – safety from external enemies, law, order, and economic growth. Moreover, by taking the higher aim of character formation off the table, the modern philosophers removed what they saw as the chief cause of internal and external conflict, namely, religion. Machiavelli taught that the interests of the prince and the people could coincide if the prince provided good laws and order and the people were armed. Hobbes taught that fear and rational self-interest would lead people to the social contract, which would lead to peace and prosperity. Neither of these thinkers had the aim of saving men's souls or leading them to higher virtues.

Leo Strauss describes the Hobbesian turn as "respectable, pedestrian hedonism, sobriety without sublimity and subtlety, protected or made possible by 'power politics.'"[13] He observed that modern political thought greatly reduced the purview of government, lowering its aims, and abandoning the character-forming function of government in exchange for increasing the chances for peace. In this volume, Simpson writes in a similar vein of this lowering of aims:

> Tame the beast of infinite passion by the equal coercion of all. Make such coercion, and not infinite pursuit, the object and measure of politics. Overthrow the ancient tradition of political thought, which aimed politics at the comprehensive good of happiness. Replace it with the novelty

of liberalism, which aims politics at securing for all the pursuit of their own vision of happiness in conditions of peace guaranteed by the power of the state.[14]

This critique alone might give us insight into how the Islamic world, which still highly values the pronouncements of scholars, and scholars of religion in particular, might view the advances of the West towards modern thinking.[15] The modern way of thinking on this issue has, by this time, been thoroughly ingrained in the Western mind. But for Islamic fundamentalists, who insist on Shari'a law, the modern way is foreign. For them, it is unnatural to think of government as limited only to the protection of safety, rights, and the setting of economic rules, and the idea of relegating the most important things in life to the random and arbitrary decisions of individuals seems too risky.

The American Way

Like all founders, the American statesmen of 1787 desired a society which would help Americans to be better people. A significant part of this goal involved stability – designing a republic that would endure. In fact, it is arguably the case that the deliberations of 1787 were more concerned with stability than virtue. Madison studied the sources of failure of past republics, including the recent calamities in the states under the Articles of Confederation, and discovered that tyranny resulting from faction was the principal reason that past republics had not survived. These republics had suffered from a shortage of the better motives, or virtues. What was to be done? The conventional wisdom would have involved some variation on the approach of Aristotle, which promoted virtue. In fact, the notion of a republic absent classical virtue was entirely alien to most at the time of the American founding.

Of interest to us in Madison's argument about how to control the effects of faction is where theocracies would fall in his scheme, relative to how liberal democracies would fall. Madison thought that there were two options for controlling factions: removing their causes or controlling their effects. There were, in turn, two possible ways to address faction at its root cause. The first of these, later to be followed by both the French and the Russians, is to turn to some sort of a dictatorship. Madison rejected this solution out of hand because it "is worse than the disease."[16] The second approach for confronting faction at its cause was to encourage everyone, or most everyone, to have the same opinions and passions. Although this may strike us today as absurd, this is close to the pre-modern approach championed by, among others, Aristotle. This is nothing other than deciding upon a particular ethic and publicly promoting it. In the intellectual context of his day, this type of unanimity could be imagined through some sort of Rousseauian civil religion, censorship, and so on. If all citizens (or even almost all) freely agreed, which is the theocratic ideal, there would be no problem of faction and the problem of oppression would also be solved.

Madison rejected this second attack on faction at its source because he believed that diversity of opinion was the natural state for human beings. Our very nature as rational creatures with the power of speech gives us the ability to form and communicate opinions. We are rational creatures with free will, and therefore incapable of anything even close to unanimity. "By rejecting the promotion of uniformity of opinion," Licht writes, "Madison rejects the Aristotelian solution."[17] Madison then turns to a consideration of solving the dilemma of factions by focusing upon dealing with their effects. First, he enumerates the several possible bases for factions including "opinion," "passion," and "interest." Second, he considers the implications of each type of faction for being able to deal successfully with the problem of tyranny. This results in a typology of sorts of desirable and undesirable factions, depending upon their likelihood of avoiding destructive tyranny.

The very idea that any sort of faction, and thus disagreement, could be desirable was arguably revolutionary at the time of the founding and is also at odds with some twenty-first-century Islamic ideology. So long as the public business focuses upon ethical/religious matters, differences of opinion are unacceptable and conflict can take on a life-and-death character. However, if the public focus is turned away from regime ethos, disagreement (faction) becomes more acceptable and may lead to competition rather than all-out conflict.

Three types of factions are clearly undesirable to the founders. First, they feared the effects of factions based upon strongly held opinions concerning issues of right and wrong, and a "zeal for different opinions concerning religion."[18] The world, of course, has a long history of religious conflict. The severity of the conflict stems from the fact that religion deals with singularly important matters (the afterlife among others) based largely upon faith, and is therefore not readily subject to compromise.[19]

While religion is the principal and obvious focus of the founder's concerns, other sources of ethical disagreement would also be of concern. For example, liberal thinkers starting with Hobbes rejected aristocratic honour for the same reason they wanted to "mute" religious motivations – both caused people to risk their lives. In the case of honour, one's reputation and self-concept, or one's dignity, are more important than mere life. In the case of religious zeal, one's immortal soul is more important. Why fight over honour or faith when there would never be an end to the argument, and in the case of religion at any rate, one could not actually force another person to have a particular faith inwardly (Locke) anyway?

But these liberal thinkers also had deep questions about both honour and faith beyond these practical considerations. While they argued that they should be defined and controlled by the sovereign (Hobbes) or tolerated by the government and people (Locke), both also argued that there was no way to reach the truth about either one of them, that in fact we could see them as essentially human constructs. For Hobbes, honour was a designation that was made by whomever was in power and could change, depending upon who was in power or the priorities of the time. He distinguished between natural religion and conventional religion, arguing that the many differences in doctrine, prayer, and worship among religions were merely superficial, and so no one need object if the sovereign arbitrarily set an official faith. For Locke, honour was an outdated and dangerous motivation that should be replaced by something more useful, namely, the commercial spirit with its corresponding virtues (or as Tocqueville later mused, even a new commercial honour).[20] He argued, much the same as Hobbes, that religious differences that people had fought and died for were merely conventional – but he argued that because these differences were much less important than people believed, they should be willing to tolerate them. Both men saw honour and faith as essentially political problems, and both were deeply sceptical about the truth of either one, or at least any particular definition of either one. This is the modern attitude towards honour and religion in a nutshell, and it is the mirror opposite of the Islamic theocratic view of both. Why fight over honour or faith when there would never be an end to the argument, and in the case of religion at any rate, one could not actually force another person to have a particular faith?

Theocracies often have a single man or an elite few at the helm, an Ayatollah, a group of mullahs, or a charismatic public figure, for instance. When they are successful, these men garner faith and loyalty by associating themselves with God's will on earth. But Madison was concerned about factions forming around attachments to charismatic, but ultimately demagogic, leaders "ambitiously contending for pre-eminence and power"[21] He was able to see the potential benefit in such attachments for drawing people out of narrow self-interest and mediocrity towards something greater than themselves, leading them to emulate truly admirable virtues displayed by the leader. Be that as it may, the love of leaders is more dangerous than it is helpful, Madison concluded, because they create factions of people willing to go to war for their man.

The third and fourth categories of faction involve economic interest, which Madison identified as the most frequent and reliable source of faction. There are property divisions based on class – the haves and have-nots – and there are divisions based on economic motives: "a landed interest, a manufacturing interest, a mercantile interest, a monied interest, with many lesser interests ... actuated by different sentiments and views."[22] If people divided themselves up by who was rich and who was poor, the result could be class warfare. As in ancient times, the poor would try to use their numbers to overwhelm the rich and take their property, and the rich would try to use their economic might to keep the majority in check. This too was an undesirable type of faction from the perspective of the founders. So Madison hoped to encourage the development and political impact of another type of interest-based division based on economic sectors, a type that could produce many factions whose interests could check each other.

With many factions, created by the existence of many ways to make money in a growing economy, it would be difficult for any one faction to get enough power on its own. Self-interested people within these factions would be forced by their circumstances to engage in coalition building on issues, and they would have to compromise. No one faction would get everything it wants, and all would have some influence in the political process. Because all had some influence, the envy and hatred that arise in economic class differences would not emerge (or at least not with enough force) with a multiplicity of interest-based factions. Because the issues involved in their political activity are interest based and not about human dignity, or eternal reward or damnation, the passions involved, while strong, would not spur people to engage in life-or-death struggles to make sure they achieve their total vision. Because they stood to prosper with the system intact, they would be willing to accept compromise.

So the trick is to turn people's minds away from their class identity, or indeed any other identity, such as their religion, and to have them think of themselves as members of particular economic interest groups, because then, compromise becomes a routine necessity in order to get anything done. This is a sort of divide and conquer strategy, and this is how those who advocate for theocracy might see the modern, liberal, commercial state – its members divided and conquered by the sins of materialism and egalitarianism.

Egalitarianism is just as problematic as materialism: Islamic theocracy is extremely patriarchal and masculinist, and liberal democracy has become by contrast extremely gender-neutral when it comes to political and economic involvement. Insomuch as "do or die" opinion tends to come from the masculine gender, the theocrat might (and does) see Western societies as feminized, unmanly, lacking in virility because lacking in strong convictions. Even for defenders of liberalism like Diamond and Strauss, there is some loss as well as some gain in this lack of virile opinion. They note with some trepidation this departure from the ancient, Aristotelian perspective – politics becoming a mere means to mundane ends, not a good in itself, with aims that are "solid but low." Politics becomes the mere means by which we can achieve peaceful private lives and the pursuit of self-interest; the private life becomes more important than the public or societal life.

In order to make sure that politics was defanged, Madison and the founders incorporated a number of particular elements into the Constitution which essentially called forth this diversity of interests and brought it into play politically. Most important is the American version of federalism, whereby the central government is superior to the states with respect to some areas of responsibility, while the states continue to be sovereign in other areas. This not only focuses some important political conflict at the national level, but does so within the context of the coalition building required when a great variety of interests are involved in politics. In this situation, it would be highly unlikely for a majority to agree upon truly serious matters.

In addition, the founders also proposed an elaborate system of checks and balances in order to create even more divisions based upon self-interest, to further guarantee that no one or group within our representatives would become tyrannical. The bicameral structure of the legislative branch as well as the separation of powers would provide mechanisms by which power-seeking politicians would jealously guard their constitutionally provided prerogatives. According to Madison's chilling discussion in Federalist No. 51 there needs to be an interaction between the vice of power and the constitutional safeguards designed to harness it for good:

> Ambition must be made to counteract ambition. The interests of the man must be connected with the constitutional rights of the place. It may be a reflection on human nature that such devices should be necessary to control the abuses of government. But what is government itself but the greatest of all reflections on human nature. If we were angels, no government would be necessary. If angels were to govern men neither external or internal controls on government would be necessary.[23]

For the moderns, having lived through seemingly endless religious wars which were at least in part about the securing of the greatest good of immortality, better motives should not be the goal of governments, but rather comfortable self-preservation. Notice that the ancient highly defined "happiness" gave way to the modern gutting of the term: Lindsay notes: "The reduction of government's task chiefly to the regulation of commerce is made possible by the reduction of happiness or the good life to comfortable self-preservation."[24] And Diamond insists that this is not a case of Madison and other modern liberal thinkers believing that in the end, in the "free marketplace of ideas," the higher ideas and motivations would win the day without government support, but rather that they needed opinion to be "toned down in order that democratic factionalism not rip society apart."[25]

Defence of the Bourgeois Virtues

Republican theory had always assumed that virtuous citizens capable of looking beyond self or class were needed in order to avoid the cycle of faction, tyranny, and decline. To the contrary, Diamond acknowledges that the American way encourages "self-serving political ambition" in the public realm, and pursuit of narrow self-interest in the form of acquisitiveness and the qualities associated with it in the private realm, exactly the sorts of activity which had previously been "ethically censored." Madison's strategy "deliberately risks magnifying and multiplying in American life the selfish, the interested, the narrow, the vulgar, and the crassly economic."[26] Such assumptions about human nature and behaviour do not sit well with thinkers who are more progressive in their orientation.

Diamond addresses specifically the objections of Richard Hofstadter because his views are "in the spirit of Charles Beard," the famous socialist critic of American democracy.[27] Hofstadter sees in the realistic liberalism developed by Madison too much of an indictment of human nature. As Thomas Scorza explains, "Mr. Diamond's portrait of the Founders' modern realism disappointed those modern 'idealists' who would be loyal only to a democracy formed according to the promise of their own 'brilliant and easily realized dream.'"[28] Hofstadter labels the founders' view as "Hobbesian," and therefore too pessimistic about people's potential to transcend self-interest. Diamond responds that if the Hobbesian realism that Hofstadter sees was all there was to the founders' thought, it would be hard to defend their political ideas, because they would truly aim too low. But, he says, Americans instinctually know there is more to it than that. So, he turns to discovering what makes America better than a regime founded upon the pursuit of crass self-interest.

Diamond argues that associated with the self-interested pursuit of commerce are instrumental behaviours which are virtues of a sort. He insists, in defence of the American way, that "the American political order rises respectably high enough above the vulgar level of mere self-interest in the direction of virtue – if not to the highest reaches of the ancient perspective, still toward positive human decencies or excellences."[29] He distinguishes between crass avarice and acquisitiveness, insisting that what the founders wanted to encourage was acquisitiveness. The distinction is that avarice focuses on having, whereas acquisitiveness focuses on getting. "Equally a manifestation of self-interest," writes Lindsay, "acquisitiveness nonetheless differs from avarice in the manner of getting from hoarding, and dynamic from static – as embodied in the different ways of life of the entrepreneur and the miser. Acquisitiveness, then, is avarice rationalized; and rationalized avarice is superior to unreflective avarice."[30]

While this distinction may seem very fine, and indeed is arguable, these scholars are arguing that in America the excitement comes from the process of building and growing businesses, not just in the pleasure of piling up money. This is quite close to what Tocqueville describes as a uniquely American commercial honour, a bold and adventuresome attitude towards enterprise which turns it into a creative act and moves it beyond simple materialism.[31] It is the earning, and even the way of earning – it must be justly and independently earned – that gives Americans the pleasure in their economic activity. So, in order to achieve this higher pleasure, Americans develop certain instrumental virtues. These are not the highest virtues of faith, charity, loyalty, and self-sacrifice, but they are virtues nonetheless. For instance, the American may not display rage at having his character impugned, and may avoid conflict over insults – and thus from the aristocratic perspective, forfeits his honour. But he instead exhibits a great deal of self-control, refusing to allow himself to be driven by his passions, and this for the sake of his long-term goals. Other virtues that follow from the desire to acquire are honesty, generosity (or the rejection of miserliness at any rate), and agreeableness.

The key to understanding the bourgeois virtues is that they fulfil the goals of acquisitiveness. We are honest because honesty is better for business. The merchant who is not miserly with customers will keep them coming back. The business owner who is polite, whose customers are always right, will prosper. Reputation is everything in business, and the bourgeois virtues are necessary to build and maintain a good reputation.

Diamond also argues that the commercial republic encourages additional forms of virtue beyond those needed for successful commerce. First, borrowing from Tocqueville, he tells us that Americans' bourgeois virtues are supplemented by a higher republican virtue, because they are also citizens who participate in the democratic process. They develop the habit of self-governance, which also forms men's characters, making them stretch themselves beyond their own self-interest to consider the common good, or at least a compromise. This impulse is especially strong at the subnational/state level owing to the role afforded to the states by the Constitution's federal structure. Decisions made at this level are of particular interest to citizens and they are easily grasped since they involve matters which are both familiar and pertinent. As Schambra points out, such local decisions "impinge tangibly upon citizens' commercial interests ... and the individual is drawn gradually, almost imperceptibly, into public life." As a consequence, "he begins to acquire the taste and capacity for republican self-government and, through habit, some degree of self-transcending, public spirited attachment to the good of the community."[32] The citizen impulse might not be as strong as the commercial drives in America, but it is certainly there, and involves many people in thinking about and cooperating for the common good. Diamond also points out that individuals are not compelled, but are free to develop the so-called higher order virtues privately with the help of religion, education, family upbringing, and voluntary associations. He argues that the founders assumed a natural, albeit weak, inclination towards certain virtues even in the absence of "political tutelage in the ancient mode."[33]

Commercial Republic versus Theocratic Regime

One is hard-pressed to find common ground between liberal and theocratic regimes. While both agree that society is characterized by a shortage of the better motives, they are clearly at odds concerning what's to be done about it. Liberalism is grounded in individualism and all that flows from it, including rights, limited government, faction, toleration, egalitarianism, materialism, and suspicion of authority. Rights accrue to the individual and therefore predate society. For the theocrat, duty is paramount, the community is more important than the individual, hierarchy is necessary, and both faction and toleration are unacceptable.

Recall Madison's argument in Federalist 10 about mitigating the destructive impact of tyranny. He tells us that we may address faction in terms of either its root causes or its effects. The liberal and the theocratic regime could not be further apart. The founders choose to focus upon the effects of factions, thereby allowing them to form and prosper. Theocracies, to the contrary, address faction at its cause by following exactly those two strategies against which Madison argued strenuously. A dictatorship, or at least an oligarchy, is required – along with the pursuit of virtue – to, in Madison's words, give "everyone the same opinions, interests and passions."[34]

More generally, American liberalism and the theocratic regime differ with respect to the greatest or common good as well as to how it can be achieved. For the theocrat, the greatest good is eternal life, and the only way to achieve the greatest good is obedience to the will of God in all things. This notion of the common good assumes that the government has a responsibility to provide its citizens with the ability to develop the higher virtues, and the instruction in and practice of religion, to be right with God, even preventing people from going astray by force of law. The idea that acquisitiveness should drive society, that the bourgeois virtues are good enough, and that somehow people's characters will be positively shaped by arguing with each other over issues in a democratic setting – issues that are minor by comparison with eternal reward or punishment – does not make much sense to the theocrat. He is likely to see such ideas as excuses for following a life of sin and disregarding God's will.

Looked at from either the Aristotelian or the theocratic perspective, politics in American society had become abstracted from the previously supremely important function of character formation. This is the ultimate departure from the ancient, Aristotelian perspective – politics becomes merely a means to mundane ends, it is not a good in itself, and its aims are "solid but low." Politics becomes the mere means by which we can achieve peaceful private lives and seek our individual self-interest; the private life becomes more important than the public or social life.

Potential greatness involving some sort of fundamental change in the human condition was rejected as a goal by the founders as they instead sought a safe, stable, and enduring government. In essence, the statesmen of 1787 were

> deliberately sacrificing the best of human possibilities to escape the terrible worst, they secured a decent life for ordinary citizens according to their common nature. After the Founding – the short summer of creation – there would be no need, no room for great men, great cities, great thoughts, great faiths and great deeds. All would be busily and endlessly engaged in securing their inalienable rights to life, liberty, and the pursuit of happiness.[35]

Since it was the task of the laws to create a way of life or to nurture among citizens certain qualities of character, then the laws necessarily had to penetrate every aspect of a community's life; there could be no separation of state or government and society, and no limitation of the former with respect to the latter.[36] For the Islamic theocrat, it is unnatural to think of government as limited only to the protection of safety, rights and the setting of economic rules. The idea of relegating the most important thing in life to the random and arbitrary decisions of individuals seems too risky. In a theocracy, the wise and the best-qualified rule and the masses are deferential. To the contrary, in a liberal regime the masses are not deferential; in fact, they are the ultimate source of sovereignty and may or may not select wise leadership. Diamond offers somewhat of a counterargument to this theocratic attack when he comments that, despite its pragmatic tendencies, the American regime not only fosters republican virtues, but is not hostile to the love of learning (though this is probably due to an indifference towards it). He also says that the founders, while creating a regime in which lower virtues are encouraged in the pursuit of what theocrats would call a vice – acquisitiveness –, nonetheless also created an arena in which various levels of moral character would emerge. The better sort of men in a free society would rise to the surface, and this is what the founders expected.

But the theocrat would question the degree of respect Americans have for intellectuals, and how many of their elected officials can be called a part of Jefferson's "natural aristocracy?" A theocrat would argue that those who are most learned – theologians and scholars – are not well respected in America and seem actually to be resented, to the extent that they do not conform to the inclinations of the majority. Gordon Wood is helpful with respect to this point.[37] He contrasts the statesmen of the founding with public figures today and argues that they were in fact the wise ones to whom the public deferred. However, the democratic culture they set in motion was one that would eventually turn its back on deference to wisdom. He would in all likelihood agree with the theocrat that such figures find their proper place only in a theocracy. There, wise leaders are sought out, and the majority acknowledges that it needs to be led. Wisdom and the higher virtues are sources of authority, and democratic Americans ultimately do not want to acknowledge any true authority to which they should defer.

Summing Up

Clearly, the theocrat would not only disagree with the principles of the American founding, grounded as they are on individual self-interest, egalitarianism, and materialism, but he would also question just how well the American regime has produced the milder, self-controlled sort of person who displays the bourgeois virtues. Islamic theocrats, of course, emphasize and no doubt exaggerate the "decadence" of the American culture, but they could certainly point to the trends in family breakup and financial misconduct as prime examples that the moderate and prudent citizens expected by the founders are not as numerous as they would have liked. They might also question whether our elected officials tend to represent a "natural aristocracy" that voters can look up to with respect and trust. After all, not only are our politicians not theologians or philosophers, but they are often a reflection of the popular will rather than shapers of that will.

To an Islamic thinker, much like to Aristotle, the American regime might not look like a regime at all. The American regime fails to listen to wisdom. Unlike the regimes of the Middle East which have theocratic tendencies, there is no religious scholar, no *"ulama,"* to guide political authorities. Licht's description of the proper relationship between the philosopher and political authority, according to Aristotle, could easily be applied to the proper relationship between the *ulama* and political authorities, assuming of course that the *ulama* bear the wisdom in their societies:

> The teaching contained both a "wisdom" and the way to wisdom, which was to be filtered down to the lawgivers and to potential lawgivers by the very transmission of the tradition of political philosophy ... The lawgiver, or statesman so educated through Aristotle becomes in some sense a "knower" of what is good for man as such, and what human excellence is, not only for the best men, but for the various kinds of men.[38]

There is no arguing that despite its economic tumult in recent years, America remains the wealthiest and most powerful country in the world. From that measure, the American regime appears successful. From the critic's perspective, this success reflects well Diamond's view of America's priorities in commercial success, but it may not reflect the founders' true intent.[39] It may also be argued, and it has been argued, that the "bourgeois virtues" are not to be seen as so "low" as they have been depicted here, but as the foundation for a decency which elevates mankind from his base and animalistic state and gives him dignity in freedom and in the ability to participate in the political process. But from the theocrat's perspective, even individual freedom and political participation, when not thoroughly anchored in an understanding and acceptance of man's proper aims, are simply powerful lures away from God.

Is there reason to hope that liberalism and Islamic fundamentalism might come to tolerate one another? On the face of things, it seems much more likely that, given its toleration of different points of view with respect to domestic policy matters, American liberalism would be able to accept and ignore the massive difference between the two ideologies. However, as Diamond points out, "the American Way" is a "particular relationship" between ethics and politics, but part of the particular American way is its universalizing tendency. More than most peoples, Americans do not think of their ideology as applying just to them. Americans' religious heritage may have something to do with this: "Our tendency to understand moral principles in universal terms may also be furthered by the lingering influence of the Biblical heritage which lays down moral principles applicable to all men in all countries."[40] In addition, we see this universalism in our Declaration of Independence and its theory of natural rights. The idea is not that the three primal rights are particular to the American experience, but are common to all humans.

This tendency of Americans to see their political values as universal sets up a potential conflict with other ways of life, in particular those competing ideologies which also claim to be true for all. Such is the Islamic theocratic view: its origins are in a religion that claims to be good for all, even including the return of the Caliphate. The ethics and politics of these two universal ideologies are very different, setting up the potential for deep and lasting conflict.

In all, when we look clearly upon the modern foundations of the "American Way" and the rather "ancient" assumptions of some Islamists, we have to admit that the differences between the two are very stark and concern the most important things – the path to happiness, the nature of the soul, morality, and truth itself. In the West, we have found a way around our long history of religious conflict with the promotion of tolerance, but with the price of putting these important things in the background, relativizing, individualizing, and deprioritizing them. As far as religion is concerned, it is not that Western liberals necessarily are of the opinion that religion is not important. Rather, there seems to be a growing ecumenical tendency in the West not to believe that one religion is more important than the next. This is perhaps clearest among the various Protestant sects. However, the gulf in terms of dogma between Roman Catholicism and Protestantism seems much less critical in today's times. In the Middle East, some societies are going in the opposite direction, not because (or not only because) they dislike America, but because they truly value, sometimes in very misguided ways, the public pursuit of these most important things. For Islam, one religion is not as good as the next. Matters of faith are not subject to compromise. Moreover, this is not mere rhetoric. Until we are able to understand that, we will not be able to deal with the challenges these societies pose to us with the level of sophistication required to find solutions.

NOTES

1 On continuity and change between the Bush and Obama Middle East foreign policies see Andreas Krieg, "Externalizing the Burden of War: The Obama Doctrine and U.S. Foreign Policy in the Middle East," *International*

Affairs 92.1 (2016): 97–113. Some research indicates that democratic reforms can be completely compatible with the establishment of *shari'a* law. Sabri Ciftci, "Secular-Islamic Cleavages, Values and Support for Democracy and Shari'a in the Arab World," *Political Research Quarterly* 66.4 (2012): 781–93.

2 Martin Diamond, "Ethics and Politics: The American Way," in *The Moral Foundations of the American Republic*, ed. Robert H. Horwitz (Charlottesville: University Press of Virginia, 1986).

3 His essay "Ethics and Politics: The American Way" is considered to be "the most ambitious work of his career," written late in that career, and so representing his mature thought on the subject. Thomas Lindsay, "Democracy, Acquisitiveness, and the Private Realm: Martin Diamond on the Reasonable Optimism of the Founding," *Political Science Reviewer* 28 (1999): 49.

4 Diamond, "Ethics and Politics," 78.

5 Aristotle, *Politics*, Book 3, ch. 4.

6 Ibid., Book 7, ch. 1. In an excellent treatment of Aristotle's views on the character-forming purposes of the polis, Neill explains in this volume, "Aristotle in the *Politics* is not only assuming that our political communities ought to be oriented toward the good life, but also that they ought to promote such a life among their members. The problem of politics is to determine the cooperative principles that would unite persons in a polis and facilitate their achievement of the good life" (84–5).

7 Diamond, "Ethics and Politics," 81.

8 Ibid.

9 Plato, *The Republic*, trans. G.M.A. Grube (Indianapolis, IN: Hackett Publishing Co., 1992), 561d.

10 In this volume Scott Hibbard defines theocracy in a useful way as "the effort to link political authority to a particular religious tradition, and to use the institutions of the state to promote one interpretation of religion at the expense of all others" (286). Not all governments that are theocratic in that sense go on to have a "clerical elite" which "rules in the name of God," however.

11 Diamond, "Ethics and Politics," 82.

12 Machiavelli, *The Prince*, trans. Leo S. de Alvarez (Irving, TX: University of Dallas Press, 1980), ch. 15, §1.

13 Leo Strauss, *What Is Political Philosophy? And Other Studies* (Chicago: University of Chicago Press, 1959), 49.

14 Simpson, "Theocracy's Challenge," (198).

15 One way to understand this conflict is an examination of how this fundamentalism comes to have greater and greater influence over

the politics of states such as Saudi Arabia. Muhammad Al Atawneh explains: "The *'ulama'* [Islamic scholars] ... managed to increase their power over time by expanding their control over other ministries and religious agencies, such as the Ministry of Justice, the Ministry of Islamic Affairs and Endowments, Call and Guidance, the Ministry of Pilgrimage, the Committee of Commanding Good and Forbidding Wrong, Preaching and Guidance of Islam at Home and Abroad, the supervision of girls' education, notaries public, the supervision of mosques and *awqaf* (charitable trusts)." Muhammad Al-Atawneh, "Is Saudi Arabia a Theocracy? Religion and Governance in Contemporary Saudi Arabia," *Middle Eastern Studies* 45, no. 5 (September 2009): 729.

In Saudi Arabia, the Wahhabi *ulama* and the Saudi royal family rule cooperatively. The *ulama* will issue a *fatawa* (religious ruling) based on *shari'a* (religious law), which is then made law by the political leaders, or the leaders will make a law which is later legitimized by the *ulama*. The political authorities are to be obeyed so long as their rule conforms to *shari'a*, which is ultimately defined by the *ulama* (ibid., 730–3). At least as it is described here, the relationship between the *ulama* and political rulers of Saudi Arabia is both illiberal and oppressive, in stark contrast to the current Western liberal view of the separation between church and state.

16 Federalist No. 10, in *The Federalist Papers*, ed. Clinton Rossiter (New York: New American Library, 2003), 73.

17 Robert A. Licht, "Reflections on Martin Diamond's 'Ethics and Politics: The American Way,'" *Publius* 8.3 (1978): 193.

18 Federalist 10, 73.

19 In this volume, Beiner provides (through an examination of the 3rd Earl of Shaftsbury's anti-clericalism and neo-paganism) an excellent discussion of what he calls anti-clericalism born of the liberal critique of religion as bullying orthodoxy and as an instigator of civil war.

20 Alexis de Tocqueville, *Democracy in America*, ed. J.P. Mayer, trans. George Lawrence (New York: Harper and Row, 1988), vol. 2, part 2, ch. 18. On honour more generally see Laurie M. Johnson, *Locke and Rousseau: Two Enlightenment Responses to Honor* (Lanham, MD: Lexington Books, 2013) and Laurie Bagby, *Thomas Hobbes: Turning Point for Honor* (Lanham, MD: Lexington Books, 2009).

21 Federalist 10, 73.

22 Ibid., 74.

23 Federalist 51, 319.

24 Lindsay, "Democracy, Acquisitiveness, and the Private Realm," 51.

25 Diamond, "Ethics and Politics," 98.

26 Ibid., 95.
27 Richard Hofstadter, *The American Political Tradition* (New York: Alfred A. Knopf, 1948). Charles Beard, *An Economic Interpretation of the Constitution of the United States* (New York: Macmillan, 1913).
28 Thomas J. Scorza, "Comment: The Politics of Martin Diamond's Science," *Interpretation: A Journal of Political Philosophy* 8.2/3 (1980): 20.
29 Diamond, "Ethics and Politics," 99.
30 Lindsay, "Democracy, Acquisitiveness, and the Private Realm," 64.
31 Tocqueville, *Democracy in America*, vol. 2, part 2, ch. 18.
32 William A. Schambra, "Introduction," in *As Far as Republican Principles Will Admit: Essays by Martin Diamond*, ed. William A. Schambra (Washington, DC: AEI Press, 1992), 9.
33 Diamond, "Ethics and Politics," 107.
34 Federalist 10. Madison decides, "There are again two methods of removing the causes of faction: the one, by destroying the liberty which is essential to its existence; the other, by giving to every citizen the same opinions, the same passions, and the same interests."
35 Marvin Meyers, "The Least Imperfect Government: On Martin Diamond's Ethics and Politics," *Interpretation: A Journal of Political Philosophy* 8.2/3 (1980): 8.
36 Diamond, "Ethics and Politics," 84.
37 Gordon S. Wood, "The Democratization of Mind in the American Revolution," in *The Moral Foundations of the American Republic*, ed. Robert H. Horwitz (Charlottesville: University Press of Virginia, 1986).
38 Licht, "Reflections on Martin Diamond's 'Ethics and Politics,'" 196–7.
39 See, for example, Alan R. Gibson, "America's Better Self: Diamond, Madison, and the Foundations of the American Regime," *The Political Science Reviewer* 28.1 (1999): 102–20.
40 Diamond, "Ethics and Politics," 75–6.

13 Religion, Tolerance, and American Theocratic Politics: Lessons for the Contemporary Era

SCOTT W. HIBBARD

Debates over the proper relationship between religion and government have been a central feature of American politics since the country's founding. At issue is whether a particular interpretation of religion ought to be given preference within the institutions of nation and state, or whether the government should be neutral in regard to matters of religion and belief. Should the United States, in short, affirm a theocratic basis of government – and recognize Protestant Christianity as the official state religion – or should no preference be given to one religion (or denomination) above all others? While the constitutional separation of church and state ostensibly settled this matter, these debates have remained a source of contention. Disputes about the proper role of religion in government have been particularly acute in recent decades, when the resurgence of an illiberal (or theocratic) religious politics has been associated with the rise of the so-called religious right. Political activists – and state leaders – associated with this movement have challenged the secular basis of American politics and called for a close relationship of religion and government, one that identifies the United States as a Christian nation and that uses the state to actively promote religious belief.

The continued salience of religion in American politics is due, in part, to the pervasive belief that Americans are a chosen people with a unique destiny in the world. This idea of American Exceptionalism (discussed below) informs popular conceptions of national identity and is deeply rooted in the country's history. The nature and meaning of this legacy, however, remains a matter of dispute. The secular vision of American nationalism reflects the Enlightenment ideas prevalent at the nation's founding, and – in this view – the effort to accommodate religious diversity defines the American experiment and the country's exceptional nature. On the other hand, those who view American history through a theocratic lens – and who argue for a more central role for conservative Protestantism in the public square – see the United States as a Christian nation dominated by un-Christian values. While the secular understanding of faith and nation is informed by a liberal or modernist interpretation of religion, the theocratic draws from the country's Puritan legacy (or, more precisely, one aspect of that legacy). In this latter context, an illiberal understanding of the religion informs an exclusive vision of national identity, and a theocratic vision of American national purpose. For conservative activists, then, the redemption of the political community requires Christians to "take back" their country from secular humanists.

The following chapter will examine the tension between these competing visions of American politics and society, and will situate this debate in its historical context. Particular attention will be given to the theocratic tendencies in the religious politics of recent years. By theocratic tendencies I am referring to the effort to link political authority to a particular religious tradition, and to use the institutions of the state to promote one interpretation of religion at the expense of all others. In reviewing this tendency, I will situate America's theocratic politics in a larger ideological context, and examine the manner in which different interpretations of religion have historically informed different visions of social life. To this end, the chapter will distinguish between two variants of secularism – the strict separation of religion and government (irreligious secularism) and a non-sectarian or "ecumenical" secularism – and the more explicitly theocratic religious nationalism.

The chapter will also examine the dangers of American theocratic politics, and the lessons to be learned from earlier writers. Historically, the theocratic tendency has been associated with the demonization of dissent, and the denigration of ethnic and religious minorities. Whether this manifests as an exclusive (and overt) religious nationalism, or a more secularized "political theology," there remains an element of intolerance in theocracy that breeds division and conflict. While the elimination of religion from the public square may appear to offer a solution, many have argued that it is precisely this alternative – defined by an innate hostility towards religion – that generated the backlash behind the resurgence of religious politics in the 1970s and 1980s. Here, then, the ancient lesson of tolerance in matters of religion and belief proves especially salient. While not without their own limitations, the lessons from earlier eras – particularly the seventeenth and eighteenth centuries – provide a useful insight into addressing the challenges of religious diversity and the issues associated with modern religious politics. The specific political philosophers to whom I will refer include John Locke and Roger Williams.

Theocratic Politics and the Secular Alternative

Historically, religious institutions have been a central part of political order and the organization of social life. In Europe, for example, the institutions of church and state were closely intertwined throughout the Middle Ages. The political authority of the state found legitimacy in the revelation safeguarded by church authorities, while the church relied upon political leaders to regulate religious belief and practice. This close affiliation of religious institutions and political authority is typical of theocratic forms of government. Theocracy is here defined as a form of government where a clerical elite – or their designate – rules in the name of God. Sovereignty, in this context, resides with the Divine, and the clerical class (or their designates) are charged with administering His/Her revealed laws.[1] The basis for this form of government is twofold. First, it is assumed that the world is an emanation of God, and that the Divine Creator has a particular intention for the right ordering of human society. Hence, there is a necessary and legitimate role for government to enforce religious law and otherwise regulate religious expression as a means of safeguarding the well-being of society. Second, the legitimacy of political authority is premised upon its ability to both understand and implement God's will in a political context. Both of these issues argue for a close association of the institutions of religion and government.

There is an important distinction to make, however, between a theocratic state – one which fuses religious and political authority entirely – and a traditionalist state with theocratic tendencies. In the first instance, religious leaders are also the political rulers, whereas in the second, the authorities are distinct, though mutually supportive. The contemporary Iranian state would be a good example of the first trend. Religious clerics in Iran hold the highest constitutional offices, and law and government policy ostensibly derive from Shia Islam. Most importantly, the ultimate interpreter of the Shia tradition is also the head of the constitutional state, thus fusing religious authority and political authority in the constitutional office of the Supreme Leader (the *Velayet-e-faqui*). In the second case – that of the traditionalist state – the state takes upon itself the responsibility of enforcing religious law, defining religious orthodoxy, and subsequently regulating religious thought and practice. There is a distinction, however, between religious authority and political authority in such instances, with the former serving as interpreter of the tradition, and the latter using the coercive mechanisms of the state to perpetuate religious conformity. In such cases, state financial support for an established church and/or religious establishment would be common. The current government of Saudi Arabia illustrates this latter tendency, as did most of the early European states.

In either instance, the arguments for using political power to promote religious uniformity are similar. These arguments are premised upon the belief that religious conformity is essential to public order, and that political unity can only be achieved through a high degree of cultural and religious homogeneity. Conversely, dissent – whether religious, political, or cultural – is seen as divisive and threatening to social order. Tolerance of dissent, in this view, particularly in matters of faith, has commonly been seen as acquiescing in heresy (wrong belief), apostasy (renunciation of belief), or atheism (unbelief). In any of these instances, tolerance puts public order at risk and the soul of the dissenter in jeopardy. It is argued, then, that there exists a legitimate and necessary role for the state to police the boundaries of acceptable opinion – prohibiting, for example, blasphemy or idolatry – and that the use of force to promote religious orthodoxy is both religiously and politically justified.

The problems with this vision of theocratic rule are many. As John Locke argued in his *Letter concerning Toleration*,[2] coercion in matters of conscience will invariably be ineffective. Given the importance of religion – and salvation – to the individual believer, and given the nature of human conscience, one cannot coerce others to believe something they intuitively know to be wrong. As Locke argued, "The care of Souls cannot belong to the Civil Magistrate, because his Power consists only in outward force; but true and saving Religion consists in the inward perswasion of the Mind ... Such is the nature of the Understanding, that it cannot be compell'd to the belief of any thing by outward force."[3] Hence, Locke believed that theocratic politics invariably bred either hypocrisy or enmity. "I cannot safely take [the Magistrate] for my Guide, who may probably be as ignorant of the way [of Salvation] as my self, and who certainly is less concerned for my Salvation than I my self am."[4] This, then, ties into a second point. Repressing dissent and coercing belief invariably leads to division and strife. Although Locke supported uniformity earlier in his life, he came to recognize how coercion in matters of belief fuelled Europe's civil wars. Particularly within multi-religious societies, tolerance was a necessary requirement for civil peace. Moreover, Locke came to the realization that it is not religion that drives theocratic tendencies, but politics. Anti-tolerance codes and other theocratic prescriptions were little more than veiled efforts to gain political control through religious submission. Such codes, in short, were "much rather Marks of Men striving for Power and Empire over one another than of the Church of Christ."[5]

Perhaps the most fundamental insight that Locke derives from his experience with the theocratic politics of his era is that it is not the business of government to regulate religious belief. Rather, government is constituted to protect and preserve "Civil Interests," and does not extend to matters of religion. In making this claim, Locke is drawing a sharp distinction between the legitimate purview of government and church authority, seeking to "settle the just bounds that lie between the one and the other."[6] It is this analysis that provides the basis for separating church and state. The state (or Magistrate), on the one hand, is responsible for "things belonging to this life," and, insofar as government holds a charge for providing order in the temporal realm, it legitimately exercises the coercive apparatus of the state. The church, on the other hand – which Locke defines as a "voluntary society of men who join together to worship God in such a manner as they judge acceptable to him and effectual to the salvation of their souls"[7] – deals solely with the realm of spirit and conscience. Individuals must be free to enter and free to leave. The role of force and coercion in such matters is illegitimate, and entirely contrary to Christian ethics.

These ideas are reflected in American thinkers such as Roger Williams and, later, Thomas Jefferson and James Madison. Williams, in particular, is significant because he was a Puritan dissenter, exiled from the Massachusetts Bay colony for his views on church–state relations and individual belief. Informed by John Calvin's differentiation between the "inward" forum of conscience and the "outward" forum of public life, Williams preceded Locke in arguing against established churches (or what he referred to as "National religions"). Williams's view was based in large measure on the belief that individual morality did *not* require religion – a central assumption of the theocratic view – but, rather, that moral laws are accessible through the inner light of conscience. More to the point, fundamental belief ought to be regulated by "spiritual power" – that is, religious and rational argumentation – not the sword. Governmental power, by contrast, is in its very essence temporal in nature, and ought therefore to be limited to the realm of human affairs. Insofar as individuals did not violate basic norms of social order – and did not infringe upon others' rights – they "may – and should – be left free to determine their religious beliefs as their conscience dictates."[8] To do otherwise – that is, to persecute citizens based upon their religious beliefs – will simply "fill the streams and rivers with blood."[9]

It is this differentiation between realms that provides a basis for the secular tradition in the Western (and specifically the American) context. It is important here to differentiate between two forms of secularism and secular rule. The root word, "secular," typically refers to worldly or temporal affairs. That is, not ecclesiastical or clerical, nor involving a separate realm of reality held to be sacred. When we look to secular rule, what we are referring to is a differentiation between spheres – temporal and transcendent – and a corresponding separation of authorities, with political authorities governing the temporal and religious authorities the realm of belief. The process of secularization need not require the eradication of religion, but it certainly demands a differentiation of spheres. Secularism has, nonetheless, come to be seen as the antithesis of religion. In this context, secularism is commonly understood as a moral and political doctrine that is rationalist in orientation, and concerned solely with worldly affairs. Morality is derived not from scriptural commandments (or the Divine), but, rather, from the requirements of an innate humanism.

We can therefore distinguish between two very distinct but related interpretations of secularism, both of which are evident in the American experience.[10] The first, *irreligious secularism*, is best understood as hostility to religion, and may be summarized as "a doctrine oriented toward human earthly well-being that excludes all consideration of religious belief and practice."[11] The emphasis here is on the exclusion of religion from public life. This understanding is rooted in an aspect of the Enlightenment project that saw organized religion as one of the forms of tyranny that ought to be overthrown. Hence, government should remove religion from the public sphere and diminish religious belief among its subject population. The alternative rendering of secularism is one defined by neutrality in matters of religion, not hostility. Secularism, in this view, is sympathetic but impartial towards religion and fundamental belief, neither privileging nor excluding particular religions or denominations. This alternative, *ecumenical secularism*, can be defined as "a doctrine oriented toward human earthly well-being in a narrow or restricted sense that otherwise supports protection of religious belief and practice."[12] Each of these positions – both religious and secular – can be found in the American experience, and it is to this topic that the following section will now turn.

Religion in American Politics

Historical Context

The early colonial period preceding the formation of the United States was defined by a close affiliation of religion and state. The original settlers of New England came to the New World in order to escape religious persecution, and to find a sanctuary where they could freely practise religion as they saw fit. These early settlers saw themselves as a "new Israel" in exodus from a country dominated by religious error. Although searching for religious freedom, neither the Pilgrims (who arrived at Plymouth Rock) nor the Puritans of Massachusetts Bay, sought to extend the principle of religious freedom to others. Nor did they see a reason to do so. As discussed above, the assumption at the time was that religion provided the moral basis of society; hence, civil law was needed to promote religion and to persecute heresy. Moreover, since their interpretation of Christianity was assumed to be uniquely correct, tolerance of religious dissent was inappropriate. Heterodox views were perceived as a threat to both social order and personal salvation. Hence, many of the early settlers saw it as entirely legitimate to use the coercive mechanisms of government to regulate religious thought and practice. This close association of religious authority and political power was replicated in Virginia, which established the Church of England in its colony.[13]

Religious freedom as it is understood today derived not from Virginia or New England, but from the emerging pluralism of the mid-Atlantic region. In these colonies, the diversity of religious denominations demanded a greater degree of religious tolerance. This was facilitated by the pragmatism of local merchants – who were motivated more by profit than religion – and by religious idealists like Roger Williams and William Penn. Both Williams and Penn established colonies that provided a haven for dissident sects. Williams, in particular, was driven by a conviction that freedom of conscience was required for religious purposes. He had been exiled from the Massachusetts Bay Colony because of his view that civil powers had no right to coerce individuals in matters of belief. Williams argued that to do so was not just a violation of the individual's liberty of conscience, but was also "against the testimony of Christ Jesus."[14] Moreover, Williams did not believe that civil magistrates ought to be in the business of promoting religion in the first place; rather, this "task belongs to God's scattered saints."[15] The subsequent separation of church and state in Williams's Rhode Island was intended to protect religion from political intrusion.

The influence of Enlightenment philosophy was similarly important to religious freedom in America. While recognizing the significance of religion to public morality, colonial leaders were nonetheless distrustful of both civil and religious authorities as arbiters of religious truth. This trend reflected the influence of Deism – a religious perspective shaped by the Enlightenment – which gave priority to reason as a means of interpreting God's will (as opposed to revelation). Deism also rejected the literalist belief in the inerrancy of scripture, and questioned human authority on such matters. The philosophy of John Locke suited this temperament well; the role of the state from Locke's view was to protect individuals from external abuse and to enforce contracts, but to do little else. Like Roger Williams, these early Deists believed that the state ought *not* to involve itself in the business of promoting particular interpretations of religion. Nor did they believe that government should ally with religious authorities "in the joint names of Caesar and God to impose their will on the people."[16] Religion, in other words, was best left to the individual and to God.

In the aftermath of the American Revolution, these competing visions of the country's religious legacy were clearly in conflict. On the one hand, there were segments of early American society that were influenced by the theocratic ideas of their Puritan forebears (at least those in the Massachusetts Bay Colony), and sought to recognize Christianity as the official religion. The basis of their argument was that church and state are inseparable within a Christian commonwealth, and that "power and law [together] serve God's moral design."[17] Moreover, the importance of religion to both morality and society required the active support of government. This meant that Christianity ought to be a central feature of public education, public offices should be limited to Christians, and religion ought to provide a basis for the nation's laws.[18] By contrast, many of the founding fathers, such as Washington, Madison, Jefferson, and Franklin, opposed the various forms of establishment being offered, and believed that religion was best left to the private sphere. These latter individuals saw established religion as one of the forms of tyranny that the Revolution was seeking to throw off.

Their support for an explicit separation of church and state was, thus, driven by a desire to limit the ability of religious and political authorities to intrude into the realm of conscience.

The relative merits of religious freedom and establishment were debated within the various state assemblies after 1776, and in the Constitutional Convention at the national level in 1789. At the state level, these debates were extremely rancorous, and pitted dissenting sects against their Protestant brethren. At the national level, however, there was a surprising degree of unanimity. The Convention agreed to adopt a policy of secular neutrality, and subsequently removed all references to God (and Christianity) from the Constitution. The only provisions concerning religion were negative, the most significant of which was the First Amendment, which prohibits Congress from passing any laws that either proscribe religious freedom or establish a national church.[19] Supporters of secular neutrality included the Deists, as well as members of independent denominations who were *not* part of the established churches. Many Baptists, Quakers, and others were concerned about state interference in religious practice, and were critical of earlier experiments in limited tolerance. Moreover, the "New Lights" (converts) of the Great Awakening agreed with Deists like Jefferson that matters of conscience were an individual's concern. Consequently, they supported the institutional separation of church and state as the best means of ensuring religious freedom. The dangers of sectarian division, and the growing number of dissenters, also convinced many delegates to "put contending sectarians on an equal footing by giving special status to none."[20]

If the US Constitution ensured that no one denomination enjoyed preferential status within the institutions of government, Protestant Christianity nonetheless remained predominant in public life throughout the nineteenth and early twentieth centuries. More to the point, American nationalism was imbued with notions of providential mission, "chosen" status, and a firm belief in "American Exceptionalism." Exceptionalism, in this context, is the idea that the United States is different (and ostensibly better) than other nations. This belief is rooted in the country's Christian and republican heritage, and is linked to a corresponding obligation to support and promote the principles upon which the country was founded. The notion of Manifest Destiny, a term coined in 1845, reflected these sentiments, and associated settlement of the West with a providential mission to extend freedom and Christian civilization throughout the continent. This tendency to view national

purpose through a religious lens extended to the imperialist undertak-
ings in the Philippines and in Cuba, and to the country's entry into the
First World War.

If religion informed popular thinking about the country's role in the
world, there were, nonetheless, deep divisions over both religious interpretation and political action. Protestant Christianity informed both a
"priestly" affirmation of the so-called Gilded Age of the late nineteenth
century – the so-called Gospel of Wealth – as well as the "prophetic"
critique of that same status quo.[21] In the first instance, Protestantism,
corporate capitalism, and free market economic policies were closely
intertwined to provide an affirmation for a pattern of social order
defined by a high degree of social stratification. In the second instance,
Protestant teachings took the form of the "Social Gospel," which cri-
tiqued the greed, inequitable distribution of wealth, and social ills
associated with the era. These divisions also mirrored a deeper split
between the "modernist" interpretation of Christian belief and the
"fundamentalists." At issue was whether, and how, American religion
ought to accommodate modernity, particularly the modernist emphasis
on reason over revelation and material progress over spiritual development. The modernist view sought to interpret the Christian tradition
in a contemporary context, recognizing as it did the advances in science and human knowledge, while also recognizing the timeless truths
of Christ's moral teachings. The fundamentalists, by contrast, retained
their belief in the literal truth of scripture, the virgin birth, Christ's miracles, and the assumption that the Bible is the literal word of God. This
question of interpretation had enormous implications for the Christian
mission, with modernists (and advocates of the Social Gospel) focusing
on social justice in this world, while the fundamentalists placed their
emphasis on conversion and finding salvation in the next. The tensions
between these competing visions of a shared faith tradition were evident in the Scopes Monkey trial of 1925, which focused on the question
of teaching evolution theory in public schools, and represented a very
public debate between Christian fundamentalism and an increasingly
secular, liberal and modernizing society.

While the larger debate over religious interpretation hinged on the
question of reason versus revelation, there were also differences over
competing visions of social life. The liberal (and modernist) Christianity
that became predominant in the 1950s and 1960s reflected an ecumenical approach to matters of faith and politics. Rooted in the country's
Enlightenment tradition, the mainline Protestant churches embraced

a modernist theology that informed the post–Second World War liberal political consensus. Religion was an important part of mid-century American political life, but it was promoted in the context of a non-denominational, ecumenical secularism. This modernist centrism was epitomized by Eisenhower's comment that "America makes no sense without a deeply held faith in God – and I don't care what it is."[22] Eisenhower, like Roosevelt before him (and Kennedy and Johnson after), promoted an amorphous "civil religion," which combined the traditional religious elements of American nationalism – faith, providential mission, chosen status – with an inclusive conception of national identity.[23] This mix of religion and politics subsequently provided the basis for the policies of the Great Society, and informed the Civil Rights Movement (and legislation), all of which were consistent with a separation of church and state. Secularism in this context entailed non-discrimination in matters of religion and belief, not hostility.

A more theocratic vision of American religious nationalism was similarly evident in the mid-twentieth century. Evangelical preachers such as Billy Graham and Billy Hargis (among others) emerged during this period. The "crusades" and revivals of these celebrated preachers linked fundamentalist religious teachings with conservative politics. In the context of open-air revival meetings, evangelists such as Graham associated conservative political policies with God's will, and provided a religious affirmation for traditional patterns of social order. The Cold War was depicted as a religious struggle between the Christian West and godless communism, with civic loyalty and faith connected in a revivalist emphasis upon personal conversion that was central to cultivating obedience to political authority. Graham and his fellow evangelists were not alone in spreading these views. Conservative Christian organizations such as the American Council of Christian Churches (ACCC), the National Association of Evangelicals (NAE), the Christian Anti-Communist Crusade, and the John Birch Society similarly linked Christian literalism with anti-communism, free market economics and a return to "traditional values."[24] Many of these groups were especially critical of mainline (modernist) clergy who questioned the inequities associated with unregulated capitalism.[25] These conservative religious groups also preached against such things as big government, the United Nations, racial integration, and the income tax.[26] It is not surprising that many of these groups – particularly the Southern Baptist Church and the ACCC – were also opposed to the civil rights movement, arguing that racial "segregation [was] a biblically sanctioned plan of God."[27]

This ideological current laid the groundwork for the contemporary conservative movement.

Theologians such as Reinhold Niebuhr criticized this early manifestation of the religious right for conflating religion and American nationalism in a manner that he believed was nothing short of idolatry. In *Moral Man and Immoral Society*, Niebuhr wrote about the danger of subsuming individual morality to the collective, be it a tribe, nation, or ethnic group. Since nations and states act out of self-interest, even the altruistic sacrifice of the individual that is inherent within patriotic duty can be directed in a destructive, and immoral, end. Niebuhr's warning was especially relevant in the context of an assertive religious nationalism, where the self-interest of the community – and its pursuit of power and wealth – was clothed in the more palatable rhetoric of justice, morality, and freedom. Similarly, the extension of these ideas to the economic sphere was especially problematic given the tendency of religious conservatives to portray the pursuit of self-interest in a religious framework that it did not deserve. More to the point, Niebuhr saw in this broader tendency a basic misunderstanding of Christian tradition. He argued that the willingness to equate one's own goals with God's, and to claim that one's beliefs uniquely reflected God's will, was simply "wrong religion."[28] True religion, he argued, "knows first of all its own partiality and so the falsity of its spiritual pride."[29]

The Culture Wars

Contemporary religious politics in the United States has its roots in these earlier eras. For many, the resurgence of a conservative, illiberal Protestantism is the defining feature of the current trend. The 1980 presidential campaign marked a key moment when a "new era of religious politics had arrived."[30] Jerry Falwell's Christian Coalition had emerged as a significant force in the 1980 campaign, helping as it did to elect Ronald Reagan as president in an electoral landslide. What this campaign highlighted, however, was not the return of religion per se, but rather a newfound strength for the theocratic vision of American politics. Similar to their forebears in the Christian Anti-Communist movement, the new foot soldiers of the religious right consciously fused free market capitalism, Evangelical Christianity, and an unbridled patriotism in a priestly affirmation of the American system. The ideology of the Moral Majority, the Christian Coalition, and other similar groups emphasized many of the same themes as earlier fundamentalists, such as biblical literalism and the priority of personal conversion over social reform. Their assertion of moral certitude, moreover, was tied closely to the claims of an exclusive understanding of divine revelation, which, in turn, informed a conviction that they were uniquely qualified to redefine the rules governing public life.

A central feature of the movement was the belief that the ills of American society were caused by the irreligious secularism that had ostensibly banished religion from the public sphere (what Simpson refers to as "separation-creep" or "liberal theocracy"). In this regard, the resurgence of Christian activism in the 1980s and 1990s can be seen as a backlash against the politics of the previous two decades. In particular, Conservative religious activists were responding to several Supreme Court decisions that banned organized prayer in school (1962 and 1963), legalized abortion (1973), and extended the right of non-discrimination to homosexuals. Conservative Christians were also concerned about the Equal Rights Amendment (which guaranteed equal treatment of women), the vocal dissent over American military involvement in Vietnam, and the attacks upon traditional institutions that defined this turbulent era. Christian activists saw these trends as part of an overreaching secular humanism that threatened the very fabric of American society. The school prayer decisions, in particular, were perceived as an intrusion by government into matters of conscience in a clear effort to banish religion from the public sphere.

The ideological debates that defined this period – epitomized in the "Culture Wars" of the 1990s – represented two competing visions of American society. At issue was not just the proper role of religion in public life, but also a polarization of American politics along cultural lines. As in previous periods, differing interpretations of religion informed the political fault lines of this era, and reflected fundamentally different views on society and politics. Issues such as homosexual rights, abortion, the teaching of evolution, and organized prayer in public school subsequently became key sites of political contestation. Religious conservatives – whether Protestant, Catholic, or Jewish – tended to view these as moral and religious issues, and (at least in regard to the first three) as being rightfully constrained by the state. Religious liberals (or modernists), by contrast, saw these questions as a matter of individual freedom – and conscience – and did not recognize the right of either state or society to enforce conformity. Religious conservatives and religious liberals also had very different views on economic policy and the regulation (or lack thereof) of business and the economy.

At another level, however, the Culture Wars of this period – a term first coined by James Davison Hunter, and later picked up by political actors such as presidential candidate Pat Buchanan – embodied a deeper struggle to define the nation.[31] A key point of conflict in this debate was the tension between the moral absolutes of biblical literalism and the situational ethics of the liberal, modernist tradition. While the latter was tolerant of alternative world views and the inclusion of diversity, the former saw such moral relativism as an affront to both God and society. These positions echoed earlier debates from the seventeenth century over the relative merits of uniformity, with the competing visions of society – inclusive or exclusive, secular or religious – being informed by different understandings of both religion and politics. While modernists saw this debate as a matter of tolerance and equal treatment, conservatives saw it as a matter of basic morality and restoring God's rightful place in government. As one Christian activist summed up the matter: "The critical issue for our day is the relationship of Christ and His Word to our political and legal system in the United States. Who has jurisdiction over every aspect of American society, Jesus Christ or the State? Is this to be a Christian nation or a humanistic nation?"[32]

This last point is extremely important. What is ultimately at issue in these debates is whether the society (and, hence, the nation) ought to be defined by the values of inclusion and tolerance, or whether the will (and ethnic motifs) of a particular segment of the majority population ought to be predominant. This debate is not a competition between tradition and modernity, but, rather, between differing visions of modernity. Is the United States, in short, to be a religious or secular society, and, if the latter, is it be rooted in an ecumenical or an irreligious secularism? More to the point, should the dominant community – and its religious identity – be given preference in the political realm, or is there an obligation for state authorities to protect minority rights and cultural diversity? These questions pit different political forces against one another, with religious conservatives arguing for a more central role for religion in governing public morality and social life. In doing so, they offered a theocratic vision of society that looked to the state to regulate religious thought and promote political unity through a high degree of social conformity. Religious liberals, by contrast, invoked the Christian message to sanction an inclusive, ecumenical secularism (and more equitable economic policies), while anti-religious secularists were content with the exclusion of religion from the public sphere altogether.

In some respects, it is surprising that the Christian right fared so well in these debates, given their historical marginalization and the religious pluralism of American society. One of the key explanations for the political strength of Christian conservatives is the support they have received from the Republican Party, and the purposeful manipulation of conservative Christianity by mainstream political actors. This is an important, though less well known aspect of the resurgence of theocratic politics in the post–Cold War era.[33] Throughout the period in question, Republican Party operatives saw in conservative religion a tool for appealing to white, Christian voters, and splitting the New Deal coalition that had long been the basis of the Democratic Party. No one saw this better than Richard Nixon, who initiated the so-called Southern Strategy that consciously used race, religion, and culture to appeal to the white working class, particularly in the South and West. This type of right-wing populism defined the Reagan Revolution of the 1980s, the Republican takeover of Congress in 1994, and the presidential campaigns of George W. Bush in 2000 and 2004. It also figured prominently in John McCain's bid for the presidency in 2008 (particularly his selection of Sarah Palin as a vice presidential candidate). By fusing conservative religion, an assertive patriotism, and divisive social issues, Republican Party operatives sought to polarize the American electorate along cultural lines, minimize the salience of economic issues, and draw working-class whites into a coalition that catered to the interests of America's corporate elite.

A central feature of the Republican strategy – and the corresponding culture wars of the 1980s and 1990s – was the denigration of liberal (i.e., Enlightenment) norms as misguided, immoral, and culturally inauthentic. This strategy of "positive polarization" also relied upon an obfuscation of such issues as poverty, the loss of American industry, and the costs of an expansive foreign policy. In the context of hard-fought electoral campaigns, these issues were subordinated to questions of abortion, biography, and divisive wedge issues. More to the point, religion was used to sanction conservative economic and foreign policies, and situate Republican policies within a moral framework. The irony is that it was during the Reagan and Bush eras that the country witnessed the demise of its manufacturing base, and with it middle-class standards of living. While the transformation of the US economy – and America's emergence as a debtor nation under Ronald Reagan – ought to have been central topics of debate, they were surprisingly marginal. Rather, Republican Party operatives worked to co-opt the discontent associated with socio-economic dislocation, and redefine the ills of American society as a crisis of spirit, not a crisis of capitalism. To this end, they were greatly aided by conservative churches and right-wing Christian activists.

The invocation of an exclusive, theocratic politics came to fruition during the presidency of George W. Bush. Following the time-worn strategy of positive polarization, both the 2000 and 2004 Republican presidential campaigns – as well as the marketing of Administration policies – relied upon an overt blending of patriotism, conservative Christianity, and an assertive militarism. Particularly in the aftermath of 9/11, the conflation of national purpose and religious mission was clearly evident. The invasion of Afghanistan, the declaration of the war on terror, and the subsequent invasion of Iraq were all clothed in a religious rhetoric that invoked American national purpose and Exceptionalism. This type of religious nationalism commonly portrayed the war on terror as a spiritual battle against the forces of evil. Similar to the Christian anti-Communist Crusade of the 1950s, representatives of the Administration argued that the United States was a Christian nation where "God reigns supreme," and where victory depends on the nation's coming together "in the name of Jesus."[34] The 2004 presidential campaign similarly included a conscious effort to conflate religion, nationalism, and partisan politics by inculcating a belief among conservative Christians that Bush was God's choice for the White House.[35]

Ironically, it was the ideological rigidity of the Bush Administration's policies that was responsible for its ultimate demise. Driven by a mix of religious conviction and ideological certitude, the Bush Administration pursued a number of policies that ultimately proved counterproductive, bordering on disastrous. Whether it was the invasion of Iraq, the torture scandal at Abu Ghraib, the warrantless surveillance of American citizens on a large scale, or the existence of CIA secret prisons, the image of America as a Godly nation was seriously tarnished, and many in the Evangelical community felt they had been manipulated, and "used" to sanction political priorities that had little to do with their agenda. As the former head of the Bush Administration's Office of Faith Based Initiatives wrote, "[as a result of this politicization of religion,] the name 'Jesus' doesn't bring to mind the things he said he wanted associated with his followers – love for one another; love for the poor, sick and imprisoned; self-denial; and devotion to God. It is associated with anti-abortion activities, opposition to gay rights, the Republican Party, and tax cuts."[36]

Conclusion

The 2008 election of Barak Obama appeared to bring an end to the exclusive religious nationalism that had defined the post-9/11 period. The excesses of the Bush Administration had discredited many of its policies, and the 2006 and 2008 elections had served as a rejection of that record. The effort to depict Bush Administration policy as consistent with either national values or religious purpose had been shown wanting. It was simply hard to square the invocation of providential mission with the pictures of US servicemen and women abusing Iraqis held in US custody. Perhaps more significant was the religious intolerance at the heart of the theocratic message, which had alienated large segments of the population. The religious politics of this era, in short, left a bitter legacy, and a deeply divided electorate in its wake. Ironically, the theocratic politics of this era ultimately proved Locke right: religious uniformity (and intolerance) breeds division, not unity.

Against this backdrop, the ecumenical centrism of Barak Obama was a welcome reprieve. Obama had spoken eloquently of reconciling politics and faith, and he was able to offer a progressive political message in a Christian vernacular. His message was a return to the modernist civil religion of earlier decades, and represented a departure from both the irreligious secularism of the far left and the theocratic politics of the far right. In a 2006 speech, he argued that it is a mistake to disregard the influence of faith in people's lives, and that society should not "ask believers to leave their religion at the door before entering into the public square." Rather, Obama argued that a compromise needs to be found that can reconcile faith with the realities of a religiously diverse political community. Moreover, "a sense of proportion should also guide those who police the boundaries between church and state."[37]

In many respects, Obama was returning to the central challenge of this country: how to accommodate a deeply religious population that has little agreement on either theology or politics. Obama's ideas on religious tolerance reflected the kind of ecumenism inherent within the Enlightenment tradition, and in the understanding of secularism as non-discrimination. Whether influenced by the ideas of the early founders or not, his vision of religion and society mirrored the religious compromise that was at the heart of the American constitution. Obama's message also reflected the liberal consensus of the early post–Second World War years, which was defined by a commitment to equal treatment, non-discrimination, and social justice. It was at once reverential and tolerant. Obama's vision of religion and society, in short, was more akin to the thinking of Reinhold Niebuhr than Jerry Falwell.

In hindsight, it is perhaps not surprising that the reprieve was short lived. Whether it was racism, hostility to modernist thinking, or simply old-fashioned partisanship, the attacks on Obama's patriotism, his centrist principles, and his integrity came fast and furious. It is hard not to see the instrumental purpose behind the concerted effort to discredit this centrist president. Whether this was the rumour surrounding Obama's birth place, or the effort to characterize him as socialist or Muslim (or secular), the intent was to discredit the man, and depict him – and his policies – as culturally inauthentic. This smear campaign even went so far in certain Evangelical circles as to hint that Obama was the anti-Christ.

The election of Donald Trump in 2016 was part of this backlash against President Obama. Although Trump's economic populism was a central feature of his presidential campaign, so too was the candidate's white nationalism, his pandering to the "birther" movement, and a willingness to demonize immigrants and Muslims. Trump's rhetoric on the campaign trail, in short, rejected the multiculturalism and tolerance at the heart of Obama's message. Not surprisingly, Trump's anti-minority sentiment was closely associated with an "alt-right" understanding of Christianity as a "tribal marker" and the Republican Party as a "white person's populist party."[38] While many conservative Christians were concerned about losing the moral high ground by associating with racists and neo-Nazis, others embraced the Trump campaign precisely because they saw it as "a vehicle for white supremacy."[39] Central to the alt-right philosophy is a perception that the United States is engaged in a civilizational conflict with "radical Islamic terrorism," and, by extension, with Islam. Several Administration officials (and former officials) have been involved in anti-Muslim activism, and the Trump Administration's immigration ban and talk of a Muslim registry operates from the premise that liberalism and Islam are antithetical to white, Christian identity.

The depth of support that Trump received among evangelicals was surprising given the candidate's proclivity for lying and his record of marital infidelity (let alone his past ownership of casinos and strip clubs). And, yet, Trump won 81 per cent of the white Evangelical vote,[40] many of whom saw in him a steward of their values. This surprising turn was due in part to the support of those leaders of the Christian right who saw Trump as someone who could deliver on their legislative priorities and would defend Christianity from secular culture. As evangelist Franklin Graham commented after the election, Trump was the means by which

"God would change the direction that our nation was going in ... [and stop the secularists] who had gotten control of Washington [and who] had a humanistic, atheistic agenda."[41] Trump also had support from Christian ministers who embraced the Gospel of Wealth (or "prosperity gospel"). The five ministers who participated in his inauguration, for example, were united in their veneration of free market economics and the pursuit of riches, and in their shared view that wealth was a reflection of divine favour. Not surprisingly, the Trump family has a long association with the Marble Collegiate Church in New York City, whose former minister Norman Vincent Peale was a well-known spokesman for the Gospel of Wealth.[42]

While one can't doubt the sincerity of leaders like Franklin Graham, one can critique their statements. The aforementioned comment is misleading on several levels, not least of which is its conflation of ecumenical and irreligious secularism, and the assumption that secularism is by definition hostile to religion. Perhaps more disconcerting is Graham's false dichotomy between belief and unbelief, and the rather explicit assumption that only theologically conservative Christians hear God's word. What is most interesting about these trends, though, is the central paradox associated with the theocratic politics of the Republican right: that a religion of love and peace can be so readily tied to a religious politics of hate and deception. This paradox highlights two aspects of modern religious politics in the United States. First, the real challenge for the country remains intolerance – whether religious or secular – which undermines the effort to build a genuine sense of political unity amidst the country's diversity. Second, while there are many sincere believers among the Christian right, it is also clear that conservative religion has proved to be extremely useful (and pliable) in the pursuit of power, money, and interest. Theocratic politics in the United States, in short, has more to do with the lust for power than the moral teachings of Christ. As Locke rightly notes, "Who sees not how frequently the Name of the Church, which was so venerable in the time of the Apostles, has been made use of to throw Dust in Peoples Eyes, in following Ages?"[43]

NOTES

1 The *Oxford English Dictionary* defines theocracy as "a. A form of government in which God (or a deity) is recognized as the king or immediate ruler, and his laws are taken as the statute-book of the kingdom, these laws being

usually administered by a priestly order as his ministers and agents; hence (loosely) a system of government by a sacerdotal order, claiming a divine commission; also, a state so governed: esp. applied to the commonwealth of Israel from the exodus to the election of Saul as king.

b. *transf.* A priestly order or religious body exercising political or civil power."

2 John Locke, *A Letter Concerning Toleration*, ed. and intro. James H. Tully (Indianapolis: Hackett Publishing Co., 1983).

3 Ibid., 27.

4 Ibid., 37.

5 Ibid., 25.

6 Ibid., 26.

7 Ibid., 28.

8 David Little, "Calvinism, Constitutionalism and the Ingredients of Peace," in *Calvinism and Democracy*, ed. John R. Bowlin (Grand Rapids, MI: Wm. B. Eerdman Publishing, 2014), 35. Part of the argument in this section is drawn from an earlier paper written by the author. See Scott Hibbard, "Religion, Nationalism and the Politics of Secularism," in *Oxford Handbook on Religion, Conflict and Peacebuilding*, ed. Scott Appleby and Atalia Omer (New York: Oxford University Press, 2015).

9 David Little, "Calvinism, Constitutionalism and the Ingredients of Peace," in *Calvinism and Democracy*, 35.

10 For a discussion of the various forms of accommodation, see Ahmet Kuru, *Secularism and State Policies toward Religion: The United States, France and Turkey* (New York: Cambridge University Press, 2009).

11 David Little, "The Global Challenge of Secularism to Religious Freedom," in *Trends of Secularism in a Pluralistic World*, ed. Jaime Conteras and Rosa Maria Martinez de Codes (Madrid: Iberoamericana-Vervuert, 2013), 3.

12 Ibid., 4.

13 A more expansive treatment of the material in this section can be found in Scott W. Hibbard, *Religious Politics and Secular States: Egypt, India and the United States* (Baltimore: Johns Hopkins University Press), ch. 6 and 7.

14 See Frank Lambert, *The Founding Fathers and the Place of Religion in America* (Princeton: Princeton University Press, 2003), ch. 3.

15 Isaac Kramnick and R. Lawrence Moore, *The Godless Constitution: The Case against Religious Correctness* (New York: W.W. Norton and Co., 1997), 56.

16 Lambert, *The Founding Fathers and the Place of Religion in America*, 161.

17 The quote is from Edmund Burke, in his defence of religious tests for public office holders in England. Kramnick and Moore, *The Godless Constitution*, 80.

18 There were also differing modes of "establishment" proposed in these early debates, including the designation of Christianity, in general, or

Protestant Christianity as the official religion in lieu of any one particular sect or denomination.

19 The Constitution also contains a ban on religious tests for national office holders (see article 6, sect. 3).

20 Lambert, *The Founding Fathers*, 238. It should be noted that these clauses did not apply to states, which had various forms of establishment and bans on clergy in politics until the early 1800s.

21 See Frank Lambert, *Religion in American Politics: A Short History* (Princeton: Princeton University Press, 2008), ch. 3.

22 Cited in Will Herberg, *Protestant-Catholic-Jew: An Essay in American Religious Sociology* (Chicago: University of Chicago Press, 1960), 84.

23 Robert Bellah, "Civil Religion in America," in *Beyond Belief: Essays on Religion in a Post-Traditionalist World* (Berkeley: University of California Press, 1991).

24 For more on the early history of the conservative movement, see George Nash, *The Conservative Intellectual Movement since 1945* (New York: Basic Books, 1976).

25 For more on the link between Conservative Christianity, free market economics, and corporate America, see Kevin K. Kruse, *One Nation Under God: How Corporate America Invented Christian America* (New York: Basic Books, 2015).

26 See F.B. Schick, "Americanism Seminars and the Communist Challenge," *Western Political Quarterly* 15.2 (1962). Significantly, Graham did not support racial segregation, and was a key figure in providing a "colour blind" rhetoric within mainstream conservatism. Steven P. Miller, *Billy Graham and the Rise of the Republican South* (Philadelphia: University of Pennsylvania Press, 2009), 12.

27 Lambert, *Religion in American Politics*, 179.

28 Reinhold Niebuhr, interview with Mike Wallace, ABC Television, 27 April 1958. http://www.hrc.utexas.edu/multimedia/video/2008/wallace/niebuhr_reinhold.html.

29 Reinhold Niehbuhr, *Moral Man and Immoral Society: A Study in Ethics and Politics* (Louisville, KY: Westminister John Knox Press, 1960), xviii.

30 David Domke and Kevin Coe, *The God Strategy: How Religion Became a Political Weapon in America* (New York: Oxford University Press, 2008).

31 James Davison Hunter, *Culture Wars: The Struggle to Define America* (New York: HarperCollins, 1991). See also Patrick Buchanan, 1992 Republican National Convention speech, Houston, Texas, 17 August 1992.

32 Gary DeMar, a Georgia-based author and activist, cited in Lambert, *Religion in American Politics*, 186.

33 For more on this topic, see Hibbard, *Religious Politics and Secular States*, ch. 6 and 7.

34 General William Boykin, cited in editorial "The General Who Roared," *New York Times*, 22 October 2003, A22. See also Tom Teepen, "A Sectarian Stew Pot," Cox News Service, 27 October 2003.

35 See Deborah Caldwell, "Did God Intervene? Evangelicals Are Crediting God with Securing Re-Election Victory for George W. Bush," for a discussion of the conservative Christian view of the 2004 election. http://www.beliefnet.com/News/Politics/2004/11/Did-God-Intervene.aspx.

36 David Kuo, *Tempting Faith: An Inside Story of Political Seduction* (New York: Free Press, 2007), 261.

37 Barak Obama, remarks before the "Call to Renewal Speech," Washington, DC, 26 June 2006. More about this speech can be found in Peter Boyer, "Party Faithful: Can the Democrats Get a Foothold on the Religious Vote?" *The New Yorker*, 8 September 2008.

38 Sarah Posner, "Amazing Disgrace," *The New Republic*, 20 March 2017.

39 Ibid.

40 See Michelle Goldberg, "Donald Trump, the Religious Right's Trojan Horse," *New York Times*, 27 January 2017.

41 Franklin Graham, cited on Fox News, 8 January 2017. Interview available at http://insider.foxnews.com/2017/01/08/franklin-graham-god-had-hand-donald-trumps-election-prayer.

42 James Barron, "Overlooked Influences on Donald Trump: A Famous Minister and His Church," *New York Times*, 5 September 2016.

43 Locke, *Letter Concerning Toleration*, 37.

14 Shaftesbury's *Characteristics* and the Problem of Priestcraft

RONALD BEINER

1

The problem of religion and politics is still very much with us. For nearly four decades, we have had a stubbornly illiberal clerical regime in Iran. In Egypt between 2012 and 2013 we saw a popularly elected theocratic government, overthrown by what amounted to a military coup. Both Pakistan and Afghanistan are fighting deadly serious jihadist insurgencies with theocratic ambitions that may or may not be defeated. In Syria and Iraq, the jihadist movement that now calls itself "the Islamic State" (formerly ISIL or ISIS) aspires to a restored Caliphate, and was able to demonstrate, with notable military victories against the Syrian and Iraqi regimes, that those aspirations, however crazy, could be given some effect. No one surveying the scene in 2017 could confidently assert that theocracy as a possible regime has been banished to the past. Nor are such problems limited to the Islamic world. In Israel, both domestic politics and relations with the Palestinians are severely complicated by theocratic political parties. In the Balkans in 2013 we saw the Serbian Orthodox Church trying to scuttle an EU-brokered settlement between Serbia and Kosovo. Or consider recent reports of radical Buddhist monks helping to incite anti-Islamic ethnic violence in central Myanmar. The last is perhaps especially disturbing – certainly if one presumes that no religious tradition could be more politically benign than Buddhism! – since it underscores the existence of ugly forms of theocratic politics beyond the ambit of the three Abrahamic religions. It therewith teaches us that a theocratic potential exists in *all* the world religions (though one could draw the same lesson from Hindu nationalism). *One* very important way – though obviously not the only way – of nourishing our reflection on the challenges posed to contemporary political life by religion (and politicized religion in particular) is engagement with canonical texts in the Western tradition of political theory. Let's start by briefly sketching this problem in relation to a few landmarks in the history of modern political thought before turning in a more detailed way to one such landmark in particular.

A crucial puzzle that confronts scholars of the history of modern political thought is why certain great thinkers in the political theory canon who were ferociously anticlerical were nonetheless drawn to the civil religion idea as a desirable theoretical project. Leaving aside ancient antecedents,[1] this project extends roughly from Machiavelli to Hobbes (and Harrington) to Rousseau, and constitutes a significant chapter in the history of political philosophy. It would seem that for thinkers for whom Christianity and the other major religions seemed far too deeply entrenched both in human psychology and in the require-ments of social life for a secular society really to be imaginable at all,[2] the political appropriation of religion seemed to offer a viable "opening gambit" in the endeavour to domesticate religion for political purposes. Ancient polities had seemed to do this in a civically beneficial way, and the hope was to reduce Christianity to a kind of civil cult instrumental-ized to the needs of the commonwealth no less than the pagan cults had been. James Harrington offers an excellent illustration of how this project became central to the tradition of republican political thought. Harrington wrote: "It hath been a maxim with legislators not to give checks unto the present superstition, but to make the best use of it, as that which is always most powerful with the people."[3] And insofar as Hobbes was committed to this project no less than Machiavelli and Rousseau were, it's possible to regard Hobbes as an unintentional but still important contributor to the republican tradition (hence the para-doxical embrace of Hobbes as a theorist of civil religion by Harrington and Rousseau).[4] However, as the secularizing Enlightenment gained pace, this civil religion notion started to look redundant, and was dis-placed by other, bolder strategies for domesticating religion. Hence, civil religion presented itself as an attractive strategy precisely to think-ers who were deeply fearful of the damage that churches and priests could do to the commonwealth, but who were sceptical about disciplin-ing religion by means other than civil religion. In fact, it might be said that these civil-religion types – Hobbes, Harrington, Spinoza – were the ones who blasted the heavy artillery against clerical oppression, soften-ing up the opposition for later moderate liberals like Locke. Tellingly, it was Harrington, a theorist of civil religion, who coined the term "priest-craft."[5] For the republican tradition (Machiavelli, Harrington, Rousseau), the purpose of civil religion was both to domesticate religion and to mobilize people to be more robust citizens; for Hobbes, the purpose of civil religion was strictly to domesticate religion.

It is easy to assume that this civil religion theme has little or no relevance to the predicaments posed to contemporary politics by religion today, but that might well be an over-hasty judgment. Consider the recent brilliant book *Constitutional Theocracy*, by the scholar of comparative constitutionalism Ran Hirschl, which shows persuasively that in many contemporary Islamic societies, the state exerts itself to seize the political-theological initiative – by practising a form of constitutional politics that defines civic requirements as pronouncements of Islamic law – and does so precisely in order to *domesticate* Islamic politics within their societies and subordinate it to state imperatives (we can call it "Islamic Erastianism"!). That is, secularizing political elites define their state as an Islamic state as a pretext for empowering constitutional courts to rule on Islamic law, thereby favouring liberalizing interpretations.[6] Obviously, this strikes these political elites as an attractive political strategy because they are alive to the same potential threat to secular political authority that motivated Hobbes, Harrington, and Spinoza to experiment with the thought of civil religion in the seventeenth century. But needless to say, this Islamic Erastianism gets eclipsed insofar as we see Arab governments pass into the hands of (either moderate or hard-line) Islamists – that is, genuine theocrats.

Civil religion is a notable theme within our tradition of political thought because many of the leading thinkers of modernity – Machiavelli, Hobbes, Harrington, Spinoza, Locke, Pierre Bayle, Montesquieu, Rousseau, Hume, Adam Smith – came to the view that religion poses a decisive *political* problem, and were determined to seek out a variety of strategies for domesticating religion politically. Civil religion in its essence means that religion is too dangerous to be left in the hands of churches and priests, and since it cannot be simply conjured away, it ought to be deposited in the hands of the state (which would put religion to good civic purposes and guarantee religious toleration among all citizens). Not all of the thinkers listed above embraced this particular strategy, but certainly some of them did. This line of thinking may or may not have the intellectual relevance it once did; but the *problem* that elicited civil-religion theorizing certainly has lost none of its contemporary relevance. That is at least one reason why we continue to read, or ought to continue to read, the theorists who defined the civil religion tradition. The theorists of civil religion have many things to teach us, but perhaps the most important is the perennialness of theocracy as a political possibility. They thought that theocracy has the potential to be the most dangerous form of politics, and there is no reason to believe that we are now securely immune from that danger. Again, consider a few contemporary examples: the ongoing oppression of homosexuals in Africa; or the influence of Serbian Orthodox priests during the Yugoslav civil wars of the 1990s; or religious extremism in Israel and Palestine. Consider theocratic politics in Iran and Afghanistan, a veritable sinkhole of ignominy and grief; or the religious right in the United States; or countless other places where clerical political power is being abused – that is, helping to mobilize fear, hatred, and cruelty. Theocracy is neither an abstract theoretical possibility nor the memory of a long-banished past; it is a real part of the political present – not only in Iran but in Libya, Egypt, Lebanon, Syria, Palestine, Iraq, potentially in Pakistan, and elsewhere.[7] If theocracy is still a possibility (which it certainly is), then civil-religion theorizing, as practised for instance by Harrington and his followers, retains its relevance.

Needless to say, reflection on the history of political philosophy offers no magic solutions to our own twenty-first-century predicaments and dilemmas. Those we'll have to solve on the basis of our own political and intellectual resources; we can't simply read these off from some ancient text. But reading the canon can at least remind us that such predicaments and dilemmas didn't arise yesterday. They are coeval with political society, and inserting ourselves into a long tradition of debate and reflection can bring that fact home to us, and thereby help enrich the store of wisdom we'll need to solve our problems (or at least wrestle with them).

2

Shaftesbury was not the writer of treatises but rather an essayist and composer of philosophical dialogues as well as the author of commentaries on his own texts, and the rather hodge-podge character of *Characteristics* reflects this perhaps undisciplined – or perhaps attractive – many-sidedness of Shaftesbury's literary activity. Among other things, the book is an important text in the tradition of reflection on and intellectual response to the cultural and political vices of hegemonic religious authority. It is a classic of the deist tradition, and clearly had monumental influence on the philosophical culture of the eighteenth century. But it also has less visible links to the preoccupations with civil religion, the critique of priestcraft, and the Erastian domestication of Christian orthodoxy briefly encapsulated above.[8] In particular, it is intriguing to explore how Shaftesbury's thought relates to the seventeenth-century republican tradition flowing out of Harrington (including the ardent anticlericalism that is a trademark of that tradition). Shaftesbury himself flags this link back to the Harringtonian tradition in the following endorsement of the idea of a civil religion sketched in *Oceana*:

> [The soothing of religious passion by the magistrate] was ancient policy and, hence (as a notable author of our nation [namely, Harrington] expresses it), it is necessary a people should have a "public leading" in religion. For to deny the magistrate a worship or take away a national church is as mere enthusiasm as the notion which sets up persecution. For why should there not be public walks as well as private gardens? Why not public libraries as well as private education and home tutors?[9]

Private religion and public religion, so the suggestion goes, are complementary rather than contradictory, and Shaftesbury's reference to "ancient policy" makes clear that he, no less than Harrington, privileges the pagan civil-religion model. I don't wish to assimilate Shaftesbury's project to the project of Harrington and his followers, but there are nonetheless common threads that are quite interesting to trace. These common threads are symbolized by the mediating figure of John Toland, who was both a Harringtonian republican and a notable deist.[10] It is important to guard against a de-politicized reading of Shaftesbury's deism,[11] and reading *Characteristics* as a late product of a line of "neo-pagan" and anticlerical theorizing traceable back to *Oceana* helps us to avoid this. Shaftesbury echoes *both* the Erastianism and the vehement anticlericalism to be found in Harrington and in the later Harringtonians; and he also anticipates the kind of deist theology laid out fifty years later in Rousseau's "Profession of Faith of a Savoyard Vicar," which, it was hoped by both of them, would preserve religion at its best while avoiding the host of moral and political vices historically associated with Christianity.[12]

As regards Shaftesbury's Erastianism, consider the following analogy between religion and medieval heraldry: "Particular persons may design or paint, in their private capacity, after what manner they think fit, but they must blazon only as the public directs."[13] This corresponds to the historical process by which feudal clans were "reduced by law or settled practice from the power they once enjoyed," involving a reining in of their earlier privileges in deference to "the magistrate and civil power." The implication is that the same process of transfer of authority to the civil magistrate applies in the case of religion. Shaftesbury further implies that subordination to the trumping authority of the civil magistrate was necessary, in the one case as in the other, in order to eliminate a source "of civil conflict," of "defiances and mortal frays."[14]

As regards Shaftesbury's deism: one interpretive hypothesis worth exploring is the notion that Shaftesbury's project arose from the troubling thought that Christianity no longer supplied the unshakeable cultural and moral foundations that, in his view and the view of virtually all his contemporaries, were required as the condition of having a coherent society; hence the view that a more reason-based (rather than revelation-based) replacement had to be sought. This project needn't be regarded as a subversive one, any more than, say, Keynes's revision of capitalism was necessarily intended to be subversive of capitalism. Rather, on this reading, it would have been conceived as fundamentally a "propping-up" operation, so to speak (although it may well be that a subversive aspect is not lacking in the open and emphatic acknowledgment that new foundations are needed). Justin Champion classifies Shaftesbury as a "radical Freethinker,"[15] a description that plays up the more subversive side of Shaftesbury's deism. I certainly have no wish to slight this aspect, for seeing Shaftesbury as part of a Harrington-Toland lineage (at least with respect to the problem of priestcraft), as Champion and I both do, necessarily conjures up the more subversive implications of his natural religion. Nonetheless, it seems unlikely that Shaftesbury's own image of himself was one of a "radical Freethinker."[16]

With Rousseau's "Profession of Faith of the Savoyard Vicar" in mind,[17] it might be suggested that deism typically has both a negative side and a positive side (though clearly the two often work together). The negative side is the critique of revealed religion. The positive side is an account of why rational theology is true. It wouldn't be unreasonable to call the negative side – which is obviously strongly present in Shaftesbury, at least as prominent as the positive side, if not more so – the "Freethinking" side of Shaftesbury's deism. Shaftesbury spells out his "sceptical" stance towards revelation quite candidly.[18] There are echoes in that account both of Spinoza's *Theological-Political Treatise* and of Locke's *Essay Concerning Human Understanding*.[19] Near the end of *Characteristics*, Shaftesbury professes "our own steady orthodoxy,"[20] but there is scant reason to take this profession at face value, especially considering the blatantly Spinozist challenges to Scripture posed by Shaftesbury.[21]

The way that I have expressed the nature of the project seems already to cast it as a kind of civil religion, but one need in no way rule out the possibility that Shaftesbury fully believed his version of theism to be true (just as Rousseau believed his to be). Shaftesbury once confessed that "as in philosophy so in politics, I am but few removes from mere scepticism" (though he conceded that he held, "perhaps tenaciously," certain "so very few, plain, and simple" principles).[22] To be sure, part of what Shaftesbury seems to mean by "scepticism" is a Socratic willingness to consider both sides of a given issue.[23] Still, it's hard to know fully what to make of this curious avowal of "scepticism" by a thinker who so emphatically affirms the reality of moral experience, and the beauty and harmony of the created universe. For all of his reverence for Socrates, Shaftesbury certainly presents himself in his writings as more of a Platonist than a Socratic. However, Klein's study of Shaftesbury's notebooks of 1698–1704 discloses genuinely anguished reflection on the notions of natural sociability and providential deity, in stark contrast to the confident affirmations professed in Shaftesbury's published texts.[24]

Of course, it isn't impossible to see a particular religion (including deism) both as true *and* as serving a potential civil-religion function – according to some readings of Rousseau, that would be the way to read *his* deism, that is, both as a theological improvement on Christianity *and* as a civil-religious aid to morality, helping to keep us virtuous in a cultural situation where Christianity might be starting to lose traction. The same might be true of Shaftesbury. But it's not entirely out of place to ask: what reason is there to believe that a natural religion of this kind *could* fill the cultural vacuum opened up by the waning authority of orthodox versions of Christianity? Shaftesbury's version may have been at least *one* of the versions of deism that Hume had in mind when he wrote: "Philosophers, who cultivate reason and reflection, stand less in need of [religious] motives to keep them under the restraint of morals; and the vulgar, who alone may need them, are utterly incapable of so pure a religion, as represents the Deity to be pleased with nothing but virtue in human behavior."[25] But whether Hume had Shaftesbury in mind or not, this represents an interesting and powerful challenge to the cultural purposes (which one can subsume under the label of deism deployed as a civil religion) that we have been attributing to Shaftesbury.

In speaking, as we just did, of the cultural vacuum opened up by the waning authority of orthodox versions of Christianity, it should be noted that there are multiple texts in *Characteristics* where Shaftesbury indicates that this is more or less how he himself sees the cultural situation. For instance, at the bottom of page 265, Shaftesbury acknowledges the growth of unbelief. At the top of the next page, he suggests that free rational debate with unbelievers may be "suitable to times of less strictness in matters of religion and places less subject to authority." That is, his suggestion is that a new strategy of winning over the religiously sceptical may be called for – namely, a free philosophical examination of "the very grounds and principles of all religion"[26] – at a time when the old strategies (appeal to the unquestionable authority of churches and the bullying of dissidents) were starting to look as if they were losing their purchase. On page 266, Shaftesbury again says that it is a question of responding to "different circumstances" – that is, circumstances in which the full hegemony of Christian orthodoxy can no longer be taken for granted.

As regards Shaftesbury's identity as a deist, or as something midway between a Christian and a deist, one should note Theocles's hostile reference in "The Moralists" to "our modern deism."[27] That is, he associates the term "deism" with modern versions of Epicureanism that render divinity irrelevant to morality, as opposed to the morally founded theology laid out in the "Inquiry Concerning Virtue or Merit" (what he calls "realist divinity") that Theocles is committed to defending. So, clearly, Shaftesbury is anxious to distance himself from what *he* considers to be a "deist" view – namely, an Epicurean conception of deity that omits any notion of a *providential* intelligence.[28] His own theology, by contrast, is intended to supply everything that a revealed religion supplies to morality, minus the actual appeal *to* revelation.[29] However, notwithstanding Shaftesbury's more restrictive understanding of what defines deism, it is quite easy for us, looking backward three centuries, to see Shaftesbury as a bona fide part of the deist tradition.

One should be careful not to overstate Shaftesbury's contribution as a philosopher of deism: his account of it as a view of the world (let alone as a theology) hardly amounts to more than a few paragraphs in "An Inquiry Concerning Virtue or Merit"[30] (restated in "The Moralists").[31] Shaftesbury discusses, for instance, how the natural fit between the spider as predator and the fly as prey provides evidence of a universal ordering of nature.[32] It's certainly clear what conception of the world Shaftesbury *wanted* to vindicate: "a divine excellence in things" that serves to furnish evidence of "a supreme mind."[33] "A providence must be proved from what we see of order in things present" (270). The reality of God "the world alone ... by its wise and perfect order must evince." Those are the propositions that define Shaftesburian deism. But it's far from clear what exactly constitutes a convincing vindication of such propositions. "It is the province of philosophy alone to *prove* what revelation only supposes" (267; my italics). That's a fine aspiration; but how does one "prove" it?[34]

To be sure, Shaftesbury was of the view that a deist religion was morally superior to orthodox versions of Christianity, and also morally superior to atheism; but without a philosophical exhibition of its truth, that situates us once again in civil-religion territory. All his intellectual energy went into tracing how *belief* in a harmoniously ordered universe intelligently fashioned by a deist God would promote virtue; very little went into showing, or trying to show, why this was a reasonable or philosophically compelling belief. As Shaftesbury puts it, an Epicurean belief in the reign of "atoms and chance" will tend to produce a temper marked by "spleen" (especially "under the circumstances of a calamitous and hard fortune"), and this will run counter to the "affection" of beauty and harmony that generally undergirds a life of virtue.[35] Even if one were persuaded by this claim that morality (according to a Shaftesburian view of moral life) needs the assurance of "a general mind" and an ordering providence, it would hardly provide a proof of the truth of deism. And Shaftesbury's reference to the "hypothesis" of perfect theism seems to concede clearly enough that a rational demonstration is wanting by which to vindicate this hypothesis in relation to its rival Epicurean hypothesis.[36] In short: in the "Inquiry," Shaftesbury does much to argue for natural sociability, the embeddedness of morality in human nature, and virtue as a necessary constituent of human happiness, and does a respectable job of giving some plausibility to those conceptions. But he does very little indeed to argue for the universe as a created whole; the latter is almost entirely *presumed* as a supporting background for the argument about virtue.

Shaftesbury enters into a discussion of the public dimensions of religion in a dialogue between Theocles and Philocles in part 2, section 3 of "The Moralists." In the context of a critique by Theocles of what Shaftesbury, at the end of part 1, had referred to (in the voice of Philocles) as "the fierce unsociable way of modern zealots, those starched, gruff gentlemen who guard religion as bullies do a mistress,"[37] Philocles cites the zealous opinion "that 'none writ well against the atheists beside the clerk who drew the warrant for their execution.'"[38] Theocles forcefully repels this suggestion: "There is no enforcement of reason but by reason"; atheists must be "reasoned with like other men."[39] Philocles expresses scepticism that a mere contest of reasons will suffice. (Two pages later, Philocles "confesses" that he had been impersonating the views of religious zealots in order to provoke from Theocles a fuller defence of Shaftesburian deism.[40] Much later, we learn that Theocles was doing some "personating" of his own.)[41] In response, Theocles introduces a distinction between two different "characters" commonly jumbled together under the label of "atheist": the one who doubts (the agnostic), and the one who absolutely denies (the true atheist). The former "may bear a due respect to the magistrate and law." The latter, by contrast, "sets up an opinion against the interest of mankind and being of society," and hence is legitimately punishable.[42] While Theocles's preferred policy is a contest of reasons rather than coercive enforcement, this seems to open the door to legitimate coercion by the magistrate in the domain of religion. However, he insists that it would be illegitimate to extend this coercion to the doubter, the agnostic, for it is "hard to say" how agnosticism can be punished "unless the magistrate had dominion over minds as well as over actions and behavior and power to exercise an inquisition within the inmost bosoms and secret thoughts of men."[43]

This is the familiar appeal to the inviolability of intellectual conscience argued for in a common front by Hobbes, Spinoza, and Locke in the seventeenth century.[44] But if the magistrate is unable to penetrate into "the inmost bosoms and secret thoughts of men," how is he able to determine who is the agnostic (the mere doubter who it would be illegitimate to punish) and who is the atheist (the shameless denier who *can* be legitimately punished)? Despite having apparently conceded a valid prerogative (at least in certain cases) on the part of the magistrate for punitive sanctions against unbelief, the broader preference is clearly for free intellectual debate (located within the precincts of philosophy) concerning the rationality of belief. For as Philocles puts it, "The more discreet and sober part of unbelievers" will be more effectively moved by the "deliberate and gentle [pen] of philosophy" than by "the dispatching pen of the magistrate."[45] Here Shaftesbury appeals, characteristically enough, to the example of "antiquity": in pagan societies, there was certainly no distinction between the office of the magistrate and the office of "guardians of the public worship"; yet these magistrates (quite reasonably) saw no reason why suppression or censorship of "liberty of philosophizing" (to borrow Spinoza's phrase) was entailed by their office of being guardians of the public worship.[46] Theocles's point is that nothing prevents well-governed human societies from having *both* civil religion *and* "philosophical liberty"– or at least, nothing would prevent this *if* Christian societies were regulated more like pagan societies.[47]

Since the most powerful expression of the anticlericalism that joins Shaftesbury to Harrington, Neville, and Toland is the vehement critique of the ancient Egyptian priesthood in "Miscellany II," I will conclude this chapter by focusing my attention on that text.[48] There is a short but conspicuous echo of that Shaftesburian critique in Montesquieu's "Dissertation sur la politique des Romains dans la religion," a lecture delivered to the Academy of Bordeaux a mere five years after the publication of *Characteristics*.[49]

The starting point of Shaftesbury's discussion is a distinction between "enthusiasm" and "superstition."[50] This enthusiasm/superstition distinction basically correlates with the distinction between *love* and *fear*. Enthusiasm is associated with "admiration and esteem," whereas superstition is associated with "fear, melancholy, consternation." Religious zealotry draws upon "both these extravancies." This is the fundamental two-sidedness of religion, such that even a religion of love such as Christianity doesn't lack for appeals to "terrors of the deepest kind."[51] Enthusiasm (at least in its best versions) is meant to encapsulate the character of true religion, associated with ideas of order, harmony, beauty, majesty, grandeur, and above all, virtue. Shaftesbury doesn't deny that this "very natural honest passion" can also give rise to "high fanaticism": "many strange irregularities," associated with "the ecstatic way of devotion," "pretended grace and amorous zeal," "devout ecstacies."[52] "Mystics and fanatics are known to abound as well in our reformed as in the Romish churches."[53] But these pathologies, he suggests, are distortions – a mode of "over-indulgence" – of something essentially healthy and natural.[54] (Shaftesbury distinguishes between "a legitimate and a bastard sort" of enthusiasm.[55] He calls the latter "vulgar enthusiasm."[56]) The case is otherwise with superstition, Shaftesbury's account of which is allegorized in his piercing analysis of Egyptian religion.

At the beginning of Shaftesbury's narrative concerning Egypt,[57] he immediately highlights the issue of religion's relationship to the state. "The common heathen religion [was] rendered more illustrious by the munificence of the Roman Senate." The "Egyptian or Syrian religions," by contrast, tended more towards foul superstition, playing up the aspect of "mystery and concealed rites, *having less dependence on the magistrate*" (my italics). Egypt, the "motherland of superstition,"[58] fell subject to a corrupting over-supply of priests. One factor was that the priesthood turned into a hereditary guild, so that every priest gave rise to a "whole lineage" of priests (what Shaftesbury calls "propagation by descent")[59]. But the more fundamental cause of this over-supply was simply the abundant attractions of the profession itself:

> It is a tempting circumstance to have so easy a mastery over the world, to subdue by wit instead of force, to practice on the passions and triumph over the judgment of mankind, to influence private families and public councils, conquer conquerors, control the magistrate himself, and govern without the envy which attends all other government or superiority. [Again, note the crucial theme of the implicit battle for authority between priests and magistrates.] No wonder if such a profession was apt to multiply, especially when we consider the easy living and security of the professors, their exemption from all labour and hazard, the supposed sacredness of their character and their free possession of wealth, grandeur, estates and women.[60]

On Shaftesbury's account, multiplication of the number of priests inevitably swells "the quantity of superstition": "If these dealers are numerous, they will force a trade."[61] And if "the liberal hand of the magistrate" permits "swarms of this kind" to propagate, they will soon raise such a ferment in men's minds" that "the magistrate, however sensible of the grievance," will be inhibited from "proceeding to a reform."[62]

This is a classic tale of the evils of priestcraft:[63] "the property and power of the Egyptian priesthood in ancient days arrived to such a height as in a manner to have swallowed up the state and monarchy."[64] And the same story was played out in Ethiopia, "the state having been wholly swallowed in the exorbitant power of their landed [priestly] hierarchy." It is in this context that Shaftesbury quite deliberately and conspicuously cites the *Harringtonian* principle that "dominion must naturally follow property."[65] If the civil magistrate fails to "restrain the number or possessions of the sacred body," the dominion of the latter will inevitably overwhelm that of the state.[66] It was fundamentally a question of "the able and crafty" amassing the "power to gain inheritances and possessions by working on ... human weakness," namely, the weakness for superstition on the part of "the ignorant and vulgar."

Harrington's sociological analysis is alluded to again on page 363. On the same page, Shaftesbury describes the Egyptian priesthood as a "landed clergy" (a term borrowed from Harrington).[67] And on page 372,

Shaftesbury narrates how this Egyptian process of priestly accumulation of "lands and revenues" came to be replicated first by the Roman priests and then by the Christian priests. Directly relevant here is Harrington's statement in *Pian Piano* that "since the aristocratical balance of the clergy is gone [i.e., since Henry VIII's expropriation of the church], [the people] shake the yoke of the priest."[68] That is, both political *and religious* liberation hang on a concerted democratization of the distribution of landed property. According to Harrington's analysis, only with the introduction of a "popular balance" could one hope to dislodge priestcraft.

The upshot was the breeding of "a zealot people,"[69] which then inspired a similar fascination with "mysteries" and "occult sciences" among neighbouring peoples – notably the ancient Hebrews.[70] For instance, Shaftesbury offers the subversive suggestion that the Jewish adoption of circumcision was more a product of Abraham's (and later Moses's) deference to the Egyptian court than "any divine notice or revelation."[71] The broader suggestion insinuated throughout this narrative, no less subversive, is that the pervasive Egyptian influence upon the Hebrews[72] conveyed the "plague" of priestcraft[73] to the later history of Western religion. Further evidence of the sway of Egyptian superstition is provided by the story of "the great Hebrew legislator," Moses.[74] Shaftesbury interprets the information in Acts 7:22 that Moses had "imbibed the wisdom" of the Egyptian nation as a confirmation that priestly superstitions were transmitted from the Egyptians to the Hebrews.[75] Shaftesbury draws upon one of his pagan sources (Marcus Junianus Justinus) to interpret the story of Joseph in Genesis as another case of an astute and ambitious Israelite penetrating the Egyptian court by means of a thorough mastery of Egyptian sorcery.[76] Joseph, by his choice of a bride, formed an alliance with the priests, and then helped to serve their interests by prevailing upon his princely patron "not to meddle with the Church lands."[77] Here, too, there was a striking parallel between Joseph and Moses ("the great founder of the Hebrew state"), who "also matched himself with the priesthood of some of the neighbouring nations" (viz., the Midianites). Moses's "establishment of the Hebrew religion and commonwealth" was decisively guided by the advice of his father-in-law, Jethro, a "foreign [that is, Midianite] priest."[78] The net effect of these narratives – or a Shaftesburian interpretation of them – is to emphasize a view of Jewish monotheism not as the eruption of a novel dispensation in the midst of a heathen world, but *on the contrary* as continuous with Egyptian superstition and Egyptian priestly hegemony – as a product of "the wide diffusion of the priestly science" in Egypt.[79] Priestcraft among the Egyptians had shown itself to be an exceptionally profitable trade; the regulation of "sacred things" was unwisely forfeited by the magistrates, which gave free rein to the priestly class, and allowed them to get the upper hand with respect to both property and power; and finally, the reign of superstitious zealotry, fuelled by the interests of the priests, reached its culmination with the unleashing of an orgy of sectarian hatred and holy wars.[80] Shaftesbury, in "Miscellany II," chapter 1, manages to narrate all this without ever mentioning Christianity as such; but it would be nearly impossible to read his account without supposing that his primary intention was to offer an underhanded commentary on all the pathologies of *Christian* priestcraft (a rhetorical trick then picked up and imitated by Montesquieu).[81]

One of the things that is striking about this account is how the quite harsh depiction of Judaism as being in a direct line with Egyptian priestcraft represents a very sharp break with the "Erastian philo-Semitism" (as Jeffrey Collins terms it) of, for instance, Hobbes, Harrington, and Toland.[82] However, again, it is hard to believe that Shaftesbury's ultimate target is any different than that of these "philo-Semitic" thinkers, namely, Christianity. In "Miscellany II," chapter 2, Shaftesbury makes explicit his critical judgments about the legacy of Christianity, which, in succession to the relative religious toleration of the pagan religions, was one of "bigotry,"[83] "persecution,"[84] pursuit of "mutual extirpation,"[85] and "massacre and desolation."[86] Shaftesbury's cross-reference on page 377 (n. 93) back to page 356 also makes fully explicit that the religion of Moses was certainly not the only monotheistic religion to replicate the priestcraft of the Egyptians.[87] The clearest and most provocative indication of Shaftesbury's siding with paganism against Christianity is without question his ardent celebration of Julian the Apostate.[88] It would not be going too far to say that Shaftesbury presents Julian as a shining hero of toleration, enlightenment, and resistance to priestcraft. Far from *lamenting* the apostate emperor's choice of "the ancient religion" (as Shaftesbury pretends to do at the end of note 89), he clearly views it as a triumph of virtue, gallantry, elegance, wit, humour, generosity, and mildness (to cite the various adjectives he applies to Julian).[89]

It would perhaps be an overstatement to claim that Shaftesbury is a direct intellectual successor to Harrington and the Harringtonian republican tradition of civil-religious and anticlerical discourse. But our hope is that the discussion offered above has at least suggested interesting lines of thought in *Characteristics* that are indeed traceable back to a theoretical tradition flowing from Harrington, which in turn gives one reason to think that students of seventeenth-century republican thought might find it productive to reread Shaftesbury through the lens of that tradition. As we sketched in the opening pages of this essay, leading Western political thinkers have spent centuries wrestling with the problem of clerical authority as a source of bullying orthodoxy and potential political turmoil. If we read Shaftesbury alongside critics of priestcraft like Harrington, Neville, and Toland, it may turn out that this once-influential deist has not exhausted the instruction that he has to offer for contemporary reflection.[90]

NOTES

1 Some of these antecedents are explored in Ronald Weed and John von Heyking, eds, *Civil Religion in Political Thought* (Washington, DC: Catholic University of America Press, 2010); see also Jeffrey R. Collins, *The Allegiance of Thomas Hobbes* (Oxford: Oxford University Press, 2005), ch. 1. For a suggestion that Plato and Aristotle already anticipated the civil religion idea of leading modern political philosophers – in order to avoid "transferring public allegiance to a *trans-political* source," hence preventing "a political and spiritual dualism, with its inevitable consequence of divided authority and the depreciation of political life" – see Stanley Rosen, "Order and History," *Review of Metaphysics* 12.2 (December 1958): 271.

2 To cite Harrington's formulation, "Religion is every whit as indelible a character in man's nature as reason." J.G.A. Pocock, ed., *The Commonwealth of Oceana* (Cambridge: Cambridge University Press, 1992), 273.

3 *The Commonwealth of Oceana*, ed. Pocock, 245. Cf. another good (and not dissimilar) encapsulation of civil religion offered by Edward Gibbon: "The various modes of worship, which prevailed in the Roman world, were all considered by the people, as equally true; by the philosopher, as equally false; and by the magistrate, as equally useful" (*The Decline and Fall of the Roman Empire*, vol. 1, ch. 2). I consider Harrington's relevance to the themes encapsulated here in two companion articles: Ronald Beiner, "Civil Religion and Anticlericalism in James Harrington," *European Journal of Political Theory* 13.4 (2014): 388–407; and Ronald Beiner, "James Harrington on the Hebrew Commonwealth," *Review of Politics* 76.2 (2014): 169–93.

4 As regards Hobbes as a paradigmatic civil religionist, one can commend Bishop Bramwell for having hit the nail on the head: Hobbesian politics

requires the Sovereign to "approve or reject all sorts of Theologicall doctrines, concerning the kingdome of God, not according to truth or falsehood, but according to that influence which they have upon political affaires." Quoted in Collins, *The Allegiance of Thomas Hobbes*, 267.

5 J.G.A. Pocock, ed., *The Political Works of James Harrington* (Cambridge: Cambridge University Press, 1977), 372 and 384. If one looks at each of the exemplary civil religionists in turn (for instance, Machiavelli, Hobbes, Harrington, Spinoza, Rousseau), one sees that each of them was a ferocious and deliberate analyst of, and enemy of, "priestcraft."

6 Ran Hirschl, *Constitutional Theocracy* (Cambridge, MA: Harvard University Press, 2010).

7 Yvonne Sherwood, in her chapter in this volume, argues that the spectre of theocratic oppression is merely an invention of religion-despising Western liberals. This argument might be more convincing if Sherwood were prepared to consider instances of past and present theocratic authority as something other than mere projections of liberal rhetoric, or if she could show that they are in fact benign. If theocracy is "impossible," are we hallucinating when we look at Saudi Arabia and Iran and see regimes that appear very powerful and very oppressive?

8 These themes have drawn a lot of attention from historians of political thought in recent years. Notable examples include: Eric Nelson's *The Hebrew Commonwealth*, Paul Rahe's *Against Throne and Altar*, Jeffrey Collins's *The Allegiance of Thomas Hobbes*, Jonathan Israel's work on the legacy of Spinoza, Justin Champion's work on John Toland, and my own book *Civil Religion*.

9 Anthony Ashley Cooper, Earl of Shaftesbury, *Characteristics of Men, Manners, Opinions, Times*, ed. Lawrence E. Klein (Cambridge: Cambridge University Press, 1999), 11. All references to follow refer to this edition.

10 The work of Justin Champion is essential in appreciating Toland's contribution as an intellectual mediator and a disseminator of radical ideas: I have profited from Champion's illuminating commentary in his edition of John Toland, *Nazarenus* (Oxford: Voltaire Foundation, 1997) and Champion's subsequent book, Justin Champion, *Republican Learning* (Manchester: Manchester University Press, 2003), as well as Justin Champion, "Mosaica respublica: Harrington, Toland, and Moses," in *Perspectives on English Revolutionary Republicanism*, ed. Dirk Wiemann and Gaby Mahlberg (Farnham, UK: Ashgate, 2014), where Champion presents Toland as in effect encouraging a reading of Harrington through a Spinozist lens. Toland's project of putting Harrington back on the cultural-political agenda was also to some extent Shaftesbury's project,

since we know from T. Forster, *Original Letters of John Locke, Algernon Sidney, and Lord Shaftesbury* (Bristol: Thoemmes, 1990), letter 38, that Shaftesbury sought to disseminate Toland's edition of Harrington – a fact whose significance has been noted both by Margaret C. Jacob, *The Radical Enlightenment: Pantheists, Freemasons and Republicans* (London: Allen & Unwin, 1981), 230, and by Champion. Caroline Robbins treats Toland and Shaftesbury as a pair: see Caroline Robbins, *The Eighteenth-Century Commonwealthman* (Cambridge, MA: Harvard University Press, 1961), 125–33. Paul Rahe, *Against Throne and Altar* (Cambridge: Cambridge University Press, 2008), 3 and 106 n. 7, also acknowledges Shaftesbury as part of the republican tradition. On Shaftesbury's early association with the neo-Harringtonian milieu to which Toland belonged, see Lawrence E. Klein, *Shaftesbury and the Culture of Politeness* (Cambridge: Cambridge University Press, 2004), 16 and 137–8; Klein's introduction to his edition of *Characteristics*, xix; Justin Champion, *The Pillars of Priestcraft Shaken* (Cambridge: Cambridge University Press, 1992), 212; and Robbins, *The Eighteenth-Century Commonwealthman*, 6. On Shaftesbury as an ideological successor to Harrington and Neville, see Klein, *Shaftesbury and the Culture of Politeness*, 126–8, 145–6, and 161; Champion, *The Pillars of Priestcraft Shaken*, 213 n. 43; Robbins, *The Eighteenth-Century Commonwealthman*, 125; and Christopher Brooke, *Philosophic Pride: Stoicism and Political Thought from Lipsius to Rousseau* (Princeton, NJ: Princeton University Press, 2012), 119–20. See also the appeal to "old Whig" republicanism in Shaftesbury's 1706 letter to Pierre Coste discussed by Klein on pp. 176–7 of *Shaftesbury and the Culture of Politeness*. However, it should be noted that the broader thesis of chapter 7 of *Shaftesbury and the Culture of Politeness* is that Shaftesbury's ideological alignment with the neo-Harringtonian civic-republican Whigs did *not* extend beyond the 1690s (owing both to "changing political conditions and his own intellectual evolution"); see 125, 132, 138, 141, 148, 150, and 198. Champion offers no account of the post-1700 transformation in Shaftesbury's Whiggism carefully traced by Klein. For further material relevant to the reconstruction of a (fairly tangled) Harrington-Neville-Toland-Shaftesbury lineage, see also the editor's introduction to Edmund Ludlow, *A Voyce from the Watch Tower, Part Five: 1660–1662*, ed. A.B. Worden, Camden Fourth Series, vol. 21 (London: Royal Historical Society, 1978), 39–55. Finally, for a key statement by Klein of Shaftesbury's intellectual debt to Harrington, see *Shaftesbury and the Culture of Politeness*, 151.

11 Cf. Klein, *Shaftesbury and the Culture of Politeness*, 1.

12 In chapters 9 and 10 of Ronald Beiner, *Civil Religion* (Cambridge: Cambridge University Press, 2011). I trace this philosophical project back to Spinoza.

As Jonathan Israel rightly points out: "Shaftesbury argues against, but also parallels, Spinoza's ethical project." Jonathan Israel, *Radical Enlightenment* (Oxford: Oxford University Press, 2001), 68. Exactly the same judgment can be applied to Rousseau and Kant's versions of natural religion in relation to Spinoza, as I explore in *Civil Religion*, ch. 17. In the case of Shaftesbury, it might be suggested that his intellectual proximity to Bayle represents an indirect link back to Spinoza. For instance, one might interpret Shaftesbury's reference, in "Miscellany II" (*Characteristics*, 365–6), to the "martyrdom" of Vanini as gesturing towards Bayle (see *Civil Religion*, 184 n. 36, 185 n. 44, and 204 n. 19). On Shaftesbury's debt to Bayle (as well as the essential differences between them), see Klein, *Shaftesbury and the Culture of Politeness*, 52 n. 11.

13 *Characteristics*, 161–2.

14 Ibid., 162. Cf. Philocles's claim, in "The Moralists" (*Characteristics*, 301), that we rely on "our visible sovereigns," "in the common way of our religion," to guide us in the suitable worship of invisible powers. "Our lawful superiors teach us what we are to own and to perform in worship." See also *Characteristics*, 471 ("as by law established") and 480 (appointed "through the magistrate and by prince or sovereign power here on earth").

15 This is from the publisher's blurb, presumably composed by Champion, on page i of *The Pillars of Priestcraft Shaken*. Champion (*Republican Learning*, 18) also includes Shaftesbury in what he calls "the radical republic of letters." Champion no doubt has in mind Shaftesbury's close personal ties to such heterodox figures as Benjamin Furly, Toland, and Prince Eugene of Savoy. According to Champion and Margaret Jacob, this was the milieu that gave rise to the notorious clandestine work *Traité des trois imposteurs* (although other scholars have different views about the origins of the *Treatise*). See Jacob, *The Radical Enlightenment*, 25–6 and 217–31 (as well as the relevant documents collected in her appendix); Champion, *Republican Learning*, 29 and 170–3; and Abraham Anderson's edition of the *Treatise*: *The Treatise of the Three Impostors and the Problem of Enlightenment* (Lanham, MD: Rowman and Littlefield, 1997). For a very different portrayal of Shaftesbury and his legacy (one that emphasizes his conservatism rather than his radicalism), see Jonathan Israel, *A Revolution of the Mind* (Princeton, NJ: Princeton University Press, 2010), 178 and 182. As should be obvious from the account that follows, my view of Shaftesbury is a fair bit closer to Champion's than to Israel's.

16 See Klein, *Shaftesbury and the Culture of Politeness*, 157.

17 Jean-Jacques Rousseau, *Emile or On Education*, ed. Allan Bloom (New York: Basic Books, 1979), 266–313.

18 *Characteristics*, 369–70.

19 See also *Characteristics*, 382, 413–14, 437–40 (where Shaftesbury insists that Scripture would lack credibility without the "collateral testimony" of pagan sources); and 442, alluding to the Hobbesian-Spinozist thesis that the Pentateuch was in fact the work of Ezra. As regards the latter, see Noel Malcolm, *Aspects of Hobbes* (Oxford: Clarendon Press, 2002), ch. 12.

20 *Characteristics*, 471.

21 Ibid., 471–7.

22 Benjamin Rand, *The Life, Unpublished Letters, and Philosophical Regimen of Anthony, Earl of Shaftesbury* (New York: Macmillan, 1900), 367. See also *Characteristics*, 235, 369, and 395, and Klein's introduction, xiv.

23 See *Characteristics*, 241.

24 See *Shaftesbury and the Culture of Politeness*, ch. 3, esp. 70–1.

25 David Hume, *Writings on Religion*, ed. Anthony Flew (La Salle, IL: Open Court, 1992), 285. Consider also Michael Oakeshott's cutting reference to "the fairyland of Deism": "Introduction" to Thomas Hobbes, *Leviathan*, ed. M. Oakeshott (Oxford: Basil Blackwell, 1960), lxiii.

26 *Characteristics*, 265.

27 Ibid., 267.

28 Cf. Brooke, *Philosophic Pride*, 120 and 125.

29 *Characteristics*, 267–8.

30 Ibid., 168–9.

31 Ibid., 244–5, 273–6. Shaftesbury calls the last of these three texts (namely, "The Moralists," part 2, sect. 4) "a sermon upon his [meaning: Shaftesbury's own] system of divinity." Ibid., 272.

32 The account of natural design in *Characteristics* seems no less flimsy than the corresponding discussion in Rousseau's *Emile*, certainly when read through post-Darwinian eyes. Julian Barnes cites a Christian website, belief.net, where Richard Dawkins was asked his view "about the despair aroused in some by the implications of Darwinism." Dawkins gave the following reply: "If it's true that it causes people to feel despair, that's tough. The universe doesn't owe us condolence or consolation; it doesn't owe us a nice warm feeling inside. If it's true, it's true, and you'd better live with it." Julian Barnes, *Nothing to be Frightened of* (London: Jonathan Cape, 2008), 88. Shaftesbury had the luxury of living in a pre-Darwinian era when he wasn't obliged to confront such challenges. It's not clear that the truths of Darwinian science are fatal to Shaftesbury's idea of virtue (oriented to beauty and harmony); but they *do* seem fairly fatal to the view

of the natural ordering of the world that – according to the argument in the "Inquiry Concerning Virtue or Merit" – is an important buttress to virtue.

33 *Characteristics*, "The Moralists," 269.

34 Cf. Ibid., 275: "established on abundant proof." Shaftesbury may well have thought that he could demonstrate that his idea of virtue was more compelling than the ideas he associated with modern Epicureanism, and that this would prove a solid foundation for a plausible theology. But it's hard to see how he could have thought that he could "prove" the reality of a providential order with just a few sketchy examples. (One could say the same of Rousseau.) The point about the impossibility of proof is pressed by Shaftesbury himself in the voice of Philocles at the bottom of page 278 to the top of page 279. My own post-Darwinian view, I have to say, is that the challenge mounted by Philocles on page 279 (namely, that the appearance of rational form is the product of a cosmic fluke, which will one day be restored to its default position of "primitive discord and confusion" by "Old Father Chaos") seems a lot more compelling than any of the pro-deist arguments ventilated by Shaftesbury, either in his own voice or in the voice of Theocles.

35 Ibid., 190.

36 Ibid., 190 and 191; cf. 235, 268, 279, 294, 301, and 306.

37 Ibid., 246. Compare the somewhat similar image in Halifax's great aphorism: "Most men's anger about religion is as if two men should quarrel for a lady they neither of them care for" (quoted in Felix Raab, *The English Face of Machiavelli* [London: Routledge and Kegan Paul, 1965], 243). For an account of Halifax as "the first truly secular conservative," see Anthony Quinton, *The Politics of Imperfection* (London: Faber and Faber, 1978), 35–8.

38 *Characteristics*, 263.

39 Ibid.

40 Ibid., 265.

41 Ibid., 460.

42 Ibid., 264.

43 Ibid.

44 It may strike the reader as strange or surprising for us to have included Hobbes in this "common front," but see his strong declaration in chapter 47 of *Leviathan* that "there ought to be no Power over the Consciences of men." For a somewhat fuller discussion, see my essay, Ronald Beiner, "Three Versions of the Politics of Conscience: Hobbes, Spinoza, Locke," *San Diego Law Review* 4.4 (2010): 1107–24. For a contrary view, see Johan Tralau, "Hobbes Contra Liberty of Conscience," *Political Theory* 39.1 (2011):

58–84. (Tralau argues that any appearance of a Hobbesian commitment to liberty of conscience is merely "sophisticated doublespeak.") A far superior account – because it does much better justice to the genuine tension in Hobbes between his *attraction to* and *fear of* a right of free conscientious judgment – is offered by Mark Hanin in "Thomas Hobbes's Theory of Conscience," *History of Political Thought* 33.1 (2012): 55–85. However, Hanin overlooks the concern with *intellectual* conscientious judgment that I highlight in my own interpretation.

45 *Characteristics*, 264; cf. 382–6.

46 Ibid., 382–6.

47 Ibid., 265.

48 For a commentary on this text, see Klein, *Shaftesbury and the Culture of Politeness*, 169–74. Klein basically reads Shaftesbury as an early-eighteenth-century Habermasian, concerned above all with criticizing the "distorted communication" associated with a church-dominated society, and with the articulation of an ideal of free "conversation" liberated from "inequality and domination" (154; cf. 98–9 and 168–9). As Champion points out (*The Pillars of Priestcraft Shaken*, 216 n. 52), Shaftesbury's critique of the Egyptian priesthood is traceable back to Harrington's *Prerogative of Popular Government*. Klein points out an interesting difference between Shaftesbury and Toland: whereas Toland's "hermetic interests led him to see a positive model of civic religion in ancient Egypt," this was ruled out for Shaftesbury by his account of Egyptian "priestcraft"; *Shaftesbury and the Culture of Politeness*, 200 n. 10. Jan Assmann, in *Moses the Egyptian: The Memory of Egypt in Western Monotheism* (Cambridge, MA: Harvard University Press, 1998), offers a very helpful and thorough account of what is meant here by "hermetic interests."

49 Montesquieu, *Oeuvres complètes*, ed. Daniel Oster (Paris: Du Seuil, 1964), 39–43. As indicated in the previous note, Montesquieu here could have been following the lead of either Shaftesbury or Harrington (or both). Assmann (*Moses the Egyptian*, 214–15), without specifically citing Harrington or Shaftesbury or Montesquieu, refers to the theory of imposture, "very common in the seventeenth and eighteenth centuries," and its use of a constructed image of Egypt "in order to speak about the present without persecution. The model of the treacherous Egyptian priests was meant to act as a mirror of contemporary clerical institutions." In her chapter in this volume, Yvonne Sherwood writes: "In general we seem coy about applying the term theocracy, retrospectively, to powers that we regard as having made an important contribution to the foundational values of 'the West' ... We are much more inclined to apply

the term theocracy to ancient Egypt, which has never qualified as the precursor of the West." In this passage, Sherwood seems to allude to the fact that leading critics of priestcraft such as Harrington, Shaftesbury, and Montesquieu gave special attention to priestcraft in ancient Egypt. But the account she sketches here fails to offer a plausible explanation, since it is obvious that Egypt was for these critics a merely vicarious target: *Christian* priestcraft was clearly the real target.

50 *Characteristics*, 355.

51 Ibid.

52 Ibid., 354–5.

53 Ibid., 355.

54 Ibid., 354.

55 Ibid., 367.

56 Ibid., 467.

57 Ibid., 356.

58 Ibid., 357.

59 Ibid., 358.

60 Ibid., 357–8.

61 Ibid., 358.

62 Ibid.

63 Shaftesbury himself uses this term in *Characteristics*, 359 n. 29. In the same note, Shaftesbury quotes from Diodorus Siculus the same story of King Ergamenes's massacre of the priesthood narrated (with relish!) by Hobbes in *Behemoth*. Hobbes also celebrates Ergamenes's blow against priestcraft in *A True Ecclesiastical History from Moses to the Time of Martin Luther* (London: E. Curll, 1722), 15; in the Preface (calling it "the famous Slaughter of the Priests"), Hobbes cites book 4 of Diodorus Siculus as his source.

64 *Characteristics*, 359.

65 Ibid., 359–60.

66 Ibid., 360.

67 For Harrington's own critique of the Egyptian landed clergy as a spur to superstition (and the implied parallel with "Gothic" landed clergy), see *Political Works of James Harrington*, ed. Pocock, 437–8 and 537. As is underscored by Pocock ("Historical Introduction," 93), what the archetype of the Egyptian priesthood is meant to suggest is the problem of a landed clergy becoming an entrenched oligarchy in the sense of a *second aristocracy*. (But it should be noted that Harrington, in sharp contrast to Shaftesbury, denies that either Israel or Rome was influenced by Egypt in this respect.)

68 Ibid., 382.

69 *Characteristics*, 360.

70 Ibid., 360–1.

71 Ibid., 361. Similar speculations are offered by Freud in *Moses and Monotheism*. Hobbes, too, traced the Egyptian origins of Mosaic rituals: see *A True Ecclesiastical History*, 19. For a comprehensive discussion of the tradition, stretching from John Toland to Freud, of interpreting Moses according to images rooted in ancient Egypt, see Assmann, *Moses the Egyptian*. See also Champion, *Republican Learning*, 176, 180, and 184–5. Although Shaftesbury cites Genesis (*Characteristics*, 361 nn. 33 and 35), his main source is clearly Herodotus (n. 34), as well as other pagan sources. The implication is that pagan sources trump scriptural sources. Shaftesbury ramps up the subversion of scripture even further in note 37 (362) when, relying on Marcus Junianus Justinus, he suggests that the Mosaic exodus was not a story of divine liberation but rather one of Egyptian *expulsion* of the Jews for medical reasons. In a fascinating discussion in chapter 2 of *Moses the Egyptian*, Assmann traces similar narratives back to Manetho and various other ancient Egyptian historians. In other words, Shaftesbury aligns himself with a view of Moses that is emphatically pagan and Egyptian rather than biblical.

72 *Characteristics*, 362.

73 Cf. *Characteristics*, 315.

74 Ibid., 362–3. Cf. 442, where Shaftesbury deploys the familiar civic-republican trope of treating Moses alongside fellow "politicians and civil sages" like Solon and Lycurgus. For an iconic representation of this trope, see the frontispiece of Toland's 1700 edition of Harrington, as reproduced on the cover of Champion's *Republican Learning*; the top of the frontispiece features a pantheon of epic lawgivers, with Moses at one end and Numa at the other end (and Confucius in the middle!). See also Champion, *Republican Learning*, ch. 7. Very much in the spirit of Machiavelli and Hobbes (see Beiner, *Civil Religion*, 55 n. 44), Shaftesbury signals on 387 ("blood and massacre") that he is fully aware of the darker, more ruthless side of the Mosaic founding.

75 In note 40 (*Characteristics*, 363), Shaftesbury also cites Exodus 7.11, 7.22, and 8.7. According to Assmann, the verse in Acts 7:22 was of critical importance in shaping "the Moses discourse in the seventeenth and eighteenth centuries" (*Moses the Egyptian*, 10; cf. 56).

76 *Characteristics*, 363.

77 Shaftesbury cites Genesis 41:45, 47:22, and 47:26.

78 *Characteristics*, 364. This is also an important theme in Harrington, as I have discussed in the second of the two companion articles on Harrington mentioned in note 3 above.

79 Ibid.

80 Ibid., 364–5.

81 See *Characteristics*, 315 for a powerful encapsulation of how Egypt anticipates all the subsequent "desolation" wrought by religion. Egypt was the "soil, where *first* religion grew unsociable" (my italics). But the "infection" has spread far beyond Egypt. Note Shaftesbury's reference on 371 to "the polite heathens of the ancient world," which seems to carry the implication that the religion that succeeded paganism failed to rise to the same standard of politeness, and hence sociability.

82 Of course, it wasn't just radical Erastians who were philo-Semitic in the seventeenth century. S.B. Liljegren, *Harrington and the Jews* (Lund: C.W.K. Gleerups Förlag, 1932), 4, refers to "the increasing Hebraism of English religious thought, as represented by the Puritan movement"; cf. 27: "the general Hebraism of the time." Liljegren provides some useful background on this broader cultural context, which may be relevant to Harrington's preoccupation with the Old Testament.

83 *Characteristics*, 373.

84 Ibid., 375.

85 Ibid., 376.

86 Ibid., 377.

87 For Shaftesbury's judgment on the third of the Abrahamic faiths, see *Characteristics*, 437.

88 Ibid., 14, and 375–7 n. 89.

89 Shaftesbury's admiration for Julian was shared by Montesquieu: see *Spirit of the Laws*, book 24, chapter 10. I owe this reference to Ed Andrew.

90 I would like to thank Justin Champion for very helpful comments and suggestions in response to an earlier draft of this essay.

Contributors

Ronald Beiner is a Professor of Political Science at the University of Toronto and a Fellow of the Royal Society of Canada. His books include an edition of Hannah Arendt's *Lectures on Kant's Political Philosophy* (1982); *Political Judgment* (1983); *What's the Matter with Liberalism?* (1992); *Philosophy in a Time of Lost Spirit* (1997); *Liberalism, Nationalism, Citizenship* (2003); *Civil Religion: A Dialogue in the History of Political Philosophy* (2011); and *Political Philosophy: What It Is and Why It Matters* (2014). He also has a book on Nietzsche and Heidegger forthcoming with the University of Pennsylvania Press.

Fred Dallmayr is Packey J. Dee Professor Emeritus in Philosophy and Political Science at the University of Notre Dame. He holds a Doctor of Law degree from the University of Munich and a PhD degree in political science from Duke University. He has been a visiting professor at Hamburg University and at the New School for Social Research in New York, and a fellow at Nuffield College in Oxford. During 1990–1 he was in India on a Fulbright research grant. He is past president of the Society for Asian and Comparative Philosophy (SACP) and an advisory member of RESET (Rome). He has served as co-chair of the World Public Forum – "Dialogue of Civilizations" (Vienna), and is currently a member of the supervisory board of the DOC Research Institute. He has published some 35 books and over 200 articles. Among his recent book publications are *Dialogue among Civilizations* (2002); *In Search of the Good Life* (2007); *The Promise of Democracy* (2010); *Integral Pluralism: Beyond Culture Wars* (2011); *Being in the World: Dialogue and Cosmopolis* (2013); *Freedom and Solidarity: Toward New Beginnings* (2015); *Apocalypse Against* (2016); and *Democracy to Come* (2017).

James Franke is Associate Professor of Political Science at Kansas State University. He also serves as Director of Graduate Studies. His research focuses upon issues in American political thought. His recent publications include articles in the *Journal of Educational Research*, the *Journal of Political Science Education*, and *Management Decision*. He is a two-time winner of the William L. Stamey Excellence in Teaching Award.

Jeffry R. Halverson is an Associate Professor of Religious Studies in the Department of Philosophy and Religious Studies at Coastal Carolina University (USA). He previously served as an assistant research professor at Arizona State University. Halverson is also the author of four books, including *Theology and Creed in Sunni Islam* and *Searching for a King: Muslim Nonviolence and the Future of Islam*.

Houchang Hassan-Yari is a Professor Emeritus at the Royal Military College of Canada and Research Professor at the Sultan Qaboos University in Oman. His most recent publications include "Iran, Afghanistan and the Benefits of a Regional Approach," in Sten Rynning, ed., *South Asia and Great Powers International Relations and Regional Security* (2017); "Understanding Israel's Nuclear Ambiguity," in Marzieh Kouhi-Esfahani and Ariabarzan Mohammadighalehtak, eds., *Nuclear Politics in Asia* (2017); "Clashology within Islam: Not Civilisational, but Political," in Mojtaba Mahdavi and W. Andy Knight, eds., *Towards "the Dignity of Difference": Neither "the Clash of Civilizations" nor "the End of History"* (2012).

Scott W. Hibbard is an Associate Professor in the Department of Political Science at DePaul University, where he teaches courses on American Foreign Policy, Middle East Politics, and International Relations. Hibbard received his PhD from Johns Hopkins University, and holds advanced degrees from the London School of Economics and Political Science, and from Georgetown University. He taught at the American University in Cairo as part of a Fulbright award (2009–10), and was a visiting research fellow at the Kroc Institute for International Peace Studies at Notre Dame (2017). Hibbard also worked in the US government, where he served as a Program Officer at the United States Institute of Peace (1992–7) and a legislative staff member in the United States Congress (1985–92). Hibbard is the author of *Religious Politics and Secular States: Egypt, India and the United States* (2010), and co-author (with David Little) of *Islamic Activism and U.S. Foreign Policy* (1997). He is also a co-editor (with Aminah McCloud and Laith Saud) of *An Introduction to Islam in the 21st Century* (2013).

Laurie M. Johnson is Professor of Political Science, specializing in political philosophy, at Kansas State University. She is the author of several books, most recently including *Honor in America? Tocqueville on American Enlightenment*, and *Locke and Rousseau: Two Enlightenment Responses to Honor*. She is editor of the Lexington Books series *Honor and Obligation in Liberal Society: Problems and Prospects*, and director of Kansas State's Primary Texts Certificate program. She is currently working on a book on the political thought of Carl Jung.

Toivo Koivukoski is Associate Professor of Political Science at Nipissing University. His publications include *After the Last Man: Excurses to the Limits of the Technological System* (2008), and *The New Barbarism and the Modern West: Recognizing an Ethic of Difference* (2014). He is a co-editor of several collections in the *Ancient Lessons for Global Politics* series.

Mark J. Lutz is Director of the Society for Greek Political Thought and Associate Professor of Political Science at the University of Nevada, Las Vegas. He is the author of numerous journal articles and book chapters on classical and contemporary political philosophy, as well as of *Socrates' Education to Virtue* (1998) and *Divine Law and Political Philosophy in Plato's Laws* (2012).

Steven F. McGuire is the Thomas W. Smith Fellow with the Matthew J. Ryan Center for the Study of Free Institutions and the Public Good at Villanova University. He has published essays on Plato, Aristotle, Kant, Schelling, and Eric Voegelin, and is co-editor of *Concepts of Nature: Ancient and Modern*, *Subjectivity: Ancient and Modern*, and *Eric Voegelin and the Continental Tradition: Explorations in Modern Political Thought*.

Alan Mittleman is the Aaron Rabinowitz and Simon H. Rifkind Professor of Jewish Philosophy at the Jewish Theological Seminary in New York City. He is the author of seven books, most recently *Human Nature and Jewish Thought* (2015). His new study, *Holiness and Violence in Judaism: A Moral Philosophical Investigation*, is forthcoming. His work focuses on Jewish political and moral thought.

Jeremy Neill is an Assistant Professor of Philosophy at Houston Baptist University, where he has taught since 2011. He is a 2004 graduate of Wheaton College, and has taught at Saint Louis University and the University of Notre Dame. His specialties are in ethics, political philosophy, and philosophy of religion. He has published articles and reviews with journals such as *Philosophy and Social Criticism*, *Faith and Philosophy*, *Critical Review of International Social and Political Philosophy*, *Philosophia Christi*, *Res Publica*, *Review of Metaphysics*, *Social Theory and Practice*, *Political Theology*, *Schutzian Review*, and *Public Reason*.

Yvonne Sherwood is Professor of Religious Studies at the University of Kent, UK. Current obsessions – besides political theologies – include blasphemy, sacrifice, and the legal operation of the category of "belief." She obtained her PhD in 1995 and was appointed to a personal chair in 2010. She has published four monographs and six edited collections. Recent publications include *Biblical Blaspheming* (2012), and "On the Freedom of the Concepts of Religion and Belief" in *Politics of Religious Freedom* (2015).

Peter L.P. Simpson is Professor of Philosophy and Classics at the Graduate Center CUNY and at the College of Staten Island CUNY. He has written extensively on Ancient Philosophy (especially Aristotle), and on Moral and Political Philosophy.

David Edward Tabachnick is Professor of Political Science at Nipissing University. His research focuses on linking ancient political thought to contemporary ethics and politics. He is the author of *The Great Reversal: How We Let Technology Take Control of the Planet* (2013) and is a founding editor of *The Ancient Lessons for Global Politics* book series. He has published articles on the philosophy of technology. In 2015–16, he was the Harrison McCain Visiting Professor at Acadia University and writing on multiculturalism and security.

Hermínio Meireles Teixeira was born in O Porto, Portugal, and raised in Montréal, Canada. He completed his graduate studies at Carleton University, in Ottawa, Canada. His areas of scholarly research, publication, and teaching are as follows: the critical traditions of political theology, and their historical and political encounters with traditions of indigenous political thought and practice.

Index

www.ingramcontent.com/pod-product-compliance
Lightning Source LLC
Chambersburg PA
CBHW030235030426
42336CB00009B/103